# Czech Yearbook of International Law®

## Volume XI

### 2020

## Human Rights, Humanity and Sustainable Development from the International Law Perspective

## Editors

**Alexander J. Bělohlávek**
Professor
at the VŠB TU
in Ostrava
Czech Republic

**Naděžda Rozehnalová**
Professor
at the Masaryk University
in Brno
Czech Republic

## Questions About This Publication

www.czechyearbook.org; www.lexlata.pro; editor@lexlata.pro

Printed in the EU.
ISBN/EAN: 978-90-829824-1-1
ISSN: 2157-2976

Lex Lata B.V.
Mauritskade 45-B
2514 HG – THE HAGUE
The Netherlands

Typeset by Lex Lata B.V.

Czech Yearbook of International Law®

**Address for correspondence & manuscripts**

*Czech Yearbook of International Law®*

*Jana Zajíce 32, Praha 7, 170 00, Czech Republic*

**editor@lexlata.pro**

**Editorial support:**

Jan Šamlot, Dr.T.F. Lenka Němečková, Ing. Karel Nohava,
Anna Dušková, Tomáš Kauer, Jana Alexandra Krocová, Radim Zdych

Impressum

**Institutions Participating in the CYIL Project**

**Academic Institutions within Czech Republic**

**Masaryk University (Brno)**
> Faculty of Law, Department of International and European Law
> [*Masarykova univerzita v Brně, Právnická fakulta,
> Katedra mezinárodního a evropského práva*]

**University of West Bohemia in Pilsen**
> Faculty of Law, Department of Constitutional Law & Department
> of International Law
> [*Západočeská univerzita v Plzni, Právnická fakulta,
> Katedra ústavního práva & Katedra mezinárodního práva*]

**VŠB – TU Ostrava**
> Faculty of Economics, Department of Law
> [*VŠB – TU Ostrava, Ekonomická fakulta, Katedra práva*]

**Charles University in Prague**
> Faculty of Law, Department of Commercial Law, Department of
> European Law & Centre for Comparative Law
> [*Univerzita Karlova v Praze, Právnická fakulta,
> Katedra obchodního práva, katedra evropského práva & Centrum
> právní komparatistiky, PrF UK*]

**University College of International and Public Relations Prague**
> [*Vysoká škola mezinárodních a veřejných vztahů Praha*]

**Institute of State and Law of the Academy of Sciences of the Czech Republic, v.v.i.**
> [*Ústav státu a práva Akademie věd ČR, v.v.i.*]

**University of Finance and Administration, Czech Republic**
> [*Vysoká škola finanční a správní, a.s., Praha, Česká republika*]

**Non-academic Institutions in the Czech Republic**

**Office of the Government of the Czech Republic**
> Department of Legislation, Prague
> [*Úřad vlády ČR, Legislativní odbor, Praha*]

**Arbitration Court attached to the Economic Chamber of the Czech Republic and Agricultural Chamber of the Czech Republic, Prague**
[*Rozhodčí soud při Hospodářské komoře České republiky a Agrární komoře České republiky*]

**International Arbitration Court of the Czech Commodity Exchange, Prague**
[*Mezinárodní rozhodčí soud při Českomoravské komoditní burze, Praha*]

**ICC National Committee Czech Republic, Prague**
[*ICC Národní výbor Česká republika, Praha*]

**Institutions outside the Czech Republic Participating in the CYIL Project**

**Austria**

**University of Vienna** [*Universität Wien*]
Department of European, International and Comparative Law, Section for International Law and International Relations

**Poland**

**Jagiellonian University in Krakow** [*Uniwersytet Jagielloński v Krakowie*]
Faculty of Law and Administration, Department of Private International Law

**Slovakia**

**Slovak Academy of Sciences, Institute of State and Law**
[*Slovenská akadémia vied, Ústav štátu a práva*], Bratislava

**University of Matej Bel in Banská Bystrica**
[*Univerzita Mateja Bela v Banskej Bystrici*],
Faculty of Political Sciences and International Relations, Department of International Affairs and Diplomacy

**Trnava University in Trnava** [*Trnavská Univerzita v Trnave*],
Faculty of Law, Department of Labour Law and Social Security Law

| | |

*Proofreading and translation support provided by:*
*SPĚVÁČEK překladatelská agentura, s.r.o., Prague, Czech*
*Republic and Pamela Lewis, USA.*

# Contents

## BOOK REVIEWS

## NEWS & REPORTS

# BIBLIOGRAPHY, CURRENT EVENTS, IMPORTANT WEB SITES

Alexander J. Bělohlávek

All contributions in this book are subject to academic review.

# List of Abbreviations

| | |
|---|---|
| **A/RES** | General Assembly resolution |
| **AD** | Anno Domini |
| **ASEAN** | Association of Southeast Asian Nations |
| **BelCCI** | Belarusian Chamber of Commerce and Industry |
| **BIT** | Bilateral Investment Treaties |
| **BPS** | Central Bureau of Statistics |
| **CCR** | Constitutional Court of Romania |
| **CIS** | Commonwealth of Independent States |
| **CJEU** | Court of Justice of the European Union |
| **COMI** | Centre of main interests [of the debtor]. |
| **1995 Convention** | Convention of the European Communities on Insolvency Proceedings of 1995. |
| **CZK** | Czech koruna |
| **DNA** | Deoxyribonucleic acid |
| **EC** | European Communities |
| **ECJ** | Court of Justice of the EU |
| **ECPT** | European Committee for the Prevention of Torture |
| **ECHR** | European Court of Human Rights |
| **ETS** | European Treaty Series |
| **EU** | European Union |
| **Eurofood** | Judgment of the ECJ (Grand Chamber) in Case C-341/04 of 2 May 2006, Eurofood IFSC Ltd |
| **FCIArb** | Fellow of the Chartered Institute of Arbitrators |
| **FDEAW** | Framework Decision on the European Arrest Warrant |

| | |
|---|---|
| **HIV** | Human Immunodeficiency Virus |
| **HLV Report** | External evaluation of Regulation No 1346/2000/EC on Insolvency Proceedings. |
| **HR** | Human rights |
| **IACL** | International Association of Constitutional Law |
| **ICC** | The International Chamber od Commerce |
| **ICSID** | The International Centre for Settlement of Investment Disputes |
| **ILO** | International Labour Organization |
| **Interedil** | Judgment of the Court of Justice of the EU in Case C-396/09 of 20 October 2011, Interedil Srl, in liquidazione v Fallimento Interedil Srl et Intesa Gestione Crediti SpA |
| **LCIA** | The London Court of International Arbitration |
| **LLM** | Master of law |
| **MKAS** | The International Commercial Arbitration Court (ICAC) at the Chamber of Commerce and Industry of the Russian Federation [RUS], also as ICAC RF |
| **NAFTA** | North American Free Trade Agreement |
| **NGOs** | Non-Government Organizations |
| **OECD** | Organisation for Economic Co-operation and Development |
| **PCIJ** | The Permanent Court of International Justice |
| **RB** | Republic of Belarus |
| **Regulation 1346/2000** | Council Regulation (EC) No 1346/2000 of 29 May 2000 on insolvency proceedings. |
| **Regulation 2015/848** | Regulation (EU) 2015/848 of the European Parliament and of the Council of 20 May 2015 on insolvency proceedings (recast). |
| **RF** | Russian Federation |
| **RK** | Republic of Kazakhstan |
| **RM** | Republic of Moldova |
| **SCC** | The Stockholm Chamber of Commerce |
| **STM** | The Helping Society |
| **TEU** | Treaty of European Union |

| | |
|---|---|
| **TNCs** | Transnational Corporations |
| **TV** | Television |
| **UCC** | Union Carbide Corporation |
| **UML** | UNCITRAL Model Law on Cross-Border Insolvency of 1997. |
| **UN** | United Nations |
| **UNCITRAL** | The United Nations Commission on International Trade Law |
| **UNGA** | United Nations General Assembly |
| **UNO** | United Nations organisation |
| **UNTS** | United Nations Treaty Series |
| **USA** | United States of America |
| **VCCA** | Vilnius Court of Commercial Arbitration |
| **VCLT** | The Vienna Convention on the Law of Treaties |
| **VIAC** | Vienna International Arbitral Centre |
| **WALP** | World Association of Law Professors |
| **WMO** | World Meteorological Organization |
| **WTO** | World Trade Organization |

# Articles

# David Annoussamy

# The Arduous Progress of Human Rights

**Key words:**
*universal | opposition |
philosophy of life | economic
inequality | implementation
| regional declarations |
ecology | groups | basics |
order of priority*

Czech Yearbook of International Law®

David Annoussamy,
Juge honoraire, Inde;
Emeritus Member of the
International Academy of
Comparative Law.
E-mail: david.
annoussamy@gmail.com

**Abstract** | *The idea of human rights has been simmering in Europe from quite early. It came to the limelight with the declaration of independence of America and the French Revolution. It culminated in the Universal Declaration of Human rights after the Second World War. Universalisation was opposed to in principle as well as on practical considerations. They were perceived as a product of western philosophy of life. Apprehensions were nurtured by poor countries who considered the imposition of rights a veiled form of colonialism. Others felt that they may constitute a hindrance to their economic progress.*

*In order to ensure a better promotion of human rights, efforts are made by advanced countries to attune the Rights to the philosophy of life of Asian, Arabic and African countries as well. But in order to ensure the success of Human rights, it would be advisable to return to basics, namely the dignity and the welfare of men, women and children. A time bound programme towards that end by each country will be more conducive to the real application of Rights than the Universal Declaration of Rights which may remain as a guiding light.*

| | |

# I.     History of human rights

## I.1.     Emergence of human rights

**1.01.**  The European country with the longest history of human rights formulation is England. The first piece of legislation is the code of Ethelred (9th century), followed by the code of laws of Edward the Confessor (11th century). They filled the then existing vacuum of law and curtailed the hegemony of the powerful on the humbler classes. A big step forward was accomplished by the Magna Carta (1215) wrenched from the king of England by French barons.

**1.02.**  The next step was the Habeas Corpus Act of 1679 and finally the Bill of Rights of 1689. Then the scene of action shifts to America. The State of Virginia proclaims the first declaration of rights in 1776 which is followed by other States. The declaration of independence of America contains the affirmation of some essential rights. Then we have the famous declaration of the Rights of Man and the Citizen by France in 1789, which made much impact on the rest of the world. This was followed by the Bill of Rights in America and the incorporation of the French declaration in the French constitution, both in the year 1791.

**1.03.**  Though in both the documents, rights are said to be universal, neither France nor America thought that they should endeavour to have the rights applied all over the world. The characterisation of rights as universal was solely for the purpose of fortifying the case of human rights in their own countries. This position was made explicit in the words of John Quincey Adams who served as Secretary of State from 1817 to 1825: "We are friends of liberty everywhere but the custodian only of our own".

**1.04.**  There was a setback to human rights in France itself after the reactionary forces overcame the revolutionary ones. Human rights developed steadily in France only upon the reestablishment of a democratic regime after 1870 on a stable basis. Human rights spread also to other European countries with more or less of success. There were also periods of complete denial of rights, by totalitarian regimes in Germany and Italy.

## I.2.     Universalization of human rights

**1.05.**  After the First World War, the Society of Nations did not evince much interest in Rights except in respect of bonded labour, slavery, minorities or inhabitants of countries under trusteeship. After the scourge of the Second World War, the need to extend human rights to all countries was felt. This found expression in the Atlantic Chart adopted by the United States and England in 1941. Then the United Nations proclaimed their faith on human rights in the preamble of the UN Charter. The first article assigns as an aim for the world body the development and encouragement of rights. When that article was being debated, South Africa with its apartheid regime prevailing then, opposed it. Most of the newly independent States apprehended the revival of colonialism under the guise of human rights. So they accepted Article 1 of the Charter only with the addition of Article 2 proclaiming the principle of non intervention in domestic affairs of nations by the world body.

**1.06.** The Charter of the United Nations provided for the constitution of a human rights commission entrusted with the mission to prepare a Human Rights Charter, a pact through which member countries would bind themselves to uphold the rights, to adopt measures to detect cases of non-observance and to take suitable sanctions. Members of the commission who met in March 1946 found it fit to start with the formulation of a Declaration of Rights. The President of the United States deputed his wife Eleonor Roosevelt to preside over that commission. A senior U.S. senior officer who assisted the president of the commission stated that the declaration should be a carbon copy of the American Declaration of Independence and American Bill of Rights. It did not turn out so, thanks to the efforts of the draftsman of the declaration, Professor Rene Cassin from France. However, the basic philosophy is more or less the same. The commission completed its task most expeditiously. The Universal Declaration of Rights was adopted and solemnly proclaimed on the 10th December 1948.

**1.07.** Since the declaration has no binding value, it was found necessary to bring into existence a covenant for the same purpose. But a conflict arose between western countries which prioritised civil rights and communist and Asean countries which prioritised economic and cultural rights. The first ones maintained that political and civil rights should be guaranteed at all cost in any condition; the latter ones argued that implementation of human rights was not possible if socio economic conditions were not congenial. In order to get over the difficulty it was decided to split the rights. Two covenants were finalized on 16 December 1966.

**1.08.** One covenant relates to civil and political right which came into force on 23rd March 1976. It provides for the establishment of a Human Rights Committee which became thereafter the Human Rights Council. The covenant creates obligations to signatory

States to report every five years on the situation in respect of rights in their respective countries. Those reports were to be reviewed by the council whose remarks were to be published. The covenant allows also the inspection by external bodies. The Council may bring the violations to the Security Council which in turn may refer them to the International Criminal Court.

1.09.    An optional protocol was attached to this covenant. It allows individuals to make complaints to the international body against their government. This was meant to be a great leap towards internationalisation of human rights. Among countries which have signed the covenant, however, only a few have signed the protocol.

1.10.    The second covenant relates to economic, social and cultural rights. It came into force on 3rd January 1976. A committee to monitor the implementation of this covenant was established on 28 May 1985.

1.11.    Though the two kinds of rights were separated, the interdependence of the two was affirmed in the preambles of both the covenants. The United States ratified only the covenant on civil and political rights while China ratified only the covenant on socio economic rights.

1.12.    In 1993, the General Assembly of the UNO adopted a resolution establishing a post of United Nations High Commissioner for Human Rights.

## II.    Opposition to universalization

### II.1.    Expression of opposition

1.13.    There has been opposition to the very idea of human rights in Europe even at the time when it was being first advocated, the most noteworthy opponents being Jeremy Bentham and Karl Marx. Human rights policy could not fit either in the utilitarianism or the historical materialism. Independently of those doctrines, a French counter revolutionary Joseph de Maistre came out with a startling statement: "There is no such thing in the world as Man. I have seen in my life Frenchmen, Italians, Russians and so on. But as regards Man I declare I have never seen him in my life; if he exists really, I do not know him". (The French declaration referred to the right of man)

1.14.    At the time of elaboration of the declaration itself, Communist countries' position was that man reaches his highest position only in cooperation with the community and that therefore the duty of man to the community should be stated alongside. Since it was not done they abstained from voting in favour of the universal declaration whose universality was affected from the start.

1.15. Thereafter a large number of countries have joined the international body. They have in principle accepted the declaration in the euphoria of their admission to the world body without realizing its full significance and obligations arising from it. But some of them have in the course of time expressed reservations bordering sometimes on opposition. Further, the declaration does not convey the same meaning in all languages. Even the same person, for instance the intellectual African, may resort to two different readings of the French text, one inspired by his university education and another inspired by his original culture.

## II.2. Reasons for opposition

1.16. Opposing countries found that the declaration was based on the western philosophy of life and was not acceptable in its entirety to their ethos. In fact, the declarations of France and of The United states which constituted the basis of the Universal declaration were inspired by the spate of writings on political philosophy in European countries mostly France and England. From those writings one can easily gather the cultural basis of human rights. Four ideas are found to have been the leading factors.

1.17. The first and foremost element of the western political philosophy, sustaining human rights is the specificity of man. All other creatures are basically different from him because they are deprived of soul. They are meant to serve the needs of man. This conception has led to give a very high place to man, to human life and to his dignity.

1.18. The second component of human rights in Europe which is the corollary of the first one is the consideration of man for himself without any consideration of his link with any group. The State itself has come to be regarded as the sum of citizens. There have been deliberate efforts to abolish groups which individuals belonged to, for various reasons. Man was sought to be freed from his various allegiances of the past and considered for himself. This of course gave much strength to human rights.

1.19. The third element consists of giving a legal basis to the rights of man conceived as above. It resides on the belief on natural law. The adjective "natural" appears along with rights in many places in the French declaration. In the American declaration we find the word "self evident" tagged to rights. The idea behind natural law is that positive laws like customs, Roman law and canon law do not embody the entirety of law. Above these positive laws there are other laws inherent to the nature of man, which are binding on all men. This idea which dates back to Greeks has developed in the course of time in Europe and gathered strength in spite of some opposition. Blackstone, the well known British jurist of the 17th century would go to the extent of saying that only laws which are in accordance with nature deserve to be obeyed, that human laws should not be allowed to contradict natural law.

**1.20.** The last element of human rights in Europe relates to the manner of discovery of natural law. It is proposed to apprehend it with help of reason. It is therefore by thinking that one would discover the law. That law should be reasonable, viz acceptable to all minds. It is not however the result of the common thinking of people. It is propounded by some thinkers and considered as natural law when it appears evident to all.

**1.21.** These four pillars which are at the origin of human rights as they have evolved in European countries are not to be found in other countries. They differ from traditional values, social set up and formulation of law in those countries. No wonder that human rights as they emerged in Europe were not found acceptable by other countries.

**1.22.** In China the basic philosophy of Confucius implies certain relationship between the universe and the individual. According to it, the individual should follow the rule of that relationship and perfect himself in observing the prescribed rites. It shall not be good for him to look for help and protection in brandishing rights.

**1.23.** In Africa the individual is not considered separately from the group he belongs to. ASEAN (The Association of Southeast Asian Nations) countries maintained that ASEAN values were different from western values and that they were ready to forego personal freedoms for the sake of social stability and prosperity.

**1.24.** The Arab countries found themselves uneasy with the rights as expressed in the declaration and as understood by western countries. The extreme position of those countries finds a place in the declaration made by the Iranian delegation at the 39th session of the United Nations on 7th December 1984.

> "The Iranian government does not recognise any authority or power other than that of God who is All Powerful and no legal tradition other than that of Islamic law. Therefore the Iranian delegation reaffirms that conventions, or decisions, of international organisations which are contrary

to those of Islam have no validity in the Islamic Republic of Iran. The Universal Declaration of the Rights of Man which emanates from a secular conception of the Judeo-Christian tradition cannot be applied by the Muslims and does not correspond in any way to values recognised by Iran; this latter will not hesitate to transgress those dispositions, should it be necessary to choose between the Divine law of the country and the said conventions"

## II.3.    Real factors of resistance

**1.25.**    There are also other factors which nurture resistance. First, rights as they are declared matured slowly in Europe and were proclaimed in successive waves in the course of two centuries; in other countries they were all ushered in at one stroke. It is also to be remembered that in Europe, at least in some countries, people fought for rights; on the contrary rights were practically thrusted upon other countries.

**1.26.**    Secondly, the remembrance of the colonialism and semi colonialism of the past to which the other countries were subjected still lingers. So human rights are felt as an attempt of revival of the past domination. Even now there is a big disparity between rich countries and the others and the temptation to dictate by the former. So there is a risk of the intervention of the world body dominated and financed by rich nations in the matter of rights to be felt as an encroachment on their freedom hardly won.

**1.27.**    Thirdly, there is still a great economic inequality between the two sides. Advanced countries with the sale of sophisticated arms and high tech products at high cost suck the economy of other countries which is resented by the latter.

**1.28.**    Fourthly, for the implementation of rights there are obstacles to be surmounted, mainly paucity of funds and lack of trained manpower. In addition, there is social resistance; some rights run against the vested interest of individuals or groups.

## II.4.    Divergences

**1.29.**    Consequently, regional declarations happened to be framed like the Arab charter on Human Rights, the African Charter of Human and People's Rights, and the ASEAN Human Rights Declaration.

**1.30.**    As far as India is concerned, no conceptual difficulty was voiced; the essential rights were incorporated in its Constitution. The government of India has followed in this matter its typical course in matter of new ideas: to accept any foreign idea, leaving it to take its relative place in the Indian mentality in the course of time. The common man is not yet wedded to rights. So though there is no official opposition there is a tacit non adherence to the rights as they appear in international documents.

1.31. The champions of universality were sad over these developments but in order to save the universal declaration from total collapse they made an attempt in the world conference on human rights in Vienna in 1993. But that ended with an equivocal statement:

> "While the significance of national and regional particularities and various historical, cultural and religious backgrounds have to be borne in mind, it is the duty of States, regardless of their political, economic and cultural systems to promote and to protect all human rights and fundamental freedoms."

1.32. This kind of ambiguous statement is often resorted to by international assemblies; it leaves all delegates comforted in the belief that their viewpoint has been accepted. In practice each country interprets the approved document in its own fashion.

## III.   Towards a Solution

### III.1.   Attuning of aims by western countries

1.33. European countries are now slowly realising the close link of mankind with the rest of the animal kingdom. The scientific community has been distancing more and more from the religious viewpoint that man was substantially different from animals. Its firm opinion is that man is only one of the branches of the evolutionary tree. Modern science has found that great apes have an intelligence and conscience very close to those of men. Following this trend, New Zealand has taken steps to make a law giving great apes rights against imprisonment and torture.

1.34. It is to be recalled that in western countries people are prone to treat their pets like human beings and communicate with them as such. In such cases the proclaimed fundamental difference between men and animals gets blurred.

1.35. On the other side it is now being realized by advanced countries that blind pursuit of human interests may lead to the deterioration of the earth which will ultimately prove detrimental to man. The strongest proponents of human rights themselves are veering round the idea of harmony with nature by proclaiming the human right for a healthy environment which will entail balanced ecology and protection of animals and trees against their destruction by man. Destruction of forests, degradation of the soil and disappearance of species one after the other have prompted western countries to bring in strict laws. At their behest, international conventions on protection of animal and trees have also seen the light of the day.

1.36.    Further, the fact that groups are necessary has also been realised in European countries. They constitute the best protection of the man against the anonymous and powerful State. In fact groups did not altogether disappear in Europe though the individual has emerged stronger. Further, new groups got formed, the most pro-eminent of them being trade unions. Associations with various objectives and spiritual or quasi-religious bodies are flourishing. Experiences of community life are popular among young people.

1.37.    More importantly, the countries which want to encourage human rights all over the world are not fully implementing those rights. When America was assailing China for scant respect for human rights that country counter attacked in pinpointing the failures of America in that field.

1.38.    To sum up, though international organisations dominated by western countries are keen on the implementation of rights in other countries, there are reservations and failures in those countries themselves to some extent.

## III.2.    Existence of human rights in cultures of other countries

1.39.    On the other side, the principles inherent to human rights have been present in one form or the other in other countries as well. For instance in India, the idea of natural law is present in the concept of Dharma which is conceived as the set of moral laws which govern men, like the physical laws governing the universe and which are like the latter, permanent in nature.

1.40.    The concept of svadharma, viz dharma inherent in every person and forming part of the overall dharma would require the protection and self-realization of each human being, whatever his position in life.

1.41.    The important ethical work in Tamil language, known as Tirukurral, which dates back to the second century AD is based on reason. Many of its teachings preach human rights. For example regarding the right for food the Tirukural states vehemently:

> If he that shaped
> the world desires that men should begging go
> Through life's long course,
> let him a wanderer be and perish so.

**1.42.** Tirukural is not for the free distribution of food at the doorstep of the needy. It is more modern in its approach and advocates the right to earn one's livelihood as follows:

> Nothing is sweeter than to taste the toil-won cheer,
> Though mess of pottage as tasteless as the water clear.

**1.43.** So when we compare the culture of European countries with those of other countries in this matter there are not insurmountable difficulties in bringing them together in a large measure.

## III.3.  Prospects

**1.44.** Proclamation of rights is easy, it gives immediate moral and intellectual satisfaction; but implementation is laborious. What is important to man is not the way in which the rights are formulated but the extent to which they are made available to all men on a sustained basis. Further proclamation of human rights creates an uneasy situation: it makes people aware of their rights and prone to vindicate them without the possibility for the State to satisfy them, thereby causing frustration; they are ultimately counterproductive.

**1.45.** In order to get over the tangle it is necessary to return to the basics. Human rights constitute only a means. The ultimate aim is the dignity and welfare of man, of all men all over the world. Therefore all countries would strive to reach that goal spontaneously sooner or later. This will necessarily entails duties to the State and individuals.

**1.46.** Two ways are open in order to promote implementation of human rights. The first one would consist in reaffirming the old values present in each country supporting human rights, with such adaptation as may be found necessary. This will correspond to the mindset of the people and receive better support from the social body.

**1.47.** The second way to wade through successfully in this delicate field would be to establish an order of priority, taking into account the importance of each right to man, its cultural appeal, the cost of its implementation, the possibility of making available trained manpower. Instead of projecting rights in the hollow form of a declaration, it would be better to present them as a program of action anchored on the locally accepted values. Nothing can be permanently achieved in the field of human rights without full acceptance and participation of the people.

1.48. A five year or six year minimum programme may be prepared. The United Nations Human Rights Council would do a very useful job in helping in the preparation of such programme. It should not act as the imperative old day school master but as an understanding adviser who is sensitive to the local difficulties. In its audit it should not aim at pinpointing the violations of civil and political rights with reference to the declared rights, it should rather assess the achievements in respect of all rights of each nation with reference to its own programme.

1.49. It is well known that civil and political rights cannot progress without the economic and social development. The sensitivity of people to civil rights depends on the amount of enjoyment of socio-economic benefits. In the social body all elements interact. So, all rights may be made to progress harmoniously in order to promote the dignity and welfare of all men. Thus all available energy could be harnessed for the advancement of man, avoiding unnecessary controversies and confrontations.

| | |

## Summaries

FRA [*Les difficiles progrès dans le domaine des droits de l'homme*]
*En Europe, l'idée des droits de l'homme est née il y a longtemps. Elle est devenue centrale au moment de la déclaration d'indépendance des États-Unis, ainsi que pendant la Révolution française, pour trouver son paroxysme dans la Déclaration universelle des droits de l'homme, après la Seconde Guerre mondiale. L'universalisation des droits de l'homme a suscité des objections, tant de principe que d'ordre pratique. Les droits de l'homme étaient considérés comme un produit de la philosophie de l'Occident, et les pays pauvres craignaient que la consécration officielle de ces droits ne soit qu'une forme dissimulée de colonialisme. D'autres estimaient qu'il s'agit d'une entrave potentielle à leur développement économique.*
*Les pays développés cherchent à promouvoir les droits de l'homme, conscients de la nécessité de les adapter à la philosophie des pays asiatiques, arabes et africains. Toutefois, la véritable adoption des droits de l'homme passe par le retour aux valeurs fondamentales que sont la dignité et le bien-être des hommes, des femmes et des enfants. Un programme en ce sens, délimité*

*dans le temps et réalisé par chaque pays individuellement, a plus de chances d'aboutir que la Déclaration universelle des droits de l'homme, qui peut néanmoins continuer de remplir sa fonction de référence.*

CZE  **[Svízelný pokrok v oblasti lidských práv]**
*Myšlenka lidských práv se v Evropě zrodila již poměrně dávno. Středem pozornosti se stala v době vyhlášení nezávislosti Ameriky a v období Velké francouzské revoluce. Svého vrcholu pak dosáhla ve Všeobecné deklaraci lidských práv po druhé světové válce. Proti univerzalizaci byly vznášeny principiální i praktické námitky. Lidská práva byla považována za produkt životní filozofie Západu. Chudé země se obávaly toho, že závazné zakotvení těchto práv je jen zastřenou formou kolonialismu. Jiní je považovali za potenciální překážku jejich ekonomického rozvoje. Ve snaze zajistit lidským právům větší podporu usilují vyspělé země o to, aby byla lidská práva přizpůsobena i životní filozofii asijských, arabských a afrických zemí. Úspěšné přijetí lidských práv však vyžaduje spíše návrat ke kořenům, tedy k důstojnosti a blahobytu mužů, žen a dětí. Časově omezený program zaměřený na dosažení tohoto cíle a realizovaný každou jednotlivou zemí povede ke skutečnému uplatňování práv spíše než Všeobecná deklarace práv, která může nicméně i nadále sloužit jako určité vodítko.*

| | |

POL  **[Kłopotliwe postępy w dziedzinie praw człowieka]**
*Stosowanie Deklaracji praw człowieka nie obywa się bez problemów i komplikacji. Deklaracja opiera się na życiowej filozofii Zachodu. Dlatego tak trudno przenika do świadomości mieszkańców krajów pozaeuropejskich. Co więcej, niektóre państwa otwarcie ją odrzucają. Większość krajów uważa ich implementację za problematyczną, ponieważ priorytetem jest dla nich rozwój gospodarczy. Wydaje się, że lepiej byłoby, zamiast obstawać przy wdrażaniu praw w ich aktualnej postaci, wezwać każdy kraj do opracowania i wdrożenia ograniczonego w czasie programu wspierania praw człowieka.*

DEU  **[Mühsamer Fortschritt im Bereich der Menschenrechte]**
*Die Umsetzung der Menschenrechtserklärung geht mit Schwierigkeiten und Komplikationen einher. Diese Erklärung basiert auf der Lebensphilosophie des Westens. Daher ist es schwierig, sie in das Bewusstsein der in außereuropäischen*

*Ländern lebenden Menschen zu bringen. Einige Länder lehnen die Erklärung sogar direkt ab. Außerdem betrachten die meisten Länder deren Implementierung als problematisch, da sie ihrer wirtschaftlichen Entwicklung Vorrang einräumen. Es wäre nur von Vorteil, wenn das Beharren auf der Implementierung der Rechte in ihrer heutigen Form durch die Aufforderung an jedes Land ersetzt würde, ein zeitlich begrenztes Programm zur Förderung der Menschenrechte zu erstellen und einzuführen.*

RUS  [*Трудный прогресс в области прав человека*]
*Применение Декларации прав человека сопровождается трудностями и осложнениями. В основе данной Декларации лежит жизненная философия Запада. По этой причине она с трудом проникает в сознание жителей других стран. Некоторые страны даже напрямую ее отвергают. Более того, большинство стран считают проблематичным внедрение Декларации, поскольку приоритетным для них является собственное экономическое развитие. Возможным решением проблемы было бы создание и внедрение в каждой стране ограниченной по времени программы, направленной на поддержку прав человека. Это было бы действенней защиты имплементации прав в нынешнем виде.*

ESP  [*Difícil progreso en materia de los derechos humanos*]
*La aplicación de la Declaración Universal de Derechos Humanos se enfrenta a dificultades y obstáculos. Como la Declaración parte de la filosofía vital de Occidente, su aceptación por parte de las personas del ámbito geográfico no europeo tropieza con dificultades presentes incluso en países que la rechazan directamente. Además, la mayoría de los países considera su implementación cuestionable, dándole preferencia al desarrollo económico. Sería muy beneficioso que en vez de insistir en la implementación de los derechos humanos en su forma actual, se instara a los países a que crearan y pusieran en práctica programas temporales para promover los derechos humanos.*

| | |

Badaruddin | Ermansyah

# Potential of Social Capital for Empowerment of Village Communities

*Key words:*
*Law Number 6 Year 2014 on Village | village community empowerment | social capital*

**Abstract |** *Law no. 6 Year 2014 about the Village states that one of the things that must be done by the Village Government is to empower the village community. This research aims to identify and analyze the potential of social capital that can be utilized to support successful village development, especially in relation to the empowerment of village communities in order to support the implementation UU no. 6 of 2014 on the Village. The approach used in this research is a combination of qualitative and quantitative approaches. The study was conducted in 5 villages located in five districts in North Sumatera Province. Qualitative data was obtained by in-depth interview techniques of informants, while quantitative data was obtained through a survey to 250 respondents. This study found that in general every research village has the potential of social capital, both potential of institutional social capital and potential of social capital of value. Institutional social capital such as STM, Kenajiran Mosque, Church Stewardship, Association of Marga, Karang Taruna and Youth (Naposo Nauli Bulung), can potentially be utilized for rural development. The potential of social capital of value, such as trust is also still strong enough at the village level and it is very supportive for village development efforts, especially those related to the empowerment of rural communities as mandated in Law No. 6 of 2014 on Villages.*

**Prof. Badaruddin,** a senior lecturer at Universitas Sumatera Utara, Medan, Indonesia. He has done some research regarding potential of village community. This article is the last research before ending 2019. He is also as the corresponding author of this article. E-mail: drbadaruddin04@gmail.com

**Dr. Ermansyah**, a senior lecturer Universitas Sumatera Utara, Medan, Indonesia. He has done some research regarding potential of village community. This article is the last research before ending 2019. E-mail: drbadaruddin04@gmail.com

| | |

Czech Yearbook of International Law®

# I.    Introduction

**2.01.**    Development essentially aims to improve society in an equitable manner. Rural development also has the same goal of welfare for the whole village community. Rural development has traditionally been fostered by the government, but the effort has not produced satisfactory results. Data released by the Indonesian Central Bureau of Statistics (BPS) shows that as of September 2016, the rural population number in the villages is about one million or 13.96%. The amount is greater when compared with the urban poor who amounted to million people or 7.73%.[1] The data indicates that there has been a rural-urban development gap. Darmajanti, et al. in Wirotomo (2015) states that in general, the gap between the village and the city can be observed from per capita income; contrasting rural and urban income ratios (rough income index). In addition, public facilities such as education, clean water, medicine, electricity, and housing in the city are more available and of higher quality compared to those in the village, including banking access.

**2.02.**    According to Badaruddin, et al., Law no. 6 Year 2014 on the Village brings new hope for the village community to realize the ideals of the nation towards a just and prosperous society. The presence of the Village Law is expected to accelerate village development so that rural-urban development gaps can be minimized. The Village Law that requires the Central Government to allocate Village Funds will be able to reduce village gaps - if Village Governance and Villagers are able to utilize them properly. Conversely, if the village management is not done well, then the opposite will happen, the village will lag even further behind the progress of the city, and will in fact create new conflicts in the village.

**2.03.**    In Law no. 6 Year 2014 on the Village, the empowerment of the village community is defined as an effort to develop the independence and welfare of the community by improving knowledge, attitude, skills, behavior, ability, awareness and utilizing resources through the utilization of policies, programs, activities and mentoring in accordance with the essence of the problem and priority needs of the villagers. Through the efforts of village community empowerment, it can be expected to improve the village faster so that the development goals can be realized immediately. The empowerment of rural communities (including village officials) is important so that village laws can be implemented properly.

[1]    Available at: www.bps.go.id (accessed on 27 January 2020).

**2.04.** Zubaedi argues that empowerment contains two trends. First, the process of giving or transferring some of the power or ability to the community to become more empowered. This process is complemented by building material assets to support the development of their independence through the organization. This type of empowerment tendency is called the primary tendency of empowerment. The second trend is the process of performance awareness. It is a process of understanding and gaining awareness of the current situation, in relation to political, economic, and social relations. A person is in a state of awareness if he/she is able to analyze their problems, identify their causes, set priorities and acquire new knowledge independently. Within this framework, empowerment is identified by the individual's ability to control his environment.

**2.05.** According to Badaruddin, et al., Village Law no. 14 Year 2014 on the Village will only be implemented properly if there is awareness and willingness together (villagers - village officials - external forces) for the progress and welfare of the village. The awareness and mutual willingness to progress and increase the prosperity of the village will only emerge if the available elements of existing social capital can be utilized and accumulated in such a way through village management and village development. Such social capital provision is part of local wisdom. One of the efforts that can be done to realize the successful implementation of Law no. 6 Year 2014 About the Village is to empower the village community by utilizing social capital. The success of organizations and development that utilize social capital has been recognized by many parties.

**2.06.** Ostrom when attempting to analyze development programs in Third World countries using the social capital concept suggested that development using social capital demonstrates better success rates, thus concluding that social capital is one of the prerequisites for the success of a development program. Meanwhile Rose in her research in Russia found that social capital is a key element for the working of informal organizations in society as an alternative to formal organization. The result of a Badaruddin study found that the success of *Polongan Dua* Residents of Rao Sub-District, Pasaman District of West Sumatera, builds collective cooperation of rubber sale of auction system based on the availability and ability of local people to utilize and accumulate social capital. This research will identify and analyze the potential of social capital that can be utilized to support the success of village development, especially those related to the empowerment of rural communities in order to support the implementation of Law no. 6 of 2014 on the Village.

## II. Review of Literature

2.07.   According to Badaruddin, et al., the issuance of Law no. 6 Year 2014 on villages is expected to accelerate village development so that rural-urban development gaps can be reduced. The Village Law actually allows the village government to make village development policies more autonomous by taking into account the potential of the village and local wisdom. In addition, the Village Law also mandates the central government to allocate village funds gradually to reach 2 billion rupiahs per village as operational and rural development funds. Gradually, in the first year (2015) the new Central Government is able to allocate around Rp 300 million per village, and in the second year (2016) the central government increases it to around Rp 700 million to Rp 800 million per village. However, the results of research conducted (Badaruddin, et al. (2015)) indicate that in the first year that this Law was implemented, most of the village officials did not understand the Law of the Village very well. The same conditions are also found in the community. Most of the funds are still allocated for infrastructure development such as trenching and road hardening. The results of Dura study concluded that the allocation of village funds, village policies, and village institutions significantly influence the welfare of the community. This shows that community empowerment is one of the prerequisites for successful development (including the implementation of the Village Law).

2.08.   Ostrom uses the concept of social capital to highlight the phenomenon of development in Third World Countries. In his study using this concept of social capital, Ostrom noted that development using social capital showed better success rates, so he concluded that social capital is one of the prerequisites for the success of a development program. Meanwhile, Woolcock and Narayan mention that social capital is formed from norms and networks that can enhance togetherness (collectivity).

2.09.   Meanwhile Fukuyama mentions that trust is the core element of social capital. Associated with the organizational phenomenon, Rose in her research in Russia found that social capital is a key element for the working of informal organizations in society as an alternative to formal organization. Rose's findings show that social capital is an important prerequisite for organizational success. The Village Law Year 2014 shows explicitly the formal village organization as part of the Implementation of the Act.

In addition, the Village Law in 2014 also requires the growth of informal organizations in the village as a support for the emergence of good governance in village government.

2.10. If the results of study and research findings from Ostrom and Rose are linked to this research plan, the implementation of the Village Law Year 2014 should be colored by the workings of social capital in its organizing process, whether through formal organizations such as village administration (Village Head and village apparatus and Village Consultative Bodies) or through informal organizations such as recitation associations, Union Help Society (STM) and others. Elements of social capital must also be present in the village development program for the success of the development. Puspitasari states that efforts to increase the development and economic independence of the community must be made holistically, especially for policy makers by utilizing all the potential that exists including the potential of social capital of society. It further mentioned that the empowerment of society by involving cultural dimension and utilizing the role of social capital in society can optimize the result of empowerment process.

## III.    Methodology

2.11. The approach used in this research is a combination of a qualitative and quantitative approach with a combination model using a dominant-less dominant design (Creswell, 1994;[2] Badaruddin, et al., 2017[3]). Primary data obtained through in-depth interview technique and observations for a qualitative approach. As for the quantitative approach, primary data is collected through survey techniques by distributing a semi open ended questionnaire. The study is made of the families who reside in the area. The size of the research sample from the family group was determined by 50 heads of households from each village studied so that the total sample was 250 families. For qualitative data, the source of data is from informants. The informants in this study are village government officials (village head, village secretary, village consultant, custom leaders, and religious leaders). The study will be conducted in 5 villages

---

[2]    JOHN CRESWELL, RESEARCH DESIGN QUALITATIVE AND QUANTITATIVE APPROACHES, Sage Pubn: Thousand Oaks, London-New Delhi (1994).

[3]    Badaruddin, Erika Revida, Ermansyah, Iskandar Muda, *Village Governance With Implementation of Law Number 6 of 2014 on the Village and Village Administration*, 14(17) INTERNATIONAL JOURNAL OF ECONOMIC RESEARCH (2017), available at: https://www.semanticscholar.org/paper/Village-Governance-with-Implementation-of-Law-6-of-Badaruddin-Revida/0d183c40a54b041ec284a9f11a2fc708 7a751984 (last accessed on 21 January 2020).

located in five districts in North Sumatera Province, namely 1) Karang Anyar Village, Sicanggang Sub-district, Langkat District; 2) Lubuk Bayas Village, Perbaungan Sub-district, Serdang Bedagai District; 3) (Nagori) Pematang Sidamanik Village, Sidamanik Sub-district, Simalungun District; 4) Muara Purba Nauli Village, Batang Angkola Sub-district, Tapanuli Selatan District; and 5) Sei Kamah II Village, Sei Dadap Sub-district, Asahan District.

## IV.    Research Results and Discussion

### IV.1.    The Potential of Social Capital in Supporting the Success of Village Development According to the mandate of Law no. 6 Year 2014 about the Village

2.12.    There are at least two main objectives of the passing of Law no. 6 Year 2014 about the Village, first is the provision of legal recognition and clarity for the village government as a unit of government. This objective is stated in the Village Law Article 4 Letter a: „to give recognition and respect for an existing Village with its diversity before and after the establishment of the Unitary State of the Republic of Indonesia"; and Letter b: „to clarify the status and legal certainty of the Village in the constitutional system of the Republic of Indonesia in order to bring about justice for all Indonesian people". Based on the principle of recognition-subsidiarity, the recognition and clarity of this status is a form of autonomy for the village to regulate the governance, development implementation, fostering and empowering of the village community. The second objective is to encourage the acceleration of development for the welfare of rural communities. As stated in Article 4 Letter d to i, this regulation aims to improve public services and economic welfare of rural communities in order to overcome the gap of national development through a participatory development movement. According to the Ministry of Village, Development of Disadvantaged Areas and Transmigration, Village Building is the spirit of Law No. 6 Year 2014 About Village. Where spirit is the foundation of the Village Law to encourage the acceleration of development. Sutoro, one of the initiators of the initiative of the birth of this Law that the Village Driven Development paradigm is different from the old paradigm of Rural Development. The old paradigm, he argues, is a state-centric (autocratic, top-down, centralistic and hierarchical) village development model whereas with this new paradigm the village development is achieved with principles that are more society centric (democratic, bottom up, autonomy, independence, locality, participatory, emancipator). In relation to the implementation of Law no. 6 Year 2014, it seems that social capital can be a major force for rural communities to reduce poverty and improve welfare. The problem is how social capital has an important function in reducing the risk of failure of the development process, and how to develop it in the future. This study found the potential of social capital in the five villages studied based on elements of social capital.

### IV.1.1. Trust

2.13.    Trust is a lubricant that supports the existence of groups or communities to be efficient (Pretty and Ward, 1999). In other words, trust is an important element that encourages the realization of development in accordance with the spirit of the Village Law that is participatory development. With the element of trust, can be seen the individual's willingness to prioritize the interests of the community. From the result of social capital potency assessment conducted on 250 respondents in five villages studied, the data found that there is some form of habit or activity of a society which can potentially encourage the formation of social capital especially related with a trust element as an important element in realizing development according to Law -No. 6 Year 2014 About the Village.

### IV.1.2. Reciprocity Relationships

2.14.    Social capital is always colored by the tendency of mutual exchange (reciprocity) between individuals within a group or group itself in society (Hasbullah, 2006). This pattern of exchanges is not something that is done in the same way as buying and selling, but it is a combination of short and long term in the nuances of altruism (the spirit to help and emphasize the interests of others). The result of the research shows that the respondents' assessment on the community in the five villages studied still have the habit of helping each other in neighboring, this can be seen from the public trust to lend money or goods to neighbors or relatives in need.

2.15.    Table 1 shows that in all five villages studied, all respondents gave an average rating of 2.29 (which means being in an „adequate" position) that assessed that fellow villagers still lend each other money or goods to the needy villagers. The results of field research also indicate that the potential of social capital is a form of religious values (especially Islam) which is the most widely held religion by the community in the five villages studied.

### Table 1. Reciprocal Relationships

| Indicator | Village | | | | | Average value |
|---|---|---|---|---|---|---|
| | Karang Anyar | Lubuk Bayas | Pematang Sidamanik | Muara Purba Nauli | Sei Kamah II | |
| Citizens trust each other in terms of borrowing or lending money | 2,28 | 2,46 | 2,30 | 2,20 | 2,30 | 2,31 |
| Citizens trust each other in terms of borrowing or lending of goods | 2,20 | 2,38 | 2,32 | 2,16 | 2,32 | 2,28 |
| Average value | 2,24 | 2,42 | 2,31 | 2,18 | 2,31 | 2,29 |
| Total Average Rating | 2,29 | | | | | |

Source: Primary Data 2017 (Processed)

**2.16.** This finding also reflects that the communities in the five villages studied still have a good level of social awareness, mutual help and mutual care. The findings of the quantitative data are reinforced by interviews with informants:"... although the mutual trust between fellow citizens in this village is not as it used to be, but I see that generally this trust is still pretty good in this village, because I see that people still want to help each other with their neighbors. Besides, in this village some of the people still have relation (relative) with one another". These findings indicate that the potential for creating an independent community and working together in development is still quite strong and wide open.

### IV.1.3. Trust in the Village Government

**2.17.** Putnam reveals that social capital is as a mutual trust valuable between members of society and society against their leaders (Putnam: 1993 in Mariana: 2006: 1).[4] Concerning beliefs to village government, informants generally put trust (some say: „I am a fool, so I just follow what the village government says"). All informants generally consider leaders who have been selected to run the wheels of government as a village tool to

---

[4]    Robert D. Putnam, *The prosperous community: Social capital and public life*, 4(13) THE AMERICAN PROSPECT (1993).

must have responsibility for development programs undertaken in the village for the progress of rural communities. Informants strongly believe in the work that is the responsibility of the village government, both related to the program / project and leadership in the village, because according to the informant there has never been any objection from the community or the rejection of the performance done by the village government. According to Pandapotan (2019)[5] the role of government bureaucracy and nongovernmental organizations is to facilitate the improvement of the quality of social capital. All the programs conducted by the village government are also for the benefit of the village community as a whole, although there are programs that are not running due to funding reasons. As described in the previous section, the results of the interviews are in line with the results of a survey conducted with 250 respondents in five villages studied, as summarized in Table 2.

**Table 2. Trust against the Village Government**

| Indicator | Village | | | | | Average value |
|---|---|---|---|---|---|---|
| | Karang Anyar | Lubuk Bayas | Pematang Sidamanik | Muara Purba Nauli | Sei Kamah II | |
| Accepting Development Programs Offered by Village Officials | 1,98 | 2,74 | 2,52 | 1,90 | 2,42 | 2,31 |
| Village Government Officials Manage Village Development Programs Well and In Accordance with Village Desires | 2,08 | 2,60 | 2,44 | 1,84 | 2,08 | 2,21 |
| Belief in the Village Head | 1,84 | 1,94 | 2,00 | 1,90 | 1,90 | 1,92 |
| **Average value** | **1,96** | **3,64** | **2,32** | **1,88** | **2,13** | **2,14** |
| **Total Average Rating** | **2,14** | | | | | |

Source: Primary Data 2017 (Processed)

**2.18.** Table 2 illustrates that average respondents rated „good enough" levels of public confidence in village governance. This can be

5   Sihar Pandapotan, Hernawi Silalahi, *Social Capital as a Local Wisdom of Farmer in Managing Agricultural Resources in Lubuk Pakam Sub-district, Deli Serdang District*, 2(4) BIRCI-JOURNAL, Budapest International Research and Critics Institute (2019).

seen from the average score of respondents' assessment being: 2.14. The village community's confidence in village governance is in line with the democratic process of village head elections directly elected by villagers through the Village Head Election, in which the elected Village Head Candidates are those who obtain the most votes. That is, the elected Village Head is the best choice of the villagers, and of course the elected Village Head will gain considerable trust from his or her citizens. One informant from community leaders mentioned: „The elected village head in this village is the result of the election conducted by the villagers against the candidates for the village head. The chosen village head is the one who gets the most support from the villagers, so that the current Village Head is supported by the villagers.

2.19.     The strong support of the citizens is a capital that can be utilized by a village head in increasing the participation of the villagers in village development. On the one hand, the village democracy process has resulted in a leader who gets support from the people, but on the other hand, leads to the splitting of villagers which may result in the emergence of conflicts between supporters in the village. Consolidation of elected Village Heads becomes crucial for the full support and participation of citizens for the development and empowerment of rural communities.

### IV.1.4. The Culture of the Egalitarian Society

2.20.     Conceptually, egalitarian attitudes view all social classes as the proportions of the same elements. The egalitarian term became famous during the French Revolution which resulted in the creation of the Declaration *des droits de l'homme et du Citoyen* (Statement of Human Rights and Citizens) in 1789, with the motto: *Liberte, Egalite, Fraternite* (Independence, Equation, Fraternity) Human Rights (HAM) is included in the French constitution. The egalitarian attitude of the villagers, especially the village elites (village government officials and village leaders) will foster the growth and development of trustworthy elements of social capital. If village elites are able to play an egalitarian role, the support of villagers will be stronger.

2.21.     This also resulted in the level of public confidence in the village government in the five villages studied to be high enough. This will certainly affect the successful implementation of the Village Law. The egalitarian attitude of the leaders in the five villages studied can be seen from the extent to which the community is involved in the development process. The involvement of villagers by village officials in running the village development

Czech Yearbook of International Law®

is one of the egalitarian attitudes of the village apparatus, where the involvement of the villagers is one of the factors that bring citizen participation to village development activities. The higher the participation rate of villagers in rural development, the more successful the village development will be. Table 3 shows respondents' perceptions of the inclusion of villagers by village administration in village development.

2.22. The findings as shown in Table 3 show that respondents gave a „good enough" rating with a score of 2.30 to the assessment that the community was involved in the development process in their village. The findings also indicate that there has been an attempt by the leader (Village Head) in the five villages studied to demonstrate egalitarian attitudes in the development process in their village.

### Table 3. Egalitarian attitudes

| Indicator | Village | | | | | Average value |
|---|---|---|---|---|---|---|
| | Karang Anyar | Lubuk Bayas | Pematang Sidamanik | Muara Purba Nauli | Sei Kamah II | |
| Villagers in this village are involved in designing / planning village development programs | 1,82 | 2,58 | 2,52 | 2,06 | 2,52 | 2,30 |
| Villagers are involved in the implementation of village development village | 1,82 | 2,66 | 2,50 | 2,04 | 2,50 | 2,30 |
| Average value | 1,82 | 2,62 | 2,51 | 2,05 | 2,51 | 2,30 |
| Total Average Rating | 2,30 | | | | | |

Source: Primary Data 2017 (Processed)

2.23. The implementation of the Village Development Planning Meeting (Musrenbangdes) is one of the forums for the participation of the villagers in village development, especially in the case of village development planning. One informant mentioned that: „Development in this village is good enough and has involved villagers. Development planning already involves the community starting from the Dusun level because before the Musrenbangdes is implemented at the village level, each sub-village has organized Musyawarah Village (Musdus) to discuss what development programs they will propose at the village level. Of course citizens will propose according to their needs, although there is still direction from the government.

2.24. For example, between 2015 and 2017 Village Funds originating from the center were directed to infrastructure development, whereas citizens may need capital assistance. But whatever is programmed is the result of mutual agreement'. The inclusion of community members in the village development process is a way that can strengthen the potential of social capital that exists in the midst of society. The involvement of citizens in the village development process shows that mutual trust is still strong enough in the midst of society, and that potential should continue to be utilized.

### IV.1.5.  Values and Norms

2.25. Values essentially sets of ideas that are deemed true and important by community members inherited from generation to generation. These values include a strong work ethic (hard work), harmony, competition and achievement. As an idea, values also serve as a driving force for community members. The values of solidarity are the ideas that move the members of the community to conduct activities together. In many communities, the value of achievement is the driving force that strengthens its members to work harder to achieve proud results.

2.26. Social norms have consequences. The disobedience to norms or behaviors that do not conform to the norms that cause a person to be penalized. The form of sanction from a violation of the norm may be an Law of punishment and may be in the form of social sanctions which are more often indicated in the form of attitudes, such as rejection or not involving a person who violates the norm to engage in community activities.

### IV.1.5.1.  Norms of Importance of Cooperation

2.27. The strong desire of group members to engage and Law in groups is one of the most important elements of social capital. Proactive action is not limited to participation in the sense of being and becoming part of a group but more of a contribution in various forms. The awareness of the importance of working together will encourage cooperative efforts, if the consciousness has not arisen, it will be difficult to expect cooperation efforts. Table 4 shows that the respondents in the five villages studied have potential social capital in the form of norms about the importance of cooperation.

## Table 4. Collaboration and Collective Action

| Indicator | Village | | | | | Average value |
| --- | --- | --- | --- | --- | --- | --- |
| | Karang Anyar | Lubuk Bayas | Pematang Sidamanik | Muara Purba Nauli | Sei Kamah II | |
| Villagers work together to create village events / events (such as the 17 August event, religious events, etc.) | 1,65 | 1,88 | 2,28 | 1,74 | 2,28 | 1,95 |
| Villagers work together in village development activities (such as road construction, irrigation, etc.) | 1,99 | 2,10 | 2,24 | 1,80 | 2,24 | 2,02 |
| Average value | 2,26 | 1,99 | 2,26 | 1,77 | 2,26 | 1,98 |
| Total Average Rating | 1,98 | | | | | |

Source: Primary Data 2017 (Processed)

2.28.　Table 4 shows that the dimension of cooperative norms is a significant element of social capital in the communities in the five villages studied. Assessment of respondents in the five villages studied showed an average score of 1.98 which means the respondents considered that the people in their village had „sufficient" cooperation value in the activities of religious holidays as well as in village development, road improvement and irrigation. Although the quantitative data indicate that the respondents' assessment is in the „adequate" category, some informants (Village Heads) point out that there has actually been a decrease in the willingness of village cooperation in the sense of cooperation and sincere collective action. Citizens have been heavily influenced by the material rewards for whatever will be done. The value of mutual cooperation that has been strong in the village community has according to them started to decline. Mutual cooperation will only be done when invited, not on self awareness.

### IV.1.5.2. Norms about the Importance of Organizing

2.29.　Village organization / institution is one of the potential social capital that is owned to support participatory village development. Table 5 shows that in general all respondents from the five villages studied mentioned that joining groups or organizations is their need. These findings suggest that one potential social capital (the desire to organize) is an element that can contribute to rural development.

### Table 5. Potential on the Importance of Organizing

| Indicator | Village | | | | | Average value |
|---|---|---|---|---|---|---|
| | Karang Anyar | Lubuk Bayas | Pematang Sidamanik | Muara Purba Nauli | Sei Kamah II | |
| Joining groups / organizations (e.g., farmer groups, arisan, religious groups, ethnic groups, etc.) is a necessity | 1,84 | 2,30 | 2,04 | 2,06 | 2,04 | 2,05 |
| Total Average Rating | 2,05 | | | | | |

Source: Primary Data 2017 (Processed)

2.30.  In a development perspective, groups / communities / organizations are considered to be very strategic in promoting social participation, facilitating the learning process, and even as a joint venue in channeling aspirations. In line with this view, in the life of the people in the five villages studied, there are several groups / communities / organizations engaged in various fields (religious, political, social, cultural), especially religious and political organizations.

2.31.  The subject discussed in a meeting of members of a religious organization is a community problem. Such as the relationship between people and the relationship between people with the creator. The Helping Society (STM) is an institution that functions economically and also functions socially in religious rituals, especially at the time of death. The economic function of the Society Helps can be seen from the sums of money collected, both voluntarily and compulsorily donated by its members .The social function of the Society of Helping Society can be seen in the form of solidarity from fellow citizens who feel the same desire to work together in implementing and doing something.

2.32.  The livelihoods of the five villages studied are mostly farmers, so in this region there are also farmer groups. This group does not meet every day, only at certain times when they need them. For example, when they want to plant. They hold a meeting to get the seed, because this is usually coordinated by one person. Meetings are also conducted when there are certain events such as when there are water problems. Residents meet to find

Czech Yearbook of International Law®

solutions to the problem. More they meet between individuals only because the area of their rice fields close together. Arisan as a tool for the reduction of poverty in society. The existence of arisan as an institution, indicates that social capital is strategic enough in overcoming various problems of society, where arisan gives the community the ability to: (1) build consensus, (2) set goals, (3) build social networks (4) knit the institutions and build trust.

## IV.1.6. Equation of Principles in Organizing

2.33. A person will want to do anything for the community / organization if he / she believes that the community / organization will bring it towards the better or the direction he wants. Table 6 shows on what basis respondents want to engage in a group (organization). The data in Table 6 found that the basis of respondents (communities) in organization is one of the potential social capital to support rural development in the five villages studied. This can be seen from the average value of the assessment of 250 respondents to the 3 indicators tested which shows the results are in the category of „enough".

**Table 6. Connection / Partition Binders**

| Indicator | Village | | | | | Average value |
|---|---|---|---|---|---|---|
| | Karang Anyar | Lubuk Bayas | Pematang Sidamanik | Muara Purba Nauli | Sei Kamah II | |
| Become a member of a group because it has the same purpose. | 1,88 | 2,30 | 2,24 | 2,06 | 2,24 | 2,14 |
| Become a member of the group as interested in the benefits. | 1,92 | 2,22 | 2,16 | 2,14 | 2,16 | 2,12 |
| Become a member of the group because of the existence of justice in the group. | 2,14 | 2,26 | 2,26 | 2,14 | 2,26 | 2,21 |
| **Average value** | **1,98** | **2,26** | **2,22** | **2,11** | **2,22** | **2,16** |
| **Total Average Rating** | **2,16** | | | | | |

Source: Primary Data 2017 (Processed)

## IV.1.7. Social Network

### IV.1.7.1. Tolerance in Compound Life

2.34. Conceptually, tolerance is identical to the attitude of self-defense against another approved party. In practical terms, tolerance is often an exception for a person who cannot meet the rules that have been approached with humanitarian or accountable considerations. The awareness of tolerance from members of the visible group is so high that no one dares to fight against what the group does to them. The tolerance of the group to its members is a method to create harmony and togetherness. Table 7 shows the respondent's tolerance to the neighborhood based on ethnicity, religion, and occupation. Table 7 shows that in general most respondents have tolerant attitudes toward people of different ethnicity, religion, and occupation / profession. The average value of tolerance of 2.39 illustrates that the tolerance attitude of respondents to ethnic, religious and occupational differences is „good enough". This indicates that villagers have the potential of social capital that can be used to build social networks in the context of village development, particularly those related to community empowerment programs.

**Table 7. Tolerance of Living Environment Based on Ethnicity, Religion and Work**

| Indicator | Village | | | | | Average value |
|---|---|---|---|---|---|---|
| | Karang Anyar | Lubuk Bayas | Pematang Sidamanik | Muara Purba Nauli | Sei Kamah II | |
| Tolerance of different ethnicities. | 2,24 | 2,54 | 2,62 | 2,62 | 2.66 | 2.54 |
| Tolerance towards people of different religions. | 1,76 | 2,28 | 2,58 | 1,90 | 2,12 | 2,13 |
| Tolerance to people of different professions / occupations. | 2,20 | 2,52 | 2,80 | 2,44 | 2,66 | 2,52 |
| Average value | 2,06 | 2,44 | 2,66 | 2,32 | 2,48 | 2,39 |
| Total Average Rating | 2,39 | | | | | |

Source: Primary Data 2017 (Processed)

Czech Yearbook of International Law®

## IV.1.7.2. Participation

2.35.　The ability of people or individuals or members of the community to engage in a social network is one key to success in building social capital. People have the freedom to behave and to define themselves in social networks and to synergize the existing power so that directly or indirectly, it will add strength to the network. By contrast, by becoming an active part of a network, one will gain additional power from the network. In this context, the participation of villagers is necessary for the success of village development. The greater citizen participation is in rural development, the greater benefit of development can the citizens enjoy. Table 8 shows the potential participation of respondents in various activities of village activities. Table 8 shows that respondents generally are in the „good enough" category in terms of participation in various activities in the village such as, attending a meeting held by the Village Administration, present in extension activities, present when asked to assist neighbors. These findings suggest that the potential of social capital associated with community participation in rural development is still quite reliable. That is, the opportunity to involve people in village development activities is still quite large, and this is one element of social capital that can be utilized in the framework of the implementation of Law no. 6 Year 2014 on the Village for the empowerment of rural communities.

### Table 8. Potential Participation in Various Village Activities

| Indicator | Village | | | | | Average value |
|---|---|---|---|---|---|---|
| | Karang Anyar | Lubuk Bayas | Pematang Sidamanik | Muara Purba Nauli | Sei Kamah II | |
| Attend in an event or meeting made by the Village Government. | 2,48 | 3,04 | 2,88 | 3,38 | 2,88 | 2,93 |
| Attend the meeting held by the extension team from outside the village. | 2,54 | 3,12 | 2,92 | 2,22 | 2,92 | 2,74 |
| Attend when asked to help the neighbors who are making events such as circumcision, marriage, thanksgiving, etc. | 1,62 | 1,92 | 2,28 | 1,76 | 2,28 | 1,97 |
| Average value | 2,21 | 2,69 | 2,69 | 2,46 | 2,69 | 2,54 |

| Total Average Rating | 2,54 |
|---|---|

Source: Primary Data 2017 (Processed)

## V.    Conclusion

**2.36.** From the results of the discussion that has been done in the previous section, it can be drawn some conclusions from the results of this study. First, in general, every village studied has the potential of social capital, both potential institutional social capital and potential social capital value. The potential of institutional social capital such as STM, Mosque Kenajiran, Church Management, Association of Marga, Karang Taruna, Youth (Naposo Nauli Bulung) is that it can be utilized for rural development; Second, the potential of social capital of value, such as trust, is also still strong enough at the village level, and it is very supportive for village development efforts, especially those related to the empowerment of rural communities as mandated in Law No. 6 of 2014 Village. Third, the potential of social capital found in research can contribute to supporting rural development when utilized properly.

## VI.    Acknowledgment

**2.37.** The study is dedicated to Universitas Sumatera Utara that has provided the funding for this research in 2017.

| | |

*Summaries*

FRA    [*Le potentiel du capital social pour soutenir les communautés rurales*]

*La loi No 6 (2014) relative au milieu rural prévoit l'obligation de l'administration communale de soutenir la vie communautaire. L'objectif de la présente étude est de déterminer et d'analyser le potentiel du capital social comme instrument de développement rural, notamment dans le contexte du soutien des communautés rurales en application de la loi No 6 (2014) relative au milieu rural. La méthodologie de l'étude combine des approches qualitatives et quantitatives. L'enquête a été menée dans 5 communes se trouvant dans 5 districts différents de la province de Sumatra du Nord. Les données qualitatives ont été collectées au moyen d'entretiens approfondis avec les informateurs, alors que les données quantitatives ont été obtenues grâce à un questionnaire administré à 250 informateurs. L'étude montre que chacune des communes examinées dispose d'un capital social potentiel, et ce tant au niveau des institutions qu'au niveau des valeurs. Le capital social institutionnel (STM, Kenajiran Mosque, Church Stewardship, Association of Marga, Karang Taruna, Youth – Naposo Nauli Bulung) peut servir aux fins du développement rural. Le potentiel du capital social représenté par des valeurs, comme par exemple la confiance, s'est également avéré comme suffisamment fort en milieu rural, et peut donc jouer un rôle crucial dans le développement rural, notamment en ce qui concerne l'obligation d'apporter du soutien aux communautés rurales, prévue par la loi No 6 (2014) relative au milieu rural.*

CZE  [*Potenciál sociálního kapitálu pro posílení vesnických společenství*]

*Zákon č. 6 z roku 2014 o venkovu stanoví, že jednou z činností, kterou musí obecní správa provádět, je posilování obecního společenství. Cílem tohoto výzkumu je určit a analyzovat potenciál sociálního kapitálu, který by mohl být využit na podporu úspěšného rozvoje venkova, zejména ve vztahu k posilování venkovských společenství pro účely podpory implementace zákona č. 6 z roku 2014 o venkovu. Metodika tohoto výzkumu je kombinací kvalitativního a kvantitativního přístupu. Studie byla prováděna v 5 obcích nacházejících se v pěti okresech provincie Severní Sumatra. Kvalitativní údaje byly získávány vedením hloubkových rozhovorů s dotazovanými, zatímco kvantitativní údaje byly získávány prostřednictvím dotazníku předaného 250 respondentům. Z této studie vyplynulo, že obecně má každá ze zkoumaných obcí potenciál sociálního kapitálu, a to jak potenciál institucionálního sociálního kapitálu, tak potenciál hodnotového sociálního kapitálu. Institucionální sociální kapitál, například STM, Kenajiran Mosque, Church Stewardship, Association of Marga, Karang Taruna a Youth (Naposo Nauli Bulung), lze pro rozvoj venkova potenciálně využít. Potenciál hodnotového sociálního kapitálu, například důvěry, je na venkovské úrovni rovněž stále dostatečně silný a maximálně podporuje snahy o rozvoj venkova, zejména snahy související s posilováním vesnických společenství, jak požaduje zákon č. 6 z roku 2014 o venkovu.*

| | |

**POL** *[Potencjał kapitału społecznego we wzmacnianiu społeczności wiejskich]*
Niniejsza praca ma na celu określenie i analizę potencjału kapitału społecznego, który można wykorzystać w celu wsparcia pomyślnego rozwoju obszarów wiejskich. Z przeprowadzonych badań wynika, że każda z badanych miejscowości ma potencjał kapitału społecznego. Instytucjonalny kapitał społeczny można wykorzystać np. do celów rozwojowych. Potencjał społecznego kapitału wartości, takich jak zaufanie, w obszarach wiejskich jest nadal wystarczająco duży i w maksymalny sposób wspiera wysiłki zmierzające do rozwoju wsi, zwłaszcza w związku ze wzmacnianiem społeczności wiejskich, zgodnie z postanowieniami ustawy nr 6 z 2014 roku w sprawie obszarów wiejskich Indonezji.

**DEU** *[Das Potential des sozialen Kapitals für die Stärkung der Dorfgemeinschaften]*
Ziel dieses Beitrags ist die Bestimmung und Analyse des Potentials des sozialen Kapitals, das zur Unterstützung einer erfolgreichen ländlichen Entwicklung genutzt werden kann. Der Autor kam zu dem Schluss, dass jede der analysierten Gemeinden ein Potential des sozialen Kapitals besitzt. Institutionelles soziales Kapital kann potentiell für die ländliche Entwicklung genutzt werden. Das Potential des wertorientierten sozialen Kapitals, wie zum Beispiel des Vertrauens, ist auf ländlicher Ebene ebenfalls noch stark genug und unterstützt Bemühungen um die Entwicklung des ländlichen Raums so weit wie möglich, insbesondere das Bemühen um die Stärkung der Dorfgemeinschaften, wie dies im Gesetz Nr. 6 aus dem Jahr 2014 über den ländlichen Raum in Indonesien vorgeschrieben ist.

**RUS** *[Потенциал социального капитала для укрепления сельских общин]*
Цель данной статьи заключается в определении и анализе потенциала социального капитала, который можно использовать для поддержки успешного развития сельских районов. В этой статье приводится вывод о том, что каждый из рассмотренных населенных пунктов обладает потенциалом социального капитала. Институциональный социальный капитал потенциально можно использовать для развития сельских районов. Потенциал ценного социального капитала, например доверие, еще достаточно силен на уровне сельских районов и в максимальной степени поддерживает планы по развитию сельских районов, прежде всего, планов по

*укреплению сельских общин в соответствии с Законом № 6 (2014 год) «О сельских районах Индонезии».*

ESP   [*Capital social como mecanismo para potenciar las comunidades rurales*]
*El objetivo de este estudio es determinar y analizar el potencial del capital social para promover el desarrollo del campo indonesio. La investigación llega a la conclusión de que cada una de las localidades examinadas dispone del capital social potencial, incluido el capital social institucional o los valores sociales como la confianza, en cantidad suficiente como para fomentar al máximo el desarrollo rural y potenciar las comunidades rurales, según lo estipulado en la ley 6 del 2014, de las zonas rurales.*

| | |

## *Bibliography*

BADARUDDIN, MODAL SOSIAL DAN PENGEMBANGAN MODEL TRANSMISI MODAL SOSIAL DALAM UPAYA PENINGKATAN KESEJAHTERAAN KELUARGA (STUDI PADA TIGA KOMUNITAS PETANI KARET DI KECAMATAN RAO KABUPATEN PASAMAN SUMATERA BARAT), Research Report, Hibah Bersaing, DP2M-Dikti, Mendiknas (2006).

BADARUDDIN, ERIKA REVIDA, ERMANSYAH, MODEL IMPLEMENTASI UNDANG-UNDANG NOMOR 6 TAHUN 2014 TENTANG DESA BERBASIS MODAL SOSIAL DI SUMATERA UTARA, LAPORAN PENELITIAN UNGGULAN PERGURUAN TINGGI (PUPT), DRPM-Dikti, Menristek dan Dikti (2015).

Badaruddin, Erika Revida, Ermansyah, Iskandar Muda, *Village Governance With Implementation of Law Number 6 of 2014 on the Village and Village Administration*, 14(17) INTERNATIONAL JOURNAL OF ECONOMIC RESEARCH (2017).

Badaruddin dan Ermansyah, *Village Community Development And Social Capital. Proceedings of International Conference on Public Policy, Social Computing, and Development 2017 (ICOPOSDev 2017)*, 141 ADVANCES IN SOCIAL SCIENCE, EDUCATIONS AND HUMANITIES RESEARCH, ATLANTIS PRESS (2018).

JOHN CRESWELL, RESEARCH DESIGN QUALITATIVE AND QUANTITATIVE APPROACHES, Sage Pubn: Thousand Oaks, London-New Delhi (1994).

FRANCIS FUKUYAMA, TRUST: THE SOCIAL VIRTUES AND THE CREATION OF PRSPERITY, New York: The Free Press (1995).

JOUSAIRI HASBULLAH, SOCIAL CAPITAL (MENUJU KEUNGGULAN BUDAVA MANUSIA INDONESIA), Jakarta: MR-United Pres (2006).

Dura Justita, *Pengaruh Akuntabilitas Pengelolaan Keuangan Alokasi Dana Desa, Kebijakan Desa, dan Kelembagaan Desa Terhadap Kesejahteraan Masyarakat (Studi Kasus Pada Desa Gubugklakah Kecamatan Poncokusomo Kabupaten Malang)*, 10(1) JURNAL JIBEKA (2016).

ELINOR OSTROM, CRAFTING INSTITUTION, SELF-GOVERNING IRRIGATION SYTEMS, San Fancisco: ICS Press (1992).

Sihar Pandapotan, Hernawi Silalahi, *Social Capital as a Local Wisdom of Farmer in Managing Agricultural Resources in Lubuk Pakam Sub-district, Deli Serdang District*, 2(4) BIRCI-JOURNAL, Budapest International Research and Critics Institute (2019).

Dewi Cahyani Puspitasari, *Modal Sosial Perempuan Dalam Peran Penguatan Ekonomi Keluarga*, 1(2) DALAM JURNAL PEMIKIRAN SOSIOLOGI (2012).

Robert D. Putnam, *The prosperous community: Social capital and public life*, 4(13) THE AMERICAN PROSPECT (1993).

RICHARD ROSE, *Getting Things Done in an Antomodern Society: Social Capital Networks in Rusia*, SOCIAL CAPITAL: A MULTIFACETED PERSPECTIVE, Washington: The World Bank (Partha Dasgupta Dan Ismail Serageldin ed., 1999).

EKO SUTORO AT EL, DESA MEMBANGUN INDONESIA, Yogyakarta: Forum Pengembangan Pembangunan Desa (FPPD) (2014).

MICHAEL WOOLCOCK, DEEPA NARAYAN, *Social Capital: Implications of Development Theory, Research, and Policy*, 15(2) THE WORLD BANK RESEARCH OBSERVER 225 (2000).

SIRAJUDDIN ZUBAEDI, PENGEMBANGAN MASYARAKAT: WACANA DAN PRAKTIK, Jakarta: Kencana Prenadamedia Group (2nd ed. 2014).

Czech Yearbook of International Law®

Alexander J. Bělohlávek

ORCID iD 0000-0001-5310-5269
https://orcid.org/0000-0001-5310-5269

*Key Words:*
*access to court | centre of*
*main interests of the debtor*
*| checking court jurisdiction*
*| claim | COMI | COMI-*
*Shifting | creditor | debtor*
*| establishment | fair trial |*
*forum shopping | bankruptcy*
*tourism | insolvency*
*proceedings | insolvent debtor*
*| international jurisdiction |*
*judgment opening insolvency*
*proceedings | main insolvency*
*proceedings | ordre public*
*| procedural guarantee |*
*recognition of a decision |*
*reservation of public policy*
*| secondary insolvency*
*proceedings | universality*

# The Determination of International Jurisdiction as an Important Aspect in the Protection of the Right of Access to Justice and the Right to a Fair Trial: Defence Mechanisms against the Decision on International Jurisdiction in EU Insolvency Proceedings [Regulation (EU) 2015/848 of European Parliament and of Council on Insolvency Proceedings]

**Abstract** | *The EU conflict-of-laws rules on the international jurisdiction of courts to open main insolvency proceedings are based exclusively on a single connecting factor, i.e. the centre of main interests (COMI) of the debtor. This connecting factor, whether or not the determination thereof is to be based on objective facts perceivable by third parties, often depends on a subjective assessment of a number of circumstances. Moreover, the COMI may – and often does – vary in time. Under a previous law, this variability of the COMI*

Alexander J. Bělohlávek,
Univ. Professor, Prof. zw.,
Dr. iur., Mgr., Dipl. Ing.
oec (MB), prof. hon., Dr.
h. c. Lawyer (Managing
Partner of Law Offices
Bělohlávek), Dept. of Law,
Faculty of Economics,
Ostrava, Czech Republic;
Dept. of Int. law, Faculty
of law, West Bohemia
University, Pilsen, Czech
Republic; Vice-President
of the International
Arbitration Court at

Czech Yearbook of International Law®

*often used to be the subject of an abuse of rights. The COMI was artificially transferred to other States whose legal regime was more favourable to the debtor. In extreme cases, it was the subject of an abuse of rights or even a criminal offence. Previous rules incorporated in Council Regulation (EC) No 1346/2000 were unable to respond to such abuse. The variability of the COMI and the high risk of subjective elements in the assessment of the localisation of the COMI were a principal threat to the right to a fair trial as incorporated in the right of access to court. Selected instruments incorporated in Regulation (EU) 2015/848 of the European Parliament and of the Council are designed to respond to the threat. The most significant of such instruments include the review mechanism under Article 5(1) of Regulation 2015/848, which is an autonomous procedure under EU law, independent of any other mechanisms provided for in the national law of the state where the insolvency proceedings are conducted, in line with lex fori concursus. Except for the requirement that the grounds for applying such a procedure must concern international jurisdiction, the grounds for which the debtors, as well as any creditors, may avail themselves of this mechanism are entirely unlimited. Similarly, no deadline has been stipulated by which the creditors or the debtor may initiate such a procedure. It is a unique and autonomous procedure, which may represent an important element of protection afforded to the main parties in insolvency proceedings conducted in the EU Member States (except Denmark), i.e. including the protection of their right of access to courts or, as applicable, their right to a fair trial.*

the Czech Commodity Exchange, Arbitrator in Prague, Paris (ICC), Vienna (VIAC), Moscow, Vilnius, Warsaw, Minsk, Almaty, Kiev, Bucharest, Ljubljana, Sofia, Kuala Lumpur, Harbin (China), Shenzhen (China) etc., Arbitrator pursuant to UNCITRAL Rules. Member of ASA, DIS, ArbAut etc. Immediately past president of the WJA – the World Jurist Association, Washington D.C./USA. E-mail: office@ablegal.cz

## | | |

## I. Introduction: Importance of International Jurisdiction of Courts in Cross-border Insolvency Proceedings, EU Law and International Standards

**3.01.** The volume of cross-border obligations has skyrocketed over the past several decades. As a consequence of such developments, a debtor's insolvency is connected with international elements that must be addressed in the insolvency proceedings. At the same time, a debtor's activities and property are not always concentrated in the territory of a single State.

In such circumstances, it is by no means exceptional for the requirements for opening insolvency proceedings, as prescribed by the national *leges concursus*, to be fulfilled in several States that simultaneously claim jurisdiction to conduct the insolvency proceedings. The need for international regulation in this area is undeniable, and the endeavour to adopt such regulation dates back to the 1960s. Nonetheless, for a long period of time, the results were rather questionable. The relevant laws include the EU (EC) rules and the rules adopted under the auspices of the UNCITRAL, i.e. the UNCITRAL Model Law on Cross-Border Insolvency of 1997 (UML). The latter currently represents the primary inspiration in this area, and introduces the mechanism of effective cooperation and coordination of insolvency proceedings conducted in different States.

3.02.   The conflict-of-laws rules on insolvency proceedings represent a key component of the judicial cooperation of EU Member States. Insolvency proceedings opened in any of the EU Member States (except Denmark) on or after 26 June 2017 are now governed by Regulation 2015/848,[1] which replaced the preceding law, namely Regulation 1346/2000,[2] which applies to insolvency proceedings opened in the EU Member States (again, except Denmark) from 31 May 2002 to 25 June 2017 (incl.). Regulation 1346/2000 principally copied the Convention of the EC on Insolvency Proceedings of 1995,[3] which never entered into force and was replaced five years later by Regulation 1346/2000.

3.03.   International jurisdiction to open main insolvency proceedings under EU law is based on a single connecting factor, namely the centre of main interests (COMI) of the debtor. Hence, the centre of main interests (COMI) represents the sole conflict-of-laws criterion for the determination of international jurisdiction to open main insolvency proceedings (Article 3 of Regulation 2015/848,[4] as well as its predecessor, Article 3 of Regulation

---

[1]   Regulation (EU) 2015/848 of the European Parliament and of the Council of 20 May 2015 on insolvency proceedings (recast). Published in: Official Journal of the European Union, L 141, 05 June 2015, et. 19-72. [EUR-Lex: 32015R0848]. (Regulation 2015/848).
[2]   Council Regulation (EC) No 1346/2000 of 29 May 2000 on insolvency proceedings. Published in: Official Journal, L 160, 30 June 2000, et. 0001-0018. [EUR-Lex: 32000R1346]. (Regulation 1346/2000).
[3]   Council of the European Union Print No. 12830/95, Brussels, 1995 and Council of the EU, Document No. 6500/96, DRS 8 (CFC), Brussels, 03 May 1996 (1995 Convention).
[4]   Article 3 of Regulation 2015/848 (quote):
        [International jurisdiction] – 1. The courts of the Member State within the territory of which the centre of the debtor's main interests is situated shall have jurisdiction to open insolvency proceedings ('main insolvency proceedings'). The centre of main interests shall be the place where the debtor conducts the administration of its interests on a regular basis and which is ascertainable by third parties. (-)In the case of a company or legal person, the place of the registered office shall be presumed to be the centre of its main interests in the absence of proof to the contrary. That presumption shall only apply if the registered office has not been moved to another Member State within the 3-month period prior to the request for the opening of insolvency proceedings. (-)In the case of an individual exercising an independent business

1346/2000[5]). This connecting factor **includes business (commercial, trade) and other professional, for-profit, economic activities.**[6] In other words, it is the place of the main economic interest in terms of the creation and management of the debtor's property values, as opposed to the place of habitual residence,[7] which is connected with the territory to which a particular person has their closest relationship. Although these two instruments are formally separate, it does not necessarily follow that the COMI could be identical in the case of natural

---

or professional activity, the centre of main interests shall be presumed to be that individual's principal place of business in the absence of proof to the contrary. That presumption shall only apply if the individual's principal place of business has not been moved to another Member State within the 3-month period prior to the request for the opening of insolvency proceedings. (-)In the case of any other individual, the centre of main interests shall be presumed to be the place of the individual's habitual residence in the absence of proof to the contrary. This presumption shall only apply if the habitual residence has not been moved to another Member State within the 6-month period prior to the request for the opening of insolvency proceedings. 2. Where the centre of the debtor's main interests is situated within the territory of a Member State, the courts of another Member State shall have jurisdiction to open insolvency proceedings against that debtor only if it possesses an establishment within the territory of that other Member State. The effects of those proceedings shall be restricted to the assets of the debtor situated in the territory of the latter Member State. 3. Where insolvency proceedings have been opened in accordance with paragraph 1, any proceedings opened subsequently in accordance with paragraph 2 shall be secondary insolvency proceedings. 4. The territorial insolvency proceedings referred to in paragraph 2 may only be opened prior to the opening of main insolvency proceedings in accordance with paragraph 1 where (a) insolvency proceedings under paragraph 1 cannot be opened because of the conditions laid down by the law of the Member State within the territory of which the centre of the debtor's main interests is situated; or (b) the opening of territorial insolvency proceedings is requested by: (i) a creditor whose claim arises from or is in connection with the operation of an establishment situated within the territory of the Member State where the opening of territorial proceedings is requested; or (ii) a public authority which, under the law of the Member State within the territory of which the establishment is situated, has the right to request the opening of insolvency proceedings. (-)When main insolvency proceedings are opened, the territorial insolvency proceedings shall become secondary insolvency proceedings.

5    Article 3 of Regulation 1346/2000 (quote):
[International jurisdiction] - The courts of the Member State within the territory of which the centre of a debtor's main interests is situated shall have jurisdiction to open insolvency proceedings. In the case of a company or legal person, the place of the registered office shall be presumed to be the centre of its main interests in the absence of proof to the contrary. 2. Where the centre of a debtor's main interests is situated within the territory of a Member State, the courts of another Member State shall have jurisdiction to open insolvency proceedings against that debtor only if he possesses an establishment within the territory of that other Member State. The effects of those proceedings shall be restricted to the assets of the debtor situated in the territory of the latter Member State. 3. Where insolvency proceedings have been opened under paragraph 1, any proceedings opened subsequently under paragraph 2 shall be secondary proceedings. These latter proceedings must be winding-up proceedings. 4. Territorial insolvency proceedings referred to in paragraph 2 may be opened prior to the opening of main insolvency proceedings in accordance with paragraph 1 only: (a) where insolvency proceedings under paragraph 1 cannot be opened because of the conditions laid down by the law of the Member State within the territory of which the centre of the debtor's main interests is situated; or (b) where the opening of territorial insolvency proceedings is requested by a creditor who has his domicile, habitual residence or registered office in the Member State within the territory of which the establishment is situated, or whose claim arises from the operation of that establishment.

6    Cf. Daniel Friedemann Fritz, Rainer M. Bähr, *Die Europäische Verordnung über Insolvenzverfahren. Herausforderung an die Gerichte und Insolvenzverwalter*, 11(6) DEUTSCHE ZEITSCHRIFT FÜR WIRTSCHAFTS- UND INSOLVENZRECHT (2001), 221 et seq. (here especially et. 224).

7    See the fourth subparagraph of Article 3(1) of Regulation 2015/848.

persons other than traders.[8] Conversely, compared to the rules incorporated in Regulation 1346/2000, Regulation 2015/848 expanded the rules defining the COMI by this rebuttable presumption.[9]

## II.    Modified Universality and Parallel Proceedings against the Same Debtor

3.04.    The issue of the conflict-of-laws criteria applicable to the determination of the State court with jurisdiction to open main insolvency proceedings, as well as the conditions for conducting the insolvency proceedings with respect to one and the same debtor in other Member States, is one of the crucial issues most discussed in connection with Regulation 1346/2000, and resulted in a review thereof and the adoption of a new law. Indeed, the HLV Report itself devoted the most attention to Article 3 of Regulation 1346/2000 and the proposed amendments thereto, and Article 3 is also the most intensively discussed provision in relation to Regulation 2015/848.

3.05.    The reason is that the EU law on insolvency proceedings is based on the principle of universality. However, universality is subject to principal corrections by the elements of plurality manifested in the possibility of conducting particular insolvency proceedings in the individual States. From this perspective, the concept of universality cannot be perceived as producing universal or uniform insolvency proceedings, but only as universal effects of specific national proceedings opened in a Member State. Member States have refused the possibility of uniform insolvency proceedings, arguing that the differences in substantive law effectively preclude the introduction of insolvency proceedings with general effects throughout the entire EU; this would, conversely, give rise to many practical difficulties.[10] Hence, the EU legislature has chosen the alternative

---

[8]    Regulation 1346/2000 and Regulation 2015/848 both apply regardless of whether the debtor is a natural person or a legal person, a trader or a different entity. Insolvency capacity is governed by the *lex fori concursus* in terms of Article 7(2)(a) of Regulation 2015/848 or, as applicable, see also Article 4(2)(a) of Regulation 1346/2000.

[9]    See the fourth subparagraph of Article 3(1) of Regulation 2015/848.

[10]    See Recital 22 of Regulation 2015/848 (quote):
[T]his Regulation acknowledges the fact that as a result of widely differing substantive laws it is not practical to introduce insolvency proceedings with universal scope throughout the Union. The application without exception of the law of the State of the opening of proceedings would, against this background, frequently lead to difficulties. This applies, for example, to the widely differing national laws on security interests to be found in the Member States. Furthermore, the preferential rights enjoyed by some creditors in insolvency proceedings are, in some cases, completely different. At the next review of this Regulation, it will be necessary to identify further measures in order to improve the preferential rights of employees at European level. This Regulation should take account of such differing national laws in two different ways. On the one hand, provision should be made for special rules on the applicable law in the case of particularly

of conflict-of-laws rules regulating jurisdiction, recognition and the law applicable to insolvency proceedings. It would not be appropriate to question these arguments, but one must ask whether, and to what extent, the true reason was indeed practical problems, or whether the insolvency proceedings have fallen victim to the political interests of the representatives of the individual Member States.

**3.06.** The justification would be more persuasive if the EU legislature had put forth actual problems that such universal insolvency proceedings would cause. For instance, one problem would be the more difficult opening of insolvency proceedings for smaller creditors from a Member State different from the State of the court which would have jurisdiction to open the universal insolvency proceedings. If the debtor has sufficient assets in the other State to satisfy domestic creditors, it would appear questionable, to say the least, if these creditors were forced to conduct investigations to determine the State in which the universal insolvency proceedings should be opened, including the corresponding conditions for the opening thereof. Indeed, even the preceding Regulation 1346/2000 operated on the premise, fully adopted by Regulation 2015/848, that territorial insolvency proceedings (Article 3(4) of Regulation 2015/848) may be conducted without the opening of main insolvency proceedings.

**3.07.** Hence, the EU insolvency law clearly emphasises that there are certain situations in which insolvency proceedings covering assets of the debtor in all Member States are not only unnecessary, but may even prove counterproductive. The inability of one establishment out of many, as the term is specifically defined in the EU rules on insolvency proceedings,[11] to pay its debts

---

significant rights and legal relationships (e.g. rights in rem and contracts of employment). On the other hand, national proceedings covering only assets situated in the State of the opening of proceedings should also be allowed alongside main insolvency proceedings with universal scope.)

and Recital 11 of Regulation 1346/2000 (quote):

[T]his Regulation acknowledges the fact that as a result of widely differing substantive laws it is not practical to introduce insolvency proceedings with universal scope in the entire Community. The application without exception of the law of the State of opening of proceedings would, against this background, frequently lead to difficulties. This applies, for example, to the widely differing laws on security interests to be found in the Community. Furthermore, the preferential rights enjoyed by some creditors in the insolvency proceedings are, in some cases, completely different. This Regulation should take account of this in two different ways. On the one hand, provision should be made for special rules on applicable law in the case of particularly significant rights and legal relationships (e.g. rights in rem and contracts of employment). On the other hand, national proceedings covering only assets situated in the State of opening should also be allowed alongside main insolvency proceedings with universal scope.).

[11] See Article 2(10) of Regulation 2015/848 (quote): [...] *"establishment" means any place of operations where a debtor carries out or has carried out in the 3-month period prior to the request to open main insolvency proceedings a non-transitory economic activity with human means and assets;*[...].

need not necessarily trigger the opening of main insolvency proceedings under Article 3(1) of Regulation 2015/848, especially if the debtor's assets located in the State where the establishment is located are sufficient to settle the creditors' claims. In connection with this, it is necessary to point out the impact that Regulation 2015/848 has had with regard to one of the comments made with respect to Regulation 1346/2000, i.e. that the law envisages only such insolvency proceedings that result in the liquidation of the debtor (Regulation 2015/848 no longer adopts the premise), whereas the proper functioning of the internal market would benefit much more from an endeavour to rescue economically viable undertakings in hardship.

3.08. But the Preamble to Regulation 2015/848 mentions no such reasons, and paradoxically, invokes examples that confirm that, rather than the practical impossibility of creating uniform insolvency proceedings, the true reason is the unreadiness of the individual Member States to reach a compromise, and their insistence on their own national laws. The Preamble declares that one of the two methods employed by the Insolvency Regulation in dealing with differences in the laws of the individual Member States is the adoption of special rules on applicable law in the case of particularly significant rights and legal relationships,[12] which may in itself complicate the main insolvency proceedings, not to speak of the different approach to selected creditors. This *de facto* confirms that the diversity of laws is not generally insurmountable. It depends entirely on the Member States' political will to determine which specific issues they insist on their sovereignty and which they refuse unification. In other words, the underlying premise is that unified universally effective systems of insolvency law still operate in the territories of the individual Member States, and that national insolvency proceedings opened in a particular State have universal effects.[13] In the context of the EU insolvency law, one may speak of a modification of universality in the form of the so-called combined model.[14]

---

[12]   See Recital 22 of Regulation 2015/848 (quoted above in this paper).
[13]   STEFAN SMID, EUROPÄISCHES INTERNATIONALES INSOLVENZRECHT. Wien: Manzsche Verlags- und Universitätsbuchhandlung / Center of Legal Competence (2002), et. 39, marg. 30.
[14]   Cf. also Stefan Leible, Ansgar Staudinger, *Die europäische Verordnung über Insolvenzverfahren*, 61 KONKURS, TREUHAND, SANIERUNG (2000), 533 et seq. (here especially page 537). The authors refer to *modified universality*.

## III. Shifts in Definition of Centre of Main Interests (COMI) of Debtor and Increased Importance of Predictability

**3.09.** It may appear at first sight that the rules on international jurisdiction to open insolvency proceedings incorporated in Regulation 2015/848 have introduced far-reaching changes. On closer inspection, it is fairly easy to observe that the changes mostly do not reject the previous law, but codify the case law that has gradually developed with respect to Article 3 of Regulation 1346/2000. But when one refers to the previous existing case law, it is also necessary to point out that this means the case law of the Court of Justice. The need for a clear and unambiguous definition of the criteria for the determination of international jurisdiction arises especially due to the fact that, despite the existing case law of the Court of Justice of the European Union, the interpretations differ in practice of the centre of main interests (COMI) of the debtor as the sole connecting factor for determining the international jurisdiction to open main insolvency proceedings by national courts. Considering the above, as well as the fact that the definition of the COMI has undergone no major changes that would lay down clear and unambiguous criteria, the situation is understandable.

**3.10.** Regulation 2015/848 further enhances the principle that the court seized by the request to open insolvency proceedings is obliged to examine its international jurisdiction of its own motion;[15] hence, the pressure will continue forcing the court not to make do with the application of the presumption in Article 3 of Regulation 2015/848 (registered office or residence as the rebuttable presumption of the COMI) and take into account any and all circumstances. Further, it will exclude the possibility that the COMI could be located in a different State, even in the absence of any express objection that the presumption of existence of the COMI cannot stand in the particular case.

**3.11.** Compared to Regulation 1346/2000, no principal changes have been made to the principles governing the determination of international jurisdiction. The main insolvency proceedings affecting all assets of the debtor located in a Member State (universality of the main insolvency proceedings) may still be

---

[15] This obligation is new explicitly provided for in Article 4 of Regulation 2015/848; the court is obliged to examine the issue of international jurisdiction *ex officio* (of its own motion), and on top of that, must justify its conclusions in the judgment opening insolvency proceedings. Consequently, Articles 4 and 5 of Regulation 2015/848 represent a novelty compared to Regulation 1346/2000, although, for instance, the obligation to examine the court's own jurisdiction of its own motion (now explicitly stipulated in Article 4 of Regulation 2015/848) could have been inferred even from the previous law and the gradually expanding case law.

opened exclusively in the state where the debtor's COMI is located. However, compared to Regulation 1346/2000, Article 3(1) of Regulation 2015/848 now includes a definition[16] that in one form or another permeates any attempts at creating an effective international system of insolvency law. The rule is that the COMI is defined as the place where the debtor conducts the administration of their interests on a regular basis and which is ascertainable by third parties. This definition was articulated in the decision of the ECJ in C-341/04 (*Eurofood*),[17/18] as the conclusions made in the *Eurofood* case were subsequently also confirmed by the Court of Justice of the EU in C-396/09 (*Interedil*).[19/20] It follows from the above that this definition of

---

[16]  See the second sentence of the first subparagraph of Article 3(1) of Regulation 2015/848.

[17]  Judgment of the ECJ (Grand Chamber) in Case C-341/04 of 02 May 2006, *Eurofood IFSC Ltd*. ECR 2006, I-3813 et seq. [ECLI:EU:C:2006:281]. [EUR-Lex: 62004CJ0341]. (*Eurofood*).

[18]  *Eurofood*, paragraphs 32 and 32 (quote):

> (32) The scope of that concept is highlighted by the 13th recital of the Regulation, which states that "the 'centre of main interests' should correspond to the place where the debtor conducts the administration of his interests on a regular basis and is therefore ascertainable by third parties".
> (33) That definition shows that the centre of main interests must be identified by reference to criteria that are both objective and ascertainable by third parties. That objectivity and that possibility of ascertainment by third parties are necessary in order to ensure legal certainty and foreseeability concerning the determination of the court with jurisdiction to open main insolvency proceedings. That legal certainty and that foreseeability are all the more important in that, in accordance with Article 4(1) of the Regulation, determination of the court with jurisdiction entails determination of the law which is to apply.

[19]  Judgment of the Court of Justice of the EU in Case C-396/09 of 20 October 2011, *Interedil Srl, in liquidazione* v. *Fallimento Interedil Srl* et *Intesa Gestione Crediti SpA*. ECR 2011, I-09915 et seq. [ECLI:EU:C:2011:671]. [EUR-Lex: 62009CJ0396]. (*Interedil*).

[20]  *Interedil*, paragraphs 47 and 49. In the original Italian version (quote):

> (47) Benché il regolamento non fornisca alcuna definizione della nozione di centro degli interessi principali del debitore, la portata di quest'ultima nozione è tuttavia chiarita, come rilevato dalla Corte al punto 32 della citata sentenza Eurofood IFSC, dal tredicesimo 'considerando' del regolamento, ai sensi del quale «per "centro degli interessi principali" si dovrebbe intendere il luogo in cui il debitore esercita in modo abituale, e pertanto riconoscibile dai terzi, la gestione dei suoi interessi». [...] (49) Con riferimento al medesimo 'considerando', la Corte ha peraltro precisato, al punto 33 della citata sentenza Eurofood IFSC, che il centro degli interessi principali del debitore deve essere individuato in base a criteri al tempo stesso obiettivi e riconoscibili dai terzi, per garantire la certezza del diritto e la prevedibilità dell'individuazione del giudice competente ad aprire la procedura di insolvenza principale. Si deve ritenere che tale esigenza di obiettività e tale riconoscibilità risultino soddisfatte qualora gli elementi materiali presi in considerazione per stabilire il luogo in cui la società debitrice gestisce abitualmente i suoi interessi siano stati oggetto di una pubblicità o, quanto meno, siano stati circondati da una trasparenza sufficiente a far sì che i terzi - vale a dire, segnatamente, i creditori della società stessa - ne abbiano potuto avere conoscenza.

English translation (quote):

> (47) While the Regulation does not provide a definition of the term "centre of a debtor's main interests", guidance as to the scope of that term is, nevertheless, as the Court stated at paragraph 32 of Eurofood IFSC, to be found in recital 13 in the preamble to the Regulation, which states that "the 'centre of main interests' should correspond to the place where the debtor conducts the administration of his interests on a regular basis and [which] is therefore ascertainable by third parties". [...] (49) With reference to that recital, the Court also stated, at paragraph 33 of Eurofood IFSC, that the centre of a debtor's main interests must be identified by reference to criteria that are both objective and ascertainable by third parties, in order to ensure legal certainty and foreseeability concerning the determination of the court with jurisdiction to open the main insolvency proceedings. That requirement for objectivity and that possibility of ascertainment by third parties may be considered to be met where the material factors taken

the COMI is inherently incapable of eliminating the problems relating to the insufficient definition of this instrument, and it depends on each individual court or, as applicable, the individual circumstances of each case as to how the court assesses the place of administration and its quality of being ascertainable by third parties.

**3.12.** The place where the debtor's main interests are concentrated is the place where the debtor conducts the administration of their interests on a regular basis and which is ascertainable by third parties. Consequently, the COMI connecting factor is based on two main conceptual features. The first one is internal, while the other is external. It needs to be emphasized that the COMI must – always and as a rule – be identified on an individual basis and with due regard to all circumstances of the case. It is also necessary to bear in mind that the Court of Justice tends towards an objective approach, as the Court has demonstrated in the decision of the European Court of Justice (ECJ) in **C-341/04 (*Eurofood*)**[21] and in the decision of the Court of Justice of the EU in **C-396/09 (*Interedil*).**[22/23]

---

into account for the purpose of establishing the place in which the debtor company conducts the administration of its interests on a regular basis have been made public or, at the very least, made sufficiently accessible to enable third parties, that is to say in particular the company's creditors, to be aware of them.

[21] *Eurofood*, paragraphs 32 and 33. Quoted above.

[22] *Interedil*, paragraph 59, English translation (quote):

[...] a debtor company's main centre of interests must be determined by attaching greater importance to the place of the company's central administration, as may be established by objective factors which are ascertainable by third parties. Where the bodies responsible for the management and supervision of a company are in the same place as its registered office and the management decisions of the company are taken, in a manner that is ascertainable by third parties, in that place, the presumption in that provision cannot be rebutted. Where a company's central administration is not in the same place as its registered office, the presence of company assets and the existence of contracts for the financial exploitation of those assets in a Member State other than that in which the registered office is situated cannot be regarded as sufficient factors to rebut the presumption unless a comprehensive assessment of all the relevant factors makes it possible to establish, in a manner that is ascertainable by third parties, that the company's actual centre of management and supervision and of the management of its interests is located in that other Member State.

In the Italian version:

La seconda parte della prima questione, la seconda questione e la prima parte della terza questione devono pertanto essere risolte affermando che, per individuare il centro degli interessi principali di una società debitrice, l'art. 3, n. 1, seconda frase, del regolamento deve essere interpretato nei termini seguenti: (-) il centro degli interessi principali di una società debitrice deve essere individuato privilegiando il luogo dell'amministrazione principale di tale società, come determinabile sulla base di elementi oggettivi e riconoscibili dai terzi. Qualora gli organi direttivi e di controllo di una società si trovino presso la sua sede statutaria e qualora le decisioni di gestione di tale società siano assunte, in maniera riconoscibile dai terzi, in tale luogo, la presunzione introdotta da tale disposizione non è superabile. Laddove il luogo dell'amministrazione principale di una società non si trovi presso la sua sede statutaria, la presenza di attivi sociali nonché l'esistenza di contratti relativi alla loro gestione finanziaria in uno Stato membro diverso da quello della sede statutaria di tale società possono essere considerate elementi sufficienti a superare tale presunzione solo a condizione che una valutazione globale di tutti gli elementi rilevanti consenta di stabilire che, in maniera riconoscibile dai terzi, il centro effettivo di direzione e di controllo della società stessa, nonché della gestione dei suoi interessi,

**3.13.** The objective approach to the qualification of the COMI must be emphasized in connection with the protection of the right to a fair trial and, consequently, the protection of access to justice as such. The reason is that the process of identifying and determining the COMI as the fundamental and sole connecting factor for the determination of the international jurisdiction to open main insolvency proceedings is specific to the fact that the dividing line between objective aspects and subjective evaluation is often nearly obscured. Considering the fact that the opening of insolvency proceedings constitutes a major interference in the affairs of any entity, one must conclude that Regulation 1346/2000 contained essentially no, or only minimal, mechanisms of protection against an erroneous determination of international jurisdiction, let alone such excesses as the abuse of a right. The argument that Regulation 1346/2000 contained a reservation of public policy (*ordre public*) as a defence mechanism cannot stand in view of, inter alia, the restrictive approach of the European Union to the application of this reservation. Hence, as concerns the protection of the fundamental right to a fair trial in terms of access to justice, it is only Regulation 2015/848 that has introduced the first acceptable defence mechanisms in the EU insolvency law, although, naturally, it still remains to be seen how effective these mechanisms actually are.

## IV.      Determination of International Jurisdiction to Open Main Insolvency Proceedings and Right to Fair Trial

**3.14.** The need for predictability, i.e. the requirement stipulating that the COMI must be ascertainable by third parties, is already emphasized in Recital 13 of Regulation 1346/2000 as one of its main aspects. This particular aspect, together with ascertainability by third parties, is also provided for and

---

è situato in tale altro Stato membro; (-) nel caso di un trasferimento della sede statutaria di una società debitrice prima della proposizione di una domanda di apertura di una procedura di insolvenza, si presume che il centro degli interessi principali di tale società si trovi presso la nuova sede statutaria della medesima.

23    See External evaluation of Regulation No 1346/2000/EC on Insolvency Proceedings, JUST/2011/JCIV/PR/0049/A4 (*External Evaluation of Regulation No. 1346/2000/EC on Insolvency Proceedings*) prepared by Institute of Foreign and International Private and Business Law, Ruprecht-Karls-Universität Heidelberg [DEU] and the Institute for Civil Procedure, Universität Wien [AUT]. Also referred to as the "*Heidelberg – Vienna Report*", "*Heidelberg – Luxemburg – Vienna Report*" etc. in legal resources and literature (the "HLV Report"). Available at: http://ec.europa.eu/justice/civil/files/evaluation_insolvency_en.pdf. (accessed on 24 January 2020). References to the HLV Report are references to this material published in electronic form. Here HLV Report, marg. 2.4, et. 16.

In the original English version (quote): 'The COMI must be determined in accordance with the circumstances of each individual case; according to the objective approach of the ECJ it must be identified by reference to criteria ascertainable by third parties.'

underlined in Recitals 28 and 30 [of Regulation 2015/848], as well as Article 3(1) [of Regulation 2015/848]. Hence, the quality of being ascertainable by third parties is currently also explicitly stipulated in Article 3(1) of Regulation 2015/848, which further enhances the importance of this evaluation criterion.

**3.15.** The Preamble to Regulation 2015/848 expressly refers to the interest of the creditors and their opinion on where the debtor manages their interests. If the COMI changes, the creditors must be informed in a timely manner, for example by drawing their attention to the change of address in commercial correspondence, or through other appropriate means. Predictability must also generally be considered one of the fundamental requirements imposed on the law from the perspective of the protection of fundamental rights. From the perspective of Regulation 2015/848, or indeed the EU and international insolvency law, this predictability is primarily reflected in the predictable connecting factor for the determination of international jurisdiction to conduct insolvency proceedings. Hence, as concerns the EU rules incorporated in Regulation 2015/848, this applies to the main insolvency proceedings.

**3.16.** As mentioned above, the localisation of the COMI as the connecting factor thus also represents a key moment from the perspective of the protection of fundamental rights in terms of the right to a fair trial. Potential changes of the COMI in the course of time, as well as the subjective factors involved in the identification and determination of the COMI, which cannot be eliminated in any decision-making processes and which are exceptionally powerful specifically in the determination of international jurisdiction in EU insolvency proceedings, are the reason why predictability and ascertainability of the COMI require special attention. However, another essential factor is the reinforcement of additional control mechanisms.

**3.17.** The European Court of Justice has already elaborated on this issue in its decision in *Eurofood*, namely from the perspective of the review and recognition by a court of the jurisdiction of another Member State's court to open insolvency proceedings. In compliance with Article 16 of Regulation 1346/2000,[24] the

---

[24]    Cf. Article 19 of Regulation 2015/848 (quote):
          1. Any judgment opening insolvency proceedings handed down by a court of a Member State which has jurisdiction pursuant to Article 3 shall be recognised in all other Member States from the moment that it becomes effective in the State of the opening of proceedings. (-) The rule laid down in the first subparagraph shall also apply where, on account of a debtor's capacity, insolvency proceedings cannot be brought against that debtor in other Member States. 2. Recognition of the proceedings referred to in Article 3(1) shall not preclude the opening of the proceedings referred to in Article 3(2) by a court in another Member State. The latter proceedings shall be secondary insolvency proceedings within the meaning of Chapter III.

ECJ ruled that the principle of mutual trust requires that the courts of other Member States recognise the jurisdiction of the court that already opened the insolvency proceedings. But it is also necessary to mention the ECJ's explanation that it is inherent in that principle of mutual trust that the court of a Member State carefully check that it has jurisdiction to open the insolvency proceedings pursuant to Regulation 1346/2000. According to the decision in *Eurofood*, the court of a Member State that opens the proceedings is to (quote):

> [...] check that it has jurisdiction having regard to Article 3(1) [of Regulation 1346/2000], i.e. examine whether the centre of the debtor's main interests is situated in that Member State. In that regard, it should be emphasised that such an examination must take place in such a way as to comply with the essential procedural guarantees required for a fair legal process.[25]

3.18.   This decision and the interpretation provided by the Court of Justice in its following case law thus clearly indicate that the courts opening the insolvency proceedings pursuant to Regulation 1346/2000 are obliged to objectively assess whether the debtor has their establishment or directly their COMI in their territory, i.e. materially examine their jurisdiction to open and conduct the insolvency proceedings. Only rigorous respect for this principle may legitimately justify Article 16 of Regulation 1346/2000,[26] which reflects the principle of mutual trust. The mere fact that the registered office represents a rebuttable presumption of the COMI does not justify failure to examine and fulfil the investigative obligation of the court to examine its jurisdiction and check whether and what conditions of its jurisdiction are fulfilled or, conversely, lacking. Indeed, this conclusion is now explicitly confirmed by Article 4 of Regulation 2015/848,[27] and also follows from the decision in

---

[25]   *Eurofood*, paragraph 41.
[26]   Cf. Article 19 of Regulation 2015/848 (quoted above).
[27]   Article 4 of Regulation 2015/848 (quote):
   [Examination as to jurisdiction] 1. A court seised of a request to open insolvency proceedings shall of its own motion examine whether it has jurisdiction pursuant to Article 3. The judgment opening insolvency proceedings shall specify the grounds on which the jurisdiction of the court is based, and, in particular, whether jurisdiction is based on Article 3(1) or (2). 2. Notwithstanding paragraph 1, where insolvency proceedings are opened in accordance with national law without a decision by a court, Member States may entrust the insolvency practitioner appointed in such proceedings to examine whether the Member State in which a request for the opening of proceedings is pending has jurisdiction pursuant to Article 3. Where this is the case, the insolvency practitioner shall specify in the decision opening the proceedings the grounds on which jurisdiction is based and, in particular, whether jurisdiction is based on Article 3(1) or (2).

*Interedil,* which provides a more detailed specification of the COMI, as well as other case law concerning the requirements imposed on an establishment in terms of the EU insolvency law.

## V. Revolutionary Change Consisting of the Review of International Jurisdiction of Court to Conduct Main Insolvency Proceedings Incorporated in Article 5 of Regulation 2015/848

**3.19.** Principal reform in the deficiencies associated with the provision of judicial protection in connection with the determination of the debtor's COMI now appears to have been introduced in Article 5 of Regulation 2015/848. Article 5 of Regulation 2015/848 (quote):

> [Judicial review of the decision to open main insolvency proceedings] 1. The debtor or any creditor may challenge before a court the decision opening main insolvency proceedings on grounds of international jurisdiction. 2. The decision opening main insolvency proceedings may be challenged by parties other than those referred to in paragraph 1 or on grounds other than a lack of international jurisdiction where national law so provides.

**3.20.** Indeed, no rules analogous to Article 5 of Regulation 2015/848, and especially Article 5(1) of Regulation 2015/848, were contained in any previous international initiatives or EU legislative initiatives concerning the harmonisation of international insolvency law from the perspective of the determination of international jurisdiction. Likewise, no such rules were present in Regulation 1346/2000. Consequently, Article 5 of Regulation 2015/848 represents an important and revolutionary *novum.*

**3.21.** The provisions of Article 5 of Regulation 2015/848 only relate to a decision to open main insolvency proceedings. Hence, it does not cover any other proceedings falling within the scope of Regulation 2015/848, i.e. it does not relate to secondary insolvency proceedings. The said provision thus fails to address, inter alia, problems concerning assets that fall under two or more jurisdictional sovereignties. More precisely, it fails to address the problem of those creditors who have a claim against the estate outside the scope of jurisdiction of the court in the main proceedings.[28]

 28   Amir Adl Rubordeh, AN ANALYSIS AND HYPOTHESIS ON FORUM SHOPPING IN INSOLVENCY

# VI. Purpose and Development of Case Law in Selected Countries in Review of Court Jurisdiction to Open and Conduct Main Insolvency Proceedings

## VI.1. Purpose of Rule Incorporated in Article 5 of Regulation 2015/848

**3.22.** Article 5 of Regulation 2015/848 thus newly provides for the possibility of challenging before a court the decision opening main insolvency proceedings[29] on grounds of international jurisdiction. The purpose of the provision is to enhance the protection and legal certainty of the debtor and of the debtor's creditors in those areas where the rules incorporated in Regulation 1346/2000 were ineffective or entirely insufficient.

**3.23.** The new law is primarily connected with the phenomenon of forum shopping or insolvency/bankruptcy tourism, i.e. situations in which one of the parties to the insolvency proceedings endeavours to open the proceedings[30] in a State in which the party would have a more favourable position under the State's domestic legislation. At the same time, the new law is usually associated with the concept of COMI shifting, i.e. the frequently artificial, fictitious and ostensible transfer of the debtor's COMI between States for the purpose of securing advantages in the insolvency proceedings. The procedure under Article 5 of Regulation 2015/848 thus endeavours to introduce a mechanism that would provide an additional protection against such conduct.

**3.24.** However, the objective of Article 5 of Regulation 2015/848 is substantially broader than just protection against the artificial, fictitious and ostensible transfer of the COMI by the debtor. It also provides the same protection and legal standing to the debtors themselves. Consequently, and as mentioned above, this provision may be labelled as revolutionary for the extent of its effects on the decision on international jurisdiction in terms of the possibility to review the decision, both due to the fact that it prescribes essentially no limitations on the grounds for which the judgment opening insolvency proceedings may be challenged for lack of international jurisdiction, and with regard to the fact

---

LAW. FROM THE EUROPEAN INSOLVENCY REGULATION TO ITS RECAST [online], International Insolvency Institute (2016), et. 52. Available at: https://www.iiiglobal.org/sites/default/files/media/RUDBORDEH%2C%20Amir%20-%20An%20Analysis%20%26%20Hypothesis%20on%20Forum%20Shopping%20in%20Insolvency%20Law%20%28EU%29.pdf (accessed on 12 August 2019).

29   See Article 2(7) of Regulation 2015/848.
30   See also Article 2(7) and (8) of Regulation 2015/848.

that this procedure is not subject to any temporal limitations (see below). It represents a substantive, directly applicable law. It is important to note that Article 5(1) of Regulation 2015/848 makes no reference to the *lex fori concursus*,[31] even though it provides for a procedure that could only be applied in the State where main insolvency proceedings are opened. Although there is as yet no or only marginal experience with the application of this instrument, it is – without exaggeration – one of the most important amendments of the law as compared to Regulation 1346/2000. At the same time, however, it is one of the basic instruments reinforcing the judicial protection of the main parties, i.e. creditors and the debtor.

3.25. Such protection, now represented by Article 5 of Regulation 2015/848, previously only depended on the procedural mechanisms afforded by the national legal systems of the EU Member States, namely the law of the State in which the main insolvency proceedings were opened. In some cases, though, the creditors and/or the debtor experienced major limitations in the application of such national procedural mechanisms; sometimes such procedural protection was entirely absent. This situation was the cause for major alarm from the perspective of the protection of fundamental rights, primarily the right to a fair trial, especially because the determination of the COMI in individual cases does not depend on objective criteria or, as applicable, only on criteria of an objective nature. Consequently, the determination of the COMI in individual cases was in fact often surprising in practice, despite the proclaimed basic criterion for the determination of the COMI, i.e. its ascertainability and predictability. Although there are political reasons preventing the EU from essentially admitting that the interests of the parties were consistently being jeopardised as a result of the unpredictable determination of the COMI, the reality in cross-border cases was frequently the opposite. But the EU structures or, as applicable, the EU legislation were obviously well aware of the fact, because Regulation 2015/848 also introduced other instruments protecting foreign creditors. Hence, the mechanism of protection against the determination of international jurisdiction, i.e. the determination of the debtor's COMI, as envisaged in Article 5 of Regulation 2015/848, may represent one of the fundamental turning points as regards the securing of judicial protection in cross-border insolvency

---

[31] Cf. Peter Mankowski, In: PETER MANKOWSKI, MICHAEL F. MÜLLER, JESSICA SCHMIDT, EUINSVO 2015: EUROPÄISCHE INSOLVENZORDNUNG 2015. KOMMENTAR, München: C. H. Beck (2016), commentary on Article 5 of Regulation 2015/848, marg. 1, et. 153.

proceedings in EU law. In this regard, one must also bear in mind that the scope of the instrument laid down in Article 5 of Regulation 2015/848, including its temporal perspective (see below), is indeed very broad, and one may only hope that the rule meets the general expectations.

## VI.2. Practices in Selected Member States as a Template for the Introduction of a New Defence Mechanism against Judgment Opening Insolvency Proceedings

**3.26.** As mentioned above, the changes in EU insolvency law were necessitated primarily, though not exclusively, by the increasing practice of forum shopping, when debtors picked out a more favourable forum and tried to fictitiously transfer the place of their main interests to States with a law that was more favourable to them. Gradually, over the course of the application of Regulation 1346/2000, England became an exceptionally popular destination for opening insolvency proceedings and attracted a number of debtors from other Member States, because its laws on insolvency proceedings allow for discharge within a year. Debtors in England may actually ask for an even faster discharge, which could be completed within several months. The reason is that insolvency proceedings in England are opened on the basis of information obtained from the debtor, without any closer examination of the corresponding factual background. If the debtor fails to truthfully describe their personal and financial situation, the creditors or insolvency practitioners may demand the cancellation of the insolvency order, but they must prove that the insolvency order was based on misleading or false statements of the debtor. Indeed, most of the remedies lodged in cross-border cases argue that the debtor's COMI is actually located in a country different from England.[32] In the interesting case of *Official Receiver* v. *Mitterfellner,* the court held that it suffices for the cancellation of the insolvency order if the debtor supplied the court with false information. This applies even if the debtor's statements are not relevant from the perspective of the assessment of the COMI.[33]

**3.27.** The possibilities of insolvency tourism and fictitious transfers of the COMI to England, as a very popular destination especially for German debtors, were undermined primarily in the 2011

---

[32] HLV Report, et. 150-151.
[33] REINHARD BORK, RENATO MANGANO, EUROPEAN CROSS-BORDER INSOLVENCY LAW, Oxford: Oxford University Press (2016)., et. 101.

decision in *Steinhardt* v. *Eichler*,[34] when this particular procedure used by insolvent German debtors and the existing approach of English courts were beginning to represent a major problem of not only legal and financial dimensions, but also political ones.

3.28. Although the destination of such fictitious transfers of the COMI was not only England, but also Luxembourg and other countries, England became very popular in this regard. Transfers of the COMI were unexceptionally offered by specialised agencies in the form of various packages of services, and sometimes these services were even advertised in the media. There are two grounds for which this decision must be perceived as important. It was the decision in *Steinhardt* v. *Eichler* that resulted in the introduction of two new requirements for the transfer of the COMI in the decision-making practice, at least as concerns the approach adopted by English courts. Firstly, the debtor must present evidence to the court proving that the debtor's COMI is undoubtedly located in England. Secondly, the debtor must inform their creditors that the debtor's insolvency status has changed regarding the location, and that the debtor intends to file for insolvency in the State to which the debtor has transferred their COMI. The purpose of this requirement is to persuade the creditors to take steps against the debtors before the judgment opening insolvency proceedings is issued, primarily in the State in which the COMI is currently located in the eyes of the creditors.

3.29. Indeed, the decision in *Steinhardt* v. *Eichler*[35] was followed by an increased number of cases in which the creditors (usually from Ireland or Germany)[36] challenged in English courts the debtor's statement regarding the debtor's habitual residence or, as applicable, regarding the alleged location of the debtor's COMI in England. Hence, the expanding insolvency tourism ultimately encountered resistance from the judiciary and the creditors even in England itself, although the media and political pressure from other Member States, from which the debtors fictitiously relocated to England, certainly played their part.

3.30. However, as mentioned above, the problem was not limited to transfers of the COMI to England, although this practice apparently concerned the largest number of cases so far, at least those cases which were recorded and publicised. Judgments

---

[34] Decisions of *Chief Registrar Baister* of 30 June 2011 and 27 July 2011 in *Steinhardt* v. *Eichler*, neutral citation: [2011] BPIR 1293.

[35] Decisions of Chief Registrar Baister of 30 June 2011 and 27 July 2011 in *Steinhardt* v. *Eichler*, neutral citation: [2011] BPIR 1293.

[36] See also statistical overviews in: IAIN RAMSAY, PERSONAL INSOLVENCY IN THE 21st CENTURY: A COMPARATIVE ANALYSIS OF THE US AND EUROPE, Oxford: Bloomsbury Publishing (2017), et. 131 (for more details see elsewhere in this commentary on Article 5 of Regulation 2015/848).

opening insolvency proceedings under Regulation 1346/2000 were also challenged in other States. For instance, the French Court of Appeal in Colmar (*Cour d'appel Colmar*) delivered a decision in a case opened by an action lodged by a creditor, whereby the court cancelled the debtor's discharge on grounds that the debtor had achieved the discharge as a result of the abuse of a right.[37] The French court held that the debtor unlawfully pretended that their place of residence was in France. In actual fact, however, the debtor – who lived and worked in Germany [DEU] – had only rented his apartment in France in order to open insolvency proceedings in France and enjoy the benefits offered by the French Commercial Code, which he would not have enjoyed under German law.[38]

**3.31.** In another case in Germany, a creditor of a Greek debtor – a subsidiary of a German company – requested a review of the judgment opening insolvency proceedings against the Greek company by a German court. The court, however, denied the request and ruled that German insolvency proceedings had universal effects vis-à-vis the debtor's assets all over the world.[39]

**3.32.** The new rule enshrined in Article 5(1) of Regulation 2015/848 thus primarily has regard to the practice of courts in selected countries, although the rule will for some time apparently meet with obstacles consisting in the procedures applied in selected Member States. Regardless of the fact that this rule may be controversial from the perspective of certain countries, it undoubtedly enhances legal certainty and helps to prevent unfair transfers of the COMI, especially for creditors. But its advantages are undeniable even in those cases where the procedure is employed by the debtors themselves as persons with legal standing directly under Article 5(1) of Regulation 2015/848.

**3.33.** The possibility of challenging the decision opening main insolvency proceedings under Regulation 1346/2000 only according to the *lex fori concursus* was, in most Member States (according to the available information), only favourable to the debtors themselves or to those creditors who filed a request for opening insolvency proceedings. Hence, Article 5 of Regulation 2015/848 is often deemed important specifically for the extension of the category of persons or entities who may employ

---

[37] Judgment of the Court of Appeal in Colmar (*Cour d'appel Colmar*), case no. 1 and 11/01869 of 13 December 2011. Here according to: CHRISTOPH G. PAULUS, EUROPÄISCHE INSOLVENZVERORDNUNG: KOMMENTAR (Frankfurt a. M.: Fachmedien Recht und Wirtschaft / dfv Mediengruppe 5th ed., 2017), commentary on Article 33 of Regulation 2015/848, marg. 12, et. 386, note 40.
[38] See HLV Report, et. 195.
[39] See HLV Report, et. 140.

the applicable defence mechanisms – it now covers all creditors. Similarly to the expansion of the unfair insolvency tourism of debtors, statements regarding the location of the COMI were often abused by the creditors as well. This was frequently facilitated by the inconsistent, sometimes almost lax approach of the insolvency courts, which, at least in certain countries, often opened the main insolvency proceedings automatically and without a rigorous, or indeed any, examination of the COMI. The opening of insolvency proceedings in *insolvency* cases thus often became a *chase* for the earliest opening of the main insolvency proceedings based on the priority of earlier proceedings,[40] with no effective defence against such decisions. Hence, awarding legal standing to **all creditors, as well as debtors,** is fully adequate.

3.34.    Article 5(1) of Regulation 2015/848 thus simultaneously represents a mechanism supporting the adherence to and application of the procedure under Article 4 of Regulation 2015/848 (quoted above), as well as protection against a – by no means exceptional and, unfortunately, very frequent – abuse of the artificially established COMI, i.e. a connecting factor that varies in time, and that, depending on the circumstances, could be perceived very subjectively. These negative effects of the definition of the COMI are not entirely eliminated by Article 5 of Regulation 2015/848, but the provision at least provides another possible defence against the abuse of the rules on international jurisdiction under the EU insolvency law.

## VII.    The Nature of Law and of the Instrument of Challenging a Judgment Opening Insolvency Proceedings

3.35.    Contrary to the obligations of insolvency courts under Article 4 of Regulation 2015/848 quoted above, Article 5 provides for a court review of jurisdiction at the request of the debtor or any of the creditors. As I shall analyse in greater detail in connection with the relationship between the procedure under Article 5(1) of Regulation 2015/848 and the *lex fori concursus*, the mechanism laid down in Article 5(1) of Regulation 2015/848 is a fully independent and autonomous instrument provided for in directly applicable EU legislation. In other words, it is not a remedy in terms of the procedural mechanisms under the *lex fori concursus*. The application and scope of application of the procedures under the *lex fori concursus* are governed only

---

40    See Article 3(3) of Regulation 2015/848 or Article 3(3) of Regulation 1346/2000, as applicable.

by Article 5(2) of Regulation 2015/848, not by Article 5(1) of Regulation 2015/848, because the essence of the mechanism under Article 5(1) of Regulation 2015/848 is independent of the national law applicable to the insolvency proceedings.

**3.36.** These new rules in the EU insolvency law are based on a Commission Proposal, and they regard a series of judgments (see especially the decisions in *Sparkasse Hannover*,[41] *Sparkasse Hilden Ratingen*,[42] *Steinhardt v. Eichler*,[43]

---

[41] Decision of *Chief Registrar Baister* of 15 February 2011 in *Sparkasse et Hannover Bank* v. *The Official Receiver et Peter Johann Joseph Körffer*, neutral citation [2011] BPIR 775 / [2011] BPIR 768.

[42] Decision of England and Wales High Court of Justice, Chancery Division, Birmingham District Registry (Judge *Purple QC*) [GBR], No. 957 of 2010, in *Sparkasse Hilden Ratingen Velbert* v. *Horst Konrad Benk* et *The official Receiver* of 29 August 2012, neutral citation: [2012] EWHC 2432, available at: http://www.bailii.org/ew/cases/EWHC/Ch/2012/2432.html (accessed on 10 August 2019).

[43] Decisions of Chief Registrar Baister of 30 June 2011 and 27 July 2011 in *Steinhardt* v. *Eichler*, neutral citation: [2011] BPIR 1293. In this case, the Registrar cancelled its own 2007 decision opening insolvency proceedings and issued a separate decision four years later in which the Registrar declared that the debtor's COMI was not located in England and Wales.

Similarly also:

Decision in *Schrade* v. *Sparkasse Ludenchild*, neutral citation [2014] EWHC 1049 (ch), or

Decision of High Court of Justice, Chancery Division, Birmingham District Registry (Justice *Purple QC*) [GBR], No 957 of 2010, in *Sparkasse Hilden Ratingen Velbert* v. *Horst Konrad Benk* et *The Official Receiver* of 29 August 2012 neutral citation: [2012] EWHC 2432; the decision is available at: http://www.bailii.org/ew/cases/EWHC/Ch/2012/2432.html (accessed on 10 August 2019).

Decisions of Recorder Neil Cadwallader of 19 May 2010 and 07 June 2010 in *Hagemeister*, neutral citation: [2010] BPIR 1093. This decision is annotated in greater detail below. See *Sealy, L., S. et Milman, D.* Annotated Guide to the Insolvency Legislation. London: Sweet& Maxwell, 2011, et. 265, 272, or

Decision in *Hunt* v. *Fylde BC*, neutral citation: [2008] BPIR 1368. See *Sealy, L., S. et Milman, D.* Annotated Guide to the Insolvency Legislation. London: Sweet& Maxwell, 2012, et. 330.

In all four last mentioned cases cf. also IAIN RAMSAY, PERSONAL INSOLVENCY IN THE 21st CENTURY: A COMPARATIVE ANALYSIS OF THE US AND EUROPE, Oxford: Bloomsbury Publishing (2017), et. 181, marg. 137. The same author also offers an interesting statistical overview concerning insolvency tourism with attempts to transfer the registered office to England and Wales in the period from 2008 to 2013. This overview, adopted from *The Insolvency Service*, indicates that the persons who attempted such insolvency tourism to England and Wales in the respective period were primarily debtors from Germany [DEU] (numbers: 2008 – 43 debtors, 2009 – 107 debtors, 2010 – 103 debtors, 2011 – 141 debtors, 2012 – 141 debtors and 2013 – 63 debtors), whereas the numbers from other countries are zero or close to zero. The second-ranking country (after Germany, but with significantly lower numbers) is only Ireland in 2011 – 2013.

*Irish Bank* v. *Quinn*,[44] *Official Receiver* v. *Mitterfellner*[45]) in which especially, though not exclusively, the English courts or indeed courts of the *common law* countries, reviewed their jurisdiction and held of their own motion that a transfer of the centre of main interests was unfair.[46] At the same time, these States allowed a separate request for cancelling the decision opening main insolvency proceedings, especially if new circumstances transpired or if the creditor was unable to defend their interests before the decision opening the main insolvency proceedings became final. These mechanisms are primarily connected with the specific aspects of opening insolvency proceedings, especially under English law, where the decision on the request for opening proceedings is in principle made immediately, and it is often permitted to prove the location of the COMI merely

---

[44] Decision of High Court of Justice in Northern Ireland, Chancery Division (Bankruptcy) [GBR] Case No 2011 No. 133303, of 10 January 2012, in *Irish Bank Resolution Corporation Ltd* v. *John Ignatius Quinn (also known as Sean Quinn)*, neutral citation [2012] NICh 1. In this case, the court refused to recognise an attempt of an Irish businessman to transfer the COMI to England in view of a much shorter time needed for debt discharge. See also PETER STONE, EU PRIVATE INTERNATIONAL LAW (Edward Elgar Publishing 3rd ed., 2014), et. 530.

Similarly also in:

Decision of England and Wales High Court, Chancery Division, London No 1789 et 1794 of 2012, of 21 December 2012, in *Brian O'Donnell et Mary Patricia O'Donnell* v. *The Governor and Company of the Bank of Ireland*, neutral citation [2012] EWHC 3749 (Ch), available online at: http://www.bailii.org/cgi-bin/format.cgi?doc=/ew/cases/EWHC/Ch/2011/3749.html&query=(.2012.)+AND+(EWHC)+AND+(3749) (accessed on 10 August 2019). The decision also indicates that the debtor is authorised to transfer the COMI to another State, but he or she is obliged to provide evidence thereof that proves, inter alia, that the change of the COMI was also known to third parties at the time of the transfer. Any debtor transferring their COMI to another State should, for instance, consider an announcement to the debtor's creditors or any other measure to make such transfers public. However, as the decision in *Sparkasse Hilden Ratingen Velbert* v. *Horst Konrad Benk et The Official Receiver*, mentioned elsewhere in this article, indicates, it is necessary to provide such information or make it publicly available to all creditors. Selective choice of informed creditors may be classified in individual cases as fraudulent conduct;

Decision of High Court of Justice, Chancery Division, Birmingham District Registry (Justice Purple QC), No 957 of 2010, in *Sparkasse Hilden Ratingen Velbert* v. *Horst Konrad Benk* et *The Official Receiver* of 29 August 2012 neutral citation: [2012] EWHC 2432; the decision is available at http://www.bailii.org/ew/cases/EWHC/Ch/2012/2432.html (accessed on 10 August 2019). In this case, the German debtor (Mr Benk) claimed the transfer of his COMI to England, where he succeeded with his request for opening insolvency proceedings. *Sparkasse Hilden Ratingen Velbert* subsequently requested the cancellation of the judgment opening insolvency proceedings, arguing that Mr Benk's COMI de facto remained in Germany at the relevant time and claiming a lack of international jurisdiction of the English court. The court performed a detailed examination of all circumstances relevant for the COMI and found, for instance, that the insolvent debtor announced the transfer of his COMI to a number of creditors by registered letter, but failed to inform *Sparkasse Hilden Ratingen Velbert*, to which he owed approx. EUR 3 mil.;

Decision of *High Court of Justice, London, Chancery Division*, in *Sparkasse Bremen AG* v. *Armutcu*, neutral citation [2012] EWHC 4026 (Ch);

See also PETER STONE, EU PRIVATE INTERNATIONAL LAW, (Edward Elgar Publishing 3rd ed., 2014), et. 530.

[45] Decision of Chief Registrar Baister in *Official Receiver* v. *Mitterfellner* of 10 June 2009, neutral citation [2009] BPIR 1075.

[46] REINHARD BORK, RENATO MANGANO, EUROPEAN CROSS-BORDER INSOLVENCY LAW, Oxford: Oxford University Press (2016), et. 99.

by a Statement of Affairs presented by the debtor or claimant themselves.

**3.37.** Hence, Article 5(1) of Regulation 2015/848 provides the debtor and/or the debtor's creditors with the possibility (right) of challenging the decision opening main insolvency proceedings. The provision is a directly applicable EU rule, which applies regardless of whether or not the debtor or the creditors enjoy that right under the *lex fori concursus*.

## VIII. The Legal Standing to Make Use of the Mechanism under Article 5(1) of Regulation 2015/848

**3.38.** The mechanism under Article 5(1) of Regulation 2015/848 benefits solely (i) the creditors and (ii) the debtor.

**3.39.** In this regard, Regulation 2015/848 does not distinguish between domestic and foreign creditors and debtors. Hence, the right to challenge the judgment opening insolvency proceedings also benefits domestic creditors, i.e. all creditors other than those who may be subsumed under the definition of a foreign creditor.[47] An analogous conclusion holds true for a debtor who has their COMI in the State in which the court is located that issued the decision opening the proceedings. It is irrelevant if the case exhibits a special cross-border element of any kind at the moment at which the judgment opening the insolvency proceedings is challenged. Regulation 2015/848 applies to that case as well (with specific exceptions). Indeed, the Regulation itself does not refer to foreign creditors in Article 5 of Regulation 2015/848, although it otherwise consistently uses this term, even in the sense of the above-mentioned definition of a foreign creditor.[48] Consequently, any creditors may fully avail themselves of the mechanism envisaged in Article 5(1) of Regulation 2015/848.

**3.40.** This means that the decision opening main insolvency proceedings may conceivably be challenged by a domestic creditor or a domestic debtor seeking a positive decision confirming that the proceedings were opened. After all, the fact itself that a domestic creditor or a *domestic debtor* challenge the jurisdiction of the court using the mechanism under Article 5(1) of Regulation 2015/848 means that the creditor or the debtor, respectively, invoke cross-border aspects or the absence

---

[47] See Article 2(12) of Regulation 2015/848 (quote): [...] *'foreign creditor' means a creditor which has its habitual residence, domicile or registered office in a Member State other than the State of the opening of proceedings, including the tax authorities and social security authorities of Member States;* [...].
[48] See Article 2(12) of Regulation 2015/848.

thereof, because a domestic creditor must logically claim that the debtor's COMI is not located in the State of their domicile.

**3.41.** Article 5(1) of Regulation 2015/848 does not specify the category of creditors who may invoke the procedure provided for in that provision. The word *creditor* with no adjective attached only emphasizes that it may indeed be any of the debtor's creditors. It must be a person who has or asserts their own claim. In this connection, Prof. Mankowski points out the potentially special status of claimants filing class actions, such as persons representing a particular class of claims (such as employment claims).[49] It is important to establish in this regard whether the assignment of the particular person involved in the insolvency proceedings is to assert and enforce a particular claim or claims. Prof. Paulus correctly emphasizes that the person must be a creditor connected to the proceedings[50] in which the international jurisdiction is challenged.

**3.42.** It is unimportant, in this respect, whether the creditor invoking Article 5(1) of Regulation 2015/848 has already asserted their claim or succeeded in doing so. Indeed, it would be unacceptable if, for instance, a creditor who has already filed their claim would lose their status as a creditor in the particular insolvency proceedings in the course of the proceedings initiated under Article 5(1) of Regulation 2015/848 on grounds of a successful denial of the creditor's claim. This would result in a corresponding dismissal of the creditor's petition under Article 5(1) of Regulation 2015/848 only and without any examination of the merits, due to the absence of the creditor's legal standing. Naturally, legal standing must be examined as a preliminary issue in the proceedings under Article 5(1) of Regulation 2015/848, but the assessment thereof cannot depend on whether or not such a claim is recognised in the insolvency proceedings themselves or in any potential incidental dispute. It is therefore sufficient if a person, for the specific reason of proving legal standing under Article 5(1) of Regulation 2015/848, presents sufficient evidence that they are or may be a creditor with relation to a particular, unambiguous and clearly specified claim. Indeed, despite the need to examine the claimant's legal standing, the purpose of the proceedings under Article 5(1) of Regulation 2015/848 is not the assessment of the claimant's claim.

---

[49] PETER MANKOWSKI, MICHAEL F. MÜLLER, JESSICA SCHMIDT, EUINSVO 2015: EUROPÄISCHE INSOLVENZORDNUNG 2015. KOMMENTAR, München: C. H. Beck (2016), commentary on Article 5 of Regulation 2015/848, marg. 8, et. 154.

[50] CHRISTOPH G. PAULUS, EUROPÄISCHE INSOLVENZVERORDNUNG: KOMMENTAR. (Frankfurt a. M.: Fachmedien Recht und Wirtschaft / dfv Mediengruppe 5th ed., 2017), commentary on Article 5 of Regulation 2015/848, marg. 4, et. 213-214, here et. 214.

## IX. The Judgment Opening Insolvency Proceedings as an Object of Procedure under Article 5(1) of Regulation 2015/848

**3.43.** The object challenged by the procedure under Article 5(1) of Regulation 2015/848 is always a judgment opening insolvency proceedings. The *judgment opening insolvency proceedings* is a term defined in Article 2(7) of Regulation 2015/848.[51] Article 2(7) of Regulation 2015/848 indicates that a judgment opening insolvency proceedings denotes a situation in which the court has arrived at a positive conclusion regarding its international jurisdiction, which resulted in the opening of the insolvency proceedings. The fact that this involves cases in which the court decision under Article 2(7) of Regulation 2015/848 is positive and the court declares or confirms its jurisdiction to open and conduct main insolvency proceedings follows relatively clearly from all of the language versions of Regulation 2015/848.[52]

**3.44.** Article 5(1) of Regulation 2015/848 thus does not apply to cases in which the court[53] made a contrary ruling, i.e. that it lacks international jurisdiction, and issued a corresponding decision denying the request for opening insolvency proceedings. Such a negative decision of the court may only be challenged by instruments provided for under the *lex fori concursus*, if the law applicable to the decision allows any remedy or any other procedural defence mechanism. This conclusion is only logical, because one can assume that in many cases the request for opening insolvency proceedings will be filed in another State after a negative court decision. whereby it refuses its international jurisdiction, and it is necessary to make sure that the only bodies authorised to examine their own jurisdiction are the authorities of the other State. Indeed, the mechanism under Article 5(1) of Regulation 2015/848 may in such case be used in that other State which ultimately confirms its international jurisdiction and opens the insolvency proceedings.

**3.45.** The cases adjudicated in selected countries before the adoption of Regulation 2015/848 demonstrate that analogous mechanisms based on the national law of these States are also

---

51 Article 2(7) of Regulation 2015/848 (quote): " ,judgment opening insolvency proceedings' includes (i) the decision of any court to open insolvency proceedings or to confirm the opening of such proceedings; and (ii) the decision of a court to appoint an insolvency practitioner; [...]."

52 For an identical opinion, see also PETER MANKOWSKI, MICHAEL F. MÜLLER, JESSICA SCHMIDT, EUINSVO 2015: EUROPÄISCHE INSOLVENZORDNUNG 2015. KOMMENTAR, München: C. H. Beck (2016), commentary on Article 5 of Regulation 2015/848, marg. 4, et. 154. In this regard, Prof. Mankowski makes a comparison with the English version of Regulation 2015/848 and emphasizes the word *opening* in the phrase *judgment opening insolvency proceedings*.

53 In this case, however, it means the court pursuant to Article 2(6)(ii) of Regulation 2015/848.

applicable in these countries against negative decisions relying on the conclusion as to the lack of the court's own international jurisdiction.[54] If the *lex fori concursus* of a State also allows a decision to be challenged denying the opening of insolvency proceedings on grounds of a lack of international jurisdiction, such a procedure may naturally be applied in the particular case. But it is not the procedure under Article 5(1) of Regulation 2015/848, it is a procedure governed exclusively by the *lex fori concursus*. As we shall see below, in the paragraphs dealing with the relationship between the procedure under Article 5(1) of Regulation 2015/848 and other defence mechanisms against a decision on a request for opening insolvency proceedings, these are two entirely separate, mutually independent and parallel procedures. This makes it even less permissible to make the procedure under Article 5(1) of Regulation 2015/848 dependent, for instance, on the issue of whether the claimant, i.e. a person with legal standing, exhausted all other measures under the *lex fori concursus*. The assessment of whether the mechanism under Article 5(1) of Regulation 2015/848 may be applied must be governed exclusively by this particular provision, and under no circumstances may it be limited by the *lex fori concursus*.

**3.46.** Whether the decision in a particular case is indeed a judgment opening insolvency proceedings in terms of Article 2(7) of Regulation 2015/848 must always be assessed on a case-by-case basis, according to the actual contents of the decision and from the perspective of the definition provided for in Article 2(7) of Regulation 2015/848. Some situations may raise certain doubts, such as certain preliminary or interim measures[55] issued at the stage at which the court is deciding on the request for opening insolvency proceedings. Such moot cases therefore require that one first answer the question of whether or not the contested decision is a judgment opening insolvency proceedings pursuant to Article 2(7) of Regulation 2015/848.

**3.47.** The procedure under Article 5(1) of Regulation 2015/848 shall also not apply to actions deriving from insolvency proceedings

---

[54] See also decision of High Court of Justice in Northern Ireland, Chancery Division No 2002 No: 032346, of 07 February 2017, in the case of the debtor *Antonio Macari* Neutral citation: [2017] NICh 5, of 07 February 2017. Available online at: http://www.bailii.org/cgi-bin/format.cgi?doc=/nie/cases/NIHC/Ch/2017/5.html&query=(Mitterfellner) (accessed on 10 August 2019). The action in the said case was filed by the debtor himself against the decision whereby the opening of insolvency proceedings was refused in Northern Ireland on the grounds of absence of the COMI. The court dismissed the action, because the transfer of the COMI from Ireland to Northern Ireland was proven neither in the said proceedings, nor in connection with the request itself for opening insolvency proceedings.
[55] Cf. also Peter Mankowski, In: PETER MANKOWSKI, MICHAEL F. MÜLLER, JESSICA SCHMIDT, EUINSVO 2015: EUROPÄISCHE INSOLVENZORDNUNG 2015. KOMMENTAR, München: C. H. Beck (2016), commentary on Article 5 of Regulation 2015/848, marg. 4, et. 154.

and closely linked with them.[56/57] Hence, Article 5, together with Article 4 of Regulation 2015/848, are directly linked and only cover judgments opening insolvency proceedings. This case also requires a precise definition of the *judgment opening insolvency proceedings* under Article 2(7) of Regulation 2015/848, in conjunction with Article 3 of Regulation 2015/848, and its application to the particular case. It is also necessary to re-emphasise the purpose of the mechanism under Article 5(1) of Regulation 2015/848 (see also the separate section in this article below). Consequently, Article 5(1) of Regulation 2015/848 only relates to decisions opening main insolvency proceedings. Its application to secondary[58] or territorial[59] proceedings is excluded. This is also associated with the fact that the purpose of that mechanism is to afford sufficient protection against those decisions in which the court arrives at a positive conclusion regarding the existence of the COMI in the State where the court that opened the main insolvency proceedings is located. This is the only State in which the procedure may be used.

3.48. The court in which the decision opening main insolvency proceedings under Article 5(1) of Regulation 2015/848 may be challenged must be a court in the strict sense of the word, i.e. a court as an authority with judicial power.[60] In those cases where its jurisdiction in individual States is also or may be examined

---

[56] See Article 6 of Regulation 2015/848 (quote):
        1. The courts of the Member State within the territory of which insolvency proceedings have been opened in accordance with Article 3 shall have jurisdiction for any action which derives directly from the insolvency proceedings and is closely linked with them, such as avoidance actions. 2. Where an action referred to in paragraph 1 is related to an action in civil and commercial matters against the same defendant, the insolvency practitioner may bring both actions before the courts of the Member State within the territory of which the defendant is domiciled, or, where the action is brought against several defendants, before the courts of the Member State within the territory of which any of them is domiciled, provided that those courts have jurisdiction pursuant to Regulation (EU) No 1215/2012. (-)The first subparagraph shall apply to the debtor in possession, provided that national law allows the debtor in possession to bring actions on behalf of the insolvency estate. 3. For the purpose of paragraph 2, actions are deemed to be related where they are so closely connected that it is expedient to hear and determine them together to avoid the risk of irreconcilable judgments resulting from separate proceeding.

[57] In this connection, Prof. Mankowski also highlights the structure of Regulation 2015/848 and the importance of the fact that the rules regulating the defence mechanism under Article 5 of Regulation 2015/848 precede Article 6 of Regulation 2015/848. Peter Mankowski, In: PETER MANKOWSKI, MICHAEL F. MÜLLER, JESSICA SCHMIDT, EUINSVO 2015: EUROPÄISCHE INSOLVENZORDNUNG 2015. KOMMENTAR, München: C. H. Beck (2016), commentary on Article 5 of Regulation 2015/848, marg. 7, et. 154.

[58] See Article 3(2) of Regulation 2015/848. Article 3 of Regulation 2015/848 is quoted above in this paper.

[59] See Article 3(4) of Regulation 2015/848. Article 3 of Regulation 2015/848 is quoted above in this paper.

[60] See Article 2(6)(i) of Regulation 2015/848 (quote):
        [...]''court'' means: (i) in points (b) and (c) of Article 1(1), Article 4(2), Articles 5 and 6, Article 21(3), point (j) of Article 24(2), Article 36 and 399, and Articles 61 to 77, the judicial body of a Member State; (ii) in all other articles, the judicial body or any other competent body of a Member State empowered to open insolvency proceedings, to confirm such opening or to take decisions in the course of such proceedings;[...].'

under the *lex fori concursus* by a private-law entity before which the proceedings are opened, it is always an authority with judicial power that has this jurisdiction under Article 5(1) of Regulation 2015/848. Which particular court this is in any given State is to be determined according to the rules on jurisdiction of the *lex fori concursus*. In most cases, this court will be identical to the court with jurisdiction to hear all other issues relating to the given insolvency proceedings, but it need not always be the case. Just like in all similar cases, Regulation 2015/848 does not interfere with the issue of jurisdiction of a particular judicial authority competent to rule on a petition under Article 5(1) of Regulation 2015/848.

## X. Grounds for Challenging a Judgment Opening Insolvency Proceedings under Article 5(1) of Regulation 2015/848

### X.1. Grounds for Challenging a Judgment

**3.49.** The grounds for reviewing a prior judgment opening insolvency proceedings for a lack of jurisdiction are entirely unlimited. New evidence may appear concerning the debtor's COMI, or the opening of main insolvency proceedings may be tainted by fraud, including such extreme situations as a decision opening main insolvency proceedings and, consequently, recognition of the COMI in the State of the main proceedings achieved by way of corruption. Hence, the main insolvency proceedings may have been opened on the basis of misleading and fabricated facts, as a result of insufficient information or because of the withholding of key facts of the case.[61]

**3.50.** Consequently, the factual grounds for challenging the judgment opening insolvency proceedings under Article 5(1) of

---

[61] *Wessels, B.* EU Cross-Border Insolvency Court-to-Court Cooperation Principles, March 2014 version. Available online at http://bobwessels.nl/site/assets/files/1654/2014-03-21-first-public-draft-eu-judgeco-principles.pdf (accessed on 10 August 2019). The author invokes Principle 10 of court-to-court cooperation regarding the correction of already issued decisions (et.50) (quote):

1. Where *main insolvency* proceedings are pending in another State, the court that is deciding whether to open secondary proceeding may postpone its decision where it becomes aware of evidence which warrants such action. Such evidence may include evidence that (i) there was fraud in the opening of the foreign *main insolvency* case, or that (ii) the foreign *main insolvency* case was opened in the absence of international jurisdiction as provided in Article 3 of the EIR. 2. Where *main insolvency* proceedings are pending in another State, the court that has opened secondary proceeding may postpone a hearing where it becomes aware of evidence in the meaning of paragraph 1 or may in such a case revoke its decision if national law allows such revocation.

*Wessels, B.* invokes, inter alia, the decisions of Chief Registrar Baister of 30 June 2011 and of 27 July 2011 in *Steinhardt* v. *Eichler*, neutral citation [2011] BPIR 1293, primarily marg. 190 and 191 of the decision.

Czech Yearbook of International Law®

Regulation 2015/848 may vary, but they must always concern international jurisdiction.[62] Regulation 2015/848 intentionally desists from any limitation of the grounds, because these cases are essentially incapable of being fully subsumed under a clearly and unambiguously articulated rule. These grounds may also consist in the erroneous or unusual application of the law by the court if, for instance, other main insolvency proceedings are erroneously opened against the same debtor and no other mechanism exists or is available due to the stage of the insolvency proceedings that would ensure proper application of the principle of precedence of the main insolvency proceedings that had been opened earlier.[63]

**3.51.** The grounds for applying this procedure usually rely on factual issues.[64] However, this may also involve cases, as mentioned above, in which the information provided by the debtor with respect to the centre of main interests (COMI) of the debtor is incorrect, misleading or incomplete (see also the decisions in *Hiwa Huck*,[65] *Sparkasse et Hannover Bank* v. *The Official Receiver et Peter Johann Joseph Körffer*,[66] *Sparkasse Hilden Ratingen Velbert* v. *Horst Konrad Benk* et *The Official Receiver*,[67]

---

[62] Naturally, it is not prohibited to challenge other types of jurisdiction, such as subject-matter, territorial or institutional jurisdiction within the limits of a particular Sate, but the procedure in such cases is always governed by the *lex fori concursus*. The procedure under Article 5(1) of Regulation 2015/848 applies only to international jurisdiction. Cf. also Peter Mankowski, In: PETER MANKOWSKI, MICHAEL F. MÜLLER, JESSICA SCHMIDT, EUINSVO 2015: EUROPÄISCHE INSOLVENZORDNUNG 2015. KOMMENTAR, München: C. H. Beck (2016), commentary on Article 5 of Regulation 2015/848, marg. 6, et. 154.

[63] Decisions of Recorder Neil Cadwallader of 19 May 2010 and 07 June 2010 in *Hagemeister*, neutral citation: [2010] BPIR 1093. In *Hagemeister* the English court did not have international jurisdiction to open main insolvency proceedings, because the main proceedings had been previously opened in Germany. The decision opening main insolvency proceedings was therefore cancelled by the English court upon a separate motion. The procedure applied in this case was necessary from the procedural perspective in order to allow the conduct of the previously opened insolvency proceedings.

[64] REINHARD BORK, RENATO MANGANO, EUROPEAN CROSS-BORDER INSOLVENCY LAW, Oxford: Oxford University Press (2016), et. 99.

[65] Decision of Chief Registrar Baister of 10 December 2010 in *Official Receiver* v. *Hiwa Huck*, neutral citation [2011] BPIR 709. See also Bankruptcy and Personal Insolvency Reports, available at: http://www.jordanpublishing.co.uk/practice-areas/insolvency/news_and_comment/re-hiwa-huck-official-receiver-v-hiwa-huck-2011-bpir-709#.V7SNoyiLTIW (accessed on 05 April 2019). See also HLV Report, et. 214-215. The decision is annotated elsewhere in this paper, because the respective case has a closer connection to Article 5(2) of Regulation 2015/848 than to Article 5(1) of Regulation 2015/848 from the perspective of legal standing and grounds. But the decision mentions a broad spectrum of the grounds that may be invoked specifically in the case of actions filed by creditors or by the debtor under Article 5(1) of Regulation 2015/848.

[66] Decision of *Chief Registrar Baister* of 15 February 2011 in *Sparkasse et Hannover Bank* v. *The Official Receiver et Peter Johann Joseph Körffer*, neutral citation [2011] BPIR 775 / [2011] BPIR 768.

[67] Decision of High Court of Justice, Chancery Division, Birmingham District Registry (Justice *Purple QC*) [GBR], No 957 of 2010, in *Sparkasse Hilden Ratingen Velbert* v. *Horst Konrad Benk* et *The Official Receiver* of 29 August 2012, neutral citation: [2012] EWHC 2432; the decision is available at: http://www.bailii.org/ew/cases/EWHC/Ch/2012/2432.html (accessed on 10 August 2019).

*The Official Receiver* v. *Mitterfellner,*[68] *Steinhardt* v. *Eichler,*[69] *Official Receiver* v. *Eichler*[70]).

## X.2.  Burden of Proof

3.52.  Article 5(1) of Regulation 2015/848 makes no reference to the claimant's burden of proof. The reason is that the broad category of situations which may occur in the application of this procedure prevent any unambiguous determination of the person or entity that has the burden of proof.

3.53.  For an interesting example of an entire series of English decisions regarding a fictitious transfer of the COMI (in this case, habitual residence), although the mechanism under Article 5(1) of Regulation 2015/848 is by no means targeted merely at the protection against such cases, see the decision in *Sparkasse et Hannover Bank* v. *The Official Receiver et Peter Johann Joseph Körffer.*[71] Mr Körffer (debtor), a German citizen, was for 33 years an employer of the creditor, the German bank Sparkasse Hannover, which had a claim against Mr Körffer in connection with the extension of a loan. Sparkasse Hannover was surprised to learn in late 2008 that the debtor had filed for insolvency in England, claiming to have transferred his habitual residence to London. Sparkasse Hannover responded with an action challenging the judgment opening these insolvency proceedings. It succeeded in proving that the debtor had not transferred their COMI to England and thus managed to have the judgment opening insolvency proceedings cancelled. This decision is also significant from the perspective of the burden of proof, because the general rule is that the burden of proof lies primarily with the claimant who files a separate action contesting the debtor's COMI and, consequently, the international jurisdiction of the court which opened the main insolvency proceedings. However, this conclusion cannot be made categorically and in all cases, due to all of the potential situations that may occur. Indeed, the court held in its decision, inter alia, that despite the claimant's general burden of proof, the debtor may also not be entirely free of the burden of proof if and with respect to the circumstances that the debtor had failed to inform the debtor's creditors regarding the

---

[68]  Decision in *Official Receiver* v. *Mitterfellner*, neutral citation [2009] BPIR 1075. The court in this case made a ruling regarding the COMI when the court held that the place of the COMI also requires an element of performance/active pursuit of activity, etc.

[69]  Decisions of Chief Registrar Baister of 30 June 2011 and 27 July 2011 in *Steinhardt* v. *Eichler*, neutral citation: [2011] BPIR 1293.

[70]  Decision of Chief Registrar Baister of 19 June 2007 in *Official Receiver* v. *Eichler*, neutral citation [2007] BPIR 1636.

[71]  Decision of *Chief Registrar Baister* of 15 February 2011 in *Sparkasse et Hannover Bank* v. *The Official Receiver et Peter Johann Joseph Körffer*, neutral citation [2011] BPIR 775 / [2011] BPIR 768.

alleged relocation to another State and filing for insolvency, if one of the debtor's creditors challenges the debtor's statements regarding the COMI.[72] The procedure in *Sparkasse et Hannover Bank* v. *The Official Receiver et Peter Johann Joseph Körffer*[73] was a procedure under English law (according to the English *lex fori concursus*), and a case which was governed solely by Regulation 1346/2000 that did not provide for any mechanism analogous to Article 5(1) of Regulation 2015/848, yet it is a decision also very representative with respect to the interpretation of Article 5(1) of Regulation 2015/848, and possibly, the determination of future limits of the application thereof. The reason is that the situations fully corresponded to the purpose of Article 5(1) of Regulation 2015/848, as in a whole number of similar cases, primarily from England.

**3.54.** Hence, even though the commonly used procedural rule that stipulates that the claimant is obliged to adduce the relevant statements and bears the corresponding burden of proof is not generally excluded in the application of Article 5(1) of Regulation 2015/848, the burden of proof may transfer to another party, if the procedure applies and depending on the circumstances. As *Sparkasse et Hannover Bank* v. *The Official Receiver et Peter Johann Joseph Körffer*[74] shows, the creditor may be the claimant, but the creditor may be objectively incapable of proving their statements, as such statements consisting in a negative fact (for example, the failure to inform the creditor or the creditor's ignorance). However, the burden of proof may also lie with both parties, i.e. the debtor may be obliged to prove that the debtor informed the creditor or, as applicable, took steps as a result of which the transfer of the COMI to another Member State became known generally, including to the particular creditor. At the same time, the creditor may be obliged to prove, depending on the circumstances, that the creditor did not neglect their claims and exerted such care that could generally be requested or expected of the creditor.

**3.55.** Most of the examples described above are governed by Regulation 1346/2000 and thus rely on national insolvency mechanisms. Though they concern cases where the transfer of the COMI is challenged by the creditor, a contrary situation may happen as well.[75] Article 5(1) of Regulation 2015/848 opens this

---

[72] Decision of *Chief Registrar Baister* of 15 February 2011 in *Sparkasse et Hannover Bank* v. *The Official Receiver et Peter Johann Joseph Körffer*, neutral citation [2011] BPIR 775, marg. 68 and 69.

[73] Decision of *Chief Registrar Baister* of 15 February 2011 in *Sparkasse et Hannover Bank* v. *The Official Receiver et Peter Johann Joseph Körffer*, neutral citation [2011] BPIR 775 / [2011] BPIR 768.

[74] Decision of *Chief Registrar Baister* of 15 February 2011 in *Sparkasse et Hannover Bank* v. *The Official Receiver et Peter Johann Joseph Körffer*, neutral citation [2011] BPIR 775 / [2011] BPIR 768.

[75] See also decision of High Court of Justice in Northern Ireland, Chancery Division No 2002 No:

procedure not only to creditors, but also to debtors, to the same extent. This confirms the repeatedly mentioned broad scope of the law as concerns the factual situations to which it applies, as well as the necessity of a flexible approach to the burden of proof.

## XI. The Relationship between the Mechanism under Article 5(1) of Regulation 2015/848 and *Lex Fori Concursus*

### XI.1. The Autonomous Nature of Procedure under Article 5(1) of Regulation 2015/848 and the Parallel Application of the Mechanisms Provided for under *Lex Fori Concursus*

**3.56.** The influence of the common law and primarily the English practice and standards under the law of England and Wales is clear. It has also been invoked by the Commission in connection with the proposal for new rules now incorporated in Article 5(1) of Regulation 2015/848. This is the reason why the previous English rules may also be considered as an important, though by no means literally applicable, source of interpretation. This further increases the importance of the relationship between Article 5(1) of Regulation 2015/848 and the defence mechanisms provided for and afforded by the *lex fori concursus*.

**3.57.** Hence, the first paragraph of Article 5 of Regulation 2015/848 newly provides that the debtor or any creditor may challenge before a court the decision opening main insolvency proceedings on grounds of international jurisdiction. One may detect a certain connection to the decision in *Eurofood* in which the Court of Justice (ECJ) held that if an interested party, taking the view that the centre of main interests of the debtor is situated in a Member State other than that in which the main insolvency proceedings were opened, wishes to challenge the international jurisdiction assumed by the court that opened those proceedings, it may use, before the courts of the Member State in which they were opened, the remedies prescribed by the

---

032846, of 07 February 2017, in the case of the debtor *Antonio Macari*, neutral citation: [2017] NICh 5. Electronic version available at: http://www.bailii.org/cgi-bin/format.cgi?doc=/nie/cases/NIHC/Ch/2017/5. html&query=(Mitterfellner) (accessed on 10 August 2019). The action in the case was filed by the debtor himself against the decision whereby the opening of insolvency proceedings was refused in Northern Ireland on grounds of the absence of the COMI. The court dismissed the action, because the transfer of the COMI from Ireland to Northern Ireland was proven neither in the proceedings, nor in connection with the request itself for opening insolvency proceedings.

national law of that Member State against the opening decision.[76] But the decision in *Eurofood* concerned a broader definition of beneficiaries compared to Regulation 2015/848, and it primarily concerned a mechanism relying on the national law of the State in which the proceedings were opened. The first paragraph of Article 5 of Regulation 2015/848 thus newly provides for a unique procedure independent of the *lex fori concursus*; this clearly follows from the comparison of the two paragraphs of Article 5 of Regulation 2015/848.

**3.58.** Consequently, the principal conclusion is that the procedure under Article 5 of Regulation 2015/848 does not represent a remedy against the decision opening **main insolvency** proceedings that arises from national law,[77] but it is a unique procedure for filing a petition that has essentially been adopted from the procedural cultures of *common law*.[78] This applies in spite of the fact that the procedure under Article 5(1) of

---

[76]    *Eurofood*, paragraph 43.

[77]    See Article 2(7) of Regulation 2015/848.

[78]    Reinhard Bork et Renato Mangano refer in this regard to the following cases (REINHARD BORK, RENATO MANGANO, EUROPEAN CROSS-BORDER INSOLVENCY LAW, Oxford: Oxford University Press (2016), et. 99, note 89), when a prior decision approving the relocation of the COMI to a different state was reversed by a separate action filed by a creditor and supported with new and later evidence:

Decision of *Chief Registrar Baister* of 15 February 2011 in *Sparkasse et Hannover Bank* v. *The Official Receiver et Peter Johann Joseph Körffer*, neutral citation [2011] BPIR 775 / [2011] BPIR 768. This illustrates the British approach – even if it was proven that the COMI had actually been transferred to another state, that conclusion can be refuted later on the basis of a new (separate) action of a creditor supported by new evidence.

Decision of High Court of Justice, Chancery Division, Birmingham District Registry (Justice *Purple QC)* [GBR], No 957 of 2010, in *Sparkasse Hilden Ratingen Velbert* v. *Horst Konrad Benk et The Official Receiver* of 29 August 2012 neutral citation: [2012] EWHC 2432; the decision is available at http://www.bailii.org/ew/cases/EWHC/Ch/2012/2432.html (accessed on 10 August 2019).

Decisions of Chief Registrar Baister of 30 June 2011 and 27 July 2011 in *Steinhardt* v. *Eichler*, neutral citation: [2011] BPIR 1293. This illustrates the *common law* approach – even if it was proven that the COMI had actually been transferred to another state, that conclusion can be refuted later on the basis of a new (separate) action of a creditor supported by new evidence.

Decision of High Court of Justice in Nothern Ireland, Chancery Division c. 2011 No. 1333034, of 10 January 2012, in *Irish Bank Resolution Corporation Ltd* v. *John Ignatius Quinn (also known as Sean Quinn)*, neutral citation: [2012] NICh 1-[2012] EIRCR(A) 351, available online at http://www.bailii.org/cgi-bin/format.cgi?doc=/nie/cases/NIHC/Ch/2012/1. html&query=(.2012.)+AND+(NICh)+AND+(1) (accessed on 16 February 2020).

Decision in *Official Receiver* v. *Mitterfellner*, neutral citation [2009] BPIR 1075. Annotated below.

Other similar decisions illustrate the common law approach. Even if it was proven that the COMI had actually been transferred to another State, that conclusion can be refuted later on the basis of a new separate action of a creditor supported by new evidence:

Decision in *Official Receiver* v. *Eichler*, neutral citation [2007] BPIR 1636;

Decision of High Court of Justice in Northern Ireland, Chancery Division (Master Kelly) [GBR] No 2012/082088, of 28 January 2013, in ACC Bank PLC v. Sean McCann, neutral citation [2012] IEHC 236, available online at: http://www.bailii.org/cgi-bin/format.cgi?doc=/nie/cases/NIHC/ Master/2013/1.html&query=(ACC)+AND+(v)+AND+(McCann) (accessed on 10 August 2019). The judge in this decision has mentioned that a transfer of the COMI to another State may constitute grounds for refusing the motion to recognize the transfer of the COMI abroad on grounds of the reservation of public policy under Article 26 of Regulation 1346/2000 (Article 33 of Regulation 2015/848).

Regulation 2015/848 is in certain cases, especially in *common law* countries, identical to the procedures provided for under the *lex fori concursus*. Hence, the provision does not refer to an 'action' or any other term commonly used in national legislation, and it intentionally refers only to the possibility of challenging the decision.

3.59. Thus, the procedure under Article 5(1) of Regulation 2015/848 is no remedy. The nature and concept of the provision indicate that the decision on the petition challenging the decision opening main insolvency proceedings should primarily be rendered by the insolvency court that opened the main insolvency proceedings. Likewise, the decision on the petition under Article 5(1) of Regulation 2015/848 should be appealable to a higher tribunal. The need to provide for the possibility of review of the decision on the petition under Article 5(1) of Regulation 2015/848 follows from the very broad spectrum of grounds that the petition may invoke. These grounds may consist in the unusual or inconsistent application of the law, or in exceptional situations in which the State's power itself may have failed in its fundamental underlying principles, such as independence and impartiality. It is therefore necessary to provide for the possibility of review by a higher tribunal, despite the fact that Regulation 2015/848 itself guarantees no such review;[79] for instance, a review ultimately exercised by the forum competent to unify case law in the given Member State or, as applicable, to secure a uniform interpretation of the law. Naturally, this is also without prejudice to the possibility of filing a request for a preliminary ruling with the Court of Justice with the aim of unifying the interpretation of the provision, and one may indeed assume that the interpretation of Article 5(1) of Regulation 2015/848 will become the subject matter of preliminary ruling(s) in the future, or, as the case may be, that the courts will request a preliminary ruling specifically in the proceedings under Article 5(1) of Regulation 2015/848, which cannot be confused with the proceedings opening insolvency proceedings. The reason is that the dividing line between EU law and the *lex fori concursus* is rather unclear in Article 5(1) of Regulation 2015/848, at least as concerns the application of

---

[79] See Peter Mankowski, In: PETER MANKOWSKI, MICHAEL F. MÜLLER, JESSICA SCHMIDT, EUINSVO 2015: EUROPÄISCHE INSOLVENZORDNUNG 2015. KOMMENTAR, München: C. H. Beck (2016), commentary on Article 5 of Regulation 2015/848, marg. 11, et. 155. In this regard, one may agree with Prof. Mankowski that Regulation 2015/848 provides no guarantee of such a review. But considering the objective of the law and its importance, as mentioned in this paper, and considering the fact that the corresponding procedural instruments afforded by the *lex fori concursus* must be modified for the purposes of the procedure under Article 5(1) of Regulation 2015/848, a review of lower court decisions is certainly appropriate, if not desirable.

the corresponding procedural mechanisms, or, as applicable, as to whether and to what extent even the procedures should be perceived to be fully autonomous in this regard.

3.60. The nature and the purpose of the possibility of challenging the decision opening main insolvency proceedings are rather similar to instruments such as extraordinary remedies, where the persons with legal standing were prevented from raising an effective defence or new circumstances and evidence have transpired, etc. Despite this, it is hardly possible to consider the procedure under Article 5(1) of Regulation 2015/848 as identical to any other. It is a unique mechanism relying directly on EU law.

## XI.2. The Scope of Procedure under Article 5(1) of Regulation 2015/848 and the Absence of Any Deadline Limiting the Application

3.61. The fact that it is not a remedy against the judgment opening insolvency proceedings is important from a number of perspectives. One example would be because the procedure is not subject to limitations laid down in national laws, such as the presentation of new evidence.[80] If the *lex fori concursus* provides for a remedy against the judgment opening insolvency proceedings, such a mechanism under the *lex fori concursus* exists alongside the procedure under Article 5(1) of Regulation 2015/848. Both mechanisms exist side by side, and the use of the mechanism under Article 5(1) of Regulation 2015/848 is not limited by any deadline which usually limits the filing of a remedy under national procedures. Hence, if the debtor and/or the creditors avail themselves of the remedy under the *lex fori* and such a remedy is limited by a deadline for filing the remedy, the creditors or the debtor are limited by no such deadlines when filing the petition under Article 5(1) of Regulation 2015/848.

3.62. The absence of a deadline limiting the application of the procedure under Article 5(1) of Regulation 2015/848 is sometimes criticised for being a factor contributing to legal uncertainty. The conclusion that this procedure is not tied to any deadlines, i.e. that it is not limited by any deadlines, may also be inferred from the *travail préparatoire*. Indeed, the European Parliament originally wished to stipulate a limitation in the form of a three-week time limit from the public announcement of the opening of insolvency proceedings.[81] Hence, the application of

---

[80]   REINHARD BORK, RENATO MANGANO, EUROPEAN CROSS-BORDER INSOLVENCY LAW, Oxford: Oxford University Press (2016), et. 101, marg. 3.56.
[81]   European Parliament legislative resolution No 1346/2000 on insolvency proceedings, in relation to

any deadline limiting the filing of the petition under Article 5(1) of Regulation 2015/848, for instance, by reference to the *lex fori concursus*, is out of the question.[82] Issues that are not provided for from the procedural perspective in Article 5(1) of Regulation 2015/848 may be resolved by an analogous application of similar instruments under the *lex fori concursus*, especially in procedural matters. But the *lex fori concursus* may not be applied in such a manner as to limit the application itself of Article 5(1) of Regulation 2015/848 and in excess of the wording of Article 5(1) of Regulation 2015/848 regarding the applicability thereof. The only limitations of the application of Article 5(1) of Regulation 2015/848 are the issue of legal standing and the fact that the use of this procedure must concern challenging international jurisdiction. Any other limitations, including any deadlines, would unlawfully limit the procedure itself, whose applicability is a question of EU law only.

3.63. The necessity of this measure relating to widespread unfair insolvency tourism, the abuse of the variable nature of the COMI, as well as the relatively superficial approach of a number of courts bordering on a desire to open insolvency proceedings in their own States, rather supports the need for a most extensive subject-matter and temporal applicability. Indeed, the three-week time limit originally proposed by the European Parliament was *prima facie* too short in view of all the situations that the law might cover, as well as the fact that such a time limit would be manifestly insufficient for a number of reasons. For instance, it may be expected that the said defence mechanism will mostly be used by creditors who must address foreign courts.

## XI.3. Other Formal Requirements Imposed on Claimant

3.64. The requirements that would potentially be imposed by national law on court reviews and that would potentially also be reasonably applicable to the procedure under Article 5(1) of Regulation 2015/848, must not be of such a nature as to significantly limit

---

Article 3(3) of Regulation 1346/2000 in terms of the proposal for a regulation presented by the Commission and having regard to (i) opinion of the European Economic and Social Committee of 22 May 2013, as well as (ii) report of the Committee on Legal Affairs (A7-0481/2013). The above-mentioned EP legislative resolution is available online at: http://www.europarl.europa.eu/sides/getDoc.do?pubRef=-//EP//TEXT+TA+P7-TA-2014-0093+0+DOC+XML+V0//CS (accessed on 09 September 2018).

[82] Prof. Mankowski is somewhat unclear on this point. He does refer to gaps in the law and suggests that they should be covered by the application of the *lex fori concursus*; in his opinion, these gaps also include the absence of any time limits for the application of the procedure. But he is also aware of the fact that the absence of a time limit is a very specific situation in connection with issues that are not provided for in Article 5(1) of Regulation 2015/848. Peter Mankowski, In: PETER MANKOWSKI, MICHAEL F. MÜLLER, JESSICA SCHMIDT, EUINSVO 2015: EUROPÄISCHE INSOLVENZORDNUNG 2015. KOMMENTAR, München: C. H. Beck (2016), commentary on Article 5 of Regulation 2015/848, marg. 10, et. 154-155.

the applicability of the procedure. It needs to be emphasized that Article 5(1) of Regulation 2015/848 represents an important instrument or, indeed, one of the principal instruments for the protection of creditors and debtors directly connected to one of the pillars of EU insolvency law, namely the COMI as the sole connecting factor for the determination of international jurisdiction for the opening of main insolvency proceedings. The significant enhancement of the protection of the parties, in this case creditors and debtors, was one of the main objectives of the amendment of Regulation 1346/2000, and is also reflected in Article 5(1) of Regulation 2015/848.

3.65. Consequently, any potential requirements imposed on the claimant must have regard to the objective of the law and reasonably factor in similar procedures laid down in Regulation 2015/848. For instance, it is not possible to request mandatory professional legal representation. The only limitation conceivable in this regard could be, for instance, the requirement of a mailing address in the State where the court is located.[83]

3.66. Similarly, no limiting requirements may be imposed regarding, for instance, court fees. Connected with this, it is desirable that the Member States set the court fee, if provided for by a statute or other legislation, in such an amount that corresponds to the procedure under Article 5(1) of Regulation 2015/848 and the objective thereof, namely in the minimum acceptable amount. Considering the fact that international jurisdiction and the review thereof are an absolutely fundamental condition for any proceedings, and that the examination of the court's own jurisdiction is not only a material expression of State sovereignty, but also a basic obligation of the court (at least under Regulation 2015/848),[84] the proceedings under Article 5(1) of Regulation 2015/848 should also, if possible, be exempt from court fees, or the court fee should be a minimal fixed amount covering only the basic costs incurred by the court.

---

[83]   *Paulus, Chr.* refers here to the *effet utile* of the law and the need to have regard to circumstances such as the fact that the parties to the proceedings under Article 5(1) of Regulation 2015/848 will often include foreigners, persons or entities from distant places, He mentions, for instance, procedural limits, the language of the proceedings, etc. CHRISTOPH G. PAULUS, EUROPÄISCHE INSOLVENZVERORDNUNG: KOMMENTAR (Frankfurt a. M.: Fachmedien Recht und Wirtschaft / dfv Mediengruppe 5th ed., 2017), commentary on Article 5 of Regulation 2015/848, marg. 3, et. 213.

[84]   See Article 4 of Regulation 2015/848 (quoted above).

## XI.4. The Consequences of Challenging a Decision on a Request for Opening Main Insolvency Proceedings

**3.67.** It is necessary to mention that Article 5(1) of Regulation 2015/848 only provides for the right to challenge the judgment opening insolvency proceedings. It does not set forth the consequences of such procedure, and these consequences are left entirely to the national law.[85]

## XII. The Procedure Adopted by Persons or Entities Other than Creditors and Debtors as Part of a Defence against a Decision on International Jurisdiction of Insolvency Court: the Exclusive Application of *Lex Fori Concursus*

### XII.1. The Objective and Nature of the Procedure under Article 5(2) of Regulation 2015/848

**3.68.** Contrary to the first paragraph of Article 5 of Regulation 2015/848, the second paragraph guarantees legal standing to a much broader class of persons or entities to challenge the above-mentioned decision for a lack of international jurisdiction of the court or for other reasons, provided that the national law enables such a procedure. The second paragraph of Article 5 of Regulation 2015/848 stipulates as follows (quote): 'The decision opening *main insolvency* proceedings may be challenged by parties other than those referred to in paragraph 1 or on grounds other than a lack of international jurisdiction where national law so provides.' Hence, the main purpose of this second paragraph is the clarification of the relationship between the rights awarded by national law and the rights awarded by international law, or more precisely, the explanation that these rights are not mutually exclusive.[86]

**3.69.** However, Article 5(2) of Regulation 2015/848 is rather a confirmation and guarantee of the fact that the decision opening

---

[85] See:

Recital 34 of Regulation 2015/848 (quote): [*I*]*n addition, any creditor of the debtor should have an effective remedy against the decision to open insolvency proceedings. The consequences of any challenge to the decision to open insolvency proceedings should be governed by national law.* REINHARD BORK, RENATO MANGANO, EUROPEAN CROSS-BORDER INSOLVENCY LAW, Oxford: Oxford University Press (2016), et. 99, marg. 3.52.

[86] Cf. REINHARD BORK, RENATO MANGANO, EUROPEAN CROSS-BORDER INSOLVENCY LAW, Oxford: Oxford University Press (2016), et. 99, marg. 3.53; GABRIEL MOSS, IAN FLETCHER, STUART ISAACS, THE EC REGULATION ON INSOLVENCY PROCEEDINGS: A COMMENTARY AND ANNOTATED GUIDE, Oxford: Oxford University Press (2002), marg. 8.584, et. 452.

main insolvency proceedings may also be challenged by persons and entities other than those listed in Article 5(1) of Regulation 2015/848, and, as the case may be, also on grounds other than a lack of international jurisdiction of the court, provided that such a possibility is available under the *lex fori concursus*. However, Article 5(2) of Regulation 2015/848 exclusively regulates a procedure governed by the *lex fori concursus*. Hence, the second paragraph primarily emphasises the independence of the mechanism under Article 5(1) of Regulation 2015/848 of the *lex fori concursus*.

3.70. In this regard, the grounds for and the methods of challenging the decision opening main insolvency proceedings under the national or domestic legal systems are highly variable. For instance, in England, the decision opening main insolvency proceedings may also be challenged by the insolvency practitioner.[87/88]

## XII.2. The Subject-matter, Scope and Object of Procedure under Article 5(2) of Regulation 2015/848

3.71. Article 5(2) of Regulation 2015/848 also exclusively targets the positive decision opening main insolvency proceedings. In this regard, the scope of Article 5(2) of Regulation 2015/848 is no different from similar issues concerning Article 5(1) of Regulation 2015/848. Article 5(2) of Regulation 2015/848 also explicitly refers to the main insolvency proceedings, and it is also necessary to consider whether this means a judgment opening insolvency proceedings under Article 2(7) of Regulation 2015/848. The difference is that the application

---

[87]    HLV Report, et. 150.
[88]    See also the decision of Chief Registrar Baister of 10 December 2010 in *Official Receiver* v. *Hiwa Huck*, neutral citation [2011] BPIR 709. See also Bankruptcy and Personal Insolvency Reports, available at: http://www.jordanpublishing.co.uk/practice-areas/insolvency/news_and_comment/re-hiwa-huck-official-receiver-v-hiwa-huck-2011-bpir-709#.V7SNoyiLTIW (accessed on 05 April 2019). See also HLV Report, et. 214-215.

> In the *Hiwa Huck* decision, the insolvency practitioner requested the cancellation of the judgment opening insolvency proceedings (in the form of an insolvency order). The insolvency practitioner argued, firstly, that Mr Huck had not had his COMI in England when the request for opening insolvency proceedings was filed; the COMI was allegedly located in Germany, and consequently, the English courts lacked international jurisdiction. Secondly, the insolvency practitioner argued that the debtor had supplied the court with false information in the request for opening insolvency proceedings and in the debtor's Statement of Affaires. Mr Huck was unable to supply any evidence confirming that he indeed lived or lives in England. The court granted the insolvency practitioner's request. But a procedure corresponding to the procedure in *Hiwa Huck* cannot be applied in compliance with the regime under Article 5(2) of Regulation 2015/848 that refers exclusively to the *lex fori concursus* in those legal systems that do not recognize the insolvency practitioners' legal standing, at least as concerns the legal standing of the insolvency practitioner as the claimant.

of the procedures under the *lex fori concursus* need not only concern issues relating to international jurisdiction.

## XII.3. Term *Court* under Article 5(2) of Regulation 2015/848: Conceptual Error in Drafting of Czech Language Version

**3.72.** Contrary to all other language versions, the Czech version of Regulation 2015/848 uses the term *court* also in the second paragraph of Article 5 of Regulation 2015/848 (referring to 'a lack of international jurisdiction of the court'.[89] In this regard, a conceptual error has apparently occurred in the drafting of the Czech version. None of the other language versions employs the term, and they only refer to international jurisdiction, not the international jurisdiction of the court, as the Czech version does. A problem concerning the definition of a court, i.e. whether this means 'court' under Article 2(6)(i) or under Article 2(6)(ii), only arises if one uses the Czech version of Regulation 2015/848.

**3.73.** However, the definition of a *court* in Article 2(6)(i) of Regulation 2015/848[90] refers to the fact that the more restrictive concept of a court in terms of an authority with judicial power applies to the entire Article 5 of Regulation 2015/848, i.e. both paragraph 1 and paragraph 2. But the use of this narrow definition of a court makes no sense in the case of Article 5(2) of Regulation 2015/848. Rather, in this case (at least as concerns the context in which the term *court* is used in the Czech version) the term must be used in the broader sense, i.e. in the sense stipulated in Article 2(6)(ii) of Regulation 2015/848. Indeed, it was primarily in the cases well documented in international practice where there existed an interest in the possibility of reviewing the decisions of those authorities that are not an authority with judicial power, but which may still open insolvency proceedings depending on the national insolvency concept.

**3.74.** The problem should be resolved by a potential future amendment of the Czech language version by omitting the word *court* in Article 5(2) of Regulation 2015/848. After all, the term is unnecessary from the perspective of the wording of the provision, and the translation service, as well as the persons charged with corrections of the Czech version, clearly failed to

---

[89] This deficiency is also not present in the Slovak version, which is otherwise closest to the Czech version, and the Czech and Slovak versions often copy each other as concerns the relevant formulations.

[90] Article 2(6)(i) of Regulation 2015/848 (quote): „[...] "court" 'means: (i) in points (b) and (c) of Article 1(1), Article 4(2), Articles 5 and 6, Article 21(3), point (j) of Article 24(2), Articles 36 and 39, and Articles 61 to 77, the judicial body of a Member State;[...]." The entire Article 2(6) of Regulation 2015/848 is quoted in the footnotes above.

have regard to the connection with Article 2(6) of Regulation 2015/848.

**3.75.** On the other hand, the wording of Article 2(6)(i) itself is also incorrect. This provision refers to Articles 5 and 6. But it would be more appropriate if the reference to Article 5 of Regulation 2015/848 were made more specific and were supplemented, i.e. that the provision would, as concerns the more restrictive definition of the term *court*, invoke only Article 5(1) of Regulation 2015/848, not the entire Article 5 of Regulation 2015/848, regardless of the paragraph in question. However, the appropriateness of a reference solely invoking Article 5(1) of Regulation 2015/848, should have been mentioned by the Czech delegation and the Czech language service if the Czech delegation also desired to have the term *court* used in the Czech version specifically in Article 5(2) of Regulation 2015/848. Consequently, it is a manifest error and oversight on the part of the Czech delegation.

| | |

## Summaries

**FRA** [*La détermination de la compétence internationale en tant qu'aspect fondamental de la protection du droit d'accès à la justice (droit à un procès équitable) : les mécanismes permettant de contester les décisions sur la compétence internationale dans la procédure européenne d'insolvabilité (règlement (UE) 2015/848 du Parlement européen et du Conseil relatif aux procédures d'insolvabilité)*]

*Les règles de conflit régissant la compétence internationale des juridictions pour ouvrir une procédure d'insolvabilité principale se fondent dans le droit de l'UE sur un seul critère de rattachement, à savoir le centre des intérêts principaux (COMI) du débiteur. Ce critère de rattachement, quoique fondé sur des faits objectifs et perceptibles par des tiers, dépend souvent d'une appréciation subjective d'un grand nombre de circonstances. De surcroît, le COMI peut évoluer dans le temps. C'est cette variabilité du COMI qui a souvent fait, selon l'ancienne législation, l'objet d'abus qui prenait la forme de transfert frauduleux du COMI dans un autre État présentant un régime de droit plus favorable pour le débiteur (COMI Shifting, « tourisme d'insolvabilité »), voire d'agissements de nature criminelle. L'ancienne législation, représentée par le règlement (CE) 1346/2000 du Conseil, n'était pas en mesure de remédier à cette situation. La variabilité du COMI et un risque élevé de subjectivité lors de sa détermination présentaient une menace considérable pour le droit à un procès équitable, et plus particulièrement le droit d'accès à la juridiction. Le règlement (UE) 2015/848 du Parlement européen et du Conseil cherche à y répondre par certains nouveaux éléments, l'un des plus importants étant le mécanisme de contrôle selon l'article 5, paragraphe 1, du règlement 2015/848, qui est une procédure autonome, régie par le droit de l'UE et indépendante de tout autre mécanisme prévu par le droit national de l'État de la procédure d'insolvabilité (lex fori concursus). Le règlement ne limite en aucune manière les motifs pour lesquels les débiteurs ou les créanciers peuvent avoir recours à ce mécanisme, à l'exception du fait qu'il doit s'agir de motifs de compétence internationale. De même, aucun délai n'est fixé pour le recours des débiteurs ou des créanciers à cette procédure. Il s'agit d'une procédure autonome et unique en son genre, susceptible de jouer un rôle crucial dans la protection des parties à des procédures d'insolvabilité menées dans les États membres de l'UE (exception faite du Danemark), et, par conséquent, dans la protection de leur droit d'accès à la juridiction, sous-catégorie du droit à un procès équitable.*

CZE    [*Určování mezinárodní příslušnosti jako významný aspekt ochrany práva na přístup ke spravedlnosti – práva na spravedlivý proces: obranné mechanismy proti rozhodnutí o mezinárodní příslušnosti v evropském insolvenčním řízení (nařízení Evropského parlamentu a Rady (EU) 2015/848 o insolvenčním řízení)*]

*Kolizní úprava mezinárodní soudní příslušnosti pro zahájení hlavního insolvenčního řízení je v právu EU postavena výlučně na jednom hraničním určovateli, a to na středisku hlavních zájmů (COMI) dlužníka. Tento hraniční určovatel, ať již jeho určení má vycházet z objektivních skutečností vnímatelných třetími osobami, závisí často na subjektivním hodnocení řady okolností. COMI navíc může být a často je v čase proměnné. Právě variabilita COMI byla doposud podle předchozí úpravy často předmětem zneužití práva v podobě účelového přesouvání COMI do jiných států s právním režimem výhodnějším pro dlužníka (COMI Shifting, insolvenční turistika) a dokonce v krajních případech i předmětem zneužití práva, či dokonce jednání s kriminálním pozadím. Dřívější úprava v podobě nařízení Rady (ES) č. 1346/2000 na to nebyla schopna reagovat. Právě variabilita COMI a vysoké riziko subjektivních prvků při hodnocení jeho lokalizace zásadním způsobem ohrožovala právo na spravedlivý proces v podobě práva na přístup k soudu. Nařízení*

*Evropského parlamentu a Rady (EU) č. 2015/848 se na to snaží reagovat některými instituty. Mezi nejvýznamnější z nich patří přezkumný mechanismus podle čl. 5 odst. 1 nařízení 2015/848, který je autonomním postupem podle práva EU nezávislým na jakýchkoli jiných mechanismech podle vnitrostátního práva státu insolvenčního řízení (lex fori concursus). S výjimkou toho, že důvody pro tento postup se musí týkat mezinárodní příslušnosti, nejsou důvody, pro které mohou dlužníci, stejně jako kteříkoli věřitelé tento mechanismus využít, jakkoli omezeny. Stejně tak není stanovena žádná lhůta, ve které by věřitelé nebo dlužník mohli tento postup iniciovat. Jde o unikátní a autonomní postup, který může představovat významný prvek ochrany hlavních stran v insolvenčním řízení vedených v členských státech EU (s výjimkou Dánska) a tedy i ochrany jejich práva na přístup k soudu, resp. práva na spravedlivý proces.*

| | |

POL  [*Określanie właściwości międzynarodowej jako istotny aspekt ochrony prawa dostępu do wymiaru sprawiedliwości – prawa do sprawiedliwego procesu: mechanizmy obrony przed orzeczeniem międzynarodowej właściwości w europejskim postępowaniu upadłościowym (Rozporządzenie Parlamentu Europejskiego i Rady (UE) 2015/848 w sprawie postępowania upadłościowego)*]

*Przepisy unijne regulujące postępowanie upadłościowe, w których określenie właściwości międzynarodowej sądu celem wszczęcia i przeprowadzenia głównego postępowania upadłościowego oparte jest na jednym decydującym parametrze – głównym ośrodku podstawowej działalności dłużnika (COMI), jak dotąd nie oferowały wystarczającej ochrony prawa stron do dostępu do sądu lub prawa do sprawiedliwego procesu. Braki te próbuje usunąć Rozporządzenie Parlamentu Europejskiego i Rady (UE) 2015/848 z dnia 20 maja 2015 r. w sprawie postępowania upadłościowego, wprowadzając nowy mechanizm ochrony praw wierzycieli i dłużnika. Za jeden z najważniejszych instytutów należy tutaj uznać instytut uregulowany w art. 5 ust. 1 rozporządzenia 2015/848.*

DEU  [*Bestimmung der internationalen Zuständigkeit als wichtiger Aspekt beim Schutz des Rechts auf Zugang zur Justiz – das Recht auf ein faires Verfahren: Abwehrmechanismen gegen internationale Zuständigkeitsentscheidungen im europäischen Insolvenzverfahren (Verordnung des Europäischen Parlaments und des Rates (EU) 2015/848 über Insolvenzverfahren)*]

*Die europäische Regelung des Insolvenzverfahrens, in der die Bestimmung der internationalen Zuständigkeit des Gerichts für die Eröffnung und Durchführung des Hauptinsolvenzverfahrens auf einer einzigen Grenzdeterminante – dem Hauptinteressenzentrum des Schuldners (COMI) – beruht, gewährleistet bisher keinen ausreichenden Schutz des Zugangsrechts der Parteien zur Justiz bzw. des Rechts auf ein faires Verfahren. Diesen Mangel soll die Verordnung des Europäischen Parlaments und des Rates (EU) Nr. 2015/848 über das Insolvenzverfahren durch die Einführung neuer Mechanismen zum Schutz der Rechte von Gläubigern und Schuldnern beheben. Das in Artikel 5 Absatz 1 der Verordnung 2015/848 vorgesehene Institut ist als eines der wichtigsten Institute anzusehen.*

RUS [*Определение международной юрисдикции как важного аспекта защиты права на доступ к правосудию — права на справедливый судебный процесс. Механизмы защиты от решений о международной юрисдикции в европейских процедурах несостоятельности (Регламент (ЕС) 2015/848 Европейского парламента и Совета «О процедурах несостоятельности»)*]

*Европейское регулирование процедур несостоятельности, в котором определение международной юрисдикции суда для возбуждения и ведения главного производства по делу о несостоятельности основано на едином граничном показателе — центре основных интересов должника (COMI), до сих пор не имело достаточной защиты права сторон на доступ к правосудию или же права на справедливый судебный процесс. Этот недостаток пытается исправить Регламент (ЕС) № 2015/848 Европейского парламента и Совета «О процедурах несостоятельности» путем внедрения новых механизмов защиты прав кредиторов и должника. Одним из важных положений следует считать положение, определенное в пункте 1 статьи 5 Регламента 2015/848.*

ESP [*Determinación de la competencia jurisdiccional internacional como un elemento importante de la protección de los derechos y acceso a la justicia – derecho a un juicio justo: los mecanismos de defensa contra la resolución de la determinación de la competencia jurisdiccional internacional en el procedimiento de insolvencia europeo*

*(Reglamento del Parlamento Europeo y del Consejo (CE) 2015/848, del procedimiento de insolvencia]*
*La normativa europea del procedimiento de insolvencia, que establece la competencia jurisdiccional internacional para la incoación y tramitación del procedimiento de insolvencia principal a base del único factor de conexión – Centro de Intereses Principales del Deudor (COMI), carecía hasta la actualidad de un mecanismo eficaz de protección del acceso de las partes a la justicia, respectivamente el derecho a un juicio justo. Este defecto pretende eliminar el Reglamento del Parlamento Europeo y del Consejo (CE) 2015/848 del procedimiento de insolvencia, por el cual se establecen nuevos mecanismos de protección de los derechos de los acreedores y los deudores. Uno de los mecanismos jurídicos más importantes se introduce en el art. 5, apartado 1 del Reglamento 2015/848.*

| | |

## Bibliography

REINHARD BORK, RENATO MANGANO, EUROPEAN CROSS-BORDER INSOLVENCY LAW, Oxford: Oxford University Press (2016).

Daniel Friedemann Fritz, Rainer M. Bähr, *Die Europäische Verordnung* über *Insolvenzverfahren. Herausforderung an die Gerichte und Insolvenzverwalter*, 11(6) DEUTSCHE ZEITSCHRIFT FÜR WIRTSCHAFTS- UND INSOLVENZRECHT (2001).

Stefan Leible, Ansgar Staudinger, *Die europäische Verordnung über Insolvenzverfahren*, 61 KONKURS, TREUHAND, SANIERUNG (2000).

PETER MANKOWSKI, MICHAEL F. MÜLLER, JESSICA SCHMIDT, EUINSVO 2015: EUROPÄISCHE INSOLVENZORDNUNG 2015. KOMMENTAR, München: C. H. Beck (2016).

GABRIEL MOSS, IAN F. FLETCHER, STUART ISAACS, THE EC REGULATION ON INSOLVENCY PROCEEDINGS: A COMMENTARY AND ANNOTATED GUIDE, Oxford: Oxford University Press (2002).

CHRISTOPH G. PAULUS, EUROPÄISCHE INSOLVENZVERORDNUNG: KOMMENTAR (Frankfurt a. M.: Fachmedien Recht und Wirtschaft / dfv Mediengruppe 5th ed., 2017).

IAIN RAMSAY, PERSONAL INSOLVENCY IN THE 21st CENTURY: A COMPARATIVE ANALYSIS OF THE US AND EUROPE, Oxford: Bloomsbury Publishing (2017).

STEFAN SMID, EUROPÄISCHES INTERNATIONALES INSOLVENZRECHT. Wien: Manzsche Verlags- und

Universitätsbuchhandlung / Center of Legal Competence (2002).

PETER STONE, EU PRIVATE INTERNATIONAL LAW (Edward Elgar Publishing 3rd ed., 2014).

# Petr Čechák | Jan Šmíd | Pavel Mates

# Human Rights and the Courts

*Key words:*
*rule of law | human rights |*
*the judiciary*

Czech Yearbook of International Law®

**Abstract** | *This article concerns itself with the origins, categorisation and stages of human rights. It explains the modern traditioin of separating natural rights into claims without any connection to responsibility. The current expansion of human rights is one of the consequences of this. Another cause is identified as legal positivism, optimistic view on the ability of mankind to comprehend human rights. In contrast to that is the sceptical view which considers a very limited circle of rights to constitute natural human rights and does not assume that mankind could achieve any new understanding in this regard. Courts are becoming the arbiters in matters of human rights in countries where the law guarantees human rights and freedoms. The role of the courts when optimising their realisation and setting the boundaries during the collision of two or more requirements is essential. Judicature is an increasingly powerfull tool for both protection and searching for specific contents and development. Even though courts have drawn up decision-making methods, which include e.g.: the use of proportionality and rationality tests, the fact that extra-legal factors may play a role during the decision-making process cannot be ruled out. Outcome of this is favorising some rights over others. Protection of individual rights is placed above wider interests such as safety, order and fight against crime. This often occurs in the name of the right to a fair trial, whereby this requirement is absolutised, which precludes the trial from achieving a fair result. The courts have therefore become the real overlords in the area of human rights, as they have a wide scope for finding their own interpretations. This is especially apparent during the interpretation of the constitution, which is usually rigid, i.e. Virtually*

**Petr Čechák** lectures on constitutional law, legal theory and legal philosophy at the University of Finance and Administration in Prague. He specialized in the above topics, which he has elaborated on in his contributions to several collections of papers. E-mail: petr.cechak@mail. vsfs.cz

**Jan Šmíd** teaches the theory of law, constitutional law and political science at the University of Finance and Administration in Prague. He also teaches political philosophy and the philosophy of law at Jan Evangelista Purkyně University in Ústí nad Labem, and teaches political ideologies at the University of Economics in Prague. He specializes in the above topics, which he has elaborated on in his contributions to several collections of papers and articles published in academic journals. E-mail: john_smid@yahoo. com

**Pavel Mates** lectures on administrative law at the University of Finance and Administration in Prague and on the theory of law at the Faculty of Socioeconomics at J. E. Purkyně University in Ústí nad Labem. He specializes in the issue of administrative criminal law and the legal regulation of e-government. He has published several

Czech Yearbook of International Law®

*politically immutable, while it is open to judicial interpretation, which means it finds itself in the hands of the courts. Constitutional judiciary limits political discourse, while the other powers usually do not have the strenght to actively resist this trend, not even when courts fail to protect citizens against serious threats. One of the reactions of this is the populistic rejection of the very concept of the constitutional judiciary. The opposite reaction is an idealised view of the constitutional judiciary as a mere interpreter of the constitution.*

monographs and dozens of articles in Czech and foreign journals on these issues. He is a member of the legislative body of the government.
E-mail: pavel.mates@ujep.cz; pmates@mail.vsfs.cz

| | |

# I.    The Genesis and Current Status of Human Rights

**4.01.**    Human rights are without doubt one of the most fundamental achievements of European civilisation and an integral part thereof.[1] They are the product of an extremely long tradition of thought which dates back to antiquity. They have further passed through every significant stage of history and contributed to the formulation of ideas, which we can now summarise under the term of 'human rights'. Even though the path has been tortuous, it can be traced through the Middle Ages, the Enlightenment, the era of industrialisation and on to the present.

**4.02.**    From a legal-philosophical point of view, it is possible to combine human rights with the theory of natural law, as it was formulated in antiquity through to the Middle Ages and in its more modern forms through to the present. Several authors have pointed to this very close connection and it is possible to consider it a historical fact. According to Michal Bartoň, the ideas of natural law are connected with 'the subjective claims of the individual, i.e. as subjective rights, as natural individual claims', albeit that the idea of subjective rights began to take shape from the theory of natural law at the beginning of the 12th century.[2] Jacques Maritain, one of the most significant natural law scholars of the 20th century, also postulated the absolute inseparability of human rights from the theory of natural law. According to Maritain, 'the same natural law which designates

---

[1]    VÁCLAV PAVLÍČEK, HELENA HOFMANNOVÁ, OBČANSKÁ A LIDSKÁ PRÁVA V SOUČASNÉ DOBĚ. Praha: Auditorium 53 (2014).
[2]    MICHAL BARTOŇ, JAN KRATOCHVÍL, MARTIN KOPA, MAXIM TOMOSZEK, JIŘÍ JIRÁSEK, ONDŘEJ SVAČEK, ZÁKLADNÍ PRÁVA, Praha: Leges 3, 31 (1st ed. 2016).

our most fundamental responsibilities and makes every just law binding is also the law which awards us our basic rights'.[3] Maritain sees the link here as being clear and unequivocal.

4.03. A dispute arose in antiquity as to the godly origins of the laws. One proponent of this was Plato who dealt with a number of associated questions in his *Laws*, such as the question of the existence of the gods (888d-899d), whether they were interested in human affairs (899d-905d) and whether the gods were able to be influenced by people (905d-907d).[4] He subsequently inferred from this that universally valid laws are possible.[5]

4.04. The Sophists opposed Plato, but even though they set the rules created by man against the laws given by nature (physis), they were responsible for a fundamental reversal in philosophy's main area of attention from nature to man, including the issue of laws and justice.

4.05. Aristotle also significantly contributed to the theory of natural law and in doing so inspired medieval scholars. Other ‚co-authors' on this long list were the Stoics, amongst whom the most important from the point of view of the philosophy of law was Cicero, who considered that a relationship existed between human nature *(natura)* and civic rights *(civile ius)*. At the same time, he postulated that human ‚civic rights' had their origins in human intellectual nature, the manifestations of which are the results of the effects of universal human reason.[6]

4.06. To a certain extent, the theory of natural law achieved its peak in the Middle Ages. Its best-known proponent was Thomas Aquinas. To this day, one of the traditions of natural law is essentially based on the development of his centuries-old ideas. Thomas Aquinas created a categorisation of laws:
   1) eternal
   2) natural
   3) human (positive)
   4) the divine.

4.07. The most important of these from our point of view is the natural law which is characterised as man's participation in the eternal law, i.e. the law which was created by God when he gave the world its rules. Part of this law is given to man as rules which determine his behaviour and are recognisable using natural

---

[3] JACQUES MARITAIN, ČLOVĚK A STÁT, Praha: Triáda, Delfín 211 (2007), et 86, 91.

[4] PLATÓN, ZÁKONY, Praha: OIKOYMENH (1997).

[5] LIDSKÁ A PŘIROZENÁ PRÁVA V DĚJINÁCH, Ústí n. Labem: Filozofická fakulta Univerzity Jana Evangelisty Purkyně v Ústí n. Labem, Acta Universitatis Purkynianae, Facultatis Philosophicae (A. Havlíček ed., 2014), et 20.

[6] LIDSKÁ A PŘIROZENÁ PRÁVA V DĚJINÁCH, Ústí n. Labem: Filozofická fakulta Univerzity Jana Evangelisty Purkyně v Ústí n. Labem, Acta Universitatis Purkynianae, Facultatis Philosophicae (A. Havlíček ed., 2014), et 36.

Czech Yearbook of International Law®

reason. The recognisability of natural law lies, of course, in the plane of potentiality, because mankind only gradually discovers the rules of the natural law.[7]

Thomas Aquinas mentions the following four precepts of natural law:

1) good is to be done and evil is to be avoided in all human acts
2) bodily health is a good to be pursued and bodily harm avoided
3) in accordance with the nature which is shared with other animals ... the natural law includes that which nature has taught all animals, namely the congress of a man and a woman, the upbringing of children and so on.
4) man has a tendency towards good according to the nature of his reason ... man has a natural tendency to recognise the truth about God and to live in society ... for example, to avoid ignorance, not to insult those with whom he must cohabit and similar matters which are associated therewith.[8]

**4.08.** The only completely unconditional requirement of natural law is the first requirement of practical reason. We admittedly infer all the others from our natural tendencies, but they are already dependent upon other circumstances. The fact that Thomas Aquinas did not speak of any other natural laws is also of great significance. He mentioned other principles of natural law which are apparent to everybody, but he did not elaborate them.[9] It is therefore possible to state that the catalogue is open, but the fundamental principle has been clearly given. In Thomas' theory, natural law essentially corresponds to moral obligations, while subjective claims are side-lined.

**4.09.** Nevertheless, other traditions of natural law have also been developed in the modern era. In this regard, Leo Strauss speaks of the divide between the so-called classic and modern concept of natural law in the works of Thomas Hobbes.[10] The relationship between the law in the sense of permission and responsibility is constructed differently in Hobbes' concept. He equated natural law with rights and stated that people's passions are the source of rights which are, moreover, not limited in any way. Hobbes

---

[7] TOMÁŠ AKVINSKÝ, TOMÁŠ AKVINSKÝ O ZÁKONECH V TEOLOGICKÉ SUMĚ (překlad Karel Šprunk), Praha: Krystal OP 65-67 (1st ed., 2003).

[8] TOMÁŠ AKVINSKÝ, SUMMA THEOLOGICKÁ II. část, Olomouc: Red Soukup PE (1938).

[9] Ingrid Hašková, *Nová teorie přirozeného zákona*, 2 DISTANCE: REVUE PRO KRITICKÉ MYŠLENÍ (2006).

[10] OTTMANN, H. GESCHICHTE DES POLITISCHE DENKENS 3 (1).: DIE NEUZEIT. 1. Stuttgart - Weimar: J.B. Metzler (2006) et 290.

departed from the tradition which combined natural law with the idea of human perfection or achieving a person's goals. Hobbes began to infer natural law from the way people really live and from what most determines their actions or the actions of most people. The majority are, of course, not determined by reason, but by passions and natural law is derived from that.[11]

> The most powerful of all passions is the fear of death and, more particularly, the fear of violent death at the hands of others ... Death takes place of the telos ... If, then, natural law must be deduced form the desire for self-preservation, if, in other words, the desire for self-preservation is the sole root of all justice and morality, the fundamental moral fact is not a duty but a right.[12]

**4.10.** Strauss further points to the fact that, if the law is an absolute and fundamental legal fact and not an obligation, it then implies that the functions and limits of civil society have to be defined using the terms of natural law and not those of natural obligations. The State is not focussed on a virtuous life, but on the protection of rights (claims – authors' of the article note).

**4.11.** Strauss then considers the transformation of natural law into a revolutionary force throughout history to be one of the logical and visible consequences of the theory of Hobbes.[13] He directly quotes Hobbes, who says that the sacred charge of rulers is no longer ‚to make the citizens good and doers of noble things‘, but to ‚study, as much as by laws can be effected, to furnish the citizens abundantly with all good things ... which are conductive to delectation‘.[14]

**4.12.** The tradition of modern natural law continues from Hobbes through to the Enlightenment, which is the period of the flourishing of natural laws as we know them today. Some publications even consider the pre-Enlightenment period to be unimportant regarding the tradition which commenced with the Enlightenment.[15/16] In any case, the contribution of the Enlightenment to the formulation of subjective human rights is somewhat essential. In England Petition of Rights (1628), the Habeas Corpus Act (1679) and the Bill of Rights (1689) began to mirror modern human rights documents in

---

[11] LEO STRAUSS, NATURAL RIGHT AND HISTORY, Chicago: Univ. of Chicago Press 180 (2005).
[12] *Ibid.*, at 181.
[13] LEO STRAUSS, NATURAL RIGHT AND HISTORY, Chicago: Univ. of Chicago Press 183 (2005).
[14] *Ibid.*, at 189.
[15] MICHELINE ISHAY, THE HISTORY OF HUMAN RIGHTS: FROM ANCIENT TIMES TO THE GLOBALIZATION ERA. 1. Berkeley: University of California Press (2004).
[16] JAMES GRIFFIN, ON HUMAN RIGHTS. 2. Oxford: Oxford University Press (2011).

their contents.[17] Within the Anglo-Saxon environment, they influenced the Virginia Declaration (1776) and an entire range of other declarations within the territories of the American colonies which culminated in the Declaration of Independence (1776) and the constitutional amendments known as the Bill of Rights (1789). These documents were clearly inspired by the theories of another natural law thinker, John Locke, and his contemporary, Thomas Paine. It was within this context that the first controversy about human rights arose between Paine and Edmund Burke. While Paine considered human rights to be truly universal and superior to the traditions and cultural and political conditions in a given country, Rudolf Kučera reports that the sceptic Edmund Burke emphasised the fact that

> a person's natural rights cannot be understood as a hammer which can be used on all existing history and against all existing structures. Natural rights as conceived by people such as Thomas Paine are essentially abstract rights which can be arbitrarily augmented and must be complied with ... To him, rights mainly meant historically acquired rights.[18]

**4.13.** Moreover, the entire debate took place within the context of the French Revolution, which gave rise to yet another fundamental human rights document: the Declaration of the Rights of Man and of the Citizen. From this historical event onwards, catalogues of human rights began to appear in various parts of Europe and later also throughout the world. Perhaps the most significant of all of these is the UN General Declaration of Human Rights dating from 1948, when the fully modern and global stage of the development of human rights started.

## II.    Expansion of Human Rights

**4.14.** Within this context, it is possible to speak of an entire series of processes associated with the area of human rights, such as their globalisation and internationalisation, but also their expansion and classification. Rights can be classified, for example, from the point of view of their contents or their historical development, whereby both categories frequently merge. The breakdown of the content may look like this, for example:

- personal rights and freedoms

---

[17]    MICHAL BARTOŇ, JAN KRATOCHVÍL, MARTIN KOPA, MAXIM TOMOSZEK, JIŘÍ JIRÁSEK, ONDŘEJ SVAČEK, ZÁKLADNÍ PRÁVA. Praha: Leges 33 (1st ed. 2016).
[18]    LIDSKÁ A PŘIROZENÁ PRÁVA V DĚJINÁCH. Ústí n. Labem: Filozofická fakulta Univerzity Jana Evangelisty Purkyně v Ústí n. Labem 235, Acta Universitatis Purkynianae, Facultatis Philosophicae (A. Havlíček ed., 2014), et. 129-130.

Czech Yearbook of International Law®

- political rights and freedoms
- economic, social and cultural rights.[19]

4.15. From a historical point of view, it is possible to classify human rights using so-called generations. This is a frequently used method of structuring these rights. However, this is not entirely without its complications.

4.16. The standard structure for the genesis of the generations of human rights has the following structure:

1) personal, civil and political rights (established in the 17th-19th centuries)

2) economic, cultural and social rights (recognised from the end of the 19th century)

3) modern rights, so-called solidarity rights (from the 1970s).[20]

4.17. The breakdown of the rights according to their generation enables their simple and clear classification, but this method has a number of critics. One such objection concerns the impression invoked by the generational breakdown that all the generations of rights are of the same nature and are just as fundamental or, on the contrary, it may seem that the older generations of rights have been superseded by the newer ones. However, the fact of the matter is that the developmentally older generations contain the most fundamental and universal rights, while the newer generations often contain rights which are highly debatable.[21]

4.18. Attempts to characterise human rights are, of course, a logical consequence of the fact that the catalogues of human rights contain increasing numbers of new entries. It is therefore advisable to categorise them in some way at least for the purpose of making them more transparent and for subsequent analyses.

4.19. The expansion, or perhaps rather the hypertrophy, of human rights constitutes one of the most fundamental problems surrounding rights in the present. It is possible to name some of the factors which could have caused this phenomenon, albeit without any ambitions of naming them all.

4.20. It is necessary to consider the fact that legal positivism in its current form is no longer an enemy of the human rights agenda. From the point of view of legal positivism, or at least for some of its forms, human rights constitute the current state of human

---

[19]   JOSEF BLAHOŽ, SJEDNOCUJÍCÍ SE EVROPA A LIDSKÁ A OBČANSKÁ PRÁVA, Praha: ASPI 46 (1st ed. 2005).
[20]   NADĚŽDA ŠIŠKOVÁ, DIMENZE OCHRANY LIDSKÝCH PRÁV V EVROPSKÉ UNII, Prague: Linde 18 (2008).
[21]   JIŘÍ KABELE, SOCIÁLNÍ PRÁVA JAKO NOVOŘEČ, Praha: Občanský institute, Studie (Občanský institut) (1st ed. 1993). SUDRE, F. MEZINÁRODNÍ A EVROPSKÉ PRÁVO LIDSKÝCH PRÁV. Brno: Masarykova univerzita 136 (1997); Eliška Wagnerová, Všeobecná deklarace lidských práv jako milník mezi epochami, 5 JURISPRUDENCE (2009).

knowledge on a given matter, usually petrified in a positive right. In the Czech environment, František Šamalík or Jiří Boguszak, for example, have assumed a conciliatory attitude to human rights. According to Šamalík, the contemporary renaissance of natural law means only the recognition of the fact that pre-State rights and freedoms exist which a democratic legal state must respect, if it wishes to be such a State.[22] Jiří Boguszak speaks of the fact that a consensus exists, which does not, however, concern the question of the origins, timelessness or historical nature of these rights.[23] As such, legal positivism need not necessarily stand in the way of human rights, despite that J. Maritain, for example, was convinced of the absolutely irreconcilable nature of both approaches.[24]

**4.21.** J. Maritain has also found further grounds for the expansion of human rights in the fact that, in his opinion, we have a far greater understanding of people than previously and we are therefore able to award other rights which we had not previously considered. We can define a person's rights not only as the rights of a person, but as the rights of a

> ...social individual who has been incorporated into the economic and cultural process and especially the rights of a person as a blue-collar individual ... The new age of civilisation will be called upon to acknowledge and define the rights of an individual with regard to his or her social, economic and cultural functions – the rights of producers and consumers ... the right of everybody to share in the legacy of upbringing and the culture of a civilised life.

**4.22.** Maritain subsequently also names several of social rights.[25]

**4.23.** Maritain is, of course, unafraid of the expansion of rights and the emancipation of so-called ‚new rights‘. He reconciles any eventual conflicts with the opinion that no right is absolute and unlimited. This enables various world-view groups to eventually find acceptable compromise solutions, despite ongoing conflicts.[26] Maritain's distinction between *holding* and *exercising* a right appears to be important, especially with regard to the current debates about human rights. We can all hold certain rights, but we are not always able to apply them. The grounds for this may be found on the part of the society which is (as of

---

[22] František Šamalík, *Právní positivismus v éře lidských práv*, 6 PRÁVNÍK (1995).
[23] Jiří Boguszak, *Vyústění antinomie jusnaturalismu a juspozitivizmu*, 6 PRÁVNÍK (1995).
[24] JACQUES MARITAIN, ČLOVĚK A STÁT, Praha: Triáda, Delfín 211 (2007) et 87.
[25] *Ibid.*, at 94-95.
[26] *Ibid.*, at 96-97.

Czech Yearbook of International Law®

yet) unable to secure them or on the part of the individual who may preclude their use through his or her conduct.[27]

**4.24.** Maritain's optimism is not shared by Stanislav Sousedík, who claims that our inspection of other human rights is not built on a firm foundation. He differentiates between natural human rights and ‚mere' human rights. While he is of the opinion that we have certainty in the area of approximately four natural human rights,[28] human rights (HR) have been the subject of significant expansion thanks to which so-called ‚new rights' have come into being. Sousedík states that there are three causes for this:

1) The softening of rights.

Involves 'voluntary ' softening which has been made possible to a significant extent by social progress. This includes, for example, respect for a criminal's right to life in a modern society, which is able to secure long-term imprisonment from both an organisational and a financial point of view, while the same criminal would have been deprived of life under previous conditions.

2) The application of natural rights to new social, economic and political situations.

This includes the rights which are typical for the onset of a capitalist society, such as the right to work, for example. This was groundlessly created in a society predominantly by independent farmers or craftsmen. It can be assumed that the requirement for the right to work will lapse, if capitalism were to one day come to an end.

3) New rights which are at odds with natural human rights.

Sousedík is of the opinion that a wide range of modern rights are merely claims which have been raised without any link to natural human rights, so it is therefore not possible to consider them to constitute a more detailed application of rights (as in groups 1 and 2), but as rights which are odds with natural HR.

**4.25.** In the case of the last, most problematic group, Sousedík points to their implausibility, purely ideological origins or the clear (cultural, civilizational and economic) conditionality of these rights which is at odds with the fundamental attribute of natural HR, i.e. their universality.[29]

---

[27] *Ibid.*, at 92-93. Within this context, Maritain even speaks of the right to life which we all hold, albeit that a criminal may lose his or her right to apply this right as a result of any antisocial act on his or her part which results in the imposition of the death penalty.

[28] It is possible to assume that they equate significantly with those defined previously by Thomas Aquinas.

[29] ALEŠ HAVLÍČEK, JIŘÍ CHOTAŠ, LIDSKÁ PRÁVA: JEJICH ZDŮVODNĚNÍ A ZÁVAZNOST, Ústí n. Labem: Filozofická fakulta Univerzity Jana Evangelisty Purkyně v Ústí n. Labem, Acta Universitatis Purkynianae Facultatis philosophicae (2016), et 41-46.

Czech Yearbook of International Law®

**4.26.** Within this context, it is necessary to add the transformation of rights in the original meaning of the word into *claims* which do not originate in God, natural givens or reason, but in passions as Thomas Hobbes postulated. Like Hobbes, it is possible to state that passions know no limits except for those imposed by positive legislation.

**4.27.** In addition to expansion, another current phenomenon in the area of human rights involves their destructive nature in relation to society if they are conceived and applied (i.e. especially as mere, yet absolute, claims) along with all that is associated therewith, i.e. society's costs for maintaining the rights. All three phenomena, i.e. expansion, the destructive nature of rights in relation to society and the costs for applying them, can lead to a reduction of credibility to the very idea of human rights which is without a doubt the opposite effect their supporters would wish.

**4.28.** It is no secret that securing an ever-expanding set of rights is subject to certain costs. A contrast is often made between classic fundamental rights and so-called new rights. James Griffin has noticed that the rights to social security and healthcare are not only highly particular (i.e. limited to members of a certain group), but also costly. Griffin points to the fact that even fundamental rights are not in absolute black-and-white contrast to ‚costly' modern rights. For example, the maintenance of a just society, whereby life in a fair society is one of the most generally acknowledged fundamental rights, also requires not insignificant funds to maintain the mechanism of justice. The same can also be said of one of the fundamental responsibilities, i.e. the responsibility to assist another whose life is at risk.[30] It is a question of degree as to how much it is possible to demand the first and the second given the outlaid expenses. We therefore do not have any simple criterion which would state, for example, that rights which cannot suffice with mere forbearance, but require active engagement, are less important. The boundary between a negative status and a positive status is not completely rigorous.

**4.29.** The fact that the idea of human rights has entered into a certain crisis in the 21st century is undisputed. Even though human rights are currently on the rise, they can still enter into a crisis generated by their falling credibility combined with the newly raised, ever increasing demands for them to be secured, albeit frequently without any reciprocal obligations. Given this situation, it is necessary to realise that human rights cannot be applied outside society. Their origins, at least in the case

---

[30] JAMES GRIFFIN, ON HUMAN RIGHTS, 2. Oxford: Oxford University Press 102 (2011).

of fundamental human rights (this would apply doubly for natural human rights), lie in the very nature of humans and are admittedly independent of society, but for all that they can only be recognised and applied within the framework of a certain society which is able to recognise and create space (either through forbearance or active assistance) for their application. It is therefore not suitable to apply them against society or the State, whether from the point of view of additional costs or the securing or alteration of the institutional framework for their functioning and other aspects. Newly raised so-called human rights need to be assessed carefully. Nevertheless, the just application of abstract norms, and human rights are highly abstract norms, presents a problem of interpretation. This even led Edmund Burke to reject abstract terms in politics and the law. If we do not wish to follow him down a similarly sceptical path, we have to be aware of the fact that, while specific norms can be applied relatively simply thanks to our awareness of them, i.e. on the basis of knowledge (episteme),[31] highly abstract, often contradictory rights can only be applied on the basis of wisdom or circumspection (phronesis). This fact was raised by Plato and then by Stanislav Sousedík 2500 years later.[32]

## III.    Do the Courts Constitute a Threat To Us?

**4.30.** The existence of an independent judiciary is one of the characteristics of a State where the rule of law functions, and therefore also of a democratic State. This is accepted by essentially everybody who defines the characteristics of such a State.[33]

**4.31.** The fundamental task of the courts is to secure the law of the land by resolving conflicts involving private entities, public authorities and the State in accordance with the designated procedural regulations. In doing so, they protect the rights of citizens and society from the breach of any rights and provide a check on public power from the point of view of the preservation of the legal order. As such, courts represent one of the most

---

[31]  LIDSKÁ A PŘIROZENÁ PRÁVA V DĚJINÁCH, Ústí n. Labem: Filozofická fakulta Univerzity Jana Evangelisty Purkyně v Ústí n. Labem 235, Acta Universitatis Purkynianae, Facultatis Philosophicae (A. Havlíček ed., 2014), et 18.

[32]  ALEŠ HAVLÍČEK, JIŘÍ CHOTAŠ, LIDSKÁ PRÁVA: JEJICH ZDŮVODNĚNÍ A ZÁVAZNOST. Ústí n. Labem: Filozofická fakulta Univerzity Jana Evangelisty Purkyně v Ústí n. Labem, Acta Universitatis Purkynianae Facultatis philosophicae (2016), et 40.

[33]  The list of authors who have provided the defining characteristics of a state with the rule of law would be, without exaggeration, almost endless. We will therefore only mention a selected few: HANS KELSEN, ALLGEMEINE STAATSLEHRE, Berlin: Julius Springer 91 (1925), VLADIMÍR KLOKOČKA, ÚSTAVNÍ SYSTÉMY EVROPSKÝCH STÁTŮ, Praha: Linde (2006), et 83 et seq, KLAUS STERN, DAS STAATSRECHT DER BUNDESREPUBLIK DEUTSCHLAND, Band I. München: C. H. Beck (1984), et 781 et seq.

Czech Yearbook of International Law®

significant institutional guarantors of rights and freedoms and as such of the orderly life of democratic States.[34]

**4.32.** As has been mentioned, the second half of the 20th century and especially its post-modern phase, is characterised as a period of the expansion of human rights which find their expression in constitutions and international treaties, while Europe has been designated as a ‚special laboratory for human rights'.[35] Its politicians, judges and legal theoreticians can be proud of this, but it is not possible to overlook the fact that many of these rights have been formulated under the influence of American doctrine, practice and constitutional texts which for that matter can be read in the justifications of both national and international judicial decisions.

**4.33.** Society is facing several of challenges which include eternal questions of a constitutional nature, such as the supervision of public authority. Another arena of questions are those associated with modern technologies, including questions about internet access (is it a fundamental right? Can its contents be subjected to inspection? Can options for its use be limited?) or the permissiveness of cameras in closed circuit television systems and unauthorised invasion of privacy thereof.[36] The resolution of these questions often passes to the courts in the last instance, with full trust in their authority. They are then required to reach a decision, because any failure to do so would mean to commit *denegatio iuris*, which is one of the most serious transgressions against the principles of the rule of law. The courts are also provided with further munition in another manner. The text of a constitution is no longer understood as merely a 'legislator's monologue' which has no relevance for courts or administrative bodies. This has been definitively established since the Second World War and as such the need has arisen to resolve the tension between the necessity of direct applicability and the predominantly general nature of the text of these regulations.[37] The catalogue of fundamental rights has been formulated within a certain period and a specific environment which are not torpid. This catalogue must therefore react to ever new impetuses and to the development, amongst other things, of the spheres of the social State. An important moment which has

---

[34] KAREL KLÍMA, TEORIE VEŘEJNÉ MOCI (VLÁDNUTÍ), Praha: ASPI (2006), et 314-315 and 354.
[35] JEAN-FRANCOIS RENUCII, DROIT EUROPÉEN DES DROITS DE L´HOMME, Paris: LGDJ (1998), et 8.
[36] For example, Eva Fialová, *Právo na přístup k internetu*, 7 PRÁVNÍK 545-557, (2018); the ruling of the European Court of Human Rights in the matter of Perry versus the United Kingdom of 2003 (the rulings have been cited according to the texts in the HUDOC European Court of Human Rights database).
[37] PAVEL HOLLÄNDER, PŘÍBĚHY PRÁVNÍCH POJMŮ, Plzeň: Vydavatelství a nakladatelství Aleš Čeněk 220 (2017).

contributed to the expansion of fundamental rights is what is known as the internationalisation of these rights. International tribunals have influenced the interpretation of rights; in Europe, this especially involves the European Court of Human Rights, whose judicature not only affects the decision-making practises of the member States of the Council of Europe, but sometimes indirectly their internal national regulations.

4.34. The regulation of fundamental rights and freedoms in the texts of constitutional documents consists of two types of legal rules. The first of them involves classic legal norms, which mainly impose responsibilities or prohibitions on public administration bodies. The ban on the death penalty or the ban on torture are examples of this. These rules have a highly specific and categorical nature and it is inadmissible for the impositions and prohibitions contained within them not to be adhered to under standard situations. However, a much more typical feature involves the regulation of human rights at a constitutional level contained in norms which have the nature of legal principles, while being associated with values. The securing of these is necessary in a democratic State. These include the right to own property, religious freedom, the protection of minorities and more. They impose the obligation of their realisation in relation to these values. This should occur to the maximum possible extent in the case of the first generation of human rights or the solid core of human rights. Further, these norms have the nature of optimisation requirements.[38] However, the situation has been complicated by the fact that this securing of human rights in constitutional regulations takes the form of a general provision in which a certain right is guaranteed, and this right can only be limited in those cases where it is necessary in order to protect other values in democratic society. The concretisation which is the precondition for the possible application of a given optimisation requirement or especially for finding any legal limits to its application can only be realised by means of legal regulations to a limited extent. They are applicable in those cases where the grounds for their limitation involve the necessity of protecting the public good, and where the designation of the boundaries for the performance of public law need not be so difficult. However, the limitation of the options for the application of one human right may also arise from the existence of a different human right which clashes with the first. Both rights may have been established in the body of laws in a manner which represents an

---

[38] Also see the following with regard to the contents of the term: ROBERT ALEXY, THE THEORY OF CONSTITUTIONAL RIGHTS, Oxford: Oxford University Press 13-18, 48-68, 102 (2002).

optimisation requirement and should therefore be realised to the greatest possible extent. The designation of the boundaries for the application of such competing human rights using legal regulations is difficult to achieve in practice. The designation of the boundaries during the clash of optimisation requirements often also incorporates the necessity of considering the circumstances for a specific case. This would lead to terribly casuistic regulations, if any modifications were made by means of legal regulations,[39] and full success would therefore not be achieved. As such, the significance of the judicature, especially the judicature of constitutional courts and the constitutional judiciary, increased after the end of the Second World War in association with the enforcement of the direct binding nature of the regulation of the fundamental rights and freedoms and as a reaction to it. This occurred together with the acceptance of the nature of at least part of the norms which enshrine human rights at a constitutional level as an optimisation requirement. This did not only apply to the judicature as a protective tool, but also as a tool for searching for the specific content and development of said rights. Legal regulations at the sub-constitutional level in the form of regular laws, which are a much ‚coarser‘ tool in comparison with the judicature, can only establish the basic limits for the application of human rights or can simply be used to protect public property against the possibility that the application of any human rights could affect said property in a manner which would be in breach of the public interest.

4.35.    Fundamental rights have therefore become judiciary rights, because it is the courts, predominantly the courts of higher instance such as constitutional and international courts, which realistically determine their content.[40] At the same time, it also follows from the very essence of the rule of law, which is characterised by the reproduction of the legal regulation of all the activities of the public authorities' bodies, that this has led to inflation not only in legislation, but also in the very act of the creation of norms and that as a consequence the resolution of

---

[39]   PAVEL HOLLÄNDER, ÚSTAVNĚPRÁVNÍ ARGUMENTACE: OHLÉDNUTÍ PO DESETI LETECH ÚSTAVNÍHO SOUDU. Praha: Linde 52 (2003).

[40]   Such an example is the right to the protection of privacy enshrined in Article 8, paragraph 1 of the European Convention for the Protection of Human Rights and Fundamental Freedoms, whose contents have been gradually expanded by the judicature of the European Court until the concept has become stabilised that they cannot merely be understood as the right to be 'enclosed' within the four walls of one's home, but also include the right of the individual to establish and develop relationships with one's neighbours, the right to be forgotten, the right to the protection of transferred data and so on (for example, the ruling of the European Court for Human Rights on the matter of *Niemietz* v. *Germany* of 1992 and *Klass et al* v. *Germany* of 1978).

ever more complicated situations has once again fallen to the courts.[41]

**4.36.** All this naturally increases the role of the courts, which are admittedly the only authority which does not strive to acquire this power. As such, politically motivated theses on the so-called judgeocracy, the judicial state (Richterstaat) and court activism have been formulated which could contribute to the weakening of their status.[42] No matter how necessary it is to concur with the requirement that this power must be depoliticised,[43] the reality is such that a judge cannot live outside the social and political reality. Their conclusions are necessarily influenced by their philosophical orientation, experience and undoubtedly also by other hidden factors. These extra-legal factors significantly influence the interpretation of the fundamental rights. The direct binding nature of the constitutional regulation of fundamental rights and freedoms is meant to bring limitations to State power, as the idea of the constitutional judiciary was established to protect the citizenry and society as a whole from the threat of tyranny. However, the implementation of this system has meant that the courts have been given de facto political power.

**4.37.** The post-modern society is global and as such it is necessarily exposed to the practices of its foes, but it cannot respond to using the same means as those resorted to by its enemies. This idea, expressed by Supreme Court judge A. Barak of the Supreme Court of Israel,[44] represents a trend which absolutizes the protection of the individual's fundamental rights, albeit that this may also result in negative impacts on the functioning of democratic society.

**4.38.** It is necessary to resolve potential conflicts between human rights and the public good, for whose protection it is necessary to limit human rights, as well as reciprocally between human rights. This has required the creation of the appropriate instruments, with whose help the courts will be able to resolve these conflicts and to apply the directly binding regulation of the human rights enshrined at the constitutional level, typically in the form of legal principles. The so-called proportionality test has become just such an instrument. Its modern form was

---

[41] Jan Kysela, *Kdopak by se „soudcovského státu" bál*, in ROLE NEJVYŠŠÍCH SOUDŮ V EVROPSKÝCH ÚSTAVNÍCH SYSTÉMECH-ČAS NA ZMĚNU?, Brno: Masarykova univerzita. Mezinárodní politologický ústav 131 (V. Šimíček ed., 2007); ZDENĚK KÜHN, APLIKACE PRÁVA VE SLOŽITÝCH PŘÍPADECH. K ÚLOZE PRÁVNÍCH PRINCIPŮ V JUDIKATUŘE, Praha: Karolinum 14 (2002).

[42] For example, SOUDCOKRACIE V ČR. FIKCE NEBO REALITA, Praha: CEP, (M. Loužek ed., 2006).

[43] According to section 80, subsection 2 of the Courts and Judges Act (Act no. 6/2002 Coll.), a judge must not be influenced by political parties, public opinion or the media when performing their function.

[44] Cited according PAVEL MOLEK, ZÁKLADNÍ PRÁVA. SVAZEK PRVNÍ-DŮSTOJNOST, Praha: Wolters Kluwer 214 (2017).

formulated in German constitutional law and subsequently adopted by constitutional courts and regular courts in other European states and by the European Court of Human Rights. Given the fact that the idea of proportionality has met with a positive response or has already taken root in States outside Europe, it is possible to postulate that it could become a global model for the test of human rights protection.[45] The courts in the USA have admittedly officially rejected the adoption of the proportionality test, but at least one of the three different tests which are used instead (the so-called *strict scrutiny* test) can be said at the very least to have a certain similarity to the basic idea of the proportionality test, in that it also requires the smallest possible intervention into human rights which enables the achievement of the given goal.

4.39.    It is also possible to speak of the various forms and modifications of the proportionality test regarding its widespread dissemination. The basic idea is, however, to measure the means and goals and the proportionality test consists of three consecutive steps in its basic form. The first is the suitability test which, if human rights are to be impinged upon, investigates whether the associated measures are suitable regarding achieving the given goal. The second step is the necessity test which investigates whether the same result can be achieved using a different measure which would have a lesser impact on any protected human rights. As such, only the smallest possible intervention is admissible. The third step involves a proportionality test in the narrower sense of the phrase, during which the values which are in mutual conflict are compared.

4.40.    The basic value of the proportionality test is usually considered to be its universal applicability which was probably the reason for its extensive use.[46] It can be used in cases involving both abstract and specific inspection of constitutionality, to resolve clashes between fundamental rights and in relation to any intervention in human rights due to the protection of the public good. On the other hand, its universality has limits associated with the need for varying intensities of the review of any intervention in human rights. The sense of this test lies in the limitation of the power of the State or executive and legislative power in relation to their ability to intervene in human rights. The use of this test in the decision-making of the Constitutional Court of the Czech Republic has mainly been associated with the interpretation of

---

[45]    PAVEL HOLLÄNDER, PŘÍBĚHY PRÁVNÍCH POJMŮ. Plzeň: Vydavatelství a nakladatelství Aleš Čeněk 198-199 (2017).

[46]    DAVID KOSAŘ, MAREK ANTOŠ, ZDENĚK KÜHN, VYHNÁNEK L. ÚSTAVNÍ PRÁVO: CASEBOOK. Praha: Wolters Kluwer 362 (2014).

the human rights enshrined in the constitution as optimisation requirements, where it was only considered admissible to impinge upon any protected human rights to the smallest possible extent. The Constitutional Court came to realise that this interpretation of human rights is not always suitable, and it began to use a rationality test, within which it grants a greater degree of freedom to legislators in relation to how they regulate a specific social right. The condition of compliance with the constitution is therefore not necessarily the smallest possible intervention in a protected right. It is sufficient if the solution chosen by a legislator does mean any intervention in the very existence of the social right and the option of implementing its essential contents is not arbitrary, but rational. This has clearly been inspired by the American doctrine which differentiates between three types of tests with differing degrees of intensity of the protection of the rights and claims which constitute the subject of the review. The proportionality test clearly does not have to be associated with the optimisation requirement category, but it can be understood as simply one of several models of this test[47] and in reality this test is used in a number of modifications in different States. Its main function is to limit State power or also to act horizontally within the framework of human rights protection. Regardless of what significance pertains to human rights protection in relation to the legitimate functioning of a democratic State with the rule of law, the entitlement to the thing which the intervention in a human right is aimed at in a specific case must be commensurate not only to the nature of the specific right, but also to the circumstances of the given case.

4.41.   As such, the only thing of importance is which of the diverse catalogues of rights the courts will give preference to in the given case or even what absolute preference they will award over other values and on what basis they will do so.

4.42.   These include the ban on torture and subjection to inhuman and degrading treatment or punishment as enshrined in Article 3 of the European Convention on the Protection of Human Rights and Fundamental Freedoms. This has been assessed more or less exclusively with the proportionality test in the case of any competition with other rights and values.[48]

---

[47]   PAVEL HOLLÄNDER, PŘÍBĚHY PRÁVNÍCH POJMŮ. Plzeň: Vydavatelství a nakladatelství Aleš Čeněk 228 (2017).
[48]   Similar guarantees or prohibitions based on the model of the European Convention appear, for example, in the texts of a number of constitutions, such as in Article 25, paragraph 2 of the Portuguese Constitution, Article 15 of the Constitution of the Kingdom of Spain or Article 21 of the Constitution of the Republic of Lithuania.

**4.43.** If the hearing already has these boundaries available, the assessment takes place with a high degree of sensitivity.[49] A slap in the face which a Belgian policeman gave a youth, because he was acting in a provocative manner at a police station, was also classed as degrading treatment. The European Court justified this by stating, amongst other things, that the individual in question could have perceived one slap, despite the absence of any serious or long-term consequences (as occurred in the given case), as degrading and it emphasised the necessity of taking into account the increased vulnerability of minors.[50]

**4.44.** A much more serious situation is the so-called ‚ticking bomb dilemma‘, as exemplified by the case of M. Gäfgen, who kidnapped a small boy and demanded a ransom for his return. After his arrest, the police endeavoured to get information about the place where the victim was being held so that they could save the boy. To this end, they threatened the offender by saying that ‚he would experience significant pain caused by an individual who had been specially trained for this purpose‘ and he was also maybe insulted. The individual eventually led the police to the place as a result of this pressure, but they only found the child's body, as the offender had murdered the boy immediately after kidnapping him. It is necessary to consider the conclusions of the European Court of Human Rights, which stated that the ban on the maltreatment of humans must be applied regardless of the conduct of the victim and the motivation of the authorities. It further emphasised the fact that torture or inhumane or degrading treatment cannot be used even in cases where the life of an individual is at stake and that no exception is permissible even in the case of the public endangerment of the life of the nation, to be critical. As such, the European Court is of the opinion that Article 3 of the European Convention does not enable any exceptions, justifying factors or balancing of interests, regardless of the conduct of the given individual and of the nature of the given offence.[51]

**4.45.** It is only possible to express astonishment here as to the fact that the right of an individual, not to be subjected to any prohibited actions on the part of the State authorities, even if they have demonstrably committed a serious criminal offence, has de facto been given precedence over an individual's right to

---

[49] The European Committee for the Prevention of Torture and Inhumane or Degrading Treatment or Punishment /CPT/ has established very strict standards in this regard, see CPT/Inf/E (2002) 1 - Rev. 2015.
[50] The ruling of the European Court for Human Rights on the matter of *Bouyid* v. *Belgium* dating from 2015. Cases such as *Soering* v. *the United Kingdom* of 1989, where the possibility of poor treatment involved extradition to the USA where the individual in question could have expected to be held on Death Row for several years awaiting execution, are a different matter.
[51] The ruling of the European Court of Human Rights in the matter of *Gäfgen* v. *Germany* dated 2010.

the preservation of life.[52] This is all the more astonishing given that other pieces of judicature have designated the right to life as the most fundamental right and the most important basic value, from which no deviation is possible. They have even declared that the State has an obligation to put in place measures aimed at protecting those whose lives are in danger, albeit that this only applies under ‚clearly defined circumstances'.[53] At the same time, its leading status among the other fundamental rights is given by the fact that the other rights would be practically meaningless without it. Admittedly, this right is not absolute and unlimited and there may exist situations where it is permissible to take a life, but for all that such a situation cannot apply to the protection of the values protected in Article 3 under all circumstances.[54]

**4.46.** The ruling of the European Court in the matter of *Saadi* v. *Italy* of 2008 had a significant impact on the assessment of the interpretation of the cited article, as well as its absolute nature. This involved a Tunisian citizen who was living in Italy where he was prosecuted for the criminal offence of falsifying documents (originally also for criminal conspiracy, but this was not able to be proven). Upon completing his sentence, he was meant to be extradited back to Tunisia, where he had been convicted in the interim to a long term of imprisonment for belonging to a terrorist organisation and abetting terrorism. The European Court which Saadi approached did not consider Tunisia's diplomatic assurances to Italy as to the fact that the individual in question would not be subjected to any maltreatment and would receive a fair trial to be sufficient. On the contrary it accepted information from various human rights organisations as to the fact that the threat of maltreatment in Tunisia was real, albeit only potentially, as decisive. It stated that the extradition, which had been suspended during the hearing of the European Court, would have constituted a breach of Article 3 of the European Convention.[55]

**4.47.** A breach of the ban on inhumane and degrading treatment and the right to a fair trial as enshrined in Article 6 of the European Convention was also found to have occurred in the case of

---

[52] Some small comfort can be taken from the fact that it only designated the approach of the police as inhumane and not as cruel which pertains to torture.

[53] For example, the ruling in the matter of *McCann et al* v. *the United Kingdom* of 1995, *Velikova* v. *Bulgaria* of 2000 and *Osman* v. *the United Kingdom* of 1998; Štěpán Hůlka, *Právo na život v mezinárodním a evropském právu*, 11 PRÁVNÍK (2004), et 1066 et seq.

[54] ELIŠKA WAGNEROVÁ, VOJTĚCH ŠIMÍČEK, TOMÁŠ LANGÁŠEK, IVO POSPÍŠIL, a kolektiv, LISTINA ZÁKLADNÍCH PRÁV A SVOBOD. KOMENTÁŘ, Praha: Wolters Kluwer 482 (2012).

[55] The ruling of the European Court of Human rights in the matter of *Saadi* v. *Italy* of 2008. In a number of aspects, the European Court followed on from and deepened the arguments which it had applied with regard to the application of the article in question in the matter of *Chahal* v. *the United Kingdom* of 1996.

Czech Yearbook of International Law®

*Jalloh* v. *Germany* of 2006. In this case, the police coerced the plaintiff, who had demonstrably swallowed a so-called ,bubble' containing drugs, to vomit it up with the assistance of a doctor using an emetic. The European Court carefully clarified why this treatment was found to have been inhumane and degrading with reference to the fact that any action which is thought out in advance, applied over several hours, causes true physical injury and intensive physical and mental suffering and induces feelings of fear, anxiety and inferiority and is capable of degrading a person and breaking his or her physical or mental resistance must be considered as such. It concluded that the actions in the given case ,had reached the minimum levels of severity necessary for them to be included within the scope of Article 3'. Amongst other things, the court argued that the intervention was not essential, because the individual in question had always only had such a small amount of drugs in his mouth that he could have not have sold them on a large scale and that less intrusive methods could have been used to acquire the evidence. In particular it would have been possible to wait until the ,bubble' had been evacuated naturally. The court reached this conclusion ex post without considering the situation in which the act had been undertaken. Here too, it also raised Article 3 above the interests of protecting the public and public order. To a certain degree it significantly complicated the fight against drug criminality, although it did state that ,trading in drugs is a serious criminal offence' and admitted that ,it was aware of the problem which States are faced with in their fight against the damages inflicted on their societies by the trade in drugs'.[56]

4.48. The protection of individual fundamental rights over wider interests such as safety, order and the fight against criminality has also been given preference in several different contexts. An example of this is the matter of *S. and Marper* v. *the United Kingdom* of 2008. This involved the compliance of the storage of DNA samples and fingerprints in police databases with the right to the protection of privacy according to Article 8 of the European Convention. The European Court reached the conclusion here and in several other similar cases[57] that there was no fair balance between the plaintiffs' privacy and the State's fight against criminality. It was not swayed by the statistical data which was used to argue that many serious criminal offences

---

[56] The extents to which the interpretation of this right can lead to are demonstrated by the ruling in the matter of *Larioshina* v. *Russia* of 2002, where the European Court acknowledged that an overly small pension could have constituted grounds for inhumane and degrading treatment, albeit that it did not find so in this specific case.

[57] For example, in the matter of *Aycaguer* v. *France* of 2017.

had been clarified based on the use of the information contained in these databases. The most important thing for the court was the fact that an individual, whose information was being stored in the database, was exposed to the risk of future stigmatisation, notwithstanding that they could also be innocent.[58]

**4.49.** The rights guaranteed by the European Convention and by national bodies of laws which stand out due to their high degree of elasticity include the right to a fair trial or to the due process of law, which are sometimes even presented as a single characteristic of the rule of law.[59] This right has significantly expanded in the application practice of the European Court and national courts. It has become superordinate to rights such as the right to access to the courts, the necessity of justifying decisions, and the adherence to the procedural rules when acquiring or collecting evidence.

**4.50.** No matter how necessary it is to recognise that rights can only be acquired or obligations can only be imposed on the basis of a fair process, in practice this requirement has been absolutized to such an extent that the very sense of the process becomes lost. It is undoubtedly possible to agree with the conclusion of the Czech Constitutional Court that part of the right to a fair trial, the rule of law and the prevention of arbitrariness includes the obligation of the courts to justify their rulings.[60] Nevertheless, no general and precise criteria exist for the situations in which the courts or administrative bodies have duly found themselves to be subject to this obligation and as such every decision may appear insufficient from this point of view. This may lead to the justification becoming an end in itself and something which takes on a life of its own. At the same time, practice has shown that justifications are much more often written in order to meet the criteria of the instances of appeal than the rights and needs of the participants in the proceedings.[61] The hypertrophy of justifications will eventually result in the fact that the decision-

---

[58] The argumentation of the Supreme Administrative Court of the Czech Republic seems more advantageous in this regard. When assessing the legitimacy of the processing of such information in similar databases in accordance with section 65 of Act no. 273/2008 Coll. on the Police of the Czech Republic, as amended, it found that the rights of individuals (in this case, individuals who have been sentenced due to a deliberate criminal offence) must end at the place where the rights of the next individual, who is protected, for example by the police, begin. The police must use their legal powers to prevent, discover and prosecute the perpetrators of criminal offences. The court also emphasised the fact that the appropriate regulation corresponds to the requirements for the protection of privacy as formulated by the European Court for Human Rights (ruling ref. no. 4 As 168/2013-40).

[59] For example, the European Court of Human Rights ruling on the matter of *Delcourt* v. *Belgium* of 1970.

[60] For example, the finding of the Constitutional Court ref. no. Pl. ÚS 1/03 and ref. no. III. ÚS 84/94.

[61] The significant German theoretician, N. Luhmann, expressed this with the words that the justification may serve much more for the subsequent inspection of decisions on the protection of the rights of the participants in the hearing (NIKLAS LUHMANN, LEGITIMATION DURCH VERFAHREN, Darmstadt: Luchterland (1975)), to which end its language and method of argumentation has been determined.

making bodies of public power ,will become increasingly distant not only from the participants in the proceedings and the public, but also from the other legal professions and indeed from the entire surrounding world.' Further, 'they will become enclosed in their own expressive world in which the participants in the proceedings are merely a disruptive element, who otherwise disrupt the fluid flow of the judicial rhetoric between the individual instances with their personal stories' and as such simply justify the internal processes which are ongoing within the framework of these bodies.[62]

**4.51.** The stated errors in the procedural processes will lead to cases where an illegal act will not be able to be prosecuted, notwithstanding the fact that it is apparent that it has occurred. If we disregard the numerous cases where the evidence has been acquired for the purposes of a criminal trial using the recording of telephonic communications or bugs in a room, for which the conditions were subsequently not found to apply, it is possible to demonstrate this conclusion using the case of one of Prague's infamous dishonest taxi drivers. The Supreme Administrative Court refused to admit an audio-visual recording of the taxi journey which ended with double the correct price being charged as evidence, because there was no legal basis for any such evidence in an administrative hearing.[63] Even though there was no doubt as to the fact that the taxi driver was in breach of the legal regulations (which, for that matter, he later admitted during the course of the appeal), the court reached the conclusion that no liability could be inferred with regard to his person. The damages in the given case amounted to a mere 289 CZK, i.e. just over 10 Euros, but for all that it is possible to pose the question as to whether this anxious adherence to the letter of the procedural regulations does not provide those who breach the law with a better standing than those who are their victims. Another example in this regard involves the finding of the Constitutional Court, file ref. Pl. ÚS 4/94, which annulled the institution of the so-called anonymous witness in criminal proceedings. In effect, the Court said that the protection of the witness (and their family) against verbal and especially violent attacks, the interruption of the ability of justice to be served as a result of witness intimidation and the protection of the lives and

---

[62] Michal Bobek, *O odůvodňování soudních rozhodnutí*, 6 PRÁVNÍ ROZHLEDY (2010), et 210.
[63] Supreme Administrative Court ruling ref. no. 1 Afs 60/2009-119. It is necessary to add that the reason for finding in favour of the plaintiff was the reference to the breach of the right to the protection of privacy according to Article 8 of the European Convention and also the insufficient justification of the amount of the sanctions. Perhaps some consolation can be found in the fact that the offender was eventually prosecuted on the basis of other evidence.

Czech Yearbook of International Law ®

property of citizens are less significant than the right to a fair trial which resided in the limitation of the right of the accused to respond to the witness testimony of a specific individual.[64]

4.52. Precisely these procedural questions can be found to be completely fundamental for the assessment of any eventual breach of any other rights guaranteed by the European Convention or the national conventions. As such, for example, the European Court found that Bulgaria was in breach of respecting the right to privacy and a family life. It had extradited an individual under the suspicion of participating in the drug trade, whereby this result was not based on an independent administrative proceeding and there were insufficient procedural guarantees.[65]

4.53. The story of the Roma Čonka family which applied for asylum in Belgium because of supposed repeated attacks on the family members by a skinhead is of interest from this point of view.[66] Even though these grounds may well have been justified, it was shown during the course of the collection of the facts of the case that these facts had, at least partially, been made up. One of the plaintiffs was sentenced to imprisonment in Belgium for theft while their application was being heard and those who were not in prison did not provide the Belgian authorities with the necessary cooperation. Despite this, the court found that an entire range of their procedural rights had been breached. For example, an insufficient number of interpreters were provided who would have been able to explain their status or rights to the plaintiffs. Likewise, there was an absence of redress and the ban on mass extradition, without in any way concerning itself with the merits of the case or whether the individuals in question were even capable of meeting the conditions for being awarded asylum. The Court awarded the plaintiffs 10,000 Euros as compensation for their moral injury and 9,000 Euros as compensation for their costs even though it was doubtful whether the plaintiffs could have outlaid such an amount.

4.54. The enshrinement of fundamental rights and freedoms in constitutional documents and international treaties is necessarily general and the terminology uses indefinite terms in great abundance. This implies that the courts have a decision-making

---

[64] Constitutional Court finding file. no. Pl. ÚS 4/94. At the same time, the Constitutional Court provided the legislators with time to adopt a constitutionally compliant regulation which occurred in the amendment to section 55, subsection 2 of the Rules of Criminal Procedure. According to these, it is required to ascertain whether circumstances indicate that the witness or any individual close the witness is in danger of suffering injury to health or any other serious breach of their fundamental rights in association with the provision of testimony. It is also required to ascertain if the reliable protection of said individual cannot be secured in a different manner. If these are found to be true, the body which is active in the prosecution will put in place measures aimed at concealing the identity and appearance of the witness.

[65] The ruling of the European Court for Human Rights in the matter of *C. G.* v. *Bulgaria* of 2008.

[66] The ruling of the European court of Human Rights on the matter of *Čonka* v. *Belgium* of 2002.

role during their application. We are reminded of G. Radbruch's comment that an interpreter may understand a law better than its creator and in doing so determine what the legislator's actual will was, because he or she is wiser than the author.[67] In practise, this means that the contents of the appropriate standards have become entirely dependent upon the way that the courts interpret them, while the necessary arguments are always found with reference to any of the methods of interpretation.

**4.55.** The potentially overly low limits to the decision-making power of the courts are based only on the courts' ability to issue a justification as to why they have resolved the conflict between the constitutionally enshrined values in a given manner. This potential is also associated with fears of the courts becoming overly powerful. In his famous work, Alexis de Tocqueville spoke of the political power of the courts in the USA, where the idea of the directly binding nature of the Constitution was implemented on the basis of a decision of the Supreme Court of the USA in the famous case of *Marbury* v. *Madison* of 1803.[68] At the same time, he warned that, if only courts have the right to interpret the Constitution, the wording of which nobody can change, the Constitution would find itself *de facto* in their hands.[69] In the situation where an amendment to a constitution is an absolutely exceptional phenomenon, this still occurs to a certain extent when every decision of the constitutional judiciary which annuls a legal regulation or any part thereof limits political discourse.[70] Given the ‚delicateness' of the other types of power as manifested in the absence of a willingness to realistically oppose judicial power and to undertake a ‚counteraction' even in the case when these other types of power are of the opinion that judiciary power has exceeded its jurisdiction,[71] the option for a correction remains up to the ability of judicial power to apply a self-correction, albeit that it is not always possible to fully rely on this.

**4.56.** The danger consists of both the populist rejection of constitutional justice, usually motivated by jealousy of the

---

[67] Archbishop Hoadley expressed this in different words in the 18th century when he wrote that the real creator of a right is the one who has absolute authority to interpret the laws and not the one who first wrote or declared them (Jan Kysela, *Kdopak by se „soudcovského státu" bál*, in ROLE NEJVYŠŠÍCH SOUDŮ V EVROPSKÝCH ÚSTAVNÍCH SYSTÉMECH-ČAS NA ZMĚNU?, Brno: Masarykova univerzita. Mezinárodní politologický ústav, (V. Šimíček ed., 2007), et 134).
[68] ALEXIS DE TOCQUEVILLE, DEMOKRACIE V AMERICE. Praha: Academia 75-77 (2000).
[69] *Ibid.*, at 76.
[70] ZDENĚK KÜHN, *Postavení soudní moci v Evropě na počátku 21. století a výhled do budoucnosti*, in: ROLE NEJVYŠŠÍCH SOUDŮ V EVROPSKÝCH ÚSTAVNÍCH SYSTÉMECH - ČAS PRO ZMĚNU? Brno: Masarykova univerzita, Mezinárodní politologický ústav 81 (V. Šimíček ed., 2007).
[71] Jindřiška Syllová, *K metodám zkoumání judicializace politiky ve střední Evropě*, 5 PRÁVNÍK (2019), et 452.

power which pertains to the constitutional judiciary, and the defence thereof which states that the constitutional judiciary merely interprets the constitution,[72] which *de facto* refutes the fact that the courts execute any political power. The protection of human rights is one of the important roles of judicial power in a democratic State. The fact that human rights are under judicial protection bestows legitimacy both to the State itself and to the decisions of judges. Courts are also active in this area and their decision-making activities can be considered one of the significant tools for the development of human rights - perhaps the most significant such tool today alongside international treaties on human rights. In the situation where the other types of power have accepted this standing of the courts, the problem may lie in the fact that they have also accepted a certain degree of exclusivity which courts demand in this area. As such they have refused to oppose the courts in those cases where it can be said that the ability to rapidly self-correct is not apparent in judicial decision-making practice and where the judicialization of politics is occurring.

4.57. The individual cases which have been mentioned cannot in and of themselves bring about the destruction of society, but there can be no doubt that P. Molek is right when he says that this presentation of the European Convention means the signatory States to it have *de facto* lost the right to protect their own citizens against the threat of serious breaches of safety and of other values. As such the concept of human rights as the protection of the individual against the State which is bound by them has been cast into doubt. Voices can be heard which are claiming the possibility of the introduction of ideology into the decision-making process, when arguments for certain conclusions with regard to breaches of human rights are found at any price.[73] No matter how necessary the independence of judicial power and its authority is, this must be associated with the long-asked question *Qui custodiet ipsos custodes?* **Similarly, it raises the issue that the citizens' trust in the courts is based on how they bring the law to life**.

---

72 ZDENĚK KÜHN, *Postavení soudní moci v Evropě na počátku 21. století a výhled do budoucnosti*, in: ROLE NEJVYŠŠÍCH SOUDŮ V EVROPSKÝCH ÚSTAVNÍCH SYSTÉMECH - ČAS PRO ZMĚNU? Brno: Masarykova univerzita, Mezinárodní politologický ústav (V. Šimíček ed., 2007), et 83.

73 PAVEL MOLEK, ZÁKLADNÍ PRÁVA. SVAZEK PRVNÍ-DŮSTOJNOST, Praha: Wolters Kluwer 243 (2017). For example, in the ruling of *D. H. et al v. the Czech Republic* of 2007, the European Court reached the conclusion that the placement of Roma pupils in special schools resulted in their indirect discrimination, which gave rise to a wide variety of polemic reactions in professional and political circles. No matter how commendable the efforts of the tribunal were regarding protecting this minority, it is not possible to avoid the impression that it reached the given conclusion at any price, including by means of the incorrect interpretation of the statistical information. See also PETR BOUDA, NEPŘÍMÁ DISKRIMINACE, Brno: Spisy Právnické fakulty Masarykovy univerzity v Brně 139-168 (2011).

**4.58.** The article was created as a result of the standard project ‚Protection of Human Rights and Militant Democracy‘, and the institutional support for long-term conceptual development of research of the University of Finance and Administration‘, Prague, Czech Republic.

| | |

## Summaries

FRA  [*Les droits de l'homme et les juridictions*]
*Le présent article examine la naissance, la catégorisation et l'évolution des droits de l'homme. Il définit la tradition moderne des droits naturels compris comme des prétentions, sans lien à une quelconque obligation. Une des conséquences de cette situation est l'essor actuel des droits de l'homme, nourri par le positivisme juridique et une vue optimiste de la capacité humaine à comprendre les nouveaux droits ayant reçu le statut de droits de l'homme. Une autre vue, sceptique, estime que la catégorie des droits de l'homme naturels englobe un ensemble restreint de droits, sans croire à l'évolution de la connaissance humaine en la matière. Dans un État de droit, ce sont les juridictions qui tranchent les questions ayant trait aux droits de l'homme. Leur rôle est d'optimiser l'application de ces droits et de définir les frontières en cas de conflit de principes. La jurisprudence s'impose progressivement comme un instrument permettant de protéger ces droits, de définir leur contenu concret et de les faire évoluer. Quoique les juridictions disposent de méthodes de prise de décision, incluant, entre autres, les tests de proportionnalité et de rationalité, on ne peut exclure que la prise de décisions soit influencée par des facteurs extra-juridiques, favorisant certains droits plutôt que d'autres. Ainsi, la protection des droits individuels peut être vue comme supérieure aux intérêts généraux comme la sécurité, l'ordre et la lutte contre la criminalité, et ce souvent au nom du droit à un procès équitable. Dans certains cas, ce droit est qualifié comme absolu, ce qui peut compromettre le résultat du procès judiciaire. Les juridictions sont les vrais « maîtres » du domaine des droits de l'homme, disposant d'une large marge d'appréciation pour trouver leurs propres interprétations. Ceci est particulièrement visible dans l'interprétation de la constitution, norme rigide, donc pratiquement inaltérable par des moyens politiques, mais ouverte à des interprétations prétoriennes. La jurisprudence*

Czech Yearbook of International Law®

*des cours constitutionnelles restreint le discours politique, les autres instances du pouvoir public n'ayant généralement pas la possibilité de s'y opposer activement, et ce même lorsque ces juridictions manquent à protéger les citoyens contre des menaces sérieuses. Une des réactions à cette situation est un refus populiste du pouvoir judiciaire constitutionnel en tant que tel. À cela s'oppose une vue idéaliste de ce pouvoir, considéré comme un simple interprète de la constitution.*

CZE    [***Lidská práva a soudy***]
*Příspěvek se zabývá vznikem, kategorizací a etapizací lidských práv. Vysvětluje vydělení novodobé tradice přirozených práv jakožto nároků, bez vazby na povinnosti. Jedním z důsledků je současná expanze lidských práv, další příčinou je právní pozitivismus a optimistický pohled na schopnost lidstva pochopit nová práva, která jsou uznána za lidská práva. Proti tomu stojí pohled skeptický, který považuje za přirozená lidská práva omezený okruh práv a nedomnívá se, že by lidstvo v tomto směru dosáhlo nového poznání. V právním státě se soudy stávají arbitrem v otázce lidských práv. Role soudů je nezbytná při optimalizaci jejich realizace a stanovení hranic při kolizi příkazů. Judikatura je stále silnějšími nástrojem ochrany i hledání jejich konkrétního obsahu a rozvoje. Ačkoliv soudy mají vypracované metody rozhodování, mezi něž patří využívání tzv. testu proporcionality či racionality, nelze vyloučit, že při rozhodování mohou sehrávat roli extralegální faktory, proto mohou být některá práva být favorizována před právy jinými. Ochrana individuálních práv bývá nadřazována nad širší zájmy, jakými jsou bezpečnost, pořádek a boj se zločinností. Často se tak děje ve jménu práva na řádný proces, přičemž je tento požadavek zabsolutizován, čímž je znemožněn řádný výsledek soudního procesu. Skutečnými „pány" nad oblastí lidských práv se stávají soudy, které mají široký prostor pro nalézání vlastních interpretací. Obzvláště patrné to je při interpretaci ústavy, která je zpravidla rigidní, tedy politickými prostředky prakticky nezměnitelná, zatímco je otevřená soudcovskému výkladu, čímž se ocitá v jejich rukou. Judikatura ústavního soudnictví omezuje politický diskurs, přičemž ostatní složky veřejné moci zpravidla nemají možnost tomuto trendu aktivně oponovat, a to ani když soudy nechrání občany před vážnými ohroženími. Jednou z reakcí je populistické odmítání ústavního soudnictví vůbec. Reakcí opačnou je*

*idealizovaný pohled na ústavní soudnictví jako pouhého interpreta ústavy.*

| | |

POL  [*Prawa człowieka i sądy*]
*Prawa człowieka należą do tradycji europejskiej i mają długą genezę. W trakcie ich istnienia zmieniało się znaczenie pojęcia praw człowieka, które nabrało charakteru roszczeniowego. Jest to współcześnie stosowanie pojęcie, zgodnie z którym prawa człowieka są postrzegane jako prawa subiektywne, a ich rozwój polega na ekspansji. Zasadniczą rolę w tym procesie odgrywają m.in. sądy, które orzekają w sprawie konkretnego stosowania ogólnych postanowień zawartych w przepisach prawa. Jednak w orzecznictwie znajdują również odzwierciedlenie czynniki pozaprawne. Często należy przypuszczać, że aplikacja przez sędziów wykracza poza granice wyznaczone przez ustawodawcę. Jednym ze skutków może być upolitycznienie orzecznictwa sądowego w dziedzinie praw człowieka lub absolutyzacja ochrony podstawowych praw jednostki. Jednocześnie trudno zmienić podejście sędziów, bowiem orzeczenia sądowe de facto zamykają dyskusję polityczną w pewnych kwestiach, aczkolwiek same orzeczenia mogą być upolitycznione. Dlatego bardzo ważne wydaje się znalezienie właściwego miejsca dla roli sądów na polu ochrony praw człowieka.*

DEU  [*Menschenrechte und Gerichte*]
*Menschenrechte stellen einen Teil der europäischen Tradition dar und sie ziehen eine lange Genese nach sich. Im Laufe der Zeit veränderte sich die Auffassung zu den Menschenrechten, die hauptsächlich zu Ansprüchen wurden. Dieses Konzept funktioniert auch in der heutigen Zeit, in der die Menschenrechte als subjektive Rechte wahrgenommen werden und ihre Entwicklung auf ihrer Expansion beruht. Eine grundsätzliche Rolle in diesem Prozess spielen namentlich die Gerichte, die über konkrete Anwendung der allgemeinen Rechtsbestimmungen entscheiden. In dieser Entscheidungsfindung spiegeln sich jedoch auch extralegale Faktoren wider, und man kann häufig davon ausgehen, dass die richterliche Anwendung die von dem Gesetzgeber festgelegten Grenzen überschreitet. Eine der Konsequenzen kann die Politisierung der gerichtlichen Entscheidungsfindung im Bereich der Menschenrechte sein, gegebenenfalls der absolute Schutz der Grundrechte der*

*Einzelpersonen. Das Korrigieren des Justizansatzes ist dabei sehr schwierig, da Gerichtsentscheidungen im Grunde und in der Regel den politischen Diskurs zu bestimmten Themen beenden, wenngleich diese Entscheidungen selbst politisiert werden können. Es erscheint daher erneut wichtig, die richtige Position für die Rolle der Gerichte beim Schutz der Menschenrechte zu definieren.*

**RUS** [*Права человека и суды*]

*Права человека являются частью европейской традиции и имеют долгую историю зарождения и последующего развития. Со временем произошли изменения в концепции прав человека, из которых сформировались некие требования. С этой концепцией работают в настоящее время, когда права человека воспринимаются как субъективные права, причем их развитие заключается в их расширении. Важную роль в этом процессе также играют суды, принимающие решения относительно конкретного применения общих положений законов. Однако в принятии решений также отражаются экстралегальные факторы, и часто возможно полагать, что судьи выходят за рамки, установленные законодателем. Последствием этого может быть политизация судебных решений в области прав человека или абсолютизация защиты основных прав человека. Исправление судебного подхода является довольно сложным, поскольку судебные решения по существу завершают политический дискурс по конкретным вопросам, несмотря на то, что эти решения сами могут быть политизированы. Поэтому снова представляется важным поиск правильного места роли судов в области защиты прав человека.*

**ESP** [*Derechos humanos y los tribunales*]

*Los derechos humanos forman parte de la tradición europea y su génesis tiene una larga trayectoria temporal, durante la cual el concepto de los derechos humanos se ha ido modificando y ha ido adquiriendo, mayoritariamente, el carácter de demandas. Este concepto sigue vigente en la época moderna. Los derechos humanos se conciben hoy en día como derechos subjetivos y su evolución, como una expansión. En este proceso desempeñan un papel decisivo los tribunales, que aplican la normativa general en situaciones concretas. En este proceso, sin embargo, intervienen factores extralegales, por lo cual resulta razonable pensar que su aplicación por parte de los tribunales va más allá de los límites trazados por el legislador. Una de las consecuencias puede ser la politización de las resoluciones judiciales en materia de derechos humanos, o eventualmente, la absolutización de la protección de los derechos fundamentales individuales. Corregir la actuación de los tribunales puede resultar muy difícil ya que básicamente las resoluciones judiciales ponen fin al discurso político sobre ciertos asuntos a pesar de ser, potencialmente, también politizadas. Por esta razón, resulta importante hallar el papel adecuado de los tribunales en materia de protección de los derechos humanos.*

| | |

## Bibliography

TOMÁŠ AKVINSKÝ, SUMMA THEOLOGICKÁ II. část, Olomouc:Red Soukup PE (1938).

TOMÁŠ AKVINSKÝ, TOMÁŠ AKVINSKÝ O ZÁKONECH V TEOLOGICKÉ SUMĚ (překlad Karel Šprunk), Praha: Krystal OP 65-67 (1st ed. 2003).

ROBERT ALEXY, THE THEORY OF CONSTITUTIONAL RIGHTS, Oxford: Oxford University Press (2002).

MICHAL BARTOŇ, JAN KRATOCHVÍL, MARTIN KOPA, MAXIM TOMOSZEK, JIŘÍ JIRÁSEK, ONDŘEJ SVAČEK, ZÁKLADNÍ PRÁVA, Praha: Leges (1st ed. 2016).

JOSEF BLAHOŽ, SJEDNOCUJÍCÍ SE EVROPA A LIDSKÁ A OBČANSKÁ PRÁVA, Praha: ASPI (1st ed. 2005).

Michal Bobek, *O odůvodňování soudních rozhodnutí*, 6 PRÁVNÍ ROZHLEDY (2010).

Jiří Boguszak, *Vyústění antinomie jusnaturalismu a juspozitivizmu*, 6 PRÁVNÍK (1995).

Petr Bouda, *Nepřímá diskriminace*, SPISY PRÁVNICKÉ FAKULTY MASARYKOVY UNIVERZITY V BRNĚ, Brno (2011).

Eva Fialová, *Právo na přístup k internetu*, 7 PRÁVNÍK (2018).

JAMES GRIFFIN, ON HUMAN RIGHTS, Oxford: Oxford University Press (2011).

Ingrid Hašková, *Nová teorie přirozeného zákona*. 2 DISTANCE: REVUE PRO KRITICKÉ MYŠLENÍ (2006).

LIDSKÁ A PŘIROZENÁ PRÁVA V DĚJINÁCH. Ústí n. Labem: Filozofická fakulta Univerzity Jana Evangelisty Purkyně v Ústí n. Labem, Acta Universitatis Purkynianae, Facultatis Philosophicae 235 (A. Havlíček ed., 2014).

ALEŠ HAVLÍČEK, JIŘÍ CHOTAŠ, LIDSKÁ PRÁVA: JEJICH ZDŮVODNĚNÍ A ZÁVAZNOST, Ústí n. Labem: Filozofická fakulta Univerzity Jana Evangelisty Purkyně v Ústí n. Labem, Acta Universitatis Purkynianae Facultatis philosophicae (2016).

PAVEL HOLLÄNDER, PŘÍBĚHY PRÁVNÍCH POJMŮ, Plzeň: Vydavatelství a nakladatelství Aleš Čeněk, (2017).

PAVEL HOLLÄNDER, ÚSTAVNĚPRÁVNÍ ARGUMENTACE: OHLÉDNUTÍ PO DESETI LETECH ÚSTAVNÍHO SOUDU, Praha: Linde (2003).

MICHELINE R. ISHAY, THE HISTORY OF HUMAN RIGHTS: FROM ANCIENT TIMES TO THE GLOBALIZATION ERA, Berkeley: University of California Press (2004).

JIŘÍ KABELE, SOCIÁLNÍ PRÁVA JAKO NOVOŘEČ, Praha: Občanský institut, Studie (Občanský institut) (1993).

HANS KELSEN, ALLGEMEINE STAATSLEHRE, Berlin: Julius Springer (1925).

ZDENĚK KÜHN, APLIKACE PRÁVA VE SLOŽITÝCH PŘÍPADECH. K ÚLOZE PRÁVNÍCH PRINCIPŮ V JUDIKATUŘE, Praha: Karolinum (2002).

Zdeněk Kühn, *Postavení soudní moci v Evropě na počátku 21. století a výhled do budoucnosti, in* ROLE NEJVYŠŠÍCH SOUDŮ V EVROPSKÝCH ÚSTAVNÍCH SYSTÉMECH - ČAS PRO ZMĚNU?, Brno: Masarykova univerzita, Mezinárodní politologický ústav (V. Šimíček ed., 2007).

KAREL KLÍMA A KOLEKTIV, ENCYKLOPEDIE ÚSTAVNÍHO PRÁVA, Praha: ASPI (2007).

KAREL KLÍMA, TEORIE VEŘEJNÉ MOCI (VLÁDNUTÍ), Praha: ASPI (2006).

VLADIMÍR KLOKOČKA, ÚSTAVNÍ SYSTÉMY, EVROPSKÝCH STÁTŮ, Praha: Linde (2006).

DAVID KOSAŘ, MAREK ANTOŠ, ZDENĚK KÜHN, LADISLAV VYHNÁNEK, *ÚSTAVNÍ PRÁVO: CASEBOOK*. Praha: Wolters Kluwer (2014).

Jan Kysela, *Kdopak by se „soudcovského státu" bál, in* ROLE NEJVYŠŠÍCH SOUDŮ V EVROPSKÝCH ÚSTAVNÍCH SYSTÉMECH-ČAS NA ZMĚNU?, Brno: Masarykova univerzita, Mezinárodní politologický ústav (V. Šimíček ed., 2007).

Václav Klaus, 52 Soudcokracie v ČR. Fikce nebo realita, Praha: CEP, (M. Loužek ed., 2006).

NIKLAS LUHMANN, LEGITIMATION DURCH VERFAHREN, Darmstadt: Luchterland (1975).

JACQUES MARITAIN, ČLOVĚK A STÁT. Praha: Triáda, Delfín (2007).

Czech Yearbook of International Law®

PAVEL MOLEK, ZÁKLADNÍ PRÁVA. SVAZEK PRVNÍ-DŮSTOJNOST, Praha: Wolters Kluwer (2017).

HENNING OTTMANN, GESCHICHTE DES POLITISCHE DENKENS 3/1.: DIE NEUZEIT, Stuttgart - Weimar: J.B. Metzler (2006).

VÁCLAV PAVLÍČEK, HELENA HOFMANNOVÁ, OBČANSKÁ A LIDSKÁ PRÁVA V SOUČASNÉ DOBĚ, Praha: Auditorium (2014).

PLATÓN, ZÁKONY, Praha: OIKOYMENH (1997).

JEAN-FRANÇOIS RENUCCI, DROIT EUROPÉEN DES DROITS DE L´HOMME, Paris: LGDJ (1998).

KLAUS STERN, DAS STAATSRECHT DER BUNDESREPUBLIK DEUTSCHLAND, Band I. München: C. H. Beck (1984).

LEO STRAUSS, NATURAL RIGHT AND HISTORY, Chicago: University of Chicago Press (2005).

FRÉDÉRIC SUDRE, MEZINÁRODNÍ A EVROPSKÉ PRÁVO LIDSKÝCH PRÁV, Brno: Masarykova univerzita (1997).

Jindřiška Syllová, *K metodám zkoumání judicializace politiky ve střední Evropě*, 5 PRÁVNÍK (2019).

František Šamalík, *Právní positivismus v éře lidských práv*, 6 PRÁVNÍK (1995).

ROLE NEJVYŠŠÍCH SOUDŮ V EVROPSKÝCH ÚSTAVNÍCH SYSTÉMECH-ČAS PRO ZMĚNU?, Brno: Masarykova univerzita, Mezinárodní politologický ústav (V. Šimíček ed., 2007).

NADĚŽDA ŠIŠKOVÁ, DIMENZE OCHRANY LIDSKÝCH PRÁV V EVROPSKÉ UNII. Praha: Linde (2008).

ALEXIS DE TOCQUEVILLE, DEMOKRACIE V AMERICE, Praha: Academia (2000).

Eliška Wagnerová, *Všeobecná deklarace lidských práv jako milník mezi epochami*, 5 JURISPRUDENCE (2009).

ELIŠKA WAGNEROVÁ, VOJTĚCH ŠIMÍČEK, TOMÁŠ LANGÁŠEK, IVO POSPÍŠIL A KOLEKTIV, LISTINA ZÁKLADNÍCH PRÁV A SVOBOD. KOMENTÁŘ, Praha: Wolters Kluwer (2012).

Rodoljub Etinski

*Key words:*
environment | public participation | due account | sufficient weight

# Due Weight and Due Account Standards of the Public Participation in Environmental Matters under the European Convention on Human Rights and the Aarhus Convention

**Abstract |** *The public participation in decision-making in environmental matters is regulated by Articles 6, 7 and 8 of the Aarhus Convention and by Article 8 of the European Convention on Human Rights. The two regulations differ in particular concerning the obligation of national authorities of the Contracting Parties relating to the interests and comments of the public. Article 6 (8) of the Aarhus Convention requires that the national authorities take due account of the result of the public discussion in decision-making. Article 8 of the European Convention on Human Rights, as interpreted by the European Court of Human Rights, stipulates that the obligation of the national authorities is to give due or sufficient weight to the interests and comments of the public in decision-making process. The standard of due or sufficient weight is more specific and more demanding that the standard of due account. The two standards produce different effects in the corresponding practices of the European Court of Human Rights and the Aarhus Convention Compliance Committee. The text discloses traces of the synergy of the two Conventions and the possibility of forum shopping.*

**(Prof., Dr.) Rodoljub Etinski** taught Public International Law, Human Rights and EU Law at the Novi Sad University until 2018. He teaches Public International Law and Human Rights at the University of Donja Gorica in Podgorica since 2019. He is the chairman of the International Law Section of the Kopaonik School of Natural Law, a member of the Scientific Council of the Romanian review on human rights - *Noua Revistă de Drepturile Omului* and the vice-president of the Serbian Branch of the International Law Association.
E-mail: etinskirodoljub@yahoo.com

| | |

# I.  Introduction

**5.01.**   The text points on a surprising fact that the European Court of Human Rights (the ECtHR or the Court) has established a higher standard of the public participation in decision-making concerning environmental matters than the Aarhus Convention Compliance Committee[1] (the Aarhus Committee or the Committee). It might be astonishing since the Court has done that by applying and interpreting the Convention for the Protection of Human Rights and Fundamental Freedoms ((adopted 4 November 1950, entered into force 3 September 1953), 5 ETS (ECHR)) whose text does not refer at all to the environment. Contrary to that, Articles 6,7 and 8 of the Convention on Access to Information, Public Participation in Decision-making and Access to Justice in Environmental Matters ((adopted on 25 June 1998, entered into force 30 October 2001) 2161 UNTS 447)) are dedicated to the public participation in the decision-making related to environmental issues. It might be expected that the Committee, as the controller of the compliance of acts of the Contracting Parties with the Aarhus Convention, a special human rights instrument in the environmental context, has gone further than the Court of general human rights competence. However, experience is opposite to that expectation.

**5.02.**   The ECtHR interprets Article 8 of the ECHR as giving rise to the obligation of national authorities to give *due* or *sufficient weight* to the interests and comments of the public in decision-making process. Interpreting Article 6(8) of the Aarhus Convention, the Compliance Committee has not gone very far from the text of the paragraph which obliges the Contracting Parties to give a *due account* to the result of the public discussion in decision-making. The standard of *due* or *sufficient weight* qualifies the standard of *due account*. It requires not only consideration and replying to the arguments of the public but also the weighing and balancing of conflicting interests. Consequently, the due or sufficient weight standard might be considered as the higher, more demanding standard in comparison with less defined and broader due account standard.

**5.03.**   The text presents the development of the interpretation of Article 8 of the ECHR concerning environmental matters and the interpretation of Article 6(8) of the Aarhus Convention in the practice of the Aarhus Committee. The focus is on the effects of the two standards in practices of the Court and the Committee.

---

[1]   Veit Koester, *The Compliance Committee of the Aarhus Convention, An Overview of Procedures and Jurisprudence*, 37(2-3) ENVIRONMENTAL POLICY AND LAW 83 (2007).

## II. Development of the Interpretation of Article 8 of the European Convention on Human Rights in the Environmental Context

5.04. Article 8 of the ECHR guarantees the right to respect for private and family life and reads as follows:

> "Everyone has the right to respect for his private and family life, his home and his correspondence.
>
> There shall be no interference by a public authority with the exercise of this right except such as in accordance with the law and is necessary in a democratic society in the interests of ...the economic well-being of the country..."

5.05. Article 8(2) enumerates *inter alia* the economic well-being of the country as a legitimate aim that justifies an interference of the public authority in the right to privacy. This is relevant for interpretation of Article 8 in the context of the environmental issues. Governments usually justify their acts inimical to the environment by referring to the economic well-being of the country. Beyond that, the ordinary meaning of the terms of the Article, the context including the preamble, the purpose and object of the ECHR or the preparatory work do not say anything on the substantive or procedural obligations of the Contracting States in respect to the protection of the right to privacy against environmental impacts. The Court, however, interprets Article 8 as imposing obligations in that respect. A short review of the development of the interpretation will be presented.

### II.1. The Extension of the Scope of Application of the European Convention on Human Rights on the Environmental Issues

5.06. In *X. and Y. v. Federal Republic of Germany,* the European Commission of Human Rights found that the application related to environmental aspects of the military use of parts of a marshland was incompatible *ratione materiae* with the provisions of the ECHR and declared the application inadmissible in 1976.[2] The Commission noted that no right to nature conservation was as such guaranteed by the ECHR. Two years later in the *Tyrer* case the Court has established an evolutive way of the interpretation of the ECHR in the sense that "the Convention is a living instrument ...which must be

---

[2]  *X. and Y. v. Federal Republic of Germany* (dec). No. 7407/76, 13 May 1976.

interpreted in the light of present-day conditions."[3] It might have a certain role in the extension of the scope of the application of the ECHR to environmental issues.[4] In 1980 the European Commission of Human Rights decided in *Arrondelle* that the United Kingdom could have been responsible for violation of the right to privacy made by excessive noise of the aircraft engines by landing and taking off at the Gatwick Airport.[5] It declared the application admissible and opened the door for the consideration of the responsibility of the Contracting States for the significant violation of human rights caused by the pollution of environment. That was not necessarily a radical change in relation to the position of the Commission in *X. and Y. v. Federal Republic of Germany*. The facts in *Arrondelle* were different. The connection between the environmental problem, the noise pollution and the right to privacy was much more direct and obvious than it was in the previous case. Possibly, rising environmental awareness had some influence. The Court has not, however, changed the finding of the European Commission from 1976:

> "Neither Article 8 nor any of the other Articles of the Convention are specifically designed to provide general protection of the environment as such".[6]

## II.2. Transposition of the Procedural Aspect of Article 8 in the Environmental Context

5.07. In several cases, the ECtHR indicated the procedural aspect of the right to privacy in the context of the environmental pollution. In *Taşkın and Others* v. *Turkey*, elaborating on the procedural aspect of Article 8, the Court refers to *McMichae* and *Hatton* as the source of information.[7] The Court stated in *McMichael* that "[W]hilst Article 8 ... contains no explicit procedural requirements, the decision-making process leading to measures of interference must be fair and such as to afford due respect to the interests safeguarded by Article 8."[8] However, the Court

---

3  *Tyrer* v. *the United Kingdom* (dec.) No. 5856/72, 25 April 1978, paragraph 31. See Kanstantsin Dzehtsiarou, *European Consensus and the Evolutive Interpretation of the European Convention on Human Rights*, 12(10) GERMAN LAW JOURNAL 1732 (2011).

4  BOJANA ČUČKOVIĆ, ZAŠTITA ŽIVOTNE SREDINE U MEĐUNARODNOM PRAVU LJUDSKIH PRAVA, Beograd: Pravni fakultet Univerziteta u Beogradu (2018), et. 127.

5  *Arrondelle* v. *the United Kingdom* (dec.) No. 7889/77, 15 July 1980.

6  *Kyrtatos* v. *Greece* (dec.) No. 41666/98),12 May 2003, paragraph 52. *Fadeyeva* v. *Russia* (dec.) No. 55723/00, 09 June 2005, paragraph 68. See Sanja Đajić, *Pravo na zdravu životnu sredinu i Evropski sud za ljudska prava*, 12(IV) PRAVNI ŽIVOT 277 (2012). Ivana Krstić, *Zaštita životne sredine u jurisprudenciji Evropskog suda za ljudska prava*, 9(I) PRAVNI ŽIVOT 645 (2012).

7  *Taşkın and Others* v. *Turkey* (dec.) No. 46117/99, 10 November 2004, paragraph 118.

8  *McMichael* v. *the United Kingdom* (dec.) No. 16424/90, 24 February 1995, paragraph 87.

stated this in the context of a parental issue. The parental issue is firmly connected with Article 8, which refers explicitly to family relationships, but it does not refer to the environmental issues. Thus, the Court transposed the procedural aspect of Article 8 from the family context to the environmental context.[9] This was despite the fact that the Court could have found support for the procedural aspect of Article 8 in the environmental context also in the development of environmental procedural law.

## II.3.     The Three Stages of the Procedural Aspect of Article 8 in the Environmental Context

**5.08.**     The Court shaped the content of the procedural aspect of Article 8 in the environmental context under the influence of environmental law. The obligation of providing essential information that enables the public to assess the risk they are exposed to has been indicated in *McGinley*[10] in 1998. The contour of the procedural aspect has been laid down in *Hatton*[11] in 2003.

**5.09.**     The obligation that a governmental decision-making process must include proper investigations and studies that will allow "to strike a fair balance between the various conflicting interests at stake" has been indicated in *Hatton*.[12] In the same case the Court noted that the public had access to the relevant study and that members of the public (the applicants and persons in a similar situation) could have made any representation they considered appropriate.[13] In *Hatton,* the Court further observed that "[H]ad any representations not been taken into account, they could have challenged subsequent decisions... in the courts."[14]

**5.10.**     In *Taşkın and Others* v. *Turkey*[15], in 2004, the Court clearly defined the three stages of the procedure. The first stage consists of appropriate investigations and studies that will enable to predict and assess a possible detrimental impact of the planned activities to the environment and individual's rights, and to facilitate the striking of a fair balance between the various conflicting interests.[16] The second step consists of providing

---

[9]     See a general review on the public interest litigation before regional human rights courts in Christian Shall, *Public Interest Litigation Concerning Environmental Matters before Human Rights Courts: A Promising Future Concept?* 20(3) JOURNAL OF ENVIRONMENTAL LAW 417 (2008).

[10]     *McGinley and Egan* v. *the United Kingdom* (dec.) Nos. 21825/93 and 23414/94, 09 June 1998, paragraph 97.

[11]     *Hatton and Others* v. *the United Kingdom* (dec. gch.) No. 36022/97, 08 July 2003.

[12]     *Ibid.*, paragraph 128.

[13]     *Ibid.*

[14]     *Ibid.*

[15]     *Taşkın and Others* v. *Turkey, supra* note 7.

[16]     *Ibid.*, paragraph 119.

the public with access to the findings of the investigations and studies which would enable the public to assess the danger to which they are exposed.[17] The last step is that "the individuals concerned must also be able to appeal to the courts against any decision, act or omission where they consider that their interests or their comments have not been given sufficient weight in the decision-making process."[18]

## II.4. The Appearance of the Due Or Sufficient Weight Standard

5.11. There are several cases related to the environmental aspect of Article 8 of the ECHR where the Court employed the standard. Concerning the procedural aspect of Article 8 in *Hatton* the Court stated that it would investigate the decision-making process to ascertain whether due weight had been accorded to the interests of the individual.[19] In *Fadeyeva v. Russia* the Court found that it could not "conclude that, in regulating the steel plant's industrial activities, the authorities gave due weight to the interests of the community living in close proximity to its premises."[20] Referring to *Hatton* in *Taşkın*, the Court repeated the standard of due weight[21] and then qualified it as *sufficient weight*.[22]

## II.5. The Contribution of International Environmental Instruments to the Building of Interpretation of Article 8 in the Environmental Context

5.12. In *Taşkın v. Turkey*, the ECtHR invoked certain international environmental instruments. The Court quoted Principle 10 of the 1992 Rio Declaration on Environment and Development which is dedicated to the participation of the concerned citizens in environmental affairs and which singles out the right to environmental information and the right of participation in the decision-making but without elaboration of their specificities.[23]

5.13. The Court informed in the same case that the Aarhus Convention implemented Principle 10 of the Rio Declaration, that it entered into force and that there were thirty countries

---

[17] *Ibid.*
[18] *Ibid.*
[19] *Hatton*, paragraph 99.
[20] *Fadeyeva v. Russia, supra* note 6, paragraph 131.
[21] *Taşkın*, paragraph 115.
[22] *Ibid.*
[23] *Ibid.*, paragraph 98.

Due Weight and Due Account Standards of the Public Participation...

Czech Yearbook of International Law®

ratified it, but Turkey had neither signed it nor acceded to the Convention.[24] The presentation of the Aarhus Convention is made by referring to the three areas that is concerned with: "[D]eveloping public access to information held by the public authorities..."; "[P]romoting public participation in decision-making concerning issues with an environmental impact..."; "[E]xtending condition of access for the courts in connection with environmental legislation and access to information".[25] Having in view that the majority of Parties to the ECHR accepted the Aarhus Convention, the fact that Turkey did not do that was not an obstacle for the ECtHR to use the Aarhus Convention for interpreting Article 8. The evolutive interpretation is relied on the prevailing practice of the Contracting Parties. It does not require unanimous practice of all Parties.

5.14.    Although the texts of ECtHR judgments are usually quite long, interpretative explanations are frequently missing. The ECtHR did not explain how it used the Aarhus Convention for interpreting the procedural aspect of Article 8 of the ECHR. However, paragraph 119 of the judgment in *Taşkın* discloses the influence of the Aarhus Convention. Thus, the words "any decision, act or omission" in paragraph 119 appear in Article 9(2) of the Aarhus Convention in the same context of the access to the courts. Article 9(2) of the Aarhus Convention provides the qualified public with the access to justice "to challenge the substantive and procedural legality of any decision, act or omission subject to the provisions of article 6..." Most probably, the ECtHR had in view Article 9(2) of the Aarhus Convention when it formulated paragraph 119 of the judgment.

5.15.    The Aarhus Convention, however, does not require the attribution of *sufficient weight* to the interests or comments of the public in the decision-making. Article 6(8) of the Aarhus Convention states: "Each Party shall ensure that in the decision due account is taken of the outcome of the public participation." The clause "due account is taken of the outcome of the public participation" in Article 6(8) has not the same meaning as the clause in paragraph 119 of the judgment which states that individuals' "interests or their comments have not been given sufficient weight in the decision-making process".

---

[24]    *Ibid.*, paragraph 99.
[25]    *Ibid.* The Court invoked the Aarhus Convention also in *Tătar* v. *Romania* (dec.) No. 67021/01, 27 January 2009, paragraph 69; *Grimkovskaya* v. *Ukraine* (dec.). No. 38182/03, 21 July 2011, paragraph 39; *Ivan Tasov* v. *Bulgaria*, (dec.) No. 12853/03, 02 December 2010, paragraph 55; and in some others. See Alan Boyle, *Human Rights or Environmental Rights? A Reassessment*, 18 FORDHAM ENVIRONMENTAL LAW REVIEW 471 (2006-2007), et. 478.

**5.16.** In the rubric of the judgment in *Taşkın*, dedicated to the relevant international texts on the right to a healthy environment, beside the Rio Declaration and the Aarhus Convention, the ECtHR invokes also Recommendation 1614 (2003) on environment and human rights adopted by the Parliamentary Assembly of the Council of Europe in 2003. The Assembly recommended to Member States *inter alia* that by protection of the life, health, family and private life, physical integrity and private property in accordance with Articles 2, 3 and 8 of the ECHR and Article 1 of Protocol no. 1 to the Convention take "particular account of the need for environmental protection..."[26]

**5.17.** The Recommendation is strengthening the interpretation of the ECtHR according to which Article 8 of the Convention covers environmental issues but does not say anything specifically about an obligation of national authorities to consider views of the public in decision-making.

## II.6. The Interpretation of the Due Account Standard in the Practice of the Aarhus Compliance Committee

**5.18.** The Aarhus Compliance Committee interprets Article 6(8) in the following way: "the authority should be able to demonstrate how the comments were considered and why it did not follow the views expressed by the public" and "while it is impossible to accept in substance all the comments submitted ... the relevant authority must still seriously consider all the comments received."[27] The Committee notes that Article 6(9) controls the fulfilment of the requirement of Article 6(8).[28] Article 6(9) ensures that the public is promptly informed of the text of the decision taken by the public authorities and with the reasons and considerations on which the decision is based. The Committee considers that the Party is obliged "to show through its written and oral submissions how the outcome of public participation was duly taken into account."[29] Thus, it states that "the obligation to take due account of the outcome of the public participation should be interpreted as the obligation that the written reasoned decision includes a discussion of how the public participation was taken into account."[30]

---

[26] *Taşkın*, paragraph 100.
[27] Findings and recommendations with regard to communication ACCC/C/2012/70 concerning compliance by the Czech Republic, 20 December 2013, paragraph 61.
[28] *Ibid.*, paragraph 62.
[29] *Ibid.*, paragraph 63.
[30] Findings and recommendations with regard to communication ACCC/C/2012/68 concerning compliance by the European Union and the United Kingdom of Great Britain and Northern Ireland, 24

Due Weight and Due Account Standards of the Public Participation...

Czech Yearbook of International Law®

**5.19.** The requirement of attaching sufficient weight to the interests and comments of the public cannot be clearly recognizable in the interpretation of the Committee. The Implementation guide for the Aarhus Convention, prepared by the experts, also does not direct to an obligation of national authorities to attach sufficient weight to the interests and comments of the public. It clarifies that Article 6(8) requires the serious consideration of substance of all comments and their inclusion in the motivation of the final decision.[31] It reads further: "It does not require the relevant authority to *accept* the substance of all comments received and to change the decision according to every comment. However, the relevant authority is ultimately responsible for the decision based on all information, including comments received, and should be able to show why a particular comment was rejected on substantive grounds."[32]

## III. The Effects of the Two Standards in the Practice of the Two Bodies

**5.20.** It seems that the two standards produce different effects in the corresponding practices. However, it should be observed that the subjects and the interests in play at the two bodies are not necessarily the same. The Court has always dealt with the conflict between the economic interest of a nation or a community and the individual interest protected by the provision of the ECHR. By weighing the two interests, the Court considers whether the Contracting State has achieved the fair balance between them. The Compliance Committee considers conflicts between a broader scale of subjects, including nations, local communities, individuals and transboundary persons[33] and between different types of interests. It investigates rather whether the result of the public participation was considered by national authorities in decision-making process and whether national authorities replied to the comments of the public in a proper form. Another difference is that the Court treats the standard as both

---

September 2013, paragraph 93.
[31]   THE AARHUS CONVENTION: AN IMPLEMENTATION GUIDE, New York and Geneva: UN Economic Commission for Europe (prepared by Stephen Stec and Susan Casey-Lefkowitz in cooperation with Jerzy Jendoska, 2000).
[32]   *Ibid.*
[33]   Individuals and local communities who are located on territory of another Contracting State are designated here as transboundary persons. Under the Aarhus Convention the Contracting Party is obliged to respect the rights guaranteed by the Aarhus Convention to persons under its territorial jurisdiction and to persons under territorial jurisdiction of other Contracting Parties. See Rodoljub Etinski, *Specific Features of Human Rights Guaranteed by the Aarhus Convention*, 47(2) PROCEEDINGS OF NOVI SAD FACULTY OF LAW 79 (2013).

substantive and procedural while the Committee treats the standard rather as procedural.

### III.1. The Effect of the Due Or Sufficient Weight Standard in the Practice of the Interpretation of Article 8 in the Environmental Context

5.21. In *Hatton,* the applicants and the Respondent State disagreed whether the government measures concerning night flights at Heathrow Airport violated their rights under Article 8 of the Convention. The applicants lived in houses a few kilometers away from the airport's runways and they alleged that the level of night noise had increased in last years and became intolerable. Allegedly, noise disturbed their sleeping, especially in summer, when windows remained open, or when wind was blowing in the direction of the houses. There was a conflict between the general national economic interests and the individual interest of affected applicants. The Court (the Grand Chamber) noted that the issue of the right balance that should have been established between "the Article 8 rights affected by the regime and other conflicting community interests depends on the relative weight given to each of them."[34] The Grand Chamber evaluated the impact of the night flights to national economy and the measures taken by the Government to mitigate the effect of night noise.[35] It noted also that "[W]here a limited number of people in an area (2 to 3% of the affected population, according to the 1992 sleep study) are particularly affected by a general measure, the fact that they can, if they choose, move elsewhere without financial loss must be significant to the overall reasonableness of the general measure."[36] Thus, the Court came to the conclusion that the national authorities did not exceed their margin of appreciation "by failing to strike a fair balance between the right of the individuals affected by those regulations to respect for their private life and home and the conflicting interests of others and of the community as a whole".[37] Accordingly, there was not a violation of Article 8.

5.22. It should be noted that the Chamber of the ECtHR came to the opposite conclusion in the same case. The Chamber concluded that the respondent State failed to reach a fair balance between the United Kingdom economic well-being and the interest of

---

[34] *Hatton*, paragraph 125.
[35] *Ibid.*, paragraphs 126, 127.
[36] *Ibid.*, paragraph 127.
[37] *Hatton*, paragraph 129.

the applicants.[38] It found that the Government did not precisely determine the contribution of night flights to national economy and their impact on the applicants.[39] Further, the Chamber opines that the measures taken by the Government to mitigate the problem were not satisfactory, especially when considering that the Government did not render "a prior specific and complete study with the aim of finding the least onerous solution as regards human rights".[40] Thus, there was a violation of Article 8. The Chamber believed that the Government should have done more in collecting data relevant for the weighing. Having in view the nature of interference in the right of privacy which was not very serious, the Grand Chamber was of the opinion that the Government enjoyed a wide margin of appreciation in this case, as in greater freedom in the methodology for weighing the conflicting interests.

5.23.    In *Taşkın*, the applicants and the Respondent State differed *inter alia* on the issue whether the extraction of gold by sodium cyanide leaching in the Ovacik mine violated the right to private life of the applicants who were living in two villages near the mine. To resolve the difference, the Court investigated the substantive and procedural aspects of Article 8 of the ECHR in the context of environment pollution. Having repeated that the Contracting Parties have enjoyed a wide margin of appreciation in cases of environmental concern in respect to the substantive aspect of Article 8, the ECtHR noted that the margin of appreciation could not comprehend the disrespect for a final decision of the national court. Since the Supreme Administrative Court of Turkey annulled a permit for operating the Ovacik mine and since the judgment of the court and the relevant procedural rules were not respected by the Respondent State, the ECtHR found that the Respondent State exceeded the margin of appreciation.[41] The non-compliance with the mentioned judgment of the Supreme Administrative Court and the procedural breaches in issuing a new permit were observed by the Court also as a breach of the procedural aspect of Article 8.[42] The reference to the sufficient weight appears in the judgment rather as obiter dictum. However, the judgment reflects the conviction of the Court that the Turkish authorities did not assign sufficient weight to the concerns of the applicants

---

[38]    *Hatton and Others* v. *the United Kingdom* (dec. ch.). No. 36022/97), 02 October 2001, paragraph 107.
[39]    *Ibid.*, paragraphs 102, 103.
[40]    *Ibid.*, paragraph 106.
[41]    *Taşkın*, paragraphs 116, 117.
[42]    *Ibid.*, paragraphs 121- 125.

which were confirmed by the judgment of the Supreme Administrative Court.

5.24. In the *Fadeyeva* case, the applicant lived in a flat in the vicinity of a steel plant in the town of Cherepovets and she and her family were exposed to dust and gases from the plant that significantly exceeded the maximal amounts permitted by national law. The local authorities adopted measures of resettlement of residents living around the steel plant, but the applicant along with others from her block of apartments were not resettled. The judgment of the regional court requiring her resettlement was not executed. The adverse effects of the pollution on health of the residents of Cherepovets and especially those leaving in the vicinity of the steel plant were established. Having accepted that the production in the steel plant was contributing to the economic well-being of the country, the Court considered "whether, in pursuing this aim, the authorities have struck a fair balance between the interests of the applicant and those of the community as a whole."[43] Due to local circumstances the applicant could not help herself by buying or renting a flat beyond the zone of pollution without carrying a heavy financial burden.[44] Analyzing the materials submitted by the Government, the Court found that the Government did not demonstrate that it had given due weight to the interests of individuals living in close proximity to the steel plant in its policy concerning the plant.[45] Thus, despite the wide margin of appreciation that the respondent Stated enjoyed in the specific circumstance of the case, the Court concluded that the State failed to strike a fair balance between the interests of the community and individual interests of the applicant as protected by Article 8 of the ECHR.[46]

### III.2. The Effect of the *Due Account* Standard in the Practice of the Aarhus Compliance Committee

5.25. *Mrs. Metcalfe* and *the Avich & Kilchrenan Community Council* alleged *inter alia* that the United Kingdom filed to comply with Article 6(8) of the Aarhus Convention concerning the Carriag Gheal wind farm and the access road to the wind farm which was planned also for timber transport.[47] Allegedly the Scottish

---

[43] *Fadeyeva*, paragraph 101.
[44] *Ibid.*, paragraph 121.
[45] *Ibid.*, paragraph 131.
[46] *Ibid.*, paragraph 134.
[47] *Christine Metcalfe and the Avich & Kilchrenan Community Council* v. *the United Kingdom and the European Union*, communication ACCC/C/2012/68, 12 March 2012. The case was complex and included many issues, but for the purpose of this text the review is limited to only one issue. Mrs Metcalfe, who was

authority did not give due account to the comments submitted to decision-making for the plan and project. The comments and concerns included *inter alia* the following issues: a detrimental effect of the project to landscape; effects on surrounding people by noise and potential pollution of their private water supply; effects on wildlife, including otters, fish, birds; effects on tourism, etc. The Government replied that it considered and answered all comments, except for those related to tourism, health and fishing. Having considered the information received by the parties, the Committee found that the United Kingdom "overall duly took into account the comments submitted by the communicant and did not fail to comply with article 6 (8), of the Convention."[48] It did not scrutinize how the national authorities had taken into account the objections of the communicator, but only noted the information of the Government that "[T]he Scottish Ministers considered all these objections and during the process they found that the benefits of the project outweighed any potential impacts."[49]

**5.26.** The Spanish non-governmental organization *Association for Environmental Justice* asserted in its communication *inter alia*, that the public participation in decision-making process concerning the land use planning and the implementation of the urbanization project in a residential area of the city of Murcia was not performed as required by Article 6 of the Aarhus Convention.[50] The public sent numerous comments related to the absence of the environmental impact assessment; the legality of the agreement between the City Council and a company; the landscape and environmental values of the land;[51] the proposed density of a building that exceeded the legal limit; the lack of green areas; not enough land for the public facilities; the lack of protection against noise and others.[52] Allegedly, neither of the objections was taken into account in decision-making. The Committee found that the system was such that "as a routine, comments of the public were disregarded or not accepted on their merits, without any explanation."[53]

**5.27.** Representing the interests of Moray Feu, residents in Edinburgh, the communicant, *the Moray Feu Traffic Subcommittee of Lord*

---

a community councilor submitted the communication on behalf of the Avich & Kilchrenan Community Council and her own. The Avich & Kilchrenan Community Council had a status of nongovernmental organization.

[48] Findings and recommendations with regard to communication ACCC/C/2012/68..., paragraph 94.
[49] *Ibid.*, paragraph 67.
[50] Findings and recommendations with regard to Communication ACCC/C/2008/24 concerning compliance by Spain, December 2009. paragraphs 1,3.
[51] *Ibid.*, paragraph 48.
[52] *Ibid.*, paragraph 49.
[53] *Ibid.*, paragraph 101.

*Moray's Feuars Committee* alleged *inter alia* that the Scottish authorities failed to provide the residents with a meaningful participation in decision-making concerning the permanent rerouting of the traffic through the center of Edinburgh in order to enable installation of two tram lines.[54] The Committee found that the United Kingdom did not fail to take into account "as much as possible the objections/comments of the communicant".[55] Having reviewed the relevant decisions of the Scottish authorities, it noted that the comments were considered.[56] They were rejected, but detailed reasoning was given, and mitigation measures were considered necessary. It was acknowledged by the authorities that there was an air and noise quality impact, although the official measurements showed that air and noise were within the United Kingdom and European Union standards.[57]

### III.3. The Difference in Effects of the Two Standards in the Practices of the Two Bodies

**5.28.** The practices of the Court and the Committee concerning the application of the standard of due or sufficient weight and the standard of due account are different but not fully divergent. In the case *Association for Environmental Justice v. Spain*, the Committee indicated its willingness to consider whether comments were accepted according to their merits. It implies certain weighing of importance of the comments. In the *Moray Feu* case, the Committee expressed its appreciation of the carefulness that the Scottish authorities dedicated to the interests of the residents. The weighing and balancing includes also an investigation whether a Contracting Party took measures at its disposal to eliminate or mitigate impact to the interest of individuals.

**5.29.** On the other hand, the Court constantly repeats that the Contracting States enjoy a wide margin of appreciation in environmental affairs.[58] The Court has to be engaged primarily in the reviewing of the procedural aspect, in examining

---

[54] Findings and recommendations with regard to communication ACCC/C/2010/53 concerning compliance by the United Kingdom of Great Britain and Northern Ireland, 28 September 2012, paragraphs 1,2.

[55] *Ibid.*, paragraph 88.

[56] *Ibid.*, paragraph 87.

[57] Ibid. See review of other cases in MARIANNE DELLINGER, TEN YEARS OF THE AARHUS CONVENTION, HOW PROCEDURAL DEMOCRACY IS PAVING THE WAY FOR SUBSTANTIVE CHANGE IN NATIONAL AND INTERNATIONAL ENVIRONMENTAL LAW (2011), Electronic copy available at: http://ssrn.com/abstract=2004513 (accessed on 31 January 2019).

[58] *Fadeyeva*, paragraph 104.

"whether the decision-making process was fair and such as to afford due respect to the interests safeguarded to the individual by Article 8 (...), and only in exceptional circumstances may it go beyond this line and revise the material conclusions of the domestic authorities..."[59] Besides, the judgments of the Court are more extensive than the findings and recommendations of the Committee and due to that reason, effects of the standard are more visible.

**5.30.** Despite certain convergence of the practices, the standard of due or sufficient weight is more demanding. It requires complex analysis of the balancing of opposite interests that include determination of the weight of each involved interest and exploration of possibilities available to individuals and to the State to resolve the conflict, the weighing of financial or other burdens that these possibilities require, the principle of proportionality etc. The standard of due account can be satisfied by careful consideration of the comments and objections and by a reasonable explanation as to why they were not accepted.

## IV. The Weighing and Balancing in the Frameworks of a Margin of Appreciation and the Rule of Law

**5.31.** The concept of the margin of appreciation reflects the understanding of the Court of its subsidiary role and its conviction that a society is primarily entitled to resolve "the inherent conflicts between individual rights and national interests..."[60] The text of the ECHR does not include terms "margin of appreciation." They will be inserted in the preamble of the Convention when Protocol No. 15 enters into force.[61] The concept originates from national law and has been introduced as an instrument of the interpretation of the Convention by the European Commission of Human Rights in the sixties of the previous century.[62] In the meantime, through many cases, the Court has defined the factors which determine the scope of the margin of appreciation. They include, "the nature of the Convention right in issue, its importance for the individual, the nature of the interference and the object pursued by the

---

[59] *Ibid.*, paragraph 105.
[60] Eyal Benvenisti, *Margin of Appreciation, Consensus and General Standards*, 31 JOURNAL OF INTERNATIONAL LAW AND POLITICS 843 (1998-1999), et. 843.
[61] Article 1 of Protocol No. 15 amending the Convention for the Protection of Human Rights and Fundamental Freedoms of 24 June 2013.
[62] Eva Brems, *The Margin of Appreciation Doctrine in the Case-Law of the European Court of Human Rights*, 56 ZEITSCHRIFT FÜR AUSLÄNDISCHES ÖFFENTLICHES RECHT UND VÖLKERRECHT 240 (1996), et. 242.

interference. The margin will tend to be narrower where the right at stake is crucial to the individual's effective enjoyment of intimate or key rights".[63] The margin is restricted where an individual's existence or identity is at stake.[64] In the absence of consensus of the member States of the Council of Europe as to the relative importance of the interest or how best to protect it, the margin is wider.[65] The Court has repeated in more cases that the State enjoys a wide margin of appreciation in decision-making concerning the environmental matters, in particular in relation to the substantive aspect.[66]

5.32.   The principle of rule of law is indicated in the preamble of the ECHR and plays a significant role in the jurisprudence of the Court. It is also a limit of the margin of appreciation. The margin of appreciation cannot include disrespect for the rule of law. The principle played an important role in *Taşkın*.[67] If by disregard of domestic environmental law or judicial decisions the State enables or tolerates the pollution of environment causing significant harm to the individual interests protected by the ECHR, it is very likely that the Court will attribute responsibility to the State.

5.33.   Two variants of giving due or sufficient weight to the interests and comments of the public are conceivable. The first variant employed by the ECtHR, strives to establish a fair balance between the interest of a community and the interest of an individual. Certain elements of this variant are indicated in case law of the ECtHR. The second variant might be the ranking of interests in specific situations. Thus, considering the question whether the dyke – building operation, which slightly reduced a habitat of protected birds, contravenes Article 4(4) of the Council Directive 79/409/EEC of 02 April 1979 on the conservation of wild birds in the *Commission* v. *Germany "Leybucht"* case, the European Court of Justice stated that "a general interest which is superior to the general interest represented by the ecological objective of the directive" could justify reduction of the habitat. [68] The economic and recreational interests are not superior to the specific environmental interest, but the interest of protection of coastal structure against the danger of flooding is superior.[69] It seems that the flooding could have endangered

---

[63]   *S. and Marper* v. *the United Kingdom* (doc.). Nos. 30562/04 and 30566/04), 04 December 2008, paragraph 102.

[64]   *Ibid.*

[65]   *Ibid.*

[66]   *Hatton* gch., paragraph 100; *Taşkın*, paragraph 116; *Fadeyeva*, paragraph 134.

[67]   Taşkın, paragraphs 124, 136.

[68]   C-57/89, *Commission* v. *Germany "Leybucht"* [1991] ECR I-883, paragraph 22.

[69]   *Ibid.*, paragraph 23.

Due Weight and Due Account Standards of the Public Participation...

Czech Yearbook of International Law®

human lives.[70] Despite of the fact that the ranking was made in the interpretation of the directive in specific circumstances, it might have a general significance. The ranking might be implied by the law protecting endangered species.

## V.    Mutual Supportiveness

**5.34.**    The concept of mutual supportiveness is born in WTO law to harmonize the protection of the environment and international trade,[71] but for the time being it did not bring fruits in that field.[72] It expresses an idea of synergy of two or more international instruments and as such it could be applicable in other legal areas. This text discloses some traces of the synergy of the ECHR and the Aarhus Convention. The Aarhus Convention contributes in the construction of the procedural aspect of Article 8 of the ECHR. The achievements of the interpretation of Article 8 by the ECtHR are not visible in the practice of the Aarhus Committee, but they are present in legal practice of the Contracting States to the ECHR and partly contribute to effectiveness of Article 6 of the Aarhus Convention.

**5.35.**    The Aarhus Convention, a relatively weak international instrument, acquires the power through the national implementing law and in particular through the implementing EU legislation.[73] Also it overlaps partly with the ECHR. That opens the possibility of forum shopping. If individuals are endangered by serious and immediate environmental risk, like in *Taşkın*, or if they are hurt by the pollution like in *Hatton, Fadeyevaa, Moray Feu* or *Association for Environmental Justice v. Spain* they can address the issue to the ECtHR or to the Aarhus Committee. On that note, if acts or failures of the State contravene to the environmental provisions, they have a good chance to get redress from the ECtHR.

## VI.    Conclusions

**5.36.**    Articles 6, 7 and 8 of the Aarhus Convention and Article 8 of the ECHR, as interpreted by the ECtHR, regulate the public

---

[70]    *Ibid.*, paragraph 8.
[71]    Riccardo Pavoni, *Mutual Supportiveness as a Principle of Interpretation and Law-Making: A Watershed for the 'WTO-and-Competing-Regimes' Debate?* 21(3) EUROPEAN JOURNAL OF INTERNATIONAL LAW 649 (2010).
[72]    Appellate Body Report, United States – Import Prohibition of Certain Shrimps and Shrimps Products, WT/DS58/AB/R, 12 October 1998, paragraphs 153 - 155.
[73]    Maria Lee and Carolyn Abbot, *The Usual Suspects? Public Participation under the Aarhus Convention,* 66(1) MODERN LAW REVIEW 80 (2003), et. 82. Kate Getliffe, *Proceduralisation and the Aarhus Convention, Does increased participation in the decision-making process lead to more effective EU law,* 4 ENVIRONMENTAL LAW REVIEW 101 (2002).

participation in decision-making in environmental matters. The two regulations differ concerning the obligation of the national authorities towards the outcome of the public discussion. Article 6(8) of the Aarhus Convention obliges the national authorities of the Contracting Parties to give due account to the result of the public discussion in decision-making process. Article 8 of the ECHR stipulates that the obligation of the national authorities of the Contracting States to give due or sufficient weight of the interests and comments of the public as expressed in the public discussion. The standard of due or sufficient weight is more specific, demanding and requires more scrupulous investigation than the standard of due account.

5.37.  The two standards produce different effects in the corresponding practices of the ECtHR and the Aarhus Committee. The Court applies the standard as both a substantive and procedural one. The Aarhus Committee applies it just as a procedural standard. The Court compares the weight of the general economic interest of the State and the weight of an individual interest, protected by the ECHR, the nature and seriousness of a hart done by the pollution of environment, the possibilities at disposal of the State and individuals to escape or mitigate the damage, the proportion of the burdens of alternative solutions etc. The Aarhus Committee can be satisfied by the careful consideration of the interests and comments of the public, rendered by the national authorities and by reasoned replies of the authorities to them.

5.38.  Despite of the difference, some converging elements can be detected in the practices of the two bodies. The Aarhus Committee has announced its willingness to explore whether the comments have been accepted by the national authorities according to their merits. That indicates the understanding of the Committee that the weight of the comment might be relevant. The Committee explores also the carefulness dedicated by the national authorities to the comments of the public and it is an element included by the Court in the weighing and balancing. On the other hand, the Court repeats constantly that the States enjoy a wide margin of appreciation in environmental and economic issues and it finds its firm ground for assessment within the procedural aspect of Article 8 rather than within the substantive one.

5.39.  The different standards might be explained by the difference between the judicial proceedings before the Court and the quasi-judicial, rather conciliatory proceedings by the Committee, by maturity of the Court and relatively young age of the

Due Weight and Due Account Standards of the Public Participation...

Czech Yearbook of International Law®

Committee and other reasons. Thus, by the evolutive practice of the interpretation of the ECHR, the Court has injected new meanings to the provisions of the Convention. Contrary to that, the Committee prefers to be focused exclusively on the text of the provisions.

5.40. The ECtHR invokes the Aarhus Convention by interpreting Article 8 of the Convention and the Aarhus Convention contributed to the interpretation of Article 8. Even though the Aarhus Committee does not refer to the practice of the ECtHR, the practice of the Court objectively strengthens the effectiveness of Article 6(8) of the Aarhus Convention in the Contracting States to the ECHR. The partial overlap of the two Conventions opens the door for the forum shopping. If individuals are seriously and directly endangered by the pollution of environment like in *Taşkın*, or if they are hurt by the pollution like in *Hatton, Fadeyevaa, Moray Feu* or *Association for Environmental Justice* v. *Spain,* they can send an application to the ECtHR or a communication to the Aarhus Committee. If an act or a failure to act of the Party related to the pollution is contrary to the environmental provisions, the chance of being redressed by the ECtHR is quite good. However, if two ecological interests are competing, like in the case related to the wind farm, only the Aarhus Committee option is available.

| | |

*Summaries*

DEU [*Die Verpflichtungen zur „gebührenden Beachtung" („due weight") und „gebührenden Berücksichtigung" („due account") in Bezug auf die Beteiligung der Öffentlichkeit an Umweltfragen im Sinn der Europäischen Menschenrechtskonvention (EMRK) und der Aarhus-Konvention*]

*Die Beteiligung der Öffentlichkeit an Umweltentscheidungen ist in den Artikeln 6, 7 und 8 der Aarhus-Konvention und in Artikel 8 der Europäischen Menschenrechtskonvention geregelt. Diese beiden Regelungen unterscheiden sich insbesondere hinsichtlich der Pflichten der nationalen Behörden der Vertragsparteien, was die Interessen und Anmerkungen der Öffentlichkeit anbelangt. Artikel 6 Absatz 8 der Aarhus-Konvention besagt, dass in der Entscheidung das Ergebnis der Öffentlichkeitsbeteiligung gebührend berücksichtigt wird. Artikel 8 der Europäischen*

*Menschenrechtskonvention, so wie er vom Europäischen Gerichtshof für Menschenrechte (EGMR) interpretiert wird, legt fest, dass es die Pflicht der nationalen Behörden ist, die Interessen und Anmerkungen der Öffentlichkeit im Prozess der Entscheidungsfindung gebührend oder hinlänglich zu beachten. Die Pflicht, etwas „gebührend oder hinlänglich zu beachten", ist konkreter und strenger als die Pflicht der „gebührenden Berücksichtigung". Diese beiden Standards wirken sich in der Praxis des Europäischen Gerichtshofs für Menschenrechte bzw. des Umsetzungsausschusses der Aarhus-Konvention unterschiedlich aus. Der Beitrag verweist auf Spuren von Synergien zwischen diesen beiden Übereinkommen und auf die Möglichkeit einer zweckmäßigen Wahl der günstigeren Gerichtsbarkeit (Forum Shopping).*

CZE [*Povinnosti „řádně dbát" („due weight") a „řádně zohledňovat" („due account") ve vztahu k účasti veřejnosti na otázkách životního prostředí dle Evropské úmluvy o lidských právech a Aarhuské úmluvy*]
*Účast veřejnosti na rozhodování v otázkách životního prostředí upravují články 6, 7 a 8 Aarhuské úmluvy a článek 8 Evropské úmluvy o lidských právech. Tyto dvě úpravy se liší především co do povinnosti vnitrostátních orgánů smluvních stran týkající se zájmů a připomínek veřejnosti. Článek 6 odst. 8 Aarhuské úmluvy stanoví, že v rozhodnutí bude náležitě zohledněn výsledek účasti veřejnosti. Článek 8 Evropské úmluvy o lidských právech dle výkladu Evropského soudu pro lidská práva stanoví, že je povinností vnitrostátních orgánů dbát v procesu rozhodování řádně či dostatečně zájmů a připomínek veřejnosti. Povinnost „řádně či dostatečně dbát" je konkrétnější a přísnější než povinnost „řádně zohledňovat". Tyto dva standardy vyvolávají v praxi Evropského soudu pro lidská práva, resp. Výboru pro plnění Aarhuské úmluvy, různé účinky. Příspěvek poukazuje na stopy synergie mezi těmito dvěma Úmluvami a na možnost účelového vybírání příznivější jurisdikce (forum shopping).*

| | |

POL [*Obowiązek „należytej wagi" („due weight") i „należytego uwzględniania" („due account") w odniesieniu do udziału społeczeństwa w sprawach związanych ze środowiskiem na*

Czech Yearbook of International Law®

*gruncie Europejskiej Konwencji Praw Człowieka i Konwencji z Aarhus]*

*Obowiązek „należytej lub wystarczającej wagi" i obowiązek „należytego uwzględniania" w odniesieniu do udziału społeczeństwa w sprawach związanych ze środowiskiem, zgodnie z postanowieniami artykułu 8 Europejskiej Konwencji Praw Człowieka i artykułu 6 ust. 8 Konwencji z Aarhus, wywołują różne skutki w orzecznictwie Europejskiego Trybunału Praw Człowieka czy Komitetu ds. przestrzegania Konwencji z Aarhus. Obowiązek „należytej wagi" stosuje się jako standard materialnoprawny i procesowy, zaś obowiązek „należytego uwzględniania" stosowany jest wyłącznie jako standard procesowy. Pierwszy z wymienionych standardów wymaga wyważenia i poszukiwania równowagi między kolidującymi ze sobą interesami narodowymi i indywidualnymi. Zaspokojenie drugiego standardu polega na należytym rozpatrzeniu uwag ze strony społeczeństwa i udzielaniu odpowiedzi z uzasadnieniem na zadane pytania.*

FRA    **[*L'obligation de « tenir dûment compte » (« due weight ») et de « prendre dûment en considération » (« due account ») dans le contexte de la participation du public aux questions relatives à l'environnement selon la Convention européenne des droits de l'homme et de la Convention d'Aarhus]***

*En ce qui concerne la participation du public aux questions relatives à l'environnement, l'obligation de « tenir dûment ou suffisamment compte » et l'obligation de « prendre dûment en considération », visées par l'article 8 de la Convention européenne des droits de l'homme et l'article 6, paragraphe 8, de la Convention d'Aarhus, produisent des effets variés dans la pratique de la Cour européenne des droits de l'homme et du Comité d'examen du respect des dispositions de la Convention d'Aarhus. L'obligation de « tenir dûment compte » est appliquée comme une norme à la fois matérielle et procédurale, alors que l'obligation de « prendre dûment en considération » est appliquée uniquement comme une norme procédurale. L'application de la première des deux normes nécessite une recherche d'équilibre entre des intérêts contradictoires aux niveaux national et individuel. La seconde norme présuppose un examen rigoureux des observations du public, suivi de réponses motivées.*

RUS    **[*Обязанности «надлежащим образом соблюдать» (due weight) и «надлежащим образом отражать» (due account) в связи с участием общественности в вопросах, касающихся окружающей среды, в свете Европейской***

*конвенции о защите прав человека и основных свобод и
Орхусской конвенции*]

*Обязанности «надлежащим образом или в достаточной
степени соблюдать» и «надлежащим образом отражать» в
связи с участием общественности в вопросах, касающихся
окружающей среды, согласно статьи 8 Европейской
конвенцией о защите прав человека и основных свобод
и пункта 8 статьи 6 Орхусской конвенции, вызывают
различные реакции в практике Европейского суда по правам
человека и в Комитете по выполнению Орхусской конвенции.
Обязанность «надлежащим образом соблюдать»
применяется в качестве стандарта материального права
и процессуального стандарта, тогда как обязанность
«надлежащим образом отражать» применяется только
в качестве процессуального стандарта. Первый из выше
перечисленных стандартов требует сбалансирования
и поиска равновесия для конфликтующих национальных
и индивидуальных интересов. Выполнение второго
стандарта достигается путем надлежащей оценки
замечаний и комментариев общественности, а также
предоставления обоснованных ответов на эти вопросы.*

**ESP** [*Obligación de «conceder la debida importancia» (due
weight) y «tomar debidamente en cuenta» (due account)
la cuestión de la participación del público en asuntos
medioambientales, conforme al Convenio Europeo de
Derechos Humanos y el Convenio de Aarhus*]

*La obligación de «conceder la debida importancia» y la
obligación de «tomar debidamente en cuenta» la cuestión de
la participación del público en materia de medio ambiente,
plasmadas en el artículo 8 del Convenio Europeo de Derechos
Humanos y en el artículo 6, apartado 8 del Convenio de Aarhus,
se reflejan de manera diferente en la actuación de la Tribunal
Europeo de Derechos Humanos y el Comité del Cumplimiento
del Convenio de Aarhus. La obligación de «conceder la debida
importancia» opera como un estándar de derecho material
y procesal; en cambio, la obligación de «tomar debidamente
en cuenta» opera solamente como un estándar procesal. En
el primer caso, se requiere balancear y equilibrar los intereses
nacionales e individuales; para cumplir con el segundo estándar,
se requiere considerar debidamente las objeciones del público y
responderlas de forma fundamentada.*

| | |

Czech Yearbook of International Law®

## Bibliography

Eyal Benvenisti, *Margin of Appreciation, Consensus and General Standards*, 31 JOURNAL OF INTERNATIONAL LAW AND POLITICS 843 (1998-1999).

Alan Boyle, *Human Rights or Environmental Rights? A Reassessment*, 18 FORDHAM ENVIRONMENTAL LAW REVIEW 471 (2006-2007).

Eva Brems, *The Margin of Appreciation Doctrine in the Case-Law of the European Court of Human Rights*, 56 ZEITSCHRIFT FÜR AUSLÄNDISCHES ÖFFENTLICHES RECHT UND VÖLKERRECHT 240 (1996).

BOJANA ČUČKOVIĆ, ZAŠTITA ŽIVOTNE SREDINE U MEĐUNARODNOM PRAVU LJUDSKIH PRAVA, Beograd: Pravni fakultet Univerziteta u Beogradu (2018).

Sanja Đajić, *Pravo na zdravu životnu sredinu i Evropski sud za ljudska prava*, 12(IV) PRAVNI ŽIVOT 277 (2012).

MARIANNE DELLINGER, TEN YEARS OF THE AARHUS CONVENTION, HOW PROCEDURAL DEMOCRACY IS PAVING THE WAY FOR SUBSTANTIVE CHANGE IN NATIONAL AND INTERNATIONAL ENVIRONMENTAL LAW (2011).

Kanstantsin Dzehtsiarou, *European Consensus and the Evolutive Interpretation of the European Convention on Human Rights*, 12(10) GERMAN LAW JOURNAL 1732 (2011).

Rodoljub Etinski, *Specific Features of Human Rights Guaranteed by the Aarhus Convention*, 47(2) PROCEEDINGS OF NOVI SAD FACULTY OF LAW 79 (2013).

Kate Getliffe, *Proceduralisation and the Aarhus Convention, Does increased participation in the decision-making process lead to more effective EU law*, 4 ENVIRONMENTAL LAW REVIEW 101 (2002).

Veit Koester, *The Compliance Committee of the Aarhus Convention, An Overview of Procedures and Jurisprudence*, 37(2-3) ENVIRONMENTAL POLICY AND LAW 83 (2007).

Ivana Krstić, *Zaštita životne sredine u jurisprudenciji Evropskog suda za ljudska prava*, 9(I) PRAVNI ŽIVOT 645 (2012).

Maria Lee and Carolyn Abbot, *The Usual Suspects? Public Participation under the Aarhus Convention*, 66(1) MODERN LAW REVIEW 80 (2003).

Riccardo Pavoni, *Mutual Supportiveness as a Principle of Interpretation and Law-Making: A Watershed for the 'WTO-and-Competing-Regimes' Debate?* 21(3) EUROPEAN JOURNAL OF INTERNATIONAL LAW 649 (2010).

Christian Shall, *Public Interest Litigation Concerning Environmental Matters before Human Rights Courts: A Promising Future Concept?* 20(3) JOURNAL OF ENVIRONMENTAL LAW 417 (2008).

# Anna Hurova

# Ensuring the Right to a Safe and Favorable Environment Using Space Remote Sensing Data

*Key words:*
*remote sensing data | right to safe environment | evidence | satellite images | disaster management | space law | sustainable development*

**Abstract** | *Global environmental changes are to be mitigated with the help of comprehensive measures, such as Earth Observation using Remote Sensing Satellites. Satellite data can be used to check if the international environmental agreements are observed, and to settle legal disputes in international courts. Some legal frameworks, however, do not sufficiently address current challenges. The international space treaties, resolutions, regional treaties and their interaction with national legislations were studied with the purpose of finding a balance between environmental interests of the "sensed States" and the other States' interests, for example, national security interests of States which exercise the jurisdiction and control over the all remote sensing activity of their private operators. Nevertheless all States can access this satellite information to guarantee their environmental interests -the other States can deny to deliver such data on the ground of its personal interests, such as State security and others. Remote sensing data is used as evidence to make reasonable court decisions. It should be noted that in this article the author uses the notion "remote sensing data" as any kind of remote sensing activity products, namely "raw data", "digital images", "geological information" etc.*

**Anna Hurova** is a PhD in Law, Univ. Professor, Research fellow at the Koretsky State and Law Institute of National Academy of Sciences of Ukraine. The area scientific interests cover legal protection of near-Earth space from littering, legal provisions for the space resources mining and the avoiding of the military conflicts in space. E-mail: a.m.hurova@gmail.com

| | |

# I.     Introduction

**6.01.**    The right to a safe and favorable environment and the right to access the information have never been as connected as they are now. They represent the latest generation of rights which are derived from the consequences of globalization. In modern conditions of social-economic development, however, the first one is increasingly difficult to achieve, but in contrast to this the second one has reached its heyday. For example, myriads of satellites are currently processing remote sensing of the Earth, giving humankind unique services connected with the protection of natural resources, detection of environmental crimes during both peace and war, management of artificial and natural disasters, etc. Therefore, remote sensing satellite data plays a key role in exercising the right to a safe and favorable environment.

**6.02.**    Since the usage of remote sensing data includes different steps, i.e. collection, access, distribution and sharing, each of which has its own special legal regime connected with national security, privacy, intellectual property rights, liability and court procedures, this research will be divided into two parts. The first part is devoted to an analysis of international and regional "hard" and "soft law" space treaties concerning the establishment of a legal regime for the collection and distribution of all types of remote sensing data. In the second part, the legal practice of using satellite images as evidence before international courts such as The International Court of Justice, The International Criminal Court and some practices in the sphere of national courts are explored. These parts reflect the gradualism of remote sensing service cycle and material, along with procedural aspects of its legal regulation.

# II.     International Regime for Creation and Utilization of Remote Sensing Data Enhances the Right to a Safe and Favorable Environment

**6.03.**    The root of legal regulation of all modern space activities is the Treaty on Principles Governing the Activities of States in the Exploration and Use of Outer Space, including the Moon and Other Celestial Bodies, 1967 (Outer Space Treaty). On the basis of these Principles, the collection and dissemination of all types of remote sensing data is carried out, namely: 1) exploration and use of outer space for the benefit and for the interests of all States; 2) recognition of outer space as a province of all mankind;

3) freedom for exploration and use of outer space on the basis of equality; 4) facilitate and encourage international collaboration (Article 1); 5) international responsibility of States for activities in outer space (Article 6).[1] Clearly it was recognized that the freedom of remotely sensing the Earth and collecting information requires international cooperation and dissemination of such collected information to all the sensed States that could possibly benefit from it. Later, these principles were reflected in the special "soft law" international act – UNGA Resolution 41/65 "Principles Relating to Remote Sensing of the Earth from Outer Space" (or Resolution 41/65), adopted in 1986. Specifically, the principles 2, 4 and 14 recall all of the mentioned freedoms.[2] It should be noted, however, that all these principles during the history of space activity were interpreted in different ways. As Ram Jakhu noted accessibility to data by the sensed State as well as the freedom of using and disseminating data gathered by a sensing State, ultimately depends on data policies adopted by the State concerned.[3] That is why he calls for a comprehensive understanding of these principles and paying closer attention to the text, namely: 1) common interests he recognizes as inclusive interest to all States, regardless of their status as the parties of the treaty; 2) province of mankind was interpreted as possession jurisdiction over all matters, related to the exploration and use of outer space, 3) and finally, he proves that freedom of space activity must be considered in light of equity of all sovereign states and admissibility of abuse and misuse of the rights.[4]

6.04. Resolution 41/65 establishes some special principles which derive from the Outer Space Treaty, these principles are: active consideration of the necessities of developing States, full and permanent sovereignty of all States and peoples over their own wealth and natural resources, and avoidance of conducting detrimental to the legitimate rights and interests of the sensed States. It reflected the balance between rights of the sensed State, which often has the status of a developing country with rich natural or other valuable resources and sensing State with

---

[1]   Treaty on Principles Governing the Activities of States in the Exploration and Use of Outer Space, including the Moon and Other Celestial Bodies, 1967 (Outer Space Treaty), United Nations publication, New York, 2002.

[2]   UNGA Resolution (1986) 41/65 "Principles Relating to Remote Sensing of the Earth from Outer Space", available at: http://www.unoosa.org/oosa/en/ourwork/spacelaw/principles/remote-sensing-principles.html (accessed on 03 December 2019).

[3]   Ram Jakhu, *International Law Regarding the Acquisition and Dissemination of Satellite Imagery*, 29(1/2) JOURNAL OF SPACE LAW 65-91 (2003).

[4]   Ram Jakhu, Isavella Vasilogeorgi, *The Fundamental Principles of Space Law and the Relevance of International Law, in* IN HEAVEN AS ON EARTH? THE INTERACTION OF PUBLIC INTERNATIONAL LAW ON THE LEGAL REGULATION OF OUTER SPACE, Institute of Air and Space Law, Cologne University, Cologne, Germany (Stephan Hobe and Steven Freeland eds. 2013).

technical capabilities for removed sensing of the Earth and extracting and using such resources. On this basis, the difficult questions of national security interests occur. Commercialization of space activity, including Earth`s remote sensing creates the additional issue of the remote sensing data price.

6.05.    The common access regime to the products of Earth`s remote sensing for the sensed states is based on non-discrimination and on reasonable cost terms. This regime was criticized in science as vague and unclear. It is evident from the examples of the questions: Is it discrimination to allow developing states better terms of satellite data access than to developed countries? Is it discrimination to allow satellite data access to allied states while refusing it to hostile ones? Is it discrimination to allow satellite data access to states that co-fund satellites on better terms than those which do not? Answering these questions allows us to make a conclusion about positive discrimination of developing States, which would most likely be the sensed States[5]. Therefore, these States have the rights on participation in remote sensing through establishing and operating data collection and storage stations and processing and interpretation facilities (principle 6), acquiring technical assistance (principle 7), request for the enter into consultations in order to make available opportunities for participation and to enhance the mutual benefits to be derived therefrom (principle 13). But the real access to the different types of space data depends on the willingness of sensing States that is grounded on their financial and security interests.

6.06.    Exceptions of the common regime of Principles Relating to Remote Sensing of the Earth from Outer Space are connected with the aim of protecting the Earth's natural environment; because the identification of information that is capable of averting any harm to the Earth's natural environment phenomenon is the reason for disclosing such information to States. Another reason for freely disclosing the information also concerns the protection of mankind from natural disasters. The States participating in remote sensing activities that have identified processed data and analyzed information in their possession that may be useful to States affected by natural disasters, or likely to be affected by impending natural disasters, have to transmit such data and information to States concerned as promptly as possible. It should be noted that in cases where there are both natural and artificial phenomenon, there is a duty to disclose

---

[5]    Frans G. von der Dunk, *European Satellite Earth Observation: Law, Regulations, Policies, Projects, and Programmes Space*, CYBER, AND TELECOMMUNICATIONS LAW PROGRAM FACULTY PUBLICATIONS, University of Nebraska – Lincoln 397-445 (2009).

Czech Yearbook of International Law®

information in the moment prior to harm. On the other, in cases of natural disasters, there is a duty to disclose information prior to the natural disaster, during its occurrence, and after it has taken place. But these provisions do not regulate cases of informational support for the elimination of consequences of natural disasters. Nevertheless, these provisions declared that the interest of the protection of environment and disaster management are higher than commercial interest. On the other hand, there are no sanctions for States that act differently.

6.07.  A mix of such legal regimes is reflected in the World Meteorological Organization's (WMO) Policy and Practice for the Exchange of Meteorological and Related Data and Products including Guidelines on Relationships in Commercial Meteorological Activities, approved by Resolution 40 (Cg-XII) in 1995. It is declared as a fundamental principle of the WMO broadening and enhancing the free and unrestricted international exchange of meteorological and related data and products. Herewith "free and unrestricted" means non-discriminatory and without charge, in turn "without charge" means at no more than the cost of reproduction and delivery, without charge for the data and products themselves[6]. Hence, all member States even in the crucial situations must pay for reproduction and delivery of such data and products and the positive discrimination of environmentally affected States is relative.

6.08.  Besides this, on the regional stage, international treaties were concluded. Special attention among them should be paid to Convention about transmission and use of Earth`s remote sensing data[7], adopted on 19 May 1978 and Charter on Cooperation to Achieve the Coordinated Use of Space Facilities in the Event of Natural or Technological Disasters[8], adopted on 20 October 2000.

6.09.  Before proceeding with the examination of these international acts, it is necessary to clarify one terminological aspect. Principles Relating to Remote Sensing of the Earth from Outer Space contain three different notions to explain the products of remote sensing activity, i.e. "primary data", "processed data"

---

[6]  WMO Policy and Practice for the Exchange of Meteorological and Related Data and Products including Guidelines on Relationships in Commercial Meteorological Activities, approved by Resolution 40 (Cg-XII) in 1995, available at: http://www.wmo.int/pages/prog/hwrp/documents/wmo_827_enCG-XII-Res40.pdf (accessed on 22 November 2019).

[7]  Конвенция о передаче и использовании данных дистанционного зондирования Земли из космоса, Москва, 19 May 1978, available at: https://zakon.rada.gov.ua/laws/show/995_498/conv/print (accessed on 22 November 2019).

[8]  Charter On Cooperation To Achieve The Coordinated Use Of Space Facilities In The Event Of Natural Or Technological Disasters Rev.3 (25/4/2000).2., available at: https://disasterscharter.org/web/guest/text-of-the-charter (accessed on 22 November 2019).

and "analyzed information", but in both of the supra regional international acts, only two notions of "space data" (Earth remote sensing data) and "information" were mentioned. Access to each of this type of remote sensing data has its own legal regime. But, legal regimes of acquiring such types of data are not extremely different, neither in Principles Relating to Remote Sensing of the Earth from Outer Space, or in Charter on Cooperation to Achieve the Coordinated Use of Space Facilities in the Event of Natural or Technological Disasters. Convention about transmission and use of Earth`s remote sensing data also reflects different physical characteristics and functional purposes of these kinds of remote sensing products, namely in Article 4, access to the data with resolution better than 50 meters is prohibited, at the same time as in Article 5, access to the information about natural resources and economic potential is prohibited. Therefore, on the international level there are no significant distinctions between raw data and processed data or analyzed information. For the protection of the environmental rights, the States supply the most appropriate information for these aims (Principles 10, 11 of Principles Relating to Remote Sensing of the Earth from Outer Space and Article 4.5 of Charter). But, on the national level, access to the different types of remote sensing data creates significant expenses. In particular, raw data consists of the sensed data that has not been transformed in any way whereas remote sensing product refers to any data or image that is created from transforming raw data in any way. Prohibiting the dissemination of raw data is based on the fact that it contains the potential to be used in many different ways; this rationale is undermined by other practical requirements. Although an entity in control of raw data has the ability to transform that data into a variety of different products – and while this, in and of itself, can be harmful in the wrong hands – the reality is that processing and transforming this raw data requires uncommon, technical expertise. Remote sensing products, on the other hand, are the result of transforming raw data into a useable form by adding new information and, unlike raw data, comprehending and using remote sensing products does not require special expertise[9]. Thus, differentiation of the remote sensing data is important for commercial and security aims, but it does not matter for enhancing ecological rights. Namely, for this aim it is necessary to supply the most

---

[9]    Ram S. Jakhu, Aram Daniel Kerkonian (2017). Independent Review of the Remote Sensing Space Systems Act. Institute of Air and Space Law Faculty of Law McGill University, available at: https://international.gc.ca/arms-armes/assets/pdfs/2017_review_of_remote_sensing_space_systems_act.pdf (accessed on 22 November 2019).

appropriate data as quickly as possible. At the same time, the parallel existence of a three-tier and two-tier system of remote system data is adversely influencing the transmission of remote sensing data between different States. Therefore, we should agree with R. Jakhu who claimed that removing the distinction between raw data and remote sensing products is feasible from a security standpoint[10].

**6.10.** The first treaty was concluded by States of the socialist block for five years with the possibility of prolongation. Nowadays it is binding just formally, de facto it is not being enforced. The interest of its provisions is stipulated by high respect to the rights of sensed State. Namely, according to Articles 4th and 5th of this Convention, any type of remote sensing data: firstly, is not heard; secondly, is not transmitted without explicit consent of sensed State and thirdly, cannot be used to cause harm to said State. By the way, there were no ecological guarantees through the use of remote sensing data, except protecting said data about the natural resources of sensed State. The aim of this act was not connected with ecological interests, only with protection of other types of national security, i.e. economic, military etc.

**6.11.** A very different mechanism was drafted in the Charter. The general principles of international cooperation and dissemination of the information collected to all the sensed States which might benefit from it have been taken seriously by States with remote sensing capabilities, and many of them are taking part in this Charter, which provides a unified system of space data acquisition and delivery to those affected by natural or man-made disasters[11]. The Charter establishes a set of cooperation mechanisms between space agencies and space system operators for the use of space facilities to pursue: a) the data supply, providing a basis for critical information for the anticipation and management of potential crises; b) participation by means of data, information and services resulting from the exploitation of the space facilities in organization of emergency assistance or reconstruction and subsequent operations (Article 2). They are executed by the means of: 1) maintaining an up-to-date list of space facilities under the management of private and public operators; 2) designing scenarios for each type of crisis, which are subject to regular updating and are the basis for an action plan in the event of crisis identification; 3) the crisis situation identification; 4) implementation of an action plan in a crisis

---

[10]  *Ibid.*, at 9.
[11]  Annelie Schoenmaker (2011) Community remote sensing legal issues. Security World Foundation's official site, available at: https://swfound.org/media/62081/schoenmaker_paper_community_remote_sensing_legal_issues_final.pdf (accessed on 22 November 2019).

Czech Yearbook of International Law®

situation, which includes, for example, access to data archives, merging of data, routing the information to users etc. (Article 4). The mechanism of application of this Charter is as follows: the authorities and bodies concerned in a country affected by disaster (beneficiary bodies) should request the interventions of the Parties of the Charter (associated bodies) in order to obtain data and information on a major disaster. In some circumstances, cooperating bodies, namely European Union, the Bureau for the Coordination of Humanitarian Affairs and other recognized national and international organizations, may also request data in the event of a disaster. Then, associated bodies: prepare an archive and its acquisition plan, that is submitted to the relevant space agency, who will set up their satellite accordingly if it is possible to meet the request; coordinates the delivery of maps and takes the data provided by member agencies and interprets this, assessing what they see from the satellites and compiling it into value added products[12]. During the existing mechanisms of this Charter, 597 activations were conducted. The last one was made for the aid to Plurinational State of Bolivia on 08 February 2019, which was affected by a landslide.[13]

6.12. So, the sensed States without any or sufficient remote sensing facilities have a wide range of guarantees to protection of their environment by the means of remote sensing facilities of sensing States. In this context, it is to be noted that, unlike the legal mechanism of Principles Relating to Remote Sensing of the Earth from Outer Space, all these activities of Charter`s Parties are voluntary, thus, no funds are being exchanged between them. Furthermore, the term "crisis" means the period immediately before, during or immediately after a natural or technological disaster, in course of which warning, emergency or rescue operations take place.

6.13. But, it is a lot harder than it seems. There is a common characteristic of Convention about transmission and use of Earth`s remote sensing data and Charter on Cooperation to Achieve the Coordinated Use of Space Facilities in the Event of Natural or Technological Disasters. Both of them are based on the principles of the Outer Space Treaty, namely on the principle of international responsibility of the states for national activities in outer space. That means that each State Party of such international acts adopts their own national mechanisms

---

[12]    Activating the Charter. The International Charter`s Space and Major Disasters official site, available at: https://disasterscharter.org/web/guest/how-the-charter-works (accessed on 22 November 2019).

[13]    Landslide in Bolivia. The International Charter`s Space and Major Disasters official site, available at: https://disasterscharter.org/web/guest/activations/-/article/landslide-in-bolivia-plurinational-state-of-activation-597- (accessed on 22 November 2019).

for regulating activity of their operators. One of the Charter's founding States, Canada, in 2000, entered into a bilateral Agreement Concerning Operation of Commercial Remote Sensing Satellite Systems with the United States to regulate the private remote sensing activities. The main idea of this act is to keep control over the private remote sensing activities by each State even after the commercialization of the industry, so as to protect the shared national security and foreign policy interests of both States. According to Annex I of this Agreement, the owner, operator or registered entity shall make available to the government of any country, including Canada, data acquired by its system concerning the territory under the jurisdiction of such a government (sensed state) in accordance with the United Nations A/RES/41/65 Principles Relating to Remote Sensing of the Earth from Space.[14] However, such data shall not be provided to the sensed state if its uncontrolled release is determined to be detrimental to Canada's national security and foreign affairs interests. It seems that this rule intends to implement the above mentioned above Charter. As R. Jakhu noted, given the sensitivity of the data collected by remote sensing systems, the Minister of Foreign Affairs of Canada has special powers to request priority access to data collected by a remote sensing space system or to order an interruption of service, should it be necessary to protect national security, national defence, foreign policy interests and/or upholding Canada's international obligations. In granting licenses, the Minister of Foreign Affairs of Canada has the authority to impose conditions or restrictions on the operation of remote sensing satellite systems, as well as on the reception, storage and dissemination of data collected by such systems[15]. Therefore, even if it will be necessary for the sensed State, all satellites of Canada under some circumstances, will not supply the remote sensing data to a State due to, for example, protection of national security, national defence, foreign policy interests. This little example mirrors the common balance between rights of sensed States, particularly their highly valued ecological rights and different types of national interests of the State which exercises the jurisdiction and control overall the remote sensing activities of their private operators. Extension of the free of charge mechanisms for the protection

---

[14] Agreement Between the Government of Canada and the Government of the United States of America Concerning the Operation of Commercial Remote Sensing Satellite Systems, E103522 - CTS 2000 No. 14, available at: https://www.treaty-accord.gc.ca/text-texte.aspx?id=103522 (accessed on 22 November 2019).
[15] Ram S. Jakhu, Aram Daniel Kerkonian (2017). Independent Review of the Remote Sensing Space Systems Act. Institute of Air and Space Law Faculty of Law McGill University, available at: https://international.gc.ca/arms-armes/assets/pdfs/2017_review_of_remote_sensing_space_systems_act.pdf (accessed on 22 November 2019).

of the right to a favorable and safe environment for people all around the world through remote sensing data, regardless of capabilities to operate the remote sensing facilities, does not make this priority higher. On the one hand, the principle of international responsibility of States for national activities in outer space allows a common agreement between States to be reached and incentivizes persons within their jurisdiction to share remote sensing data on a free of charge basis. On the other hand, such principle makes all private activity dependent on the national interests of the States and consequently, access to the sensing data by the sensed State depends on their geopolitical relationships with sensing States. Fortunately, nowadays more and more of States have gained such status, albeit with different opportunities.

## III.    Remote Sensing Data as Evidence in International Environmental Litigations

6.14.    The start of remote sensing data usage in international courts litigations takes place in the 1980s. The first litigations were connected to delimitation of national borders, which were marked by rivers and other creations of nature. Such types of court disputes are not directly related to the environment, but they nonetheless give us some legal conclusions, which essentially help us to solve the case. For example, in the case of Burkina Faso versus the Republic of Mali, the International Court of Justice stated that texts and maps possess different value and reliability[16]. Thus, the court questioned the remote sensing data in the context of different ways of their interpretation.

6.15.    The second kind of lawsuit is connected to the protection of the environment during and after military conflicts. Remote sensing data allows obtaining information about territories, which may be closed due to military conflicts. The most well-known case in this context is the case between Islamic Republic of Iran and United States of America, which was connected to the oil platforms and polluting the Persian Gulf. During oral proceedings, the United States presented the missile site photographs that were produced from original photographic data captured by U.S. intelligence satellite and the testimony of satellite imagery experts who had explained and confirmed the substance of this photo-evidence to the Court. The need for the experts` explanations can be easily explained by the

---

[16]    Case concerning the frontier dispute (Burkina Faso/Republic of Mali): International Court of Justice, available at: https://www.icj-cij.org/files/case-related/69/069-19861222-JUD-01-00-EN.pdf (accessed on 22 November 2019).

Czech Yearbook of International Law®

fact that U.S. analysts based their assessment of Iranian missile facilities on the original photographic data, which was provided by the analysts with greater detail and clarity than can be seen in the photographs that accompany this submission, but national security reasons didn't allow to submit the original photographic data to the Court. Thus, the United States had reduced the resolution of the original images using computer image processing techniques.[17] As it was mentioned above, remote space data is divided into two types at least: raw data and analyzed images. Only analyzed images can be used as court evidence. This evidence has different characteristics, which depends on data analyzing. Understanding the military issue of such lawsuits and the creation of such evidences with the help of space facilities, such data can be modified. This is why the credibility of such images cannot be guaranteed. This affects the impartiality of the court's decision. An example of this problem's solution is given by the Office of the Prosecutors of the International Criminal Court, which in the 2016-2018 years Strategic Plan stated that it had invested in internal expertise in the form of 'cyber-investigators and analysts experienced in online investigations, which had improved its ability to 'identify, forensically collect and process this new evidence'. However, the Office of the Prosecutors also noted that strategic partnerships with the law enforcement community, non-governmental organizations (NGOs) and academic institutions were crucial for keeping up with the developments in the field. Going forward, the Office of the Prosecutors outlined a strategy that combines internal capacity-building through recruiting experts and investing in specialized equipment, staff training and partnerships, in addition to increasing the use of technology for presenting its cases in the Court.[18] In this case the Space Detective Agency should be mentioned, which is a Spin-off Company that is specialized on using remote sensing data in evidential context, detect illegal wastes, tackle and deter environmental crimes, and conduct historical and environmental sites analysis.[19] The last activity is crucial in cases about environment's pollution during armed conflicts, especially in the context of Programme of Resolution 3\1 (06 December 2017) adopted by

---

[17]  Case concerning oil platforms (*Islamic Republic of Iran* v. *United States of America*) International Court of Justice, available at: https://www.icj-cij.org/files/case-related/90/8632.pdf (accessed on 22 November 2019).

[18]  Evidence Matters in ICC Trials: An International Bar Association International Criminal Court & International Criminal Law Program report providing a comparative perspective on selected evidence matters of current importance in ICC trial practice, August 2016, 72 et. 21.

[19]  Air and Space evidence: The World's First Space Detective Agency official site, available at: http://www.space-evidence.net/what-we-do (accessed on 22 November 2019).

the United Nations Environment Assembly, which concerned the pollution mitigation and control in areas affected by armed conflict or terrorism. This program stressed the need to raise greater international awareness of environmental damage and pollution resulting from armed conflicts or terrorism and to take appropriate measures to minimize and control pollution in situations of armed conflicts or terrorism.[20] Unfortunately, this problem happened in Ukraine. The experts of Conflict and Environmentally Observatory had made the conclusion that data collection during conflicts can provide opportunities for dialogue between warring parties, especially in the case of Ukraine. It appears to be a growing appetite for cooperation on common environmental risks caused by the conflict between civil society organizations and local administrations on both sides of the line of contact. These are opportunities that may be lost after the delay in environmental data collection while the conflicts take place.[21]

**6.16.** The third kind of court cases with remote sensing data usage is connected to environmental issues, i.e. between Algeria and Uruguay about huge concentration of chlorophyll; between Costa Rica and Nicaragua about environmentally harmful activity. As C. Candelmo and V. Nardone wrote, in lawsuits dealing with human rights protection, for example with environmental rights, the courts have to think of the compatibility with human rights principles, when they use such evidences in national legal proceedings, but not to judge the reasons of the admissibility and value of GPS tracking and satellite imagery only.[22] Abusing the right to access the information through remote sensing can lead to the right to privacy being violated, but sometimes such a threat is necessary. For example, when indigenous people try to restore the right to live on the lands of their origin, which has close connection to their life traditions and which was lost due to the actions of government, just like San community that lives within their traditional territory in north-central Namibia. Such community collects all kind of information about boundaries of their territory, including data from Google Maps with images

---

[20] Resolution 3\1 on pollution mitigation and control in areas affected by armed conflict or terrorism, adopted by the United Nations Environment Assembly of the United Nations Environment Programme 06 December 2017, available at: http://www.trwn.org/resolution-unea3-pollution-mitigation-and-control-in-areas-affected-by-armed-conflict-or-terrorism/ (accessed on 22 November 2019).

[21] Monitoring environmental risks and damage during conflicts is vital, the case of Ukraine highlights how it can be improved, Conflict and Environmentally Observatory, 22 December 2017, available at: https://ceobs.org/monitoring-the-monitors-studying-the-ukraine-conflicts-environmental-impact/ (accessed on 22 November 2019).

[22] Claudia Candelmo, Valentina Nardone, *Satellite Evidence in Human Rights Cases: Merits and Shortcomings Merits and Shortcomings*, 1(1) PEACE HUMAN RIGHTS GOVERNANCE 87-113, 101 (2017).

of private lands, which were previously in their ownership.[23] The use of the remote sensing data as evidence in court and its compatibility with right to the privacy is treated differently depending on the State. While Germany declared Google Street View as legal, Swiss courts ruled that Google must take action to protect privacy by blurring out faces and license plates numbers. In some States, the term "privacy" is not even translated directly and is not protected as a right as such.[24] Another example is Belgian policy in this sphere: the Privacy Commission of this country decided that the use of satellite images to detect potential breaches of planning law counts as proactive investigation, and is therefore prohibited in principle. Satellite images must comply with privacy law if they are used in non-proactive investigation. For example, their details must be no greater than is needed for the specific objective of the case, they should not be kept longer than necessary and they must be destroyed once they have no further use. However, they pose no legal problem if they are used to deter crimes or to trigger remedial administrative sanctions. Satellite images would also be permissible in proactive investigations into environmental crimes conducted by criminal organizations, such as illegal waste trafficking.[25] Regardless, the States` approach in this sphere, rapid development of space and digital services affects the courts` procedures and the assessment of the evidences regarding the right to privacy.

6.17. Therefore, there are three categories of judicial cases, dealing with the protection of environmental rights with the help of remote sensing data. Such data is used more frequently as evidence regardless of skepticism from judges. Furthermore, a special institutional infrastructure is created. All these issues show that the remote sensing data collection and its dissemination are compatible with human rights, including the right to privacy.

---

[23] Jeremie Gilbert, Ben Begbie-Clench, *"Mapping For Rights": Indigenous Peoples, Litigation And Legal Empowerment*, 1(13) ERASMUS LAW REVIEW 9-10 (2018).

[24] Annelie Schoenmaker (2011) Community remote sensing legal issues. Security World Foundation`s official site, available at: https://swfound.org/media/62081/schoenmaker_paper_community_remote_sensing_legal_issues_final.pdf (accessed on 22 November 2019).

[25] Satellite images as evidence in court: legal obstacles to their use in environmental investigations: Environmental Compliance Assurance and Combating Environmental Crime in European Commission, July 2016 Thematic Issue 56, available at: http://ec.europa.eu/environment/integration/research/newsalert/pdf/satellites_as_evidence_in_court_legal_obstacles_to_their_use_56si8_en.pdf (accessed on 22 November 2019).

## IV.    Conclusion

6.18.    One of the main environmental rights is the right to access to information about the environment, and the remote sensing is a simple way to obtain such data. On the one hand, the remote sensing helps us to understand changes of the environment, natural and artificial disasters and therefore to make reasonable decisions. On the other hand, the restricted information about hard-to-reach territories, objects and activities can be provided by the remote sensing. This shows the high value of the remote sensing data in the environment protection mission.

6.19.    Such tendencies are mirrored by the material and procedural legal basis for remote sensing activity. It was presumed in this paper, that such common principle of international space law, as international responsibility for the national space activity, affects the dissemination of remote sensing data regime in two contrary ways. First, this principle allows a common agreement between States to be reached and incentivizes persons under their jurisdiction to share remote sensing data on free of charge basis. Second, such principle makes all private activity dependent on the national interests of the States and therefore, access to remote sensing data by the State depends on their geopolitical relationships with sensed States.

6.20.    Using the remote sensing data in court as evidence requires compliance with different requirements, including probative value, adequacy, sufficiency and its compatibility with human rights. Fortunately, this evidence is being rapidly developed now, thanks to constant development of court practice, and creating the infrastructure for taking this evidence into account to make legitimate and reasonable judgments.

| | |

### Summaries

FRA    [*Garantir le droit à un environnement sûr et favorable grâce aux données satellites*]
*Une des mesures disponibles pour atténuer l'impact des changements de l'environnement mondial est l'observation de la Terre par satellite. Les données satellites peuvent être utilisées pour contrôler le respect des conventions internationales en matière d'environnement, ainsi que pour régler des litiges devant des juridictions internationales. Toutefois, certaines sources de droit ne sont pas suffisamment complètes pour remédier*

*aux problèmes actuels. L'auteur du présent article a examiné les conventions internationales, les résolutions et les traités régionaux en matière d'espace, ainsi que leurs interactions avec les normes nationales, afin de voir comment les intérêts visant la protection de l'environnement de « l'État concerné » sont conciliés avec les intérêts des autres États, et notamment les intérêts de sécurité nationale des États qui exercent le contrôle des activités d'exploration par satellite menées par leurs exploitants privés. Ces données sont accessibles à tous les États soucieux de protéger leur environnement ; certains États peuvent, toutefois, refuser de fournir ces données pour sauvegarder leurs propres intérêts, comme par exemple la sécurité nationale. Les données satellites sont utilisées comme moyens de preuve contribuant à une prise de décision raisonnable. Il convient de noter que le terme « données satellites » est utilisé dans le présent article comme englobant tout produit d'exploration à distance, dont notamment les « données brutes », les « images numériques », les « informations géologiques », etc.*

CZE  **[*Zajištění práva na bezpečné a příznivé životní prostředí s využitím údajů ze satelitního průzkumu*]**
*Globální změny životního prostředí mají být zmírněny pomocí komplexních opatření, například pozorováním Země s využitím satelitního průzkumu. Satelitní údaje lze využít ke kontrole dodržování mezinárodních dohod o životním prostředí a za účelem řešení sporů u mezinárodních soudů. Některé právní prameny však aktuální problémy neřeší dostatečně. Autorka prostudovala mezinárodní dohody týkající se kosmického prostoru, rezoluce, regionální smlouvy a jejich interakci s předpisy vnitrostátního původu ve snaze nalézt rovnováhu mezi zájmy na ochraně životního prostředí „dotčeného státu" a zájmy ostatních států, například národními bezpečnostními zájmy států, které vykonávají pravomoc a kontrolu nad veškerou činností satelitního průzkumu prováděnou jejich soukromými provozovateli. K těmto satelitním údajům však mají přístup všechny státy za účelem zajištění jejich zájmů na ochraně životního prostředí – ostatní státy mohou poskytnutí těchto dat odmítnout z důvodu svých vlastních zájmů, například bezpečnosti státu a zájmů jiných. Údaje ze satelitního průzkumu jsou využívány jako důkazní prostředky pro potřeby přijímání rozumných soudních rozhodnutí. Je potřeba podotknout, že v tomto článku používá autorka pojem „údaje ze satelitního průzkumu" ve smyslu produktů dálkového průzkumu*

*jakéhokoli druhu, čímž se míní zejména „nezpracovaná data",*
*„digitální snímky", „geologické informace" atd.*

| | |

POL [***Zagwarantowanie prawa do bezpiecznego i korzystnego***
***środowiska z wykorzystaniem danych z obserwacji***
***satelitarnych***]
*Z artykułu wynika, że poszerzanie praw państw obserwowanych*
*i umożliwienie im dostępu do informacji na temat środowiska*
*naturalnego na gruncie prawa międzynarodowego nie wyklucza*
*nadrzędności praw krajów obserwujących do określenia*
*warunków takiego dostępu. Wykorzystanie tego typu informacji*
*jako dowodów sądowych jest zgodne z prawami człowieka.*

DEU [*Gewährleistung des Rechts auf eine sichere Umwelt mithilfe*
*von Daten aus der Satellitenforschung*]
*Der Beitrag kommt zu dem Schluss, dass die Ausweitung*
*der Rechte der untersuchten Staaten auf den Zugriff zu*
*Umweltinformationen durch das internationale Recht*
*die Priorität der Rechte der untersuchten Staaten auf die*
*Bestimmungen der Zugriffsregelungen nicht ausschließt. Die*
*Nutzung dieser Informationen als forensische Beweise ist mit den*
*Menschenrechten vereinbar.*

RUS [*Обеспечение права на безопасную и благоприятную*
*окружающую среду с использованием космических*
*данных дистанционного зондирования Земли*]
*В статье делается вывод о том, что расширение за*
*международным правом прав зондируемых стран на*
*доступ до экологической информации не исключает*
*главенствующую роль прав зондирующих стран*
*устанавливать режимы такого доступа. Использование*
*такой информации как судебных доказательств является*
*совместимым с правами человека.*

ESP [*Uso de los datos obtenidos por satélite en la protección del*
*derecho al medio ambiente seguro y adecuado*]
*El artículo concluye que la ampliación de los derechos de los*
*países objeto de la observación a los datos referentes al medio*
*ambiente recurriendo al derecho internacional es compatible con*
*la prioridad concedida a los países que realizan la observación*

*con respeto al régimen de acceso a esos datos. El uso de los mismos como pruebas forenses es compatible con los derechos humanos.*

| | |

## Bibliography

Claudia Candelmo, Valentina Nardone, *Satellite Evidence in Human Rights Cases: Merits and Shortcomings Merits and Shortcomings*, 1(1) PEACE HUMAN RIGHTS GOVERNANCE 87-113, 101 (2017).

Frans G. von der Dunk, *European Satellite Earth Observation: Law, Regulations, Policies, Projects, and Programmes Space*, CYBER, AND TELECOMMUNICATIONS LAW PROGRAM FACULTY PUBLICATIONS, University of Nebraska - Lincoln 397-445 (2009).

Jeremie Gilbert, Ben Begbie-Clench, *"Mapping For Rights": Indigenous Peoples, Litigation And Legal Empowerment*, 1(13) ERASMUS LAW REVIEW 9-10 (2018).

Ram Jakhu, *International Law Regarding the Acquisition and Dissemination of Satellite Imagery*, 29(1/2) JOURNAL OF SPACE LAW 65-91 (2003).

Ram Jakhu, Isavella Vasilogeorgi, *The Fundamental Principles of Space Law and the Relevance of International Law, in* IN HEAVEN AS ON EARTH? THE INTERACTION OF PUBLIC INTERNATIONAL LAW ON THE LEGAL REGULATION OF OUTER SPACE, Institute of Air and Space Law, Cologne University, Cologne, Germany (Stephan Hobe and Steven Freeland eds. 2013).

Karel Klíma

# The Concept of the European Legal State as an Existing Human Rights Protection System in Europe

**Key words:**
*Human rights and freedoms | European Court of the Human Rights | Court of the Justice of the EU | constitutional courts | judicial law creativity | case law | a modern elements in a judicial activity | European legal state*

Czech Yearbook of International Law®

**Abstract** | *The continual decision-making of the Court of Justice of the EU and the European Court of the Human Rights have created a mode of the constitutional creativity on a territorial framework of continental Europe. This activity influenced the activity of the constitutional courts of the member States and constitutional systems. The comparison of this judicial case law activity and the judicial and procedural 'out going' extensions can reveal a mode of law modernization as an element of the modification of the quasi-constitutional position of the European courts or the national constitutional courts. It is also a question as to whether the system of the Council of Europe and also of the European Union is creating a new model of the European legal State as a new constitutional value and also as a real system of the protection of human rights.*

**Prof. et Doc (mult.) JUDr. Karel Klíma, CSc., dr. hab.**, is a University Professor specializing in constitutional law, the theory of the public power, and European law. He is also head of the Department of Legal Specializations and Public Administration at the Metropolitan University in Prague. Between 1995 and 2004, he was a member of the Executive committee of the International Association of Constitutional Law (IACL). He is also a member of the World Jurist Association Board of Governors where he holds the office of WJA President for the World Association of Law Professors (WALP). E-mail: karel.klima@ mup.cz

| | |

# I.   Introduction

7.01.   The European continent is a place where the history of human rights as a constitutional phenomenon emerged. This history is based on the philosophical thinking of Greek philosophers, the Roman law phenomenon of private law, and the values of the Christian respect for an individual. Other building blocks include the development of the concept of parliamentarianism, the development of English constitutionality, the French Revolution, as well as the influence of the developing American constitutionality (after the USA was founded in 1775). The European system of human rights is an accomplished contemporary value in terms of its inherent internationalization across Europe. This system is represented by the co-existence of national constitutional systems and a double European order, specifically in the systems of the Council of Europe and of the European Union.[1] Indeed, these two systems constitute systems of directly enforceable law of an internationally contractual nature, i.e. systems of their enforceable protection in the Member States. The protection of human rights and freedoms is one of the bases and inseparable components of constitutional democracy, and if the protection of human rights and freedoms is the fundamental 'assignment', especially in the Council of Europe system, then this concept must be classified as a European constitutional value.[2]

# II.   Whether and How the Concept of the 'European Legal State' can be Inferred

7.02.   If my hypothesis that the system of enforcement of the protection of human rights from the plateau of European authorities can serve as a basis for the conclusion that a potential concept of the European legal state exists, we must specifically examine the contractual system of the Council of Europe. Nonetheless, the European Union, primarily the expanding case law of the Court of Justice of the EU (formerly the ECJ), is also a system which cultivates public administration of the Member States from the legal perspective.[3] However, it is primarily the Council of Europe

---

[1]   For more details, see in: KAREL KLÍMA, LISTINA A JEJÍ REALIZACE V SYSTÉMU VEŘEJNÉHO NOVÉHO SOUKROMÉHO PRÁVA (TITLE IN TRANSLATION: THE CHARTER AND ITS IMPLEMENTATION IN THE SYSTEM OF PUBLIC AND NEW PRIVATE LAW), Prague: Wolters Kluwer (2014), et. 11-16.

[2]   See the author's commentary in the sub-chapter 'Common constitutional values of the Member States as the source of the European constitutionalism,' in: KAREL KLÍMA, EVROPSKÉ PRÁVO (TITLE IN TRANSLATION: EUROPEAN LAW), Plzeň: Aleš Čeněk (2011), at 38 et seq.

[3]   Cf. KAREL KLÍMA, EVROPSKÉ PRÁVO (TITLE IN TRANSLATION: EUROPEAN LAW), Plzeň: Aleš Čeněk (2011), at 319 et seq.

system which operates on the basis of the Convention for the Protection of Human Rights and Fundamental Freedoms, is based on the effect which serves the individual and on direct applicability of substantive and procedural law (especially the Convention). Moreover that law is interpreted as well as created through its own court, i.e. the European Court of Human Rights. One may refer to a constitutional mechanism *sui generis*, i.e. human rights constitutionality, because the Court renders judgments against States on the basis of orders which hold the States responsible for breaching the Convention and liable for compensation. One may refer to a European 'federal supreme' or, as applicable, a *quasi*-constitutional court *sui generis*.[4]

7.03.    Let us start with the premise that the basic element of the concept of the legal State is the statement that a public authority, primarily an administrative authority or a judicial institution, is bound by the law, especially the Constitution and statutes. This is of particular importance in decisions regarding any personal, political and other rights of individuals and legal persons. Pilot and generally binding court judgments are originally an English historical phenomenon (and with an additional American version) but these have gradually become a modern component of the continental European legal culture. Indeed, as mentioned above, their two main proponents are now the two lines of 'European law', i.e. case law of the Council of Europe and case law of the European Union, followed by constitutional or other courts of the Member States in both systems.

7.04.    Special consideration must be reserved for the concept of the 'right to a fair trial' which the European Court of Human Rights has shaped into a conceptual judicial doctrine with a multilayer interpretation. In turn, this has become intertwined with the legal systems of the Council of Europe Member States as a result of the practice of, inter alia, their constitutional and supreme courts. However, the crucial issue is that, as a result thereof, the European-continental judicial culture of 'written law' was faced with the need to define its relation to the new source of law – probably running parallel to statutes. We hypothetically acknowledge this fact and we are able to explain and accept the creation of law by European judicial institutions as well as 'national' supreme judicial institutions as judicial legislation,[5]

---

[4]    *Ibid.*, at. 460 et seq.

[5]    It is a generally known fact that the scope of the rights and freedoms enshrined in the Convention is narrower than in the Universal Declaration of Human Rights and Freedoms but the case law of the European Court of Human Rights has expanded the protection of rights to include the second generation of human rights, i.e. economic and social rights; for more details, see in: JIŘÍ KMEC, DAVID KOSAŘ, JAN KRATOCHVÍL, MICHAL BOBEK, EVROPSKÁ ÚMLUVA O LIDSKÝCH PRÁVECH. KOMENTÁŘ (TITLE IN TRANSLATION: EUROPEAN CONVENTION ON HUMAN RIGHTS. COMMENTARY),

Czech Yearbook of International Law®

often of constitutional nature.[6] Moreover, the European Court of Human Rights handles applications or complaints lodged by non-State individuals and entities against the Member States which are targeted at decisions adopted by their judicial authorities, invoking interference with human rights and freedoms enshrined in the European Convention. Hence, this type of judicial control or protection is a type of a protection of 'super constitutionalism.'

7.05.    Considering its simultaneous jurisdictional activity which develops the value context of the Convention through precedents, it may be classified as a European system of constitutional super-control. The Council of Europe has made numerous decisions and adopted many normative documents which can be classified as declarations, or charters. The contents and nature of these declarations concern both substantive law and procedural law. However, the contents of these declarations and conventions have principal features significantly identical to the constitutional laws of contemporary constitutional democracies all over the world. The reason is that these systems mostly involve parliamentary forms of government or presidential systems (e.g. the USA) or an otherwise original system (e.g. Switzerland) providing, however, they regulate rights and freedoms listed in the standard catalogue recognized from the perspective of international law.[7] Indeed, each international agreement after World War II which provided for rights and freedoms has become part of the international potential of laws regulating the standard of human rights and freedoms. The years after World War II have therefore witnessed the emergence of a common international constitutional-type value system.[8]

## III.    The System of Applications Lodged with the European Court of Human Rights

7.06.    The Council of Europe phenomenon is undoubtedly accelerating and increasing its international value because its procedural structure is based on the opportunity open to natural and legal persons to initiate Court proceedings by filing an application. These applications challenge decisions made by public

---

Prague: C. H. Beck (1st ed. 2012), et. 98.

[6]    For more details, see in: KAREL KLÍMA, O PRÁVU ÚSTAVNÍM (TITLE IN TRANSLATION: ABOUT CONSTITUTIONAL LAW), Prague: Wolters Kluwer (2012), et. 120 et seq.

[7]    See JOSEF BLAHOŽ, VLADIMÍR BALAŠ, KAREL KLÍMA, SROVNÁVACÍ ÚSTAVNÍ PRÁVO (TITLE IN TRANSLATION: COMPARATIVE CONSTITUTIONAL LAW), Prague: Wolters Kluwer (5th ed. 2015), et. 182 et seq.

[8]    For more details, see in: KAREL KLÍMA, ÚSTAVNÍ PRÁVO (TITLE IN TRANSLATION: CONSTITUTIONAL LAW), Plzeň: Aleš Čeněk (4th ed. 2010), at 173 et seq.

authorities of a Member State and thereby trigger the State's liability under international law.[9] The European Court of Human Rights then examines whether these decisions conform to the ideological values of the Convention. Hence, the European Court of Human Rights reviews the compliance of the decisions with constitutional law, usually rendered by the last national judicial authority which closes the court proceedings and the application of the 'right to a fair trial' within the respective Member State. This court is sometimes the Supreme Court, and sometimes only the Constitutional Court. Such a review is subsidiary and 'ordinate' to the constitutionality of the Member States.

7.07. The system of applications under the Convention has the nature of actions for a determination, i.e. the application seeks determination and declaration of an infringement of the Convention. Hence, if the judicial system operates on the basis of substantive and procedural provisions of the Convention, draws from and interprets the Convention through the decisions of its own court, it may be referred to as a constitutional mechanism *sui generis.*

7.08. The European Court of Human Rights adjudicates with special emphasis on the articulation of judicial doctrines. The case law of the European Court of Human Rights influences the legal systems in the individual Member States, primarily by being reflected in various departments of the national legal system. The case law in itself forms a monolithic legal system based on the multiple categories of law. Regarding constitutional-law there are domains concerning the division of powers, the legal state (Rechtsstaat), the liability of public officials and authorities, the independence of the judiciary, and the right to a fair trial. In terms of administrative law there is case law on liability for acts within the framework of a civil service relationship, and forcible interventions by authorities. Regarding criminal law there is case law on classical principles of criminal law including *nulla poena sine lege, nullum crimen sine lege*, and the presumption of innocence. Finally, there is law on the organization of the judiciary and the implementation of specific procedural principles including the equality of arms, the equal standing of the parties, the right to a defense, and the right to appeal. The Court also opens categories of private law whenever the Court develops the understanding of private life, the freedom

---

9    Concerning the developments in the Council of Europe as the control system for the protection of human rights in Europe, see in: BOŻENA GRONOWSKA, EUROPEJSKI TRYBUNAL PRAW CZLOWIEKA W POSZUKIWANIU EFEKTYWNEJ OCHRONY PRAW JEDNOTKI, Toruń (2011), at 34 et seq.

of thought, the protection of the family, the protection of media freedom and the protection of ownership.[10]

## IV.  Multilevel Constitutionalism as a Multilevel Legal State

7.09.　The analytic and synthetic activities of constitutional law allows us to organize a textbook system of *case law*, and decisions of the European Court of Human Rights.[11] The overall concept of the case law thus primarily represents a certain concept of the European model of the legal State and, consequently, the European dimension of constitutional and legal systems of the Member States.[12]

7.10.　This primarily involves the global concept of the rule of law which means that there are certain premises, criteria and principles of how to approach an assessment of the conduct of States and State authorities, primarily courts, State administration authorities and law enforcement authorities. These represent doctrinal concepts of judicial interpretation of substantive and procedural law. From this perspective, the Convention is a 'living document' because the evolving interpretation employed by the European Court of Human Rights is thereby improved. A good example is the concept of permitted restrictions of the rights and freedoms guaranteed under the Convention in the form of the so-called limitation clauses.[13]

7.11.　From the perspective of the relation of the Council of Europe system and, as the case may be, the parallel European Union system and the constitutional systems of the Member States, one may argue that all of their powers are subject to certain regulations. These include the legislative power represented by parliaments being bound by substantive and procedural law under Article 6 of the Convention in the Council of Europe system. This means that the problem of legislative excesses, if any, committed by national parliaments may be subject to double control, consisting of control exercised by national constitutional (or supreme) courts and control exercised by

---

[10]　For more details, see the concept of judgements and decisions of the European Court of Human Rights in: KAREL KLÍMA, EVROPSKÉ PRÁVO (TITLE IN TRANSLATION: EUROPEAN LAW), Plzeň: Aleš Čeněk (2011), at 483 et seq.

[11]　All 'statutory' bodies of the Council of Europe, i.e. Parliamentary Assembly, Committee of Ministers and the European Court of Human Rights, may signal a deviation from or breach of fundamental principles of the system. The same can be found in the European Union system, for instance in the notification obligation in the case of technical standards, although using a different 'mechanism'.

[12]　Cf. in: KAREL KLÍMA, EVROPSKÉ PRÁVO (TITLE IN TRANSLATION: EUROPEAN LAW), Plzeň: Aleš Čeněk (2011), at 485 et seq.

[13]　For more details see DAVID KOSAŘ *in*: EVROPSKÁ ÚMLUVA O LIDSKÝCH PRÁVECH. KOMENTÁŘ (TITLE IN TRANSLATION: EUROPEAN CONVENTION ON HUMAN RIGHTS. COMMENTARY), at 73 et seq.

the Council of Europe authorities.[14] Executive authorities (including administrative authorities, other State institutions, security services, law enforcement, and penitentiary authorities) are subject to supervision exercised primarily within the framework of parliamentary control, administrative judiciary, ombudsmen, and the complaints system. A special place is reserved for the responsibility of the judiciary for the legal State, guaranteed by the above-mentioned administrative judiciary (or legality control) and, primarily, by constitutional judiciary (or constitutionality control).

## V.    The European Concept of the Protection of Substantive Constitutional Rights

**7.12.**    From the perspective of substantive constitutional law, it is primarily the right to life which is stipulated in the Convention as the preferred European dominating feature of a 'supraconstitutional' nature. The right to life entails that the Member States are bound by a requirement within a vertical and a horizontal concept. Hence, the Member States are forbidden to cause any infringement of that right themselves on a single occasion or continuously. At the same time, they are obliged to devote all of their attention to cases in which such infringement occurs, whether in public-law or in private-law relations. The former situation involves imperial or sovereign relations between the State on the one hand and natural or legal persons subordinated to the State under public law on the other hand. The latter situation involves a relationship based on equal standing of the parties.

**7.13.**    From the perspective of procedural relations, public administration authorities are always obliged to examine, in all procedural public-law relations regulated under the law, whether all procedural requirements were fulfilled which are prescribed for the given proceedings designed to clarify the events associated with the killing or loss of life, i.e. whether the investigation was conducted properly and in a manner corresponding to the significance of the event.[15]

**7.14.**    Acts against life which involve the use of force include the defense of any person against unlawful violence in the area of horizontal rights, effecting a lawful arrest or preventing

---

[14]    For an analytic-synthetic commentary see in: KAREL KLÍMA, EVROPSKÉ PRÁVO (TITLE IN TRANSLATION: EUROPEAN LAW), Plzeň: Aleš Čeněk (2011), at 485 et seq.

[15]    For more details, see the case law regarding this concept in the Czech Republic in: ELIŠKA WAGNEROVÁ, VOJTĚCH ŠIMÍČEK, TOMÁŠ LANGÁŠEK, IVO POSPÍŠIL ET AL., LISTINA ZÁKLADNÍCH PRÁV A SVOBOD. KOMENTÁŘ (TITLE IN TRANSLATION: CHARTER OF FUNFAMENTAL RIGHTS AND FREEDOMS. COMMENTARY), Prague: Wolters Kluwer, a.s. (2012), et.186 et seq.

the attack of a detained person, and action lawfully taken by public administration authorities for the purpose of quelling a riot or insurrection in the area of vertical effect. The concept prohibiting torture, inhuman or degrading treatment primarily ensures that the State must guarantee conditions compatible with the perception of human dignity. Acts of the State must not exceed the inevitable degree of harshness and stress inflicted on the given person. The Convention allows no restrictions of the said right. It is therefore an absolutely unrestrainable right.

7.15. The right to liberty and security of the person under Article 5 of the Convention belongs to the most frequently invoked provisions in the case law of the European Court of Human Rights and of the constitutional courts of the Member States. These values (liberty and security of the person) are interpreted as guarantees provided by the State when interfering with the liberty of the individual, whether through the medium of public administration authorities or in relations with other persons. The Convention itself defines the areas of permitted interference when the individual's liberty can be encroached upon.[16] As concerns the permitted methods of interference, the Convention requires mainly legality and observance of legality in the application of national law by State authorities. Detention must be legal – this is required by the rule stipulating that the applicable procedures of the particular State must be observed. Public administration is also responsible for proper investigation of the case and even the intensity of measures adopted by public administration must comply with the requirement of due respect for the protection of values. This also applies to any measures adopted by public authorities in the prevention of and reaction to the ruthlessness of terrorism.[17]

7.16. The right to respect for one's private and family life (enshrined in Article 8 of the Convention) prohibits State authorities from interfering with a person's private and family life, their home and correspondence. According to the Court, the law which allows such interventions must be specific, unambiguous and must provide for the circumstances attending the interference with privacy as well as the precise implementation thereof. Another decisive aspect is the necessity of this measure and its proportionality in relation to a specific situation. The Court has held that private life encompasses both physical and

---

[16] For instance, by the principle that even a minor may be detained for the purpose of educational supervision.

[17] As concerns the interpretation of limitation clauses, DAVID KOSAŘ *in:* EVROPSKÁ ÚMLUVA O LIDSKÝCH PRÁVECH. KOMENTÁŘ (TITLE IN TRANSLATION: EUROPEAN CONVENTION ON HUMAN RIGHTS. COMMENTARY), at 99 et seq.

mental integrity, as well as the sphere of a person's internal deliberations and their family relations.[18] Freedom of movement and residence pursuant to Article 2 of Protocol No. 4 represents an integral part of general freedom. It *a priori* involves multiple rights including the right to a determination of one's native country, the right to move freely in the territory of the State, to freely cross borders, to freely reside and settle in any place, the right to choose one's place of residence, the freedom to travel out of the country, the prohibition of depriving a person of their citizenship, and the prohibition of preventing citizens from returning to their native country.

7.17. Protocol No. 1 stipulates that each natural or legal person is entitled to the peaceful enjoyment of their possessions. No one shall be deprived of their possessions except in the public interest and subject to the conditions provided for by law. The Convention indicates that each and every interference in ownership must comply with the law. However, the guarantee of ownership does not prohibit the State from depriving a private person of ownership, but they can only do so in the public interest. At the same time, government interference in the private sphere of ownership must preserve a reasonable relation of proportionality between the requirements of general interest of the society and the need to protect the fundamental rights of the person.

## VI. The Procedural Version of the 'European Legal State'

7.18. The case law of the European Court of Human Rights is mostly focused on the issue of judicial process rather than any substantive law issues. Hence, the case law predominantly deals with the right to a fair trial, which means the development of the guarantees of enforceability of rights and freedoms under procedural law. Considering the fact that all the issues in Article 6(1) of the Convention are concentrated in the principle of 'access to court', the Convention bases the procedural guarantees of enforceability of rights and freedoms on the concept of a functioning judiciary. This conceptually fortifies a certain autonomous public-law function of the administration of justice, and consequently synthesizes the idea of special and independent public authorities, i.e. courts. The concept of the Convention then develops the model of a high-quality judicial process based on a rigorous implementation of certain

---

[18] Cf. also the *ECtHR ruling in Khan v. United Kingdom* (2000).

principles typical for court proceedings and the right of every natural or legal person whose rights and freedoms have been breached to an effective legal remedy guaranteed under Article 13 of the Convention. The Convention thereby orders the Member States to provide effective legal instruments to persons at the national level so that they may invoke their rights which have been encroached upon before a national authority. Hence, it is for the individual constitutional systems to determine how their respective judiciary shall be organized in order to meet their commitment. First and foremost, the remedy must be effective, i.e. it must be an instrument capable of terminating or remedying any interference or error committed by a public authority or, alternatively, capable of providing an adequate compensation or satisfaction for the breach. The concept of an effective remedy can also be interpreted as a collection of various consecutive remedies.[19]

7.19.    The right to a fair trial according to the ECtHR relates to civil and administrative judicial matters as well as matters handled in criminal proceedings. Gradual cultivation of, *inter alia*, the judicial process in the doctrines of the ECtHR has facilitated the development of the concept of the legal State, the level of legality of the judicial process and the separation of the judiciary from legislative and executive power. In addition, the Court guarantees the right to a potential ex post control of the decision delivered by the first-instance court, the principle of equality of arms and delivery of a decision within a reasonable period of time. Reasonability of the period within which the decision of the court is to be made means that any circumstances and reasons are excluded which prolong the proceedings and which are caused either by the court authorities or by the parties. State power is therefore liable only for delays caused by State authorities, including pre-trial criminal proceedings, judicial proceedings, etc.

## VII.    The Criminal Limb of the European Right to a Fair Trial

7.20.    The overall concept of 'case law' of the ECtHR, as focused on the procedure adopted by State power vis-à-vis an individual, is particularly concentrated on the protection of that individual from the statutory enforcement authorities of the State. Hence, the ECtHR doctrine primarily centers on proper reasons underlying any decision of State power whereby a person's

---

[19]   Cf. the decision in *Leander* v. *Sweden* (1978).

liberty is restricted – i.e. detention, custody, imprisonment and other types of detention measures applied by the State. The Court also guarantees the right to legal assistance as early as in the pre-trial criminal proceedings, and the right to a reasonable time to prepare the defense.

7.21. The above indicates that the concept of a fair trial guarantees a minimal standard, and the States are free to provide a more extensive protection of rights and freedoms especially in the field of criminal law. The Convention safeguards a protective shield for those against whom the instruments of criminal law are targeted, i.e. especially against individuals accused of criminal offences. That being said, the interpretation of criminal law by the Court favors neither the continental or inquisitorial, nor the Anglo-American adversarial criminal procedure. One may agree that the concept of the ECtHR significantly contributes to a convergence between both types of criminal court proceedings.[20] This conclusion is based on the conviction that it is the principle of contradictory proceedings and the related principle of equality of arms which the ECtHR perceives as the essence of the right to a fair trial and, consequently, the essence of justice.[21] In this sense, the Court must always decide whether the contested proceedings, assessed as a whole, were just and fair under the Convention. The Court thereby examines whether the process meets the principles of justice which constitute principles of a constitutional nature and are also applied in the constitutional systems of the Council of Europe Member States.

## VIII. The Possibility of Inferring an EU Concept of a Legal State

7.22. The Court of Justice of the European Union (formerly the European Court of Justice) is an obvious animator and actor updating the founding treaties (presently the EU Lisbon Treaty). The Court has undoubtedly contributed to the development of integration, as well as certain original aspects of the rights and freedoms of EU citizens. There are many decisions which have changed the principles of Community law[22] and shaped the nature of the Communities and the Union towards federation.

---

[20] For more details, see in: JIŘÍ KMEC, DAVID KOSAŘ, JAN KRATOCHVÍL, MICHAL BOBEK, EVROPSKÁ ÚMLUVA O LIDSKÝCH PRÁVECH. KOMENTÁŘ (TITLE IN TRANSLATION: EUROPEAN CONVENTION ON HUMAN RIGHTS. COMMENTARY), Prague: C. H. Beck (1st ed. 2012), at 573.

[21] The concept of "fair trial" in the *right to a fair trial* was first used by the ECtHR as a designation for Article 6 of the Convention in Golder (1975), A-26.

[22] The term 'Community' from the French *'Le droit communautaire'* (Community law) as the law of the Community (the then European Economic Community).

The Court's rulings have often intervened in the relations among the authorities and helped to achieve institutional balance. The Court undoubtedly extends and expands.[23]

**7.23.** The expansive concept of the Court's activities was also enabled by the methods of interpreting the founding treaties. The reason is that national courts usually adopt the linguistic interpretation in which the natural meaning of words is assessed.[24] However, the linguistic interpretation of treaties is hampered by their generality and vague formulations. The Court thus relies primarily on the teleological interpretation which analyses the individual provisions on the basis of their objective or intent.[25] The use of the teleological interpretation has enabled the Court to 'fill out' the gaps in the founding treaties and in the secondary law and adapt them to the evolution of the European integration, the objectives of which have in time developed from purely economic to areas such as environmental protection, social protection or human rights. The Court has clearly interpreted the treaties very liberally in certain respects,[26] and sometimes the Court has partially contravened their provisions.[27] The Court has without doubt even crossed, on several occasions, the limit set by the Treaties when the Court invoked the need to preserve the rule of law in the European Union.

**7.24.** In general, the Court's procedures have often been far from neutral in terms of values, but they have played a decisive role in the strengthening of integration. In what sense, then, do we perceive the concept of modernizing features in the case law of the Court of Justice of the European Union in the tradition of the European Court of Justice? The Court has undoubtedly responded to the needs of developing the free movement of persons, goods, services and capital, whereby the Court has significantly intervened in the human rights of citizens of the EU Member States.[28]

---

[23] See the December (2014) opinion of the Court of Justice of the European Union that the European Union may not join the Council of Europe.

[24] Concerning this issue, see KAREL KLÍMA, EVROPSKÉ PRÁVO (TITLE IN TRANSLATION: EUROPEAN LAW), Plzeň: Aleš Čeněk (2011), et. 36.

[25] 'Every provision of Community law must be placed in its context and interpreted in the light of the provisions of Community law as a whole, regard being had to the objectives thereof and to its state of evolution at the date on which the provision in question is to be applied,' see *Cilfit v. Ministry of Health* (1982), ECR 3415, paragraph 20.

[26] See 22/70 *Commission v. Conseil* /ERTA) 1971.

[27] See the ruling in *Reyners v. Belgium* (1974), ECR 631.

[28] The 'famous' decision, i.e. precedent, resolving the conflict between Germany and France, *Cassis de Dijon.*

## IX. The Continental European Constitutional Judiciary as the New Phenomenon of the Concept of the Legal State

**7.25.** Supreme national judicial institutions, i.e. supreme courts or, as the case may be, primarily constitutional courts, have an undisputed special role in the development and, consequently, the promotion of the European concept of the Legal State.

**7.26.** In the continental legal culture of written law of constitutional codes, the regulatory static nature of written texts requires updating of the constitution. However, it is necessary to bear in mind that each constitution has two fundamentally different parts. These include the organization of constitutional power and, consequently, constitutional rules of organizational and founding nature on the one hand or, as applicable, a normatively different catalogue of fundamental rights, political freedoms and rights of economic, social and cultural nature.

**7.27.** Judicial legislation of, primarily, constitutional courts has a mostly positive effect contributing to the creation of the State's value system, especially regarding self-limitation of State authorities when they make decisions on the rights of citizens or legal persons. In this sense, judicial legislation has certain features of modernism and fulfils the aim of convergence of written constitutional law (and the dual European superior standard) and jurisdictional creativity of supreme courts, which is also capable of solidifying the parallel concept of the European legal state.

## X. Conclusion

**7.28.** The Convention and the jurisprudence of the European Court of Human Rights form a special and comprehensive legal system aimed primarily at the cultivation of the decisions of public authorities in matters relating to natural and legal persons or, as applicable, other imperial or sovereign interventions. The European Court of Justice itself once confirmed that fundamental rights form part of the then-Community law and their protection must be guaranteed. The adoption of the EU Charter of Rights (2009) has had a synthesizing and integrating nature as well as binding principles for secondary law adopted by European Union authorities. If the secondary law develops human-rights protection, it may also be applicable in national courts.[29] Both of these original European systems are based

---

[29] For instance, the Race Equality Directive (No. 2000/43/EC) or the Equal Treatment in Employment and

Czech Yearbook of International Law®

on the enforceability of European law in the Member States as well as the requirements for organizational, interventional and decision-making level of legal activity pursued by public authorities. One may therefore conclude and confirm that the concept of the 'European legal state' is a typical European constitutional value.

| | |

*Summaries*

DEU  [*Das Konzept der europäischen Rechtsstaatlichkeit als reales System für den Schutz der Menschenrechte in Europa*]
*Die schrittweise Entscheidungsfindung des Europäischen Gerichtshofs (EuGH) und des Europäischen Gerichtshofs für Menschenrechte (EGMR) hat insbesondere in dem kontinentalen Europa zu verfassungsrechtlicher Kreativität geführt, wie dem kodifizierten Recht. Diese Tätigkeit hat sukzessive auch die Rechtsprechung der Verfassungsgerichte beeinflusst, wie sie sich in einigen Verfassungssystemen entwickelt hat. Ein Vergleich des Stils dieser Kreativität wie auch der in Frage kommenden subjektiven Exzesse institutioneller Art ermöglicht es uns, zu beurteilen, ob diese Kreativität auch Elemente der Modernisierung und eventuell über ihre Modernisierung hinaus aufweist und die quasikonstitutionelle Position europäischer Gerichte oder die konstitutionelle Position nationaler Gerichte modifiziert. Es stellt sich die Frage, ob das von dem Europarat, gegebenenfalls auch von der EU eingerichtete System die Behauptung zulässt, dass ein Modell der „Europäischen Rechtsstaatlichkeit" als neuer Verfassungswert und reales System zum Schutz der Menschenrechte und Freiheiten existiert.*

CZE  [*Koncept evropského právního státu jako reálný systém ochrany lidských práv v Evropě*]
*Postupná rozhodovací činnost Evropského soudního Dvora a Evropského soudu pro lidská práva založila v podmínkách zejména kontinentální Evropy typu kodexového práva soudní kreativitu ústavně-právního charakteru. Tato činnost postupně ovlivnila i judikování ústavních soudů tak jak vznikaly v některých ústavních systémech. Porovnání stylu této kreativity, jakož i možných subjektivních vykročení institucionálního charakteru nám umožňuje posoudit, zda tato kreativita má prvky*

---

Occupation Directive (No. 2000/78/EC).

*modernizační a eventuálně i charakter přesahující modernizaci a modifikující quasi ústavní pozici soudů evropských anebo ústavní pozici soudů národních. Je takto otázkou, zda systém Rady Evropy, případně také Evropské unie umožňuje tvrdit, že existuje model Evropského právního státu jako nová ústavní hodnota a reálný systém ochrany lidských práv a svobod.*

| | |

POL  [*Koncepcja europejskiego państwa prawa jako realny system ochrony praw człowieka w Europie*]
*Dwa współczesne europejskie systemy międzynarodowe, przede wszystkim zaś system Rady Europy, pozostają aktywne w dziedzinie ochrony praw i swobód człowieka. Ich normy kogentne wspomagają konstytucyjne wykonywanie praw i swobód człowieka, w szczególności zaś zgodność z prawem działalności organów publicznych i wymiaru sprawiedliwości. Pojawia się zatem pytanie, czy obie Karty (Konwencje) wraz z orzecznictwem sądów w obu systemach, a w szczególności Europejskiego Sądu Praw Człowieka, w powiązaniu z rozwojem doktrynalnego pojęcia „case law" obu sądów pozwalają konstatować, iż można mówić o koncepcji europejskiego państwa prawa. Tym samym rozważamy tu oryginalną i progresywną doktrynę, opartą na zasadach legalności, proporcjonalności i samoograniczenia działalności władz państwowych, w szczególności jeżeli chodzi o ingerencję w prawa człowieka.*

FRA  [*Le concept de l'État de droit européen en tant que système réel de protection des droits de l'homme en Europe*]
*Deux systèmes internationaux sont en œuvre dans la protection des droits de l'homme et des libertés fondamentales en Europe, dont notamment le système du Conseil de l'Europe. Leurs dispositions contraignantes optimisent la réalisation constitutionnelle des droits de l'homme et des libertés fondamentales, et, plus particulièrement, la légalité de l'action de l'administration publique et de la justice. On peut alors se demander si les deux Chartes, avec la jurisprudence des Cours qui font partie des deux systèmes, en particulier celle de la Cour européenne des droits de l'homme, et compte tenu de l'évolution de la conception doctrinale de la jurisprudence des deux Cours, permettent de justifier le concept de l'« État de droit européen ». Nous proposons ainsi une doctrine originale et progressive, fondée sur les principes de légalité, de proportionnalité et d'auto-restriction du pouvoir de*

*l'État, notamment en ce qui concerne les atteintes aux droits de l'homme et aux libertés fondamentales.*

**RUS** [*Концепция европейского правового государства как реальная система защиты прав человека в Европе*]
*Существующие две европейские международные системы, прежде всего, система Совета Европы, активно работают в области защиты прав и свобод человека. Их прямо обязывающие документы способствуют конституционному осуществлению прав и свобод человека и особенно соблюдению законов органами государственного управления и правосудием. Таким образом возникает вопрос, позволяют ли обе Хартии (Конвенции) совместно с судебной практикой судов обеих систем (прежде всего, Европейского суда по правам человека) и совместно с развитием доктринальной концепции «case law» обоих судов утверждать, что это концепция Европейского правового государства? Мы, таким образом, рассуждаем об оригинальной и прогрессивной доктрине, основанной на принципах законности, пропорциональности и самоограничения деятельности органов государственной власти, особенно в случае вмешательства в права и свободы человека.*

**ESP** [*Concepto del estado de derecho europeo como sistema real de la protección de los derechos humanos en Europa*]
*Los dos sistemas internacionales europeos contemporáneos, sobre todo el sistema del Consejo de Europa, actúan en materia de protección de los derechos humanos y las libertades; su normativa vinculante cultiva la ejecución constitucional de los derechos humanos y las libertades y fomenta especialmente la legalidad de la actuación de las administraciones públicas y del sistema judicial. Cabe preguntar si precisamente la existencia de ambas Cartas (Convenciones), junto con la jurisprudencia de los Tribunales de ambos sistemas, sobre todo el Tribunal Europeo de Derechos Humanos, y el desarrollo de la doctrina de «case law», permiten afirmar la existencia del Estado de derecho europeo, como doctrina progresista y original fundamentada en los principios de legalidad, proporcionalidad y autorrestricción de poder del Estado.*

| | |

Czech Yearbook of International Law®

## Bibliography

JOSEF BLAHOŽ, VLADIMÍR BALAŠ, KAREL KLÍMA, SROVNÁVACÍ ÚSTAVNÍ PRÁVO (TITLE IN TRANSLATION: COMPARATIVE CONSTITUTIONAL LAW), Prague: Wolters Kluwer (5th ed. 2015).

BOŽENA GRONOWSKA, EUROPEJSKI TRYBUNAL PRAW CZLOWIEKA W POSZUKIWANIU EFEKTYWNEJ OCHRONY PRAW JEDNOTKI, Toruń (2011).

KAREL KLÍMA, EVROPSKÉ PRÁVO (TITLE IN TRANSLATION: EUROPEAN LAW), Plzeň: Aleš Čeněk (2011).

KAREL KLÍMA, LISTINA A JEJÍ REALIZACE V SYSTÉMU VEŘEJNÉHO NOVÉHO SOUKROMÉHO PRÁVA (TITLE IN TRANSLATION: THE CHARTER AND ITS IMPLEMENTATION IN THE SYSTEM OF PUBLIC AND NEW PRIVATE LAW), Prague: Wolters Kluwer (2014).

KAREL KLÍMA, O PRÁVU ÚSTAVNÍM (TITLE IN TRANSLATION: ABOUT CONSTITUTIONAL LAW), Prague: Wolters Kluwer (2012).

JIŘÍ KMEC, DAVID KOSAŘ, JAN KRATOCHVÍL, MICHAL BOBEK, EVROPSKÁ ÚMLUVA O LIDSKÝCH PRÁVECH. KOMENTÁŘ (TITLE IN TRANSLATION: EUROPEAN CONVENTION ON HUMAN RIGHTS. COMMENTARY), Prague: C. H. Beck (1st ed. 2012).

ELIŠKA WAGNEROVÁ, VOJTĚCH ŠIMÍČEK, TOMÁŠ LANGÁŠEK, IVO POSPÍŠIL, et al. LISTINA ZÁKLADNÍCH PRÁV A SVOBOD. KOMENTÁŘ (TITLE IN TRANSLATION: CHARTER OF FUNFAMENTAL RIGHTS AND FREEDOMS. COMMENTARY), Prague: Wolters Kluwer, a.s. (2012).

Dawid Michalski

# The Development of Children's Right to the Environment in International Law

*Key words:*
*children's rights | right to the*
*environment | international*
*law | international*
*environmental law*

Czech Yearbook of International Law®

***Abstract*** *| The relationship between human rights and environmental protection is relatively young. The international community has recognized the need to undertake organized activities on this level in response to the emerging environmental threats associated with the unlimited development of technology and industry in the contemporary world. It was noticed that by degrading the natural environment, it harms mankind itself, which means that fundamental rights are violated. It has been observed that there is a relationship that combines these at first seemingly different issues. This was reflected in the human rights to the natural environment, formulated by the international community. At present, the system of universal protection of children's rights is being developed almost in parallel. Many tried and tested solutions have been taken over from the international system of human rights protection. However, the child's right to the environment is still not expressed explicitly. However, by applying inferential rules, one could undertake the deliberations to lead to conclusions that would allow the removal of this gap in the system of public international law standards. The essence of the debate revolves around the claim that the right to the environment is one of the rights of the child, as an element universally recognized in the universal system of human rights protection. The paper presents the legal status of a child in international environmental law. At the beginning, attempts were made to define the concept of a child in international public law. Next,*

**Dawid Michalski (PhD)**
received his Master's
degrees in law as well
as political sciences.
He is an Assistant in
Department of History
of Law at the Faculty of
Law and Administration
of the University of
Gdańsk and a member
of *International Law
Association.* Moreover, he
completed an internship in
the Political and Economic
Department of the Polish
Embassy in Finland. He
is the author of several
dozen publications
in monographs and
scientific journals. His
PhD dissertation title
is: "*THE LEGAL AND
POLITICAL SYSTEM
OF FINLAND 1917-2000
AND ITS FUNCTIONING.
LEGAL, HISTORICAL
AND COMPARATIVE
STUDY*". More details on:
https://en.prawo.ug.edu.
pl/pracownik/39006/
dawid_michalski
E-mail: dawid.michalski@
prawo.ug.edu.pl

*the motives of the international community were presented, engaging in the development of international protection of children's rights. Another research goal was to present the genesis and meaning of the concept of the right to the environment. Finally, an assessment of the current legal status of the child in the context of protection of environmental rights was included. Moreover, a few postulates de lege ferenda for the international community were presented.*

| | |

## I.     Introduction

**8.01.**     The relationship between human rights and environmental protection is a relatively young relationship. The international community has recognized the need to take organized action in this area in response to emerging ecological threats associated with the unlimited development of technology and industry in the modern world. It was noticed that by degrading the natural environment, it harms mankind itself, which means that fundamental rights are violated as a consequence. It has been observed that there is a relationship linking these at first seemingly different issues. This relationship is reflected in the human right to the environment formulated by the international community.

**8.02.**     Historically, up to the beginning of the 20th century, there was no institutionalized protection of children's rights. States freely determined the rights of children. This was problematic because in many states, no legal regulations were put in place. The child was solely of interest to his parents, family or tribal communities, churches, national and international organizations. In patriarchal systems, the child was the property of the father.[1]

**8.03.**     In Roman law, paternal power, almost absolute (patria potestas), included within its scope the right of life and death (ius vitae ac necis), the possibility of selling a child (ius vendendi), as well as the possibility of surrendering a child who caused unlawful damage to someone else's property, thereby making up for that damage (noxae deditio).[2] In ancient Greece, the family was also

---

[1]     MARIAN BALCEREK, PRAWA DZIECKA, Warszawa (1986), et. 10-70. More on the historical development of universal protection system of children's rights see also: Dawid Michalski, Źródła międzynarodowej ochrony praw dziecka w Organizacji Narodów Zjednoczonych, 1 AEQUITAS (2013), et. 46-60.

[2]     WŁADYSŁAW ROZWADOWSKI, PRAWO RZYMSKIE. ZARYS WYKŁADU WRAZ Z WYBOREM ŹRÓDEŁ, Poznań (1992), et. 209-211.

headed by a father who had full rights over the child. In the first days after the birth of the child, the father decided to recognize him as his own, which meant leaving him in the family. There was, however, the possibility of earlier, public renunciation of the son. The father's authority otherwise expired when the child came of age.[3]

**8.04.** In the Middle Ages, the father of the family (pater familias) still exercised full power over children. With the conceptualization and codification of family law over centuries, the father's right to life and death became increasingly rare. From then on, the father had the right to discipline at home.[4]

**8.05.** Currently, a system of universal protection of children's rights is being developed,[5] almost in parallel with the development of general human rights protection at the international level. While the child's right to the environment has not been expressed expressis verbis, by applying inferential rules, it is possible to come to some conclusions that would allow the elimination of this gap in the system of norms of public international law.

**8.06.** The thesis of this work is that the right to the environment is one of the rights of the child, as an element widely recognized in the universal system of protection of human rights.

**8.07.** In order to achieve the intended effects, an attempt was made to answer the following research questions:

1. What is the position of the child in international environmental law?
2. What is the human right to the environment?
3. Can the human right to the environment be applied by analogy to children's rights?

## II. A Child in International Environmental Law

**8.08.** The universal, organized system of human rights protection covers many protected areas. Based on this system, a universal system of protection of children's rights is developing. The binding force of previously adopted universal acts of public international law facilitates work on creating acts to protect

---

[3] TADEUSZ MACIEJEWSKI, HISTORIA POWSZECHNA USTROJU I PRAWA, Warszawa (2007), et. 67-69.

[4] Piotr Kitowski, Natalia Radecka, *Normatywny model opieki nad sierotami w XVI-wiecznych rewizjach prawa chełmińskiego. Zarys instytucji*, LXIV(1) CZASOPISMO PRAWNO-HISTORYCZNE (2012), et. 122-123; Przemysław Dąbkowski, *Prawo prywatne polskie*, 1 LWÓW (1910), et. 214-227. A practical commentary on the function of a child's legal guardian was presented by the 16th-century Magdeburg Law glossator, a Cracovian, BARTŁOMIEJ GROICKI, OBRONA SIEROT I WDÓW, Warszawa (1958).

[5] See the example Polish regulations about the modern basic family ties in international bilateral agreements ex. Dawid Michalski, *Rodzina w artykule 11 Konkordatu z 1993 roku*, 11 CYWILIZACJA I POLITYKA (2013), et. 323-335.

the rights of the child. The freedoms and rights granted to each person also include children. The exceptions are the legislations in which the norms are explicitly addressed only to adults. An example of such rights are electoral rights, which a person only enjoys if he/she has reached a certain age. According to Leszek Wiśniewski, such acts include, in particular, the Universal Declaration of Human Rights and the International Human Rights Pacts. In the content, in addition to freedoms and rights addressed to everyone, there are also those applied only to children.[6] So why, despite the fact that universal regulations are applied to every human being, and therefore also children, the international community is activating itself in activities for the international law of children's rights?

8.09.    There are several reasons for this. The basic fact is that children should be the object of special care as a future generation. In view of their weaknesses, their protection should be particularly prioritized. The international community has recognized that children's rights should be protected by standards clearly defined and adapted to the needs of the youngest. The standards applied so far have not comprehensively regulated the obligations of adults towards children. In addition, there was a need to formulate new rights not yet taken into account. An important reason is the fact that not all the countries in the world have become parties to international agreements that form the basis of the system of universal protection of human rights. The international community has recognized that a new agreement directly regulating the protection of children's rights may encourage the accession of a state that for some reason has not joined the act of universal protection of human rights.[7] It is difficult to refuse such reasoning, especially taking into account the international situation at that time. Ideological rivalry and the way human rights were understood by communist and democratic states resulted in disputes that were difficult to overcome, which made it impossible to reach an agreement, which is necessary especially when adopting a resolution act, where consensus is the basis of law-making.

8.10.    The definition of the term 'a child', as a key concept for a separate category of right holders, has been formulated in the Convention on the Rights of the Child 1989. Any human being under the age of eighteen is considered to be a child, unless,

---

6    Leszek Wiśniewski, *Geneza Konwencji o Prawach Dziecka i stosunek jej norm do innych aktów prawa międzynarodowego*, KONWENCJA O PRAWACH DZIECKA. ANALIZA I WYKŁADNIA, Poznań (Tadeusz Smyczyński ed. 1999), et. 13.

7    *Ibidem*, et. 14.

under the law applicable to the child, he or she is of legal age.[8] Thus, the disposable norm established the proposed minimum age for recognizing a human being as an adult. The international community has come to believe that this is the best time to sufficiently recognize a person as physically and mentally mature. It is worth noting, however, that not everyone achieves this maturity in the same period of development. Postulates should be made with extreme caution to reduce the age necessary for legal recognition of the child as an adult.

**8.11.** During the preparatory work for the adoption of the Convention, numerous doubts and disputes arose as to who should be the "object" of protection and the addressee of rights. There are two main issues:

    1. Does the concept of a child also refer to the fetus?

    2. Is the child also an adolescent but still a minor?[9]

**8.12.** From an example of Strasbourg case law standards in bioethics, it is possible to distinguish the difference in the perception of the subject of protection depending on the moment of life. Due to a lack of consensus on moral and ethical issues, the tribunal granted a wide margin of appreciation. Such a margin was also granted to countries in determining when legal protection of life begins.[10] For example, in the jurisprudence of the European Court of Human Rights, the interpretation regarding the moment of protection for a conceived child varies depending on the moment in which the child is found. This difference is clearly seen in the Judgment of 10 April 2007 in the *Evans* v. *United Kingdom*[11] (life in the pre-implementation embryo phase) and Judgment of the Grand Chamber of 10 December 2010 in the case *A. B. C* v. *Ireland*[12] (protection of fetal life). On this basis, although the tribunal referred to the lack of a common, coherent, European, both in terms of scientific and in terms of a legal definition of the beginning of life, it did recognize the importance of fetal development and the possibility of its protection.

**8.13.** Insofar as there is a dispute in doctrine regarding the question of the beginning of childhood,[13] it seems that the end of childhood

8    Article 1 of the Convention on the Rights of the Child 1989.

9    Tadeusz Smyczyński, *Pojęcie dziecka i jego podmiotowość*, KONWENCJA O PRAWACH DZIECKA: ANALIZA I WYKŁADNIA, Poznań – Ars boni et aequi (1999), et. 39-42.

10    Anna Śledzińska-Simon, *Rola Europejskiego Trybunału Praw Człowieka w kształtowaniu standardów w zakresie bioetyki i biotechnologii*, PRAWA CZŁOWIEKA WOBEC ROZWOJU BIOTECHNOLOGII, Warszawa (Lena Kondratiewa-Bryzik, Katarzyna Sękowska-Kozłowska ed. 2013), et. 77-79.

11    Judgment of the European Court of Human Rights of 10 April 2007 in the case of *Evans* v. *United Kingdom*, application no. 63309/05.

12    Judgment of the Grand Chamber of the European Court of Human Rights of 10 December 2010 in *ABC* v. *Ireland*, application no. 25579/05.

13    These considerations will not be the subject to more thorough analysis, for more on this subject,

should not be questionable. It established that the upper limit of childhood is eighteen years of age which is consistent with the age used in the national legislation of most countries. In Europe, only Austria and Switzerland use a higher age, nineteen and twenty years of agerespectively. Based on Article 1 of the Convention on the Rights of the Child, the possibility of early coming of age is permitted in exceptional circumstances. Attention is drawn to the positives and negatives of such a solution. On the one hand, it can be regarded as respect for cultural and religious differences that allow such deviations. On the other hand, flexibility in this matter creates a legal loophole, as some of the provisions of the Convention may not be effective for persons under the age of eighteen.[14]

8.14. Despite the fact that the right to the environment, which is the subject of this study, has not been expressed *expressis verbis* in relation to children, treating a child as a human being, the norms contained in the acts of international protection of human rights should be used by analogy. Such conclusions can be derived even from paragraphs 1-3 of the preamble to the Convention on the Rights of the Child.[15] It has been indicated there that children's rights are human rights. The provisions of the treaty basis of the system of human rights protection in the United Nations were referred to - the United Nations Charter, Universal Declaration of Human Rights and International Human Rights Pacts.[16] Thus, it was decided that children should be treated as adults, primarily because they should be treated with the same dignity and enjoy equal rights. Due to this, children's rights, as human rights, are universal - they are enjoyed by every child. According to the general principles, they are inherent and inalienable.[17] In addition, a classic anti-discrimination clause was placed in paragraph 3, which should function analogously to the one referring to adults.

---

see: OKTAWIAN NAWROT, LUDZKA BIOGENEZA W STANDARDACH BIOETYCZNYCH RADY EUROPY, Warszawa (2011); Oktawian Nawrot, *Bioprawo*, FILOZOFIA PRAWA, Warszawa (Jerzy Zajadło, Kamil Zeidler eds., 2013); Adam Łopatka, *Kto jest dzieckiem?*, KONWENCJA O PRAWACH DZIECKA A PRAWO POLSKIE, Warszawa (Adam Łopatka ed. 1991); MARTA PRUCNAL, OCHRONA DZIECI PRZED UCZESTNICTWEM W DZIAŁANIACH ZBROJNYCH WE WSPÓŁCZESNYM PRAWIE MIĘDZYNARODOWYM, Warszawa (2012), et. 26-27.

[14] MARTA PRUCNAL, OCHRONA DZIECI PRZED UCZESTNICTWEM W DZIAŁANIACH ZBROJNYCH WE WSPÓŁCZESNYM PRAWIE MIĘDZYNARODOWYM, Warszawa (2012), et. 26.

[15] Dz.U. z 1991 r. Nr 120, poz. 526.

[16] See in particular the preamble to the United Nations Charter and the preamble to the Universal Declaration of Human Rights.

[17] MAREK PIECHOWIAK, PREAMBUŁA, KONWENCJA O PRAWACH DZIECKA. ANALIZA I WYKŁADNIA, Instytut Nauk Prawnych PAN – Ars boni et aequi (1999), et. 24.

Czech Yearbook of International Law®

## III.  A Human Right to the Environment

**8.15.**  In the contemporary world, the importance of environmental protection increases disproportionately. This is not only because of the beauty of nature and tourist values, but also because of the need to provide the society with adequate and therefore healthy living conditions. In addition, environmental values are also a good that should be rationally used so as to preserve them for the benefit of present and, above all, future generations.[18]

**8.16.**  The idea of environmental protection and the concept of human rights were jointly linked in 1972, when the United Nations adopted the Stockholm Declaration. Here, they were equated with the most important human rights recognized in public international law. An attempt was made to grant the law of the environment an exceptionally high rank. The very idea of protecting nature was not born unexpectedly. It was based on deep thoughts in the areas of: philosophy, axiology, ethics, as well as politics. Philosophical views have had a significant impact on the shape of activities of the international community and national legislation. This process is particularly visible in relation to the development of human rights. New concepts have been raised in the field of human and natural world relations. At the same time, the entity was recognized as a subject authorized to use the values that are present in the natural world. It was the result of the transformation of the idea into legal norms that took place over centuries.[19]

**8.17.**  Indirect sources of the concept of human right to the environment could be seen in the philosophical approach to human relations with nature, ecological ethics and ecological philosophy. On the other hand, direct sources can be noticed in the theory of environmental values developed on the basis of axiology and political endeavors to ensure that the individual can use these values.[20] It is obvious that proper development is not possible without ecological sustainability. A clean environment ensures unrestricted development opportunities, while ecological damage leads to degradation that prevents the full potential of land, water and air resources from being utilized. The development of philosophy, ethics, axiology and politics was the basis for formulating the concept of the human right to the environment. The new attitude to the environment

---

[18]  Jarosław Ruszewski, *Dostęp do informacji o środowisku*, 9 PROKURATURA I PRAWO (2005), et. 109.

[19]  Wojciech Radecki, *Filozoficzne i polityczne podstawy prawa człowieka do środowiska*, PRAWO CZŁOWIEKA DO ŚRODOWISKA NATURALNEGO, Wrocław-Warszawa-Kraków-Gdańsk-Łódź (Jerzy Sommer ed. 1987), et. 11-12 and 23.

[20]  *Ibidem*, et. 23; JADWIGA BOHDANOWICZ, KU CYWILIZACJI EKOROZWOJU, Gdańsk (1998), et. 27-30.

is based on a correlation of rights and obligations. Therefore, the right to the environment is a right coupled with an obligation to protect it.

**8.18.** The human right to the environment have been included into the catalog of human rights widely accepted by the international community. This was due to the perception of the close relationship, environmental relations and human rights that have developed over the centuries. They were classified as collective law - third generation law.[21] Among the four rights originally found in Karel Vasak's original proposal, in the third category (nowadays - the generation) of human rights was "the right to a decent environment" (le droit á un environnement décent). Krzysztof Drzewicki claims that the initial proposals can be reduced to two, not four types of solidarity rights - the right to peace and the right to the environment. The concept of incorporating the right to the environment (le droit á l'environnement) into the group of solidarity rights (now referred to as the third generation group of rights) appeared due to the fact that they were binding throughout the entire human community. Therefore, they cannot be realized without the joint efforts of all social life entities, ex. individuals, states and other organizations. In addition, by applying the exegesis method of already adopted international public law, it is possible to justify the existence of a human right to the environment as a third generation human right.[22]

**8.19.** The first idea from which the international community deduced the concept of the right to the environment was the right to life that was already then found in the Universal Declaration of Human Rights (Article 3) and the Covenant on Political and Civil Rights (Article 6). The relationship between human rights and ecology is also raised in the context of the right to an adequate standard of living, through which good health and well-being are to be ensured. Among other rights contained in the above documents, reference was made to the right to enjoy the highest achievable level of physical and mental health, as well as the right to adequate and satisfactory working conditions. The aforementioned laws led the thesis that a polluted, degraded and unbalanced environment is contrary to recognized human rights, and above all to the most fundamental rights: the right to life and the right to health. Although the existence of such a

---

[21] John G. Merrills, *Environmental Rights*, INTERNATIONAL ENVIRONMENTAL LAW, Oxford (Daniel Bodansky, Jutta Brunnée, Ellen Hey eds., 2008), et. 664 and 666-668.

[22] KRZYSZTOF DRZEWICKI, PRAWO DO ROZWOJU. STUDIUM Z ZAKRESU PRAW CZŁOWIEKA, Gdańsk (1988), et. 12-14; *idem*, Krzysztof Drzewicki, *Koncepcja prawa do środowiska jako prawa człowieka*, 10 PAŃSTWO I PRAWO (1985), et. 54.

natural relationship does not seem to be sufficient to establish the right to the environment *ipso facto* as a new human right, the legitimacy of the presented direction of interpretation and inference was manifested in the form of permanent promotional activities. This was reflected in the emphasis on the relationship between human rights and ecology in documents adopted by the United Nations.[23]

**8.20.** For the first time, the human right to the environment was formulated explicitly in the Stockholm Declaration 1972. The first principle stated that "man has the fundamental right to (...) live in an environment of quality that allows him to live in dignity and prosperity".[24]

**8.21.** The human right to the environment can be defined in different ways. Remigiusz Sobański proposes the following:
1. The right to demand environmental protection,
2. The right to live in an environment that provides human-friendly living conditions,
3. The right to use the value of the environment.[25]

**8.22.** In addition, the right to the environment can be seen as a group of specific environmental rights, ex. the right to clean water, the right to clean soil, the right to an uncontaminated environment. However, it can also be seen as a synthesis of these rights, ex. the right to a healthy and uncontaminated environment, the right to ecological balance, or as - the most commonly used - right to the environment.[26]

**8.23.** In practice, by literally specifying a catalog of environmental rights, there should be no interpretation problems when trying to determine when an individual's right to the environment may be violated. Recently, there is an increasing tendency of international courts and tribunals to notice violations of material environmental law.[27]

**8.24.** Therefore, the Stockholm Conference was a breakthrough with significant effects on public international law in the field of organized protection of human rights in an environmental context. In addition, from that moment one can speak of the

---

[23] Krzysztof Drzewicki, *Trzecia generacja praw człowieka*, 10 SPRAWY MIĘDZYNARODOWE (1983), et. 91-93; *Idem*, Krzysztof Drzewicki, *Koncepcja prawa do środowiska jako prawa człowieka*, 10 PAŃSTWO I PRAWO (1985), et. 55. More on development of human rights see: Dawid Michalski, *Rozwój uniwersalnej ochrony praw człowieka*, 14 CYWILIZACJA I POLITYKA (2016), et. 81-98.
[24] Rule 1 of the United Nations Conference Declaration on the Human Environment of 1972.
[25] Remigiusz Sobański, *Prawa człowieka a ekologia*, PRAWA CZŁOWIEKA W PAŃSTWIE EKOLOGICZNYM, Warszawa (Remigiusz Sobański ed. 1998), et. 318.
[26] Krzysztof Drzewicki, *Koncepcja prawa do środowiska jako prawa człowieka*, 10 PAŃSTWO I PRAWO (1985), et. 53; *idem*, Krzysztof Drzewicki, *Trzecia generacja praw człowieka*, 10 SPRAWY MIĘDZYNARODOWE (1983), et. 91.
[27] PHILIPPE SANDS, JACQUELINE PEEL, ADRIANA FABRA, RUTH MACKENZIE, PRINCIPLES OF INTERNATIONAL ENVIRONMENTAL LAW, Cambridge (2012), et. 778-780.

right to the environment as one of the third generation human rights.

8.25. Nowadays, based on the current development of the concept of the right to the environment, there is a tendency to situate the entity as an authorized entity, ex. one with a specific subject right. As Krystyna Urbańska notes, the first attempts to conceptualize the human right to the environment in the universal system were made at the end of the 1960s. The report of the group of scientists referred to as the U. Thant Report entitled "Man and the environment". It pointed to the highly adverse consequences of unlimited industrial development, progressing urbanization, chemization, as well as other phenomena typical of modern civilization and causing environmental pollution. The phenomenon of the conceptualization of the individual's right to the environment should be combined with the increasing awareness of the ongoing degradation of the environment, as well as the threats of further aggravation of this adverse phenomenon, which in turn has a negative impact on health, quality of life and, consequently, on human life.[28] However, the new ecological awareness was already clearly initiated at the Stockholm Conference in 1972, namely in the first principle of the Stockholm Declaration, where the formula of subjective individualism was adopted.

8.26. In contrast, the doctrine claims that such a solution is not practical. An individual, as part of a larger community, would be more effectively represented, for example, by international organizations, which would find it easier to use their instruments effectively. Widely understood claims resulting from social endeavors would be more easily directed to obliged entities. The correct implementation of the right to the environment is a proper obligation, first of all, on the part of the state authorities, as its representatives, as well as the organized international community. One example of a social organization that can be international, and usually has, is an ecological organization. It can act as a representative of individual entities entitled to be protected in the scope of environmental rights at both the national and international level.

8.27. In this regard, the Provincial Administrative Court in Kraków (Poland) made an attempt to define the concept of ecological organization in the judgment of 14 April 2010.[29] In the pertinent sentence on the matter in question, it stated that "an ecological

---

[28] KRYSTYNA M. URBAŃSKA, PRAWO PODMIOTOWE DO DOBREGO ŚRODOWISKA W PRAWIE MIĘDZYNARODOWYM I POLSKIM, Gdańsk (2013), et. 74-75.

[29] II SA/Kr 1774/09.

organization must be an organization whose primary goal is to take or refrain from activities that enable the preservation or restoration of natural balance. An organization which in its statute mentions as the purpose the dissemination of natural values, initiating, supporting and cooperating, as well as organizing all intentions and works related to harmonious socio-economic development, as well as ecology and spatial development, cannot be considered an ecological organization. None of these objectives can be classified as [taking or refusing to take action to preserve or restore the natural balance]." It must therefore be a "fighting" organization. As Diana Trzcińska notes in her *glosa*[30] to the ruling in question, the legislator wanted to distinguish social organizations whose purpose is environmental protection.

**8.28.** The subject of protection will be another component of every human right being reviewed. As Jadwiga Bohdanowicz notes, the quality of human life on Earth is determined by the richness and type of stimuli provided by him and the life that exists on it, because human nature is biologically and spiritually shaped by external factors.[31] Regarding the classification of the quality of the environment, Krzysztof Drzewicki is critical, claiming that it is "imprecise". Due to the problematic nature of defining the criteria for general terms, such as a healthy and sustainable environment, it is impossible to define when the object of protection is violated. The lack of efficiency of the environmental components and their minimum quality standards, as well as the lack of properly implemented procedures may also lead to the inefficiency of the system functioning.[32]

**8.29.** The international community tried to determine the determinants of a properly protected environment. In the final report for the United Nations, the Subcommittee on the Prevention of Discrimination and Protection of Minorities regarding the Principles of Human Rights and the Environment[33] listed among others: freedom from pollution, environmental degradation and harmful or life-threatening activities, health, well-being and sustainable development; protection of air, land, water, glaciers, fauna and flora, important areas necessary to maintain biodiversity and ecosystems; highest health standard; adequate construction and population; ecological access to

---

[30] See a glossa to the judgment in: Diana Trzcińska, *Pojęcie organizacji ekologicznej*, 2 GDAŃSKIE STUDIA PRAWNICZE. PRZEGLĄD ORZECZNICTWA (2011), et. 41-52.
[31] JADWIGA BOHDANOWICZ, KU CYWILIZACJI EKOROZWOJU, Gdańsk (1998), et. 16.
[32] Krzysztof Drzewicki, *Koncepcja prawa do środowiska jako prawa człowieka*, 10 PAŃSTWO I PRAWO (1985), et. 62.
[33] Final report: UN Doc. E/CN.4/Sub.2/1994/9, 74.

and protection of nature and sustainable use of its resources; protection of unique resources; pleasure from traditional life and keeping indigenous people alive. Such factors could make environmental laws comparable to other social and economic rights and lead to appropriate measures to protect them.[34]

8.30. The right to the environment was included in the Stockholm Declaration extremely broadly. Therefore, it was recognized that the right environment would be the right basis to guarantee not only the health of individuals, but also their proper spiritual and economic development. outgoing departure from traditional international environmental law can therefore be observed. The broadly understood right to the environment is also supposed to guarantee protection against other international threats, such as armed conflicts of a nuclear nature. However, such a broad approach would require appropriate cooperation of many branches of law, not only within international law but also via national regulations.[35] Therefore, guaranteeing the basic rights relevant to the literal interpretation of the concept of the environment seems sufficient for the effective implementation of rights that would be presumably protected.

8.31. The right to the environment has become a binding international legal norm only in the African and Inter-American regional system for the protection of human rights by including it in written conventions.

8.32. The African Charter on Human and Peoples' Rights guarantees all peoples "the right to a generally satisfactory natural environment favorable to their development".[36] In contrast, the Salvadoran Additional Protocol to the American Convention on Human Rights, which introduced economic, social and cultural rights, guaranteed the "right to live in a healthy environment and access to basic public services". The next paragraph provides "promotion, protection and improvement of the environment".[37]

8.33. In contrast to regional systems, at the United Nations level, ex. in the universal system, the right to the environment has been recognized as a highly significant instrument of soft law, which has a significant impact on the directions of activity under international environmental law and environmental policy (ex.

---

[34] Alan Boyle, *The Role of International Human Rights Law in the Protection of the Environment*, HUMAN RIGHTS APPROACHES TO ENVIRONMENTAL PROTECTION, Oxford (Alan E. Boyle, Michael R. Anderson eds., 1996), et. 48-49.
[35] This is indicated by Jan Jerzmański in: Jan Jerzmański, *Ochrona środowiska a prawa człowieka w prawie międzynarodowym*, in PRAWO CZŁOWIEKA DO ŚRODOWISKA NATURALNEGO: PRACA ZBIOROWA, Zaklad Narodowy im. Ossolińsklich (Jerzy Sommer ed. 1987), et. 154-155.
[36] Article 24 of the African Charter on Human and Peoples' Rights 1981.
[37] Article 11 of the Salvador Additional Protocol of 1988 to the American Convention on Human Rights 1969.

based on Stockholm Declaration or Rio Declaration). The wealth of states' activities in the form of national (and international) environmental protection law, including constitutional provisions of national legal systems recognizing the right to the environment, provides strong evidence of the emergence of environmental law as a rule of customary international law.[38]

## IV. Children's Right to the Environment as a Postulate *De Lege Ferenda*

**8.34.** The international community identifies threats through its legislation for the environment (ex. introduction of hazardous chemicals or a threat to a specific specific natural resource). Environmental treaties that relate to the protection of children's health can be grouped into the most important categories in the field of environmental protection: chemical industry and hazardous waste, water pollution, air pollution and food safety. Although none of the acts adopted by the international community relate directly to the protection of children's health, many environmental documents indicate risks that can also significantly adversely affect children.[39]

**8.35.** In the Convention on the Rights of the Child, ex. the act with the most significant legal effect, environmental issues are referred to in only one Article,[40] which guarantees children the right to the highest level of health. State parties were required to take appropriate measures to this end, taking into account environmental pollution. Even considering the degree of generality of the language of international law, it is not possible to infer on this basis the creation of a universal norm that is desirable.

**8.36.** In contemporary legal status, attempts are being made to interpret the child's right to the environment from norms in which the content does not explicitly indicate the existence of such a right. This may raise doubts as to the effectiveness of any attempt to rely on such a legal basis. It seems that more is counting on the creation of a customary norm, through whose practical application a norm of customary law would be established. Creating mechanisms of action would accustom society to the presence of certain norms and enable enriching the legal culture with norms not yet defined. As a consequence,

---

[38] Lynda Collins, *Are We There Yet? The Right to Environment in International and European Law*, 3(2) MCGILL INTERNATIONAL JOURNAL OF SUSTAINABLE DEVELOPMENT LAW AND POLICY (2007), et. 136.
[39] ANNE PERRAULT, JOANNA LEVITT, USING INTERNATIONAL LAW AND INSTITUTIONS TO PROTECT CHILDREN'S ENVIRONMENTAL HEALTH, Washington (2005), et. 26.
[40] See Article 24 of the 1989 Convention on the Rights of the Child.

by such broad and multifaceted actions it would be possible to incorporate the concept of the right of the child into the environment in the universal system of protection of children's rights.

8.37.    In this way, it is pointed out that there are attempts to interpret the child's right to the environment at the doctrinal level. Therefore, it was postulated to take appropriate legislative measures, primarily by the international community, in order to actually establish an environmental principle for the youngest. Then, the appropriate legislative framework would be available for states to take appropriate actions aimed at implanting, in national law, the guarantees previously laid down in acts of public international law. In addition, it would be desirable not only to uphold the guarantees provided for in such acts, but also to attempt to pursue further rights for the weakest. Children are a special group because it is not possible for them to present their interests at both national and international level. In this situation, rational entities are required to take action in the interest of future generations. It has been repeatedly emphasized that events witnessed during early stages of life have a great impact on mental health. Through proper legislative activity, it thus seems possible to define a catalog of potential threats and measures, as well as instruments of adequate response, which can be avoided by one and the other at the same time, in order to ensure peaceful mental and physical development of the entities under protection.

8.38.    The entire achievements of public international law to this date, in particular international human rights law and international environmental law, have been used to construct the child's right to the environment.

8.39.    In the Rio Declaration,[41] reference was made: to the creativity, ideals and courage of the world's youth, which should also be included in the decision-making process related to environmental protection due to their attributes.

8.40.    In Agenda 21[42] it was noted that children constitute one third of the population and in developed countries even half of the population, and it is worth including them to protect the environment, as well as using their commitment to effectively implement the provisions of the program. It was also noted that the state of the environment affects children's health and affects their future, especially in developed countries. Many activities and recommendations were undertaken by the international

---

[41]    See Rule 21 of the Rio Declaration, UN Doc. A / CONF.151 / 26 / Rev.l (Vol. I).
[42]    UN Doc. A/CONF.151/26/Rev.l (Vol. I).

community to ensure that children are provided with a safe and healthy future, ex. a good quality environment, improved living standards and access to appropriate education, including ecological education. Agenda 21 sets out goals that should be met by countries to improve children's living conditions. One of them is to make countries aware of the need to ensure that children's interests are taken into account in the process of environmental protection and sustainable development. To achieve the set goals, it is proposed to promote basic activities in the field of environmental protection, which are related to the needs of children in this area.

8.41.    Currently, at this stage, the achievements of the international community can be supplemented with extremely valuable experience, which is a source of knowledge about the functioning of the right to the environment in practice. Currently, it does not seem appropriate to appoint further United Nations commissions and bodies to examine the situation and develop an appropriate project. The Commission on the Rights of the Child, having the relevant reports of States Parties to the Convention on the Rights of the Child, can draw appropriate conclusions from the implementation of the rights guaranteed so far. This knowledge can be *prima facie* helpful in further attempts to construct a new child's right, which is only possible after sufficient research is undertaken.

8.42.    In a modern, dynamically developing world, where environmental issues play an important role and are often raised issues in the international forum, it is desirable that the issue of children's right to the environment should be properly developed. In addition to the obvious application of explicit agreements on the human right to the environment in relation to children, as well as the provisions proclaimed in the Rio Declaration and Agenda 21, it is worth bearing in mind that there may be countries that wish to ratify the regulations relating to the youngest, without having yet ratified the regulations intended for adults. Such hope should be at the basis of taking action for further work on developing the child's right to the environment.

## V.    Conclusions

8.43.    To sum up the above considerations, it can be stated that the activity of the international community in the second half of the 20th century is a period of development of cooperation, which has primarily created universal protection of human rights. As a result of the experience of World War II, activities have been undertaken which result in both non-binding and binding acts of public international law developed within the United Nations. Agreements contained in these documents, thanks to the influence of the philosophy of law, allowed to designate the subject and standards of its organized protection. International *consensus* has become a practical expression of theoretical conceptual aspirations. As a result, a catalog of values protected by universally recognized norms of public international law was created.

**8.44.** Using inferential rules, it was possible to recognize *prima facie* human rights as children's rights. However, due to natural mental and physical weakness, children need special protection. Despite the fact that it is now proposed to treat them primarily as the subject of their rights, it is a specific unit that must be specifically protected. For this reason, actions have been taken at the international forum to create acts specific to the protection of children's rights.

**8.45.** The widespread recognition of the right to the environment as a third generation human right is a valuable exemplification of the application of custom in public international law. Despite the formulation of this right in a non-binding normative act of environmental law, the international community has included it in the catalog of human rights. The significance of the discussed law, shaped on the basis of the resolution, is caused by the relevance of the motives that followed the work on its definition. Public, fundamental recognition has proved to be sufficient for undisputed promulgation and respect.

**8.46.** The child's right to the environment is most widely expressed in the Rio de Janeiro Declaration and Agenda 21. To ensure the effective implementation of the protection of children's rights, the international community should be required to carry out further work on developing the child's right under examination. As *de lege ferenda* postulates, we can also propose to use the existing achievements of international human rights law, international environmental law, and doctrine. With proper use of knowledge about the effectiveness of the human right to the environment, as well as the child's right to the environment existing in its current form, there are no obstacles to the further development of the child's right to the environment in the contemporary world. Of course, it is also possible to properly apply the general regulation to children, but detailed regulation, taking into account the specificity of the group of addressees, can guarantee more effective assurance of this right. Then, the values deemed important for society will be protected and a specific social order will be strengthened, which in turn means that the law will fulfill its basic function.

| | |

## Summaries

**DEU**  [*Entwicklung des Rechts der Kinder auf Umwelt im Völkerrecht*]
*Das Verhältnis zwischen Menschenrechten und Umweltschutz hat keine lange Geschichte. Die internationale Gemeinschaft hat die Notwendigkeit erkannt, bestimmte organisierte Aktivitäten auf dieser Ebene als Reaktion auf neu auftretende Umweltbedrohungen im Zusammenhang mit der uneingeschränkten Entwicklung von Technologien und Industrie in der heutigen Welt zu entfalten. Die Verschlechterung der natürlichen Umwelt hat sich als selbst für die Menschheit als schädlich erwiesen. Das bedeutet, dass die Grundrechte verletzt werden. Außerdem wurde ein Link entdeckt, der diese auf den ersten Blick scheinbar unterschiedlichen Probleme verbindet. Dies spiegelte sich auch in den von der internationalen Gemeinschaft formulierten Menschenrechten auf eine natürliche Umwelt wider.*

*Nahezu parallel entwickelt sich derzeit das System des universellen Schutzes der Kinderrechte. Viele erprobte und bewährte Lösungen wurden vom internationalen System für den Schutz der Menschenrechte übernommen. Das Recht des Kindes auf die Umwelt ist jedoch noch nicht ausdrücklich verankert. Die Anwendung der Deduktionsregeln kann aber zu Schlussfolgerungen führen, die es ermöglichen würden, diese Lücke im System der Standards des internationalen öffentlichen Völkerrechts zu schließen.*

*Das Wesentliche dieser Debatte ist die Behauptung, dass das Recht auf die Umwelt eines der Rechte des Kindes als ein Element ist, das im universellen System für den Schutz der Menschenrechte allgemein anerkannt ist. Der Beitrag beleuchtet die Rechtsposition des Kindes im Bereich des internationalen Umweltrechts. Zu Beginn versucht der Beitrag, das Konzept des Kindes im internationalen öffentlichen Recht zu definieren. Im Weiteren werden die Motive der internationalen Gemeinschaft vorgestellt, die sich der Entwicklung des internationalen Schutzes der Kinderrechte widmen. Zum weiteren Ziel der in dem Artikel präsentierten Forschung war es, die Entwicklung und Bedeutung des Rechts auf Umwelt zu skizzieren. Schließlich bietet der Autor eine Bewertung des aktuellen rechtlichen Status des Kindes im Rahmen des Umweltschutzes an. Darüber hinaus listet der Beitrag mehrere Postulate de lege ferenda für die internationale Gemeinschaft auf.*

CZE [*Vývoj práva dětí na životní prostředí v mezinárodním právu*]

*Vztah mezi lidskými právy a ochranou životního prostřední nemá dlouhou historii. Mezinárodní společenství uznalo potřebu provádět na této úrovni určité organizované činnosti v návaznosti na objevující se hrozby v oblasti životního prostředí spojené s neomezeným rozvojem technologií a průmyslu v současném světě. Zjistilo se, že zhoršování přirozeného životního prostředí poškozuje samo lidstvo, což znamená, že jsou porušována základní práva. Rovněž byla objevena vazba, která spojuje tyto na první pohled zdánlivě odlišné problémy. To se odrazilo i v lidských právech na přirozené životní prostředí formulovaných mezinárodním společenstvím. V současnosti se téměř souběžně vyvíjí systém univerzální ochrany práv dětí. Řada vyzkoušených a ověřených řešení byla převzata z mezinárodního systému ochrany lidských práv. Právo dítěte na životní prostředí však stále není zakotveno výslovně. Aplikací pravidel dedukce lze nicméně na základě těchto úvah dojít k závěrům, které by umožnily tuto mezeru v systému standardů mezinárodního práva veřejného překlenout. Podstata diskuse spočívá v tvrzení, že právo na životní prostředí je jedním z práv dítěte jako prvek všeobecně uznávaný v univerzálním systému ochrany lidských práv. Příspěvek nastiňuje právní postavení dítěte v oblasti mezinárodního práva životního prostředí. Na úvod se článek pokouší definovat koncepci dítěte v mezinárodním právu veřejném. Dále jsou předestřeny motivy mezinárodního společenství, které se věnuje rozvoji mezinárodní ochrany práv dětí. Dalším cílem výzkumu bylo nastínit vývoj a význam pojmu práva na životní prostředí. Na závěr autor nabízí posouzení současného právního postavení dítěte v kontextu ochrany práv v oblasti životního prostředí. Příspěvek navíc uvádí několik postulátů de lege ferenda pro mezinárodní společenství.*

| | |

POL [*Rozwój prawa dziecka do środowiska w prawie międzynarodowym*]
*Istotą debaty jest twierdzenie, że prawo do środowiska jest jednym z praw dziecka, jako element powszechnie uznawany w uniwersalnym systemie ochrony praw człowieka. Artykuł przedstawia status prawny dziecka w międzynarodowym prawie ochrony środowiska. Na początku próbowano zdefiniować pojęcie dziecka w międzynarodowym prawie publicznym. Następnie przedstawiono motywy społeczności międzynarodowej zaangażowanej w rozwój międzynarodowej ochrony praw dziecka. Kolejnym celem badawczym było przedstawienie genezy i znaczenia pojęcia prawa do środowiska. Na koniec uwzględniono ocenę obecnego statusu prawnego dziecka w kontekście ochrony praw środowiskowych. Ponadto, przedstawiono kilka postulatów de lege ferenda dla społeczności międzynarodowej.*

FRA [**Le droit des enfants à l'environnement dans le contexte du droit international et son évolution**]
*La discussion part du constat que le droit à l'environnement fait partie des droits de l'enfant, généralement reconnu dans le système universel de protection des droits de l'homme. Le présent article s'intéresse au statut juridique de l'enfant dans le contexte du droit international de l'environnement. Tout d'abord, il cherche à définir la conception de l'enfant dans le droit international public, pour réfléchir ensuite sur les motifs qui poussent la communauté internationale à approfondir la protection internationale des droits de l'enfant. L'étude a également pour objectif d'esquisser l'évolution et la signification du concept de droit à l'environnement. En conclusion, l'auteur examine l'actuelle situation juridique de l'enfant dans le contexte de la protection des droits relatifs à l'environnement. Par ailleurs, l'article fait quelques propositions « de lege ferenda » à l'attention de la communauté internationale.*

RUS [*Развитие права детей на окружающую среду в международном праве*]
*Суть дискуссии исходит из утверждения, что право на окружающую среду является одним из прав ребенка как общепризнанный элемент универсальной системы защиты прав человека. В статье указан правовой статус ребенка в области международного права окружающей среды. В начале статьи автор пытается определить концепцию ребенка в международном публичном праве. Далее представлены мотивы международного сообщества, связанные с развитием международной защиты прав*

Czech Yearbook of International Law®

*детей. Следующая цель исследования заключалась в том, чтобы наметить развитие и важность понятия права на окружающую среду. В заключение автор представляет оценку существующего правового статуса ребенка в контексте защиты прав в области охраны окружающей среды. В статье также приводятся постулаты de lege ferenda для международного сообщества.*

ESP [*Evolución de los derechos del niño al medio ambiente en el derecho internacional*]
*El punto fundamental de la discusión consiste en la afirmación de que el derecho al medio ambiente constituye uno de los derechos del niño generalmente reconocido en el sistema universal de la protección de los derechos humanos. En el texto se aborda la posición del niño en ámbito del derecho ambiental internacional y se pretende formular una definición del niño en el derecho público internacional. A continuación, se alegan los motivos de la protección internacional de los derechos del niño y se esbozan la evolución y la concepción del derecho al medio ambiente. En la conclusión, el autor evalúa la posición legal del niño en contexto de la protección de los derechos al medio ambiente. El texto también aporta algunos postulados de lege ferenda para la comunidad internacional.*

| | |

## Bibliography

MARIAN BALCEREK, PRAWA DZIECKA, Warszawa (1986).

JADWIGA BOHDANOWICZ, KU CYWILIZACJI EKOROZWOJU, Gdańsk (1998).

Alan Boyle, *The Role of International Human Rights Law in the Protection of the Environment*, HUMAN RIGHTS APPROACHES TO ENVIRONMENTAL PROTECTION, Oxford (Alan E. Boyle, Michael R. Anderson eds., 1996).

Lynda Collins, *Are We There Yet? The Right to Environment in International and European Law*, 3(2) MCGILL INTERNATIONAL JOURNAL OF SUSTAINABLE DEVELOPMENT LAW AND POLICY (2007).

Przemysław Dąbkowski, *Prawo prywatne polskie*, 1 LWÓW (1910).

KRZYSZTOF DRZEWICKI, PRAWO DO ROZWOJU. STUDIUM Z ZAKRESU PRAW CZŁOWIEKA, Gdańsk (1988).

Krzysztof Drzewicki, *Koncepcja prawa do środowiska jako prawa człowieka*, 10 PAŃSTWO I PRAWO (1985).

Krzysztof Drzewicki, *Trzecia generacja praw człowieka*, 10 SPRAWY MIĘDZYNARODOWE (1983).

BARTŁOMIEJ GROICKI, OBRONA SIEROT I WDÓW, Warszawa (1958).

Jan Jerzmański, *Ochrona środowiska a prawa człowieka w prawie międzynarodowym*, in PRAWO CZŁOWIEKA DO ŚRODOWISKA NATURALNEGO: PRACA ZBIOROWA, Zaklad Narodowy im. Ossolińsklich (Jerzy Sommer ed. 1987).

Piotr Kitowski, Natalia Radecka, *Normatywny model opieki nad sierotami w XVI-wiecznych rewizjach prawa chełmińskiego. Zarys instytucji*, LXIV(1) CZASOPISMO PRAWNO-HISTORYCZNE (2012).

Adam Łopatka, *Kto jest dzieckiem?*, KONWENCJA O PRAWACH DZIECKA A PRAWO POLSKIE, Warszawa (Adam Łopatka ed. 1991).

TADEUSZ MACIEJEWSKI, HISTORIA POWSZECHNA USTROJU I PRAWA, Warszawa (2007).

John G. Merrills, *Environmental Rights*, INTERNATIONAL ENVIRONMENTAL LAW, Oxford (Daniel Bodansky, Jutta Brunnée, Ellen Hey eds., 2008).

Dawid Michalski, *Rodzina w artykule 11 Konkordatu z 1993 roku*, 11 CYWILIZACJA I POLITYKA (2013).

Dawid Michalski, *Rozwój uniwersalnej ochrony praw człowieka*, 14 CYWILIZACJA I POLITYKA (2016).

Dawid Michalski, *Źródła międzynarodowej ochrony praw dziecka w Organizacji Narodów Zjednoczonych*, 1 AEQUITAS (2013).

Oktawian Nawrot, *Bioprawo*, FILOZOFIA PRAWA, Warszawa (Jerzy Zajadło, Kamil Zeidler eds., 2013).

OKTAWIAN NAWROT, LUDZKA BIOGENEZA W STANDARDACH BIOETYCZNYCH RADY EUROPY, Warszawa (2011).

ANNE PERRAULT, JOANNA LEVITT, USING INTERNATIONAL LAW AND INSTITUTIONS TO PROTECT CHILDREN'S ENVIRONMENTAL HEALTH, Washington (2005).

MAREK PIECHOWIAK, PREAMBUŁA, KONWENCJA O PRAWACH DZIECKA. ANALIZA I WYKŁADNIA, Instytut Nauk Prawnych PAN – Ars boni et aequi (1999).

MARTA PRUCNAL, OCHRONA DZIECI PRZED UCZESTNICTWEM W DZIAŁANIACH ZBROJNYCH WE WSPÓŁCZESNYM PRAWIE MIĘDZYNARODOWYM, Warszawa (2012).

Wojciech Radecki, *Filozoficzne i polityczne podstawy prawa człowieka do środowiska*, PRAWO CZŁOWIEKA DO ŚRODOWISKA

NATURALNEGO, Wrocław-Warszawa-Kraków-Gdańsk-Łódź (Jerzy Sommer ed. 1987).

WŁADYSŁAW ROZWADOWSKI, PRAWO RZYMSKIE. ZARYS WYKŁADU WRAZ Z WYBOREM ŹRÓDEŁ, Poznań (1992).

Jarosław Ruszewski, *Dostęp do informacji o środowisku*, 9 PROKURATURA I PRAWO (2005).

Tadeusz Smyczyński, *Pojęcie dziecka i jego podmiotowość*, KONWENCJA O PRAWACH DZIECKA: ANALIZA I WYKŁADNIA, Poznań – Ars boni et aequi (1999).

PHILIPPE SANDS, JACQUELINE PEEL, ADRIANA FABRA, RUTH MACKENZIE, PRINCIPLES OF INTERNATIONAL ENVIRONMENTAL LAW, Cambridge (2012).

Anna Śledzińska-Simon, *Rola Europejskiego Trybunału Praw Człowieka w kształtowaniu standardów* w zakresie bioetyki i biotechnologii, PRAWA CZŁOWIEKA WOBEC ROZWOJU BIOTECHNOLOGII, Warszawa (Lena Kondratiewa-Bryzik, Katarzyna Sękowska-Kozłowska ed. 2013).

Remigiusz Sobański, *Prawa człowieka a ekologia*, PRAWA CZŁOWIEKA W PAŃSTWIE EKOLOGICZNYM, Warszawa (Remigiusz Sobański ed. 1998).

Diana Trzcińska, *Pojęcie organizacji ekologicznej*, 2 GDAŃSKIE STUDIA PRAWNICZE. PRZEGLĄD ORZECZNICTWA (2011).

KRYSTYNA M. URBAŃSKA, PRAWO PODMIOTOWE DO DOBREGO ŚRODOWISKA W PRAWIE MIĘDZYNARODOWYM I POLSKIM, Gdańsk (2013).

Leszek Wiśniewski, *Geneza Konwencji o Prawach Dziecka i stosunek jej norm do innych aktów prawa międzynarodowego*, KONWENCJA O PRAWACH DZIECKA. ANALIZA I WYKŁADNIA, Poznań (Tadeusz Smyczyński ed. 1999).

Czech Yearbook of International Law®

Iryna Protsenko

*Key words:*
*aliens | rights of aliens | trade union | right to organize in trade unions | International Labour Organization (ILO)*

# Rights of Aliens to Organize in Trade Unions

**Abstract** | *This paper covers the problem of aliens in Ukraine with exercising the right to organize in trade unions, which is guaranteed by international law to any and all workers. For example, this right is granted to every individual according to the international legal instruments that make the International Bill of Human Rights, as well as to any and all workers according to a number of conventions of the International Labour Organization (ILO), including those deemed by ILO as fundamental. The latter, for example, includes ILO`s Freedom of Association and Protection of the Right to Organize Convention (1948) No. 87 (Co87) – where Ukraine is a participant. But despite this, aliens in Ukraine enjoy only partially the right to organize in trade unions: aliens do not have any right to establish trade unions, but may only participate in trade union activities, if provided for by their articles of association. It is worth saying that in some former USSR republics, the legal regulation of the right to organize in trade unions also fails to meet the international law requirements although certain CIS Member States can be reported to fully comply with them. The paper also emphasizes that in regulating human rights, freedoms or duties, it is typical of Ukraine to omit aliens or their specific categories and to be vague and inconsistent in regulating these matters, which also takes place with the right to organize in trade unions.*

**Iryna Protsenko,** Candidate of Law Sciences, Senior Research Associate, International law and comparative law studies Department V. M. Koretsky Institute of state and law of National Academy of Sciences of Ukraine. In 2016, Iryna defended a Candidate`s dissertation: "Private-legal framework governing trade relations in Germany". The area of Iryna`s scientific expertise covers the problems of theory of private international law and international trade law, which studies have revealed considerable weaknesses in the legal regulation of rights of aliens internationally and nationwide.
E-mail: iraprocenko@ukr.net

| | |

# I. Introduction: Overview of Problems in Regulation of Rights of Aliens by Ukrainian Law

**9.01.** The contemporary Ukrainian science of international law is focused on the problems of international legal protection of human rights to a sufficient degree. Studies are made in the areas of universal and regional (principally European) mechanisms of protection of both human rights in general and rights of separate categories of individuals like: national minorities, migrant workers, women, children, disabled, etc. At the same time, Ukrainian scientists do not focus well enough on the specific nature of international legal regulation and protection of rights of aliens, in particular of foreign nationals. An exception is probably the legal status of refugees which due to the existence of special universal international legal regulation, has enjoyed separate extended legal regulation and the applicable scientific analysis. We believe that an in-depth and comprehensive study of the specific nature of the international legal regulation of rights and freedoms of aliens overall may serve as a basis for the elimination of all those weaknesses of Ukrainian law currently effective in this area.[1]

**9.02.** In particular, Ukrainian laws in their regulation of certain rights and duties of individuals often fail to grant them to aliens or their specific categories. For example, Article 11 of The Law of Ukraine "Fundamentals of the Legislation of Ukraine on Health Care" dated 19 November 1992[2] about the legal regimes for rights and duties of aliens in the area of health care solely refers to the aliens permanently residing in Ukraine (those aliens are made equal with Ukrainian citizens in terms of rights enjoyed) and aliens temporarily staying in Ukraine (for those aliens, specific legal regulation should be developed). Still, the above Article 11 does not at all refer to those aliens who temporarily reside in Ukraine (like, for example, foreign students or foreign workers).

---

[1] To have better understanding of the legal status of aliens in Ukraine, we should focus on the specific understanding of the definition "alien" by Ukrainian laws, in particular by the law being essential for this area – Law of Ukraine "On the Legal Status of Foreigners and Stateless Persons" No. 3773-VI / 2011. In paragraph 6 of part 1 of Article 1 of this Law, a person that is not a citizen of Ukraine and is a citizen (subject) of another state or states is treated as an "alien". Thus, following Ukrainian laws, the legal definitions "alien" and "foreign national (subject)" are synonyms; in its turn, "stateless persons" is a separate category of individuals. Depending on the purpose of their stay in Ukraine, aliens and stateless persons are divided into: those permanently residing in Ukraine; those temporarily residing in Ukraine; those temporarily staying in Ukraine – and the scope of their rights and duties in Ukraine is considerably different. In this paper, "aliens" shall refer to foreign nationals (subjects) and stateless persons.

[2] Law of Ukraine "Fundamentals of the Legislation of Ukraine on Health Care" No. 2801-XII/1992, published in The Official Bulletin of the Verkhovna Rada of Ukraine under No. 4/1993, available at: https://zakon.rada.gov.ua/laws/anot/2801-12 (accessed on 29 January 2020). Abstract text of the Law in English see e.g. https://zakon.rada.gov.ua/laws/anot/en/2801-12 (accessed on 29 January 2020).

Czech Yearbook of International Law®

Also, Article 10 of the same legislation is not correct enough in legal terms. It states that Ukrainian citizens have an obligation to avoid harm to the health of other citizens (Clause *a*). This wording results in an absurd conclusion that Ukrainian citizens have the right to do harm to the health of foreign nationals and stateless persons.

**9.03.** In addition, there are contradictions and inconsistencies that exist between The Constitution of Ukraine dated 28 June 1996[3] and certain Laws of Ukraine in terms of the scope of individuals eligible for particular human rights. It is the author's opinion that these contradictions and inconsistencies are even more problematic. For example, part 1 of Article 36 of the Constitution of Ukraine provides the right to organize in political parties solely to Ukrainian citizens. The Law of Ukraine "On Political Parties in Ukraine" dated 05 April 2001[4] also speaks about the right of citizens[5] to be free to organize in such parties (Article 1) and grants the right to participate in such parties solely to Ukrainian citizens (Article 6). However, Article 314 of The Civil Code of Ukraine dated 16 January 2003[6] provides for the right to be free to organize in political parties to any and all individuals/natural persons irrespective of their citizenship. In practice this contradiction does not bring in any negative results since it is conventional in Ukraine to establish political parties on the basis of the Constitution of Ukraine and aforementioned specific Law,[7] rather than on the basis of the Civil Code. Also, contemporary Ukrainian law experts have not come to a uniform conclusion as to whether it is reasonable or not to provide aliens with the freedom to organize in political parties.[8] Despite this, it is alarming that those who developed

---

3    Constitution of Ukraine 254к/96-ВР/1996, published in The Official Bulletin of the Verkhovna Rada of Ukraine under No. 30/1996. See e.g. in English available at: https://www.legislationline.org/download/id/8233/file/Ukraine_Constitution_am2019_EN.pdf. (accessed on 29 January 2020).

4    Law of Ukraine "On Political Parties in Ukraine" No. 2365-III/2001, published in The Official Bulletin of the Verkhovna Rada of Ukraine under No. 23/2001, available at: https://zakon.rada.gov.ua/laws/show/2365-14, (accessed on 29 January 2020). Abstract text of the Law in English available at: https://zakon.rada.gov.ua/laws/anot/en/2365-14 (accessed on 29 January 2020).

5    In this Law, the definition "citizen" is used, with its nationality and state affiliation being omitted. This technical error is widespread in Ukrainian laws, and this will be repeatedly illustrated further on in this paper.

6    Civil Code of Ukraine [No. 435-IV/2003], published in The Official Bulletin of the Verkhovna Rada of Ukraine under Nos.40-44/2003, available at: https://zakon.rada.gov.ua/laws/show/435-15 (accessed on 29 January 2020). Abstract text of the Code in English available at: https://zakon.rada.gov.ua/laws/anot/en/435-15 (accessed on 29 January 2020).

7    In our opinion, it is not fair enough with respect to foreign nationals permanently residing in Ukraine to deprive them of the right to organize in political parties, since the political life of the state definitely involves them too, and so they should be able to participate.

8    Refer, for example, to Viktoriya Ivanivna Ivancho, *Right of Aliens to Organize in Political Parties and Civil Associations in Ukraine, Poland and the Federal Republic of Germany: Benchmark Analysis*, 29(1) SCIENTIFIC BULLETIN OF UZHHOROD NATIONAL UNIVERSITY, Series: Law. 70-73 (2014) (ukr.). *(PDF Download Available)*, available at: http://nbuv.gov.ua/UJRN/nvuzhpr_2014_29%281%29__18

such a critically important regulation as the Civil Code could allow such a grave inconsistency of its provisions with those of the Constitution of Ukraine, even though they were strongly sticking to the opinion that it was necessary to grant the right to be free to organize in political parties to any and all individuals residing in Ukraine.

9.04. The scope of individuals who may establish civil associations in Ukraine and be their participants is also unclear in our opinion. As the abovementioned part 1 of Article 36 of the Constitution of Ukraine states, only Ukrainian citizens have the right to be free to organize in civil associations. At the same time, the special-purpose Law of Ukraine "On Civil Associations" dated 22 March 2012[9] states that individuals/natural persons may be founders and participants of civil associations – i.e. Ukrainian citizens, aliens and stateless persons legally staying in Ukraine[10] (Articles 1, 7 and 8). In this case, the Civil Code of Ukraine follows the concept of the abovementioned Law and also provides all individuals/natural persons with the right to be free to organize in civil associations, irrespective of their nationality and state affiliation (Article 314). Consequently, a serious conflict arises between the provisions of the fundamental law of the state – the Constitution of Ukraine, and the provisions of the Law of Ukraine. In practice, the Law of Ukraine prevails in this conflict. This places doubt as to the effect of the Constitution of Ukraine. In addition, contemporary Ukrainian scientists make note of the inconsistency between the abovementioned provisions of the Constitution of Ukraine and the fundamental international legal instruments in the area of human rights. For example, V. I. Kozlov, the author of the dissertation "Collective Political Rights and Freedoms of Citizens of Ukraine: Constitutional and Legal Analysis", stated:

> "The fundamental law of the state also establishes the provisions, which contradict the requirements of international instruments and at the same time restrict the rights of citizens[11]. This refers, for example, to the right to establish civil associations

---

(accessed on 29 January 2020).

[9] The Law of Ukraine "On Civil Associations" No. 4572-VI/2012, published in The Official Bulletin of the Verkhovna Rada of Ukraine under No. 1/2013, available at: https://zakon.rada.gov.ua/laws/show/4572-17 (accessed on 29 January 2020). Abstract text of the Law in English see: https://zakon.rada.gov.ua/laws/anot/en/4572-17 (accessed on 29 January 2020).

[10] In our opinion, the mentioned articles of The Law of Ukraine "On Civil Associations" require more exact wording to specify that the rights therein are granted to the aliens permanently or temporarily residing in Ukraine, since it is not rational to grant them to the individuals temporarily staying in Ukraine (tourists, for example).

[11] This wording by V.I. Kozlov, probably, has a mistake; following the context of the whole citation, this sentence should refer to "foreign citizens" rather than just "citizens".

and to become their participants, as well as the right of freedom to peaceful assembly, armor-free, and to meetings, parades and demonstrations – which are granted by the Constitution of Ukraine to solely the citizens of our country, even though international instruments provide them to all individuals irrespective of their nationality and citizenship".[12]

**9.05.** Therefore, one and the same provision of the Constitution of Ukraine (part 1 of Article 36) provides the right of freedom to organize in political parties and the right of freedom to organize in civil associations solely to Ukrainian citizens, but this provision is very much different in its being exercised across Ukrainian laws and Ukrainian scientists believe that it contradicts fundamental international legal instruments in the area of human rights (at least where it refers to the right to freedom to organize and participate in civil associations).

## II. Specific Regulation of Rights of Aliens to Organize in Trade Unions by Ukrainian Law

**9.06.** In addition to the above illustrations, there is one further example that clearly illustrates both the inconsistency of Ukrainian laws in regulation of granting human rights to aliens and their conflict with universal international law. It refers to one of the essentials of the three trade-union rights: right to organize in trade unions.

**9.07.** It should be noted that the legal regulation of this right is generally based on the provisions of part 3 of Article 36 of the Constitution of Ukraine. According to these provisions, "Citizens shall have the right to take part in trade unions with the purpose of protecting their labour and socio-economic rights and interests. Trade unions shall be public organizations uniting citizens bound by common interests in accordance with the nature of their professional activity. Trade unions shall be formed without prior permission on the basis of the free choice of their members. All trade unions shall have equal rights. Restrictions on membership in trade unions shall be determined exclusively by this Constitution and laws of Ukraine".[13]

---

[12]  VOLODYMYR IVANOVYCH KOZLOV, COLLECTIVE POLITICAL RIGHTS AND FREEDOMS OF CITIZENS OF UKRAINE: CONSTITUTIONAL AND LEGAL ANALYSIS, Kharkiv (2009), et. 10.

[13]  Constitution of Ukraine 254к/96-BP/1996, published in The Official Bulletin of the Verkhovna Rada of Ukraine under No. 30/1996. See also in English: https://www.legislationline.org/download/id/8233/file/Ukraine_Constitution_am2019_EN.pdf (accessed on 29 January 2020).

**9.08.** When analyzing this provision, primary attention is focused on the scope of the right to organize in trade unions – the first sentence of part 3 of Article 36 of the Constitution of Ukraine only mentions only the right to participate in the activities of trade unions, rather than securing an absolute right to organize in trade unions. The right to establish trade unions is mentioned in the third sentence – where the freedom of formation of trade unions is declared (i.e. with no prior permission, on the basis of a free choice of their participants). At the same time, we should specifically emphasize the approach of the Constitutional Court of Ukraine to the definition of the nature and substance of the right to establish trade unions used by the Court during proceeding No. 1-36/2000 (freedom of formation of trade unions). This case did not refer to the right of aliens to organize in trade unions. It was still noteworthy, however. that the right to form trade unions was treated as an integral part of the right of Ukrainian citizens to freely organize in civil associations (Decision No. 11рп/2000 dated 18 October 2000), the third sentence of part 3 of Article 36 of the Constitution of Ukraine being considered by the Court as an additional – against the general provisions of part 1 of the above article – guarantee of exercising the right of the citizens bound by common professional interests to organize in trade unions.[14] This approach is in line with international law but given the inconsistencies that exist between the provisions of part 1 of Article 36 of the Constitution of Ukraine and The Law of Ukraine "On Civil Associations", it does not contribute to solving the problem outlined in this article.

**9.09.** Getting back to the problem emphasized in this paper, when analyzing part 3 of Article 36 of the Constitution of Ukraine, attention is focused on the definition used therein to outline the scope of individuals eligible for the right to participate in the activities of trade unions. This definition is "citizens".[15] Which individuals are encompassed within the definition "citizens" (to

---

[14] Refer to paragraph 3 of Clause 2.3 and paragraph 1 of Clause 3.2 of the Decision of the Constitutional Court of Ukraine on the proceeding, at the constitutional instance of people`s deputies of Ukraine and the Ukrainian Parliament Commissioner for Human Rights, for constitutional compliance of the Constitution of Ukraine (constitutionality) of Articles 8, 11, 16 of Law of Ukraine "On Trade Unions, their Rights and Guarantees of Activity" (proceeding for freedom of formation of trade unions) No. 11рп/2000 dated 18 October 2000, available at: https://zakon.rada.gov.ua/laws/card/v011p710-00 (accessed on 29 January 2020). It should be noted that the Constitutional Court of Ukraine refers in support of its arguments to certain international treaties (clause 3.3 of the Decision), meanwhile paying zero attention to the fact that such treaties extend the right to organize in trade unions to any and all individuals. Probably, the Court did so, because the subject of the case did not refer to the scope of individuals eligible for the right to organize in trade unions.

[15] In its turn, the provisions of part 3 of Article 36 of the Fundamental Law of Ukraine do not specify, which scope of individuals has the right to establish trade unions; if rely on the approach used in the abovementioned Decision of the Constitutional Court of Ukraine No. 11рп/2000 dated 18 October 2000, then it should solely refer to Ukrainian citizens.

solely Ukrainian citizens or to all individuals having citizenship of any state) is, however, not stipulated in the Constitution of Ukraine.[16] It is reasonable to suggest, however, that the above definition solely refers to Ukrainian citizens. This is because in cases where the Constitution of Ukraine grants particular rights for any and all individuals/natural persons, it refers to "all people", "every individual" etc. In addition, Article 26 of the Fundamental Law of Ukraine[17] provides for equality of aliens and stateless persons with Ukrainian citizens, except as restricted by the Constitution, laws or international treaties of Ukraine. Taking this into consideration, we may conclude that according to the Constitution of Ukraine, foreign nationals and stateless persons are provided with the rights, freedoms and duties equal to those of Ukrainian citizens, except as restricted by, for example, the Constitution of Ukraine – which, actually, does restrict their right to participate in the activities of trade unions.

9.10.   The scope of individuals eligible for the right to organize in trade unions is regulated in more detail by The Law of Ukraine "On Trade Unions, Their Rights and Guarantees of Activity" dated 15 September 1999[18] (hereinafter, the Law "On Trade Unions"), which we believe to not resolve the problem of not clear enough constitutional regulation of the above right, but rather to aggravate it. The Law states that foreign nationals and stateless persons cannot establish trade unions, but can become their participants, if provided for by the articles of association of the respective trade unions (Article 6). Still, when returning back to part 3 of Article 36 of the Constitution of Ukraine where the right to participate in the activities of trade unions is solely granted to Ukrainian citizens, then Article 6 of the Law

---

[16]   It is worth mentioning that the Basic Law for the Federal Republic of Germany also often refers to a pretty abstract definition "all German people", but it is explicated in Article 116 thereof. In particular, "German people" refer to the individuals having German citizenship or those accepted – as refugees, or as exiled German nationals or their spouses or offspring – in Germany within the boundaries existing as at 31 December 1937. Former German citizens deprived of citizenship between 30 January 1933 and 08 May 1945 due to political, ethnic or religious beliefs, as well as their offspring are subject to restoration of their citizenship at their request. They are deemed as not having lost their citizenship, if after 08 May 1945 they resided in Germany and expressed no other will of theirs. By the way, according to part 3 of Article 9 of the Basic Law for the Federal Republic of Germany, the right to form associations to safeguard and improve working and economic conditions shall be guaranteed to every individual and to every occupation or profession in Germany.
[17]   Article 26 of the Constitution of Ukraine is yet another example of inconsistent regulation of rights of aliens in Ukraine, as part 2 thereof says that Foreigners and stateless persons may be granted asylum under the procedure established by law, but such law is still missing. Only paragraph 26 of Article 106 of the Constitution of Ukraine says that the President of Ukraine shall adopt decisions on granting asylum in Ukraine.
[18]   Law of Ukraine "On Trade Unions, their Rights and Guarantees of Activity" No. 1045-XIV/1999, published in The Official Bulletin of the Verkhovna Rada of Ukraine under No. 45/1999, available at: https://zakon.rada.gov.ua/laws/show/1045-14 (accessed on 29 January 2020). Abstract text of the Law in English available at: https://zakon.rada.gov.ua/laws/anot/en/1045-14 (accessed on 29 January 2020).

"On Trade Unions" contradicts the Constitution of Ukraine. Unfortunately, some Ukrainian researchers, when studying the specific nature of granting rights to organize in trade unions, do not focus on the scope of rights provided for by the Constitution of Ukraine and by the Law "On Trade Unions" at all, which further results in wrong, and even more – mutually exclusive, conflicting conclusions. For example, the scientific and practical commentary to labour laws of Ukraine, in particular to Article 243 of the Labour Code of Ukraine, states that "the right of citizens to participate in trade unions provided for by Article 36 of the Constitution of Ukraine is detailed in Article 6 of the Law as their right to establish trade unions without any prior permission on the basis of a free choice of their members, to join and withdraw as per procedure stipulated by the articles of association of the respective trade unions".[19] In other words, as the authors of this work believe (who, by the way, declare without any evidential support that Article 6 of the Law "On Trade Unions" details Article 36 of the Constitution of Ukraine) that the right to participate in trade unions is extensive enough and covers the right to establish trade unions, the right to organize in trade unions, and the right to withdraw; and all those rights should be enjoyed solely by Ukrainian citizens. But further on, this commentary states that "since Article 26 of the Constitution of Ukraine allows that laws and international treaties of Ukraine provide for specific treatment of the legal status of aliens and stateless persons, part 2 of Article 6 of the Law allows no right for such individuals to establish trade unions, yet accepts their right to organize in the existing trade unions, if provided for by the articles of association of the respective trade unions".[20] Given the two positions above, it is totally unclear which scope of individuals should be eligible for the right to organize in trade unions and participate in their activities.

9.11. By the way, The Labour Code of Ukraine dated 10 December 1971[21] (as amended considerably) aggravates the matter with the right to organize in trade unions even further, as it totally expends this right solely to Ukrainian citizens. Its Article 243 states that "according to the Constitution of Ukraine and the

---

[19] BRONISLAV STANISLAVOVYCH STYCHYNSKYI, IHOR VOLODYMYROVYCH ZUB, VOLODYMYR HAVRYLOVYCH ROTAN, SCIENTIFIC AND PRACTICAL COMMENTARY TO LABOUR LAWS OF UKRAINE, REVISED AND EXTENDED, Kyiv: A.C.K (2 ed. 2000), et. 849.
[20] BRONISLAV STANISLAVOVYCH STYCHYNSKYI, IHOR VOLODYMYROVYCH ZUB, VOLODYMYR HAVRYLOVYCH ROTAN, *Supra* note 17.
[21] Labour Code of Ukraine No. 322-VIII/1971, published in The Official Bulletin of the Verkhovna Rada of Ukraine under Annex to No. 50/1971, available at: https://zakon.rada.gov.ua/laws/show/322-08 (accessed on 29 January 2020). Abstract text of the Code in English available at: https://zakon.rada.gov.ua/laws/anot/en/322-08 (accessed on 29 January 2020).

Law of Ukraine "On Trade Unions, Their Rights and Guarantees of Activity", Ukrainian citizens have the right to establish trade unions without any prior permission on the basis of a free choice of their members with the purpose of representing, exercising and protecting their labour and socio-economic rights and interests, to organize and withdraw as per procedure stipulated by the articles of association of the respective trade unions, and to participate in their activities".

9.12. Still, in practice it is mostly the Law "On Trade Unions" that is being relied upon when trade unions make their articles of association. For example, according to paragraph 2.1 of the Articles of Association of the Trade Union of Workers of Agro-Industrial Complexes of Ukraine, 2017, "nationals of other States working or studying in Ukraine may participate in the Trade Union ...";[22] also, according to part 2 of paragraph 8 of the Articles of Association of the Trade Union of Education and Science Workers of Ukraine, "foreign nationals legally residing in Ukraine and working or studying in the education area may participate in the Trade Union".[23] However, each of the examples above has additional weaknesses. For example, the second one should cover education and science, rather than just education; in both examples, no possibility is envisaged for stateless persons to join a trade union. Meanwhile, paragraph 3.1 of the Articles of Association of the shopfloor trade union of the Verkhnyednioprovsk College at Dnipro State Agrarian and Economic University states that "foreign nationals and stateless persons working or studying in the College may be the Trade Union members".[24]

## III. International Legal Regulation of the Scope of Individuals Eligible for the Right to Organize in Trade Unions

9.13. We believe that to select the right solution for the above conflict, the scope of individuals eligible for the right to organize in trade unions should be clearly defined by means of analysis of the universal international legal instruments in the area of human rights where Ukraine is a participant. Primarily, we refer to the Universal Declaration of Human Rights, 1948, and the

---

[22] Articles of Association of the Trade Union of Workers of Agro-Industrial Complexes of Ukraine, 2017, available at: http://profapk.org.ua/cms/charter.html (accessed on 29 January 2020).

[23] Articles of Association of the Trade Union of Education and Science Workers of Ukraine, 2016, available at: https://pon.org.ua/engine/download.php?id=1678 (accessed on 29 January 2020).

[24] Articles of Association of the shopfloor trade union of the Verkhnyednioprovsk College at Dnipro State Agrarian and Economic University, available at: http://vkddaeu.dp.ua/koledzh/kerivnytstvo/profkom-vk-ddaeu/statut-pervynnoi-profspilkovoi-orhanizatsii-vk-ddaeu.html (accessed on 29 January 2020).

International Covenants, 1966.[25] It should be noted that they are unanimous in this context, as both part 4 of Article 23 of the Universal Declaration of Human Rights, 1948, and Article 22 of The International Covenant on Civil and Political Rights, 1966, speak about the right of every individual to establish trade unions and organize in trade unions, with the only exception that the above covenant provides for cases where this right is subject to restrictions. In its turn, part 1 of Article 8 of The International Covenant on Economic, Social and Cultural Rights, 1966, states that governments should be responsible for ensuring the right of each individual to establish trade unions with the purpose of exercising and protecting their socio-economic rights and interests, and to join them on the basis of their free choice, with the only condition of observing the rules of the respective organization. The use of this right is subject to no restrictions, except as provided for by law and except those required in a democratic society to safeguard national security or civil protection, or to protect others' rights and freedoms.

9.14.  As such, the International Bill of Human Rights clearly declares that everyone is eligible for the right to organize in trade unions. However, after being subject to analysis, the above international legal instruments appear to not fully cover this right since they only speak about the right of every individual to establish trade unions and to organize but do not regulate the participation in the activities of trade unions, the in-house operations of trade unions, withdrawal etc. In addition, they provide for pretty extensive purposes of establishing trade unions, in particular: to safeguard the interests of every individual (part 4 of Article 23 of the Universal Declaration of Human Rights, 1948; Article 22 of The International Covenant on Civil and Political Rights, 1966) or to exercise and protect one's social and economic interests (part 1 of Article 8 of The International Covenant on Economic, Social and Cultural Rights, 1966). Such extensive definition of purposes pursued by organizing in trade unions, as well as any and all individuals rather than solely workers being treated as persons eligible for the right to organize in trade unions – this all may result in a pretty vague understanding of the substance of trade unions and can make it impossible to distinguish trade unions from other non-government organizations.

---

[25] Both covenants regulate the right to organize in trade unions, because, as professor V. N. Denysov said, this right "is "double" or "mixed". On the one part, they have the nature of economic and social rights, on the other part, of civil and political rights". Refer to: Volodymyr Naumovych Denysov, *On Specific Implementation of Social, Economic and Cultural Rights in the System of International Law of Human Rights,* 12 LEGAL STATE: YEARBOOK OF SCIENTIFIC WORKS OF V.M. KORETSKY INSTITUTE OF STATE AND LAW OF NATIONAL ACADEMY OF SCIENCES OF UKRAINE 511 (2001).

Therefore, it is also important to analyze the international legal regulation of this matter in the context of the International Labour Organization (ILO), which provides for a clearer and more comprehensive interpretation of this right since it is a fundamental principle of its activities and represents a "trilateral nature" concept being effective at ILO. The role of the right of freedom of association is emphasized in the Declaration of Philadelphia, which states that "freedom of expression and of association are essential to sustained progress".[26] In addition, the ILO Declaration on Fundamental Principles and Rights at Work and its Follow-up, 1998,[27] declared that all member States, even if they have not ratified the fundamental ILO Conventions, have an obligation arising from mere membership in ILO to respect, to promote and to realize, in good faith and in accordance with the ILO Constitution, the principles concerning the fundamental rights which are the subject of those Conventions – for example, freedom of association. As such, ILO treats the freedom of association not only as a right, but also as a principle of the international legal regulation of labour relations.

9.15. The right of freedom of association is regulated in more detail by two fundamental ILO Conventions: Convention No. 87 – Freedom of Association and Protection of the Right to Organize, 1948 (hereinafter, "Convention No. 87"),[28] and Convention No. 98 – Right to Organize and Collective Bargaining Convention, 1949, and Ukraine is a participant of both,[29] which means it should comply with their instructions.

9.16. To outline the scope of individuals eligible for the right of freedom of association in the labour environment, we believe it is enough to analyze Convention No. 87 as it provides for the key essence of this right. It states that "each Member of the International Labour Organization for which this Convention is in force undertakes to take all necessary and appropriate measures to ensure that workers and employers may exercise

---

[26] Declaration concerning the aims and purposes of the International Labour Organization (Declaration of Philadelphia) from 10 May 1944, available at: https://www.ilo.org/dyn/normlex/en/f?p=1000:62:0::NO:62:P62_LIST_ENTRIE_ID:2453907:NO (accessed on 29 January 2020).

[27] ILO Declaration on Fundamental Principles and Rights at Work and its Follow-up. Adopted by the International Labour Conference at its Eighty-sixth Session, Geneva, 18 June 1998, available at: https://www.ilo.org/declaration/thedeclaration/textdeclaration/lang--en/index.htm (accessed on 29 January 2020).

[28] Convention concerning Freedom of Association and Protection of the Right to Organize 1948 (No. 87), (adopted 09 July 1948, entry into force: 04 July 1950), available at: https://www.ilo.org/dyn/normlex/en/f?p=NORMLEXPUB:12100:0::NO::P12100_ILO_CODE:C087 (accessed on 29 January 2020).

[29] It should be emphasized that there are also other conventions at ILO, which regulate various matters of trade-union rights. For example, they are analyzed in the following papers: HALIVA INSAFIVNA CHANYSHEVA, COLLECTIVE RELATIONS IN LABOUR ENVIRONMENT: THEORY AND LAW MATTER, Odesa: Yurydychna literatura (2001), et. 225-241; BORYS MYKOLAYOVYCH ZHARKOV, TRADE-UNION RIGHTS AND THEIR INTERNATIONAL LEGAL PROTECTION, Moscow: Nauka (1990).

freely the right to organize" (Articles 1, 11). Each Member should ensure that "workers and employers, without distinction whatsoever, shall have the right to establish and, subject only to the rules of the organization concerned, to join organizations of their own choosing without previous authorization" (Article 2). It should be noted that the definition "organization"[30] is treated in this Convention as follows: "term organization means any organization of workers or of employers for furthering and defending the interests of workers or of employers". Convention No. 87 therefore binds the ILO Members to ensure that all workers with no distinction whatsoever may exercise their right to freely establish trade unions and to organize in trade unions. This conclusion is further proved by a number of reports of the ILO Committee on Freedom of Association, which is an integral part of ILO`s system of control over compliance with the international labour standards. In those reports, the Committee has repeatedly emphasized that Article 2 of Convention No. 87 is designed to give expression to the principle of non-discrimination in trade union matters, and the words "without distinction whatsoever" used in this Article mean that freedom of association should be guaranteed without discrimination of any kind based on occupation, sex, colour, race, beliefs, nationality, political opinion, etc., not only to workers in the private sector of the economy, but also to civil servants and public service employees in general.[31] In other words, according to the Committee, the ILO Members should guarantee the freedom to organize in trade unions to all working individuals with no discrimination whatsoever, including no nationality-based discrimination.

9.17. It is noteworthy that the ILO Committee on Freedom of Association has also emphasized in some of its reports that the right to organize in trade unions also extends to migrant workers, both officially registered and not registered. The Committee`s substantiation was as follows: "all workers, irrespective of their status, should enjoy the guarantee of being granted the right of freedom of association, to avoid creating the opportunities for abusing their insecure situation",[32] and also as follows: "all

---

[30] It should be pointed to the translation of Convention No. 87 from English to Russian or Ukrainian where the legal term "organization" is often conveyed wrong – as "association" or as "trade union", which often makes it difficult to understand the Convention.

[31] FREEDOM OF ASSOCIATION, COMPILATION OF DECISIONS OF THE COMMITTEE ON FREEDOM OF ASSOCIATION, Geneva: ILO 59 (6th edition, 2018), available at: https://www.ilo.org/wcmsp5/groups/public/---ed_norm/---normes/documents/publication/wcms_632659.pdf (accessed on 29 January 2020).

[32] Interim Report Commission on Freedom of Association No. 355, November 2009 (Case No. 2620 (Korea, Republic of)), available at: https://www.ilo.org/dyn/normlex/en/f?p=1000:50002:0::NO:50002:P50002_COMPLAINT_TEXT_ID:2911238 (accessed on 29 January 2020). Case subject: the government

Czech Yearbook of International Law®

workers, with the sole exception of the armed forces and the police, are covered by Convention No. 87".[33]

**9.18.** In addition, one more integral part of ILO`s system of control over the compliance with the international labour standards – the Committee of Experts on the Application of Conventions and Recommendations, has outlined the three essentials underlying the right of freedom of association, among which: no difference between those eligible for the right of freedom of association. This means that it is applicable to all categories of workers and employers, no difference can be made between them based on occupation, sex, colour, race, beliefs, nationality, political opinion, with the sole exception of the armed forces and the police. Besides, ILO`s regulatory authorities have repeatedly requested States to change their laws and practices of treating citizenship/nationality as a condition for establishing trade unions.[34]

**9.19.** Therefore, the freedom of every worker to organize in establishments with the purpose of protecting his/her interests is the principle declared in the ILO Constitution and it underlies ILO`s overall operations. Since this principle is declared in the ILO Constitution, each ILO Member, including Ukraine, should respect, promote and realize it. Also, according to Convention No. 87, all ILO Members, including Ukraine, should guarantee that every worker is free to exercise his/her right to organize in trade unions and this right may not be subject to any nationality-based restrictions. These provisions have been, inter alia, exercised by a number of the ILO authorities.

---

of the Republic of Korea refused to register a trade union established by the illegally employed migrant workers, arrested and subsequently deported its Presidents, which the complainants believed to be geared to create a low-wage labour force in the country.

[33] Interim Report Commission on Freedom of Association No. 371, March 2014. (Case No. 2620 (Korea, Republic of)), available at: https://www.ilo.org/dyn/normlex/en/f?p=1000:50002:0::NO:50002:P50002_COMPLAINT_TEXT_ID:3171863(accessed on 29 January 2020). It is noteworthy that this case was finished by the decision of the Supreme Court of the Republic of Korea declaring that illegally employed foreign workers may establish trade unions and organize in trade unions. The extracts from this decision are available in: Definitive Report Commission on Freedom of Association No. 377, March 2016 (Case No. 2620 (Korea, Republic of)), available at: https://www.ilo.org/dyn/normlex/en/f?p=1000:50002:0::NO:50 002:P50002_COMPLAINT_TEXT_ID:3277959 (accessed on 29 January 2020).

[34] For more detail, refer to: DAVID TAJGMAN AND KAREN CURTIS, FREEDOM OF ASSOCIATION: A USER`S GUIDE – STANDARDS, PRINCIPLES AND PROCEDURES OF THE INTERNATIONAL LABOUR ORGANIZATION, Geneva: ILO (2007), et. 14-16 (ros.), *(PDF Download Available)*, available at: https://www.ilo.org/wcmsp5/groups/public/---europe/---ro-geneva/---sro-moscow/documents/publication/wcms_307205.pdf (accessed on 29 January 2020).

## IV. Overview of the Doctrine of Compliance of the Ukrainian Law Related to Providing Aliens with the Right to Organize in Trade Unions with International Law Standards

9.20. A well-known Ukrainian labour law expert, H. I. Chanysheva, having analyzed quite a few international legal instruments that regulate various matters of trade-union rights has concluded that the effective Ukrainian laws have only one inconsistency with the provisions of such instruments, and this refers to part 2 of Article 6 of the Law of Ukraine "On Trade Unions".[35] Yu. V. Kyrychenko also comes to the same conclusion, but only with reference to part 3 of Article 36 of the Constitution of Ukraine, emphasizing that "specific about part 3 of Article 36 of the Constitution of Ukraine in effect is its being applied to solely Ukrainian citizens and thus being different from the international legal instruments, which refer to "every individual", and from constitutional practice of most European countries".[36] N. A. Tsiganchuk makes the same conclusion based on the analysis of international law standards and laws of foreign countries regulating the right to organize in trade unions. N. A. Tsiganchuk suggests that Article 36 of the Constitution of Ukraine ensures that "any and all individuals rather than just Ukrainian citizens are eligible for the right of freedom of association and the right to organize in trade unions".[37] However, Yu. V. Kyrychenko suggests a slightly different solution – to move the regulation of the right to organize in trade unions to Article 44 of the Constitution of Ukraine (refers to the right to strike) extending this right to any and all individuals rather than just citizens.[38] So many Ukrainian scientists note that the legal regulation of the right to organize in trade unions does not comply with the international law standards. However, they have not yet worked out some comprehensive solution that would cover the entire legal regulation of this matter. Ukrainian scientists tend to stop on suggestions to amend the Constitution of Ukraine and

---

[35] For more detail, refer to: HALIYA INSAFIYNA CHANYSHEVA, COLLECTIVE RELATIONS IN LABOUR ENVIRONMENT: THEORY AND LAW MATTER, Odesa: Yurydychna literatura (2001), et. 225-231.

[36] Yuriy Viktorovych Kyrychenko, *Freedom to organize in trade unionds: Compliance of Constitutional Practice of Ukraine with European Standards*, 10-1 SCIENTIFIC HERALD OF INTERNATIONAL HUMANITARIAN UNIVERSITY, Series: Legal science 71 (2014), (PDF Download Available), available at: http://www.vestnik-pravo.mgu.od.ua/archive/juspradenc10-1/part_1/21.pdf (accessed on 29 January 2020).

[37] NATALIYA ANTONIVNA TSIGANCHUK, TRADE UNIONS AS SUBJECTS OF LABOUR LAW, Kharkiv (2004), et. 11. Extended abstract of PhD dissertation. (PDF Download Available), available at: https://www.researchgate.net/publication/311330921_Profesijni_spilki_ak_sub'ekti_trudovogo_prava_Trade_Unions_as_Subjects_of_Labour_Law (accessed on 29 January 2020).

[38] Yuriy Viktorovych Kyrychenko, *Supra* note 36.

forget about the Law "On Trade Unions" and about The Labour Code of Ukraine. Here, we would like to note that prior to any amendments in Ukrainian laws, the Ukrainian doctrine should clearly define not only the scope of individuals eligible for the right to organize in trade unions, but also its substance.

**9.21.** Further, it should be emphasized that some Ukrainian scientists note rightfully the irrationality of a selective approach to granting the right to organize in trade unions to solely Ukrainian citizens. For example, O. O. Pifko accentuates that "if the restrictions for aliens in establishing political parties and in their membership in such political parties can be explained by the fact that political parties participate in establishing the government, and any aliens or stateless persons in political parties may create certain threats for the national security, then trade unions are established to represent and protect the labour, social and economic rights and interests of their participants. As such, restrictions in establishing trade unions limit the possibilities of aliens and stateless persons to protect their labour, social and economic rights and interests".[39]

**9.22.** In our opinion, the nonsense of a selective approach to defining the individuals eligible for the right to organize in trade unions is further emphasized by the fact that the right to strike in Article 44 of the Constitution of Ukraine is granted to all working individuals and by the fact that the right of employers to establish civil associations is granted to all individuals/natural persons irrespective of their nationality and state affiliation (even to stateless persons). The latter is seen from Article 2 of the Law of Ukraine "On Employer Organizations, Their Associations, and the Rights and Guarantees of Their Work" dated 22 June 2012,[40] which provides the right of association to employers irrespective of their state affiliation, and from paragraph 1 of part 4 of Article 10 of this Law where the employer-related information is described, which is subject to be provided in the list of persons participating in the founding congress, and this list is also alien-oriented. Therefore, Ukrainian laws provide foreign employers with the right to organize in their civil associations and provide foreign workers solely with the right

---

[39] Oleksandr Oleksandrovych Pifko, *The Peculiarities of the Realization of the Constitutional Right to Form and Join Trade Unions in Ukraine and in Some EU Member Countries: a Comparative Study*, 2 COMPARATIVE AND ANALYTICAL LAW 80 (2018). (PDF Download Available), available at: http://www.pap.in.ua/5_2018/20.pdf (accessed on 29 January 2020).
[40] Law of Ukraine "On Employer Organizations, Their Associations, and the Rights and Guarantees of Their Work" No. 5026-VI/2012, published in The Official Bulletin of the Verkhovna Rada of Ukraine under No. 22/2013, available at: https://zakon.rada.gov.ua/laws/show/5026-17 (accessed on 29 January 2020). Abstract text of the Law in English available at: https://zakon.rada.gov.ua/laws/anot/en/5026-17 (accessed on 29 January 2020).

to join trade unions, and the latter is even not clear enough in terms of it being consistent with the Constitution of Ukraine or not. Meanwhile, the irrationality of a selective approach to defining the individuals eligible for the right to organize in trade unions shows that it is rather an outcome of an inadequate legal culture of the draft law developers than a result of a well-thought-of government policy.

## V. Overview of Legal Regulation of the Scope of Individuals Eligible for the Right to Organize in Trade Unions in Particular CIS Member States

9.23. To remove the gaps in the Ukrainian legal regulation of the rights of aliens to organize in trade unions, it would be helpful to study the specific regulation of this matter in other countries, primarily in the CIS Member States and in Eastern Europe. In our opinion, it is important and noteworthy to research how the legal regulation of particular legal relationship was developing in the countries, which have been evolving in an environment similar to the one in Ukraine, and whose social and economic systems have a lot in common with the Ukrainian one.

9.24. When it comes to the legal regulation of the scope of individuals eligible for the right to organize in trade unions, we should note that the Republic of Belarus (RB) is similar to Ukraine in this respect. In particular, it goes about the following: the RB Constitution adopted in 1994[41] solely guarantees this right to the citizens (part 3 of Article 41), although "everyone shall have the right to freedom of association" (Article 36); at the same time, the RB Law "On Trade Unions" dated 22 April 1992[42] states that foreign nationals and stateless persons can solely organize in those trade unions established and existing in Belarus if provided for by the articles of association of the respective trade unions (part 2 of Article 2). As such, the RB legal regulation of the scope of individuals eligible for the right to organize in trade unions does not meet the international law standards – just as in Ukraine.

9.25. The regulation of the matter in Russia is even more inconsistent than in Ukraine. According to part 1 of Article 30 of the Constitution of the Russian Federation (RF) adopted in 1993,[43]

---

[41] Constitution of the Republic of Belarus 1994, available at: http://www.pravo.by/pravovaya-informatsiya/normativnye-dokumenty/konstitutsiya-respubliki-belarus/ (Ru) (accessed on 29 January 2020).
[42] RB Law No. 1605-XII "On Trade Unions", available at: http://pravo.newsby.org/belarus/zakon2/z061.htm (Ru) (accessed on 29 January 2020).
[43] Constitution of the Russian Federation 12 December 1993, available at: http://www.constitution.ru/ (Ru) (accessed on 29 January 2020).

"everyone shall have the right to ... create trade unions". However, the RF Law "On Trade Unions, Their Rights and Guarantees for Performance of Their Activities" dated 12 January 1996[44] (hereinafter, the "RF Law «On Trade Unions»") makes the regulation of the matter confusing, since on the one hand, a trade union is defined as a voluntary civil association of citizens (part 1 of Article 2) but on the other hand, everyone (i.e. not just a citizen) over 14 is eligible, on the basis of a free choice to establish trade unions for protection of his/her interests, to join trade unions, participate in trade union activities and withdraw (part 2 of Article 2). Meanwhile, part 4 of Article 2 establishes the provision that foreign nationals and stateless persons in the Russian Federation may organize in the RF trade unions, except as provided for by the RF federal laws or international treaties. Therefore, from our point of view, the matter of the scope of rights to organize in trade unions granted to aliens in the Russian Federation is still not resolved. This gives rise to the contradictory information about this matter in various legal publications. For example, when commenting on paragraph 4 of Article 2 of the RF Law "On Trade Unions", Denis Malyi expresses himself so that one can get the impression that aliens may establish trade unions in the Russian Federation. In particular, he states, "it will be difficult to substantiate the detection of cases where the rights of aliens and stateless persons to establish and organize in the Russian trade unions are restricted".[45] At the same time, the Federation of Trade Unions of the Sverdlovsk region announced in 2008 the need to establish a trade union for migrant workers, which would become a part of the regional federation of trade unions "because the law does not allow aliens establishing their own independent organizations like that in the Russian Federation, but it allows aliens joining the Russian trade unions".[46] In addition to that, there is an example where aliens in the Russian Federation are deprived of the right to be members of particular trade unions. To illustrate this, we can examine Article 6 of the Articles of Association of the Russian Trade Union of Aviation Workers[47] where only the RF

---

[44] RF Law No. 10-ФЗ "On Trade Unions, Their Rights and Guarantees for Performance of Their Activities", available at: http://www.consultant.ru/document/cons_doc_LAW_8840/ (Ru) (accessed on 29 January 2020).

[45] DENIS MALYI, CONSTITUTIONAL RIGHT TO ASSOCIATION IN THE RUSSIAN FEDERATION, St. Petersburg: Yuridicheski Tsentr Press (2003).

[46] For more detal, refer to: *Trade Union for Migrant Workers to Be Established in the Sverdlovsk Region*, 203 KOMMERSANT (Ekaterinburg) (08 November 2008), available at: https://www.kommersant.ru/doc/1054108 (accessed on 29 January 2020).

[47] Articles of Association of the Russian Trade Union of Aviation Workers, as amended and supplemented of 28 September 2016, available at: http://www.profavia.ru/o-profsoyuze/ustav?showall=1&limitstart= (Ru) (accessed on 29 January 2020).

citizens over 14 who acknowledge and adhere to the Articles of Association and pay all membership fees can become members.

**9.26.** In the Republic of Kazakhstan (RK), the legal regulation of the rights of aliens to organize in trade unions is also pretty vague. On the one hand, the RK Constitution[48] is not explicit about this right and only states, "citizens of the Republic of Kazakhstan shall have the right to freedom of forming associations" (Article 23). In our opinion, the Constitution also somewhat acknowledges trade unions as a solid political force and somewhat identifies them with political parties. For example, the Constitution of the Republic of Kazakhstan clearly states, "activities of political parties and trade unions of other states, religious parties, as well as the financing of political parties and trade unions of foreign legal entities and citizens, foreign states and international organizations shall not be permitted in the Republic" (part 4 of Article 5). On the other hand, even though the RK Law "On Trade Unions" dated 27 June 2014,[49] states that a trade union shall be established by the initiative of solely a group of the Kazakhstan citizens (part 1 of Article 8), it defines the trade union members as individuals/natural persons (paragraph 5 of part 1 of Article 1) and also establishes that its provisions shall be applicable to the aliens and stateless persons residing and working in Kazakhstan. In addition, the Law states that aliens and stateless persons shall pay trade union membership fees similar to the Kazakhstan citizens (Article 3). Hence, given the latter, we can conclude that aliens in RK may join trade unions but cannot establish them. It should be noted that the trade union membership fees are the source of financing of the trade union's activities, and therefore, the membership of aliens in the RK trade unions is in conflict with part 4 of Article 5 of the RK Constitution.

**9.27.** However, the laws regulating the matter in certain other CIS Member States show stronger compliance with the international law standards. For example, we can see this in the Republic of Moldova (RM) – where the right to freely establish or organize in trade unions is granted to: according to the RM Constitution adopted in 1994[50] – any employee (part 1 of Article 42) and according to the RM Law "On Trade Unions" dated 07 July

---

[48] Constitution of the Republic of Kazakhstan 30 August 1995, available at: http://www.akorda.kz/ru/official_documents/constitution (Ru) (accessed on 29 January 2020).

[49] Law of the Republic of Kazakhstan No. 211-V ZPK "On Trade Unions", available at: https://www.ilo.org/dyn/natlex/docs/ELECTRONIC/97827/116230/F1235650974/Kaz%2014%20211.pdf, (Ru) (accessed on 29 January 2020).

[50] Constitution of the Republic of Moldova 29 July 1994, published in the Monitorul Oficial under No. 1/12 August 1994. See also: http://lex.justice.md/viewdoc.php?id=311496&lang=2 (Ru) (accessed on 29 January 2020).

2000[51] – the RM citizens, as well as foreign nationals and stateless persons legally staying in the Republic of Moldova (part 1 of Article 7).

9.28. The laws of the Republic of Azerbaijan also meet the international law standards: Article 58 of their Constitution[52] states, "everyone has the right to establish any union, including … trade union" (by the way, this provision also extends to political parties). In its turn, the Law of the Republic of Azerbaijan "On Trade Unions" dated 24 February 1994[53] states that the right to establish trade unions, join them and be engaged in trade union activities is granted to "employees, pensioners, persons being educated" (Article 3), where the employees are individuals/natural persons (Article 1).

9.29. In the Republic of Latvia, which is not a CIS member state but is still attractive for us as a former USSR republic, the Constitution does not explicitly regulate the right to organize in trade unions. However, its Law "On Trade Unions"[54] dated 06 March 2014 states that everyone shall be free to organize in trade unions (part 1 of Article 4; part 1 of Article 7).

## VI.    Conclusions

9.30. All the above shows that the legal regulation of the right to organize in trade unions in certain CIS Member States fails to meet the international law requirements – just as in Ukraine. In those countries we again witness the inconsistent use of the legal terms "everyone" and "citizen" in the Constitutions and special laws on trade unions. Still, some former USSR republics can be proud to fully comply with the international law standards of the legal regulation of the right to organize in trade unions. This variance cannot be explained by the specific nature of the national migration policies, because, for example, RF, RB and RK have different levels of migrant workers, but still they all ensure similar regulation of migrant worker rights to organize in trade unions – migrant workers are eligible to join, but not establish trade unions. It is our belief that the under regulated

51    Law of the Republic of Moldova No. 1129 "On Trade Unions", available at: http://lex.justice.md/ru/311541/ (Ru) (accessed on 29 January 2020).

52    Constitution of the Republic of Azerbaijan 12 November 1995, available at: https://ru.president.az/azerbaijan/constitution (Ru) (accessed on 29 January 2020).

53    Law of the Republic of Azerbaijan No. 792 "On Trade Unions", available at: http://republic.preslib.az/ru_d4-53.html (Ru) (accessed on 29 January 2020). By the way, the Introduction of this Law says that the warranties provided for the trade union activities have been developed according to the Universal Declaration of Human Rights, the conventions and recommendations of the International Labour Organization, and the European Social Charter.

54    Law of the Republic of Latvia "On Trade Unions" dated 06 March 2014, available at: https://likumi.lv/ta/id/265207-arodbiedribu-likums (Latvian) (accessed on 29 January 2020).

rights of aliens to organize in trade unions in some former USSR republics have been triggered by the Soviet understanding of a trade union as a powerful political force similar to a political party, which ultimately had a bigger impact on the applicable legislative developments than the international law. Meanwhile, due to the trade union activities being far from vibrant, the problems related to their legal status are invisible in practice and as such, they do not invoke any need for bringing the legal regulation of trade unions in line with the international law requirements.

9.31.    To sum up, it is worth saying that although many Ukrainian scientists accentuate the inconsistency between the Ukrainian laws regulating the right to organize in trade unions and the international legal instruments where Ukraine is a participant; our legislative authorities are reluctant to solve this problem. We think that one of the reasons is that the legal regulation gaps do not result in practical problems. After all, the role of contemporary trade unions in the social and economic life of Ukraine is pretty poor.[55] Trade unions as an effective tool are mostly doubted by not only foreign workers, but also by Ukrainian citizens. "The major problems of today`s trade unions are as follows. First, it is a continuous decline of people`s trust in trade unions; trade unions are demotivated and unable to collaborate with the workers of privately-owned businesses; trade unions provide inadequate support to those having lost their jobs, etc."[56] This correctly stated by O. A. Triukhan, researcher of legal regulation of social dialog in labour environment and also highlights other weaknesses of trade unions. Consequently, workers often do not rely on trade unions in protecting their labour rights and that is why a number of trade union regulation problems have still not been addressed with an adequate response from lawmakers.

| | |

---

[55]    For more detail about trade union problems, refer to: Oksana Anatoliivna Triukhan, *Realization of the Right of Workers to Association to Trade Unions,* 1(2) SCIENTIFIC HERALD OF KHERSON STATE UNIVERSITY, Series: Legal sciences 96 (2016) (ukr.), (PDF Download Available), available at: http://www.lj.kherson.ua/2016/pravo01/part_2/26.pdf (accessed on 29 January 2020).

[56]    Oksana Anatoliivna Triukhan, *Supra* note 41.

## Summaries

**DEU** [*Das Recht der Ausländer, sich in Gewerkschaften zusammenzuschließen*]

*Dieser Beitrag konzentriert sich auf Probleme der Ausländerin der Ukraine bei der Ausübung ihres Gewerkschaftsrechts, das nach dem internationalen Recht allen Arbeitnehmern garantiert wird. Dieses Recht wird sowohl jeder Einzelperson zuerkannt, beispielsweise im Rahmen der internationalen Rechtsinstrumente wie etwa der Internationalen Charta der Menschenrechte, als auch allen arbeitenden Menschen im Rahmen einer Reihe von IAO-Übereinkommen, einschließlich derer, die von der IAO als wesentlich erachtet werden. Zu letzterer Gruppe gehört zum Beispiel das Übereinkommen Nr. 87 über die Vereinigungsfreiheit und den Schutz des Rechts auf Vereinigung in Gewerkschaften (1948), an dem auch Ukraine teilnimmt. Trotz dieser Tatsachen haben Ausländer in der Ukraine nur zum Teil das Recht, sich in Gewerkschaften zusammenzuschließen. Ausländer haben kein Recht, Gewerkschaften zu errichten, sondern sie können sich nur an deren Tätigkeit beteiligen, wenn dies in deren Statuten verankert ist. Es sei darauf hingewiesen, dass selbst in postsowjetischen Republiken die Gesetzgebung in Bezug auf das Recht, sich in Gewerkschaften zusammenzuschließen, nicht den völkerrechtlichen Anforderungen entspricht, obwohl einigen Mitgliedsstaaten der Gemeinschaft Unabhängiger Staaten bescheinigt werden kann, dass sie diesen Anforderungen voll und ganz entsprechen. Der Beitrag unterstreicht gleichzeitig, dass es für die ukrainische Rechtsregelung der Menschenrechte, Freiheiten oder Pflichten bezeichnend ist, dass Ausländer oder ihre spezifischen Kategorien unberücksichtigt bleiben und dass sie in diesen Angelegenheiten nur vage und inkonsistent ist, was auch für das Recht, sich in Gewerkschaften zusammenzuschließen, gilt.*

**CZE** [*Práva cizinců sdružovat se v odborových organizacích*]

*Tento příspěvek se zaměřuje na problémy cizinců na Ukrajině při výkonu práva sdružovat se v odborových organizacích, které je mezinárodním právem zaručeno všem pracujícím. Toto právo je přiznáno například každému jednotlivci podle mezinárodních právních nástrojů, které tvoří Mezinárodní listinu lidských práv, jakož i všem pracujícím na základě řady úmluv Mezinárodní organizace práce (ILO), včetně těch, které ILO považuje za základní. Do druhé z uvedených skupin patří například Úmluva č. 87 o svobodě sdružování a ochraně práva sdružovat se v odborových organizacích (1948) - jejímž účastníkem je i*

*Ukrajina. Navzdory těmto skutečnostem však cizinci na Ukrajině požívají práva sdružovat se v odborových organizacích pouze částečně: cizinci nemají právo odbory zakládat, mohou se pouze účastnit jejich činnosti, pokud je to v jejich stanovách zakotveno. Je potřeba podotknout, že ani v některých postsovětských republikách nesplňuje právní úprava práva sdružovat se v odborových organizacích požadavky mezinárodního práva, ačkoli o některých členských zemích Sdružení nezávislých států lze říci, že tyto požadavky v plném rozsahu dodržují. Příspěvek rovněž zdůrazňuje, že pro ukrajinskou právní úpravu lidských práv, svobod nebo povinností je typické, že cizince nebo jejich specifické kategorie opomíjí a je v těchto záležitostech pouze neurčitá a nekonzistentní, což platí i ve vztahu k právu sdružovat se v odborových organizacích.*

|  |  |

POL  [*Prawo obcokrajowców do zrzeszania się w organizacjach związkowych*]

*Artykuł poświęcono specyfice egzekwowania prawa obcokrajowców na Ukrainie do zrzeszania się w związkach zawodowych. Autorka podkreśla, że bez względu na fakt, że są to prawa zagwarantowane w normach prawa międzynarodowego, obcokrajowcy nie mają na Ukrainie prawa do zakładania związków zawodowych. Mogą jedynie uczestniczyć w działalności związków zawodowych, których statut dopuszcza członkostwo obcokrajowców.*

FRA  [*Le droit des étrangers de s'associer dans des organisations syndicales*]

*Le présent article se consacre aux spécificités du droit des étrangers en Ukraine de s'associer dans des organisations syndicales. L'auteur rappelle que les étrangers ne disposent pas du droit de créer des organisations syndicales en Ukraine, malgré le fait que ce droit est garanti par les normes de droit international. La seule forme d'activité syndicale qui leur est ouverte est l'adhésion à des groupements syndicaux dont les statuts autorisent l'adhésion d'étrangers.*

RUS  [*Право иностранцев на объединение в профсоюзы*]

*В статье рассмотрены особенности реализации иностранцами в Украине права на объединение в профсоюзы. В ней подчеркнуто, что несмотря на гарантию этих прав нормами международного права, в Украине иностранцы не имеют право создавать профсоюзы. Они только могут принимать участие в деятельности тех профсоюзов, уставы которых разрешают иностранцам вступить в их членство.*

**ESP** [***Derecho de sindicación de los extranjeros***]
*El texto da cuenta de la situación particular en que se desarrolla la promoción del derecho de sindicación de los extranjeros en Ucrania. La autora resalta que a pesar de que la normativa internacional ampara el derecho de sindicación, los extranjeros que residen en Ucrania no tienen derecho a establecer sindicatos y su participación en dichas organizaciones se limita a aquellas cuyos estatutos permiten que sus miembros sean extranjeros.*

| | |

## Bibliography

Volodymyr Naumovych Denysov, *On Specific Implementation of Social, Economic and Cultural Rights in the System of International Law of Human Rights*, 12 LEGAL STATE: YEARBOOK OF SCIENTIFIC WORKS OF V.M. KORETSKY INSTITUTE OF STATE AND LAW OF NATIONAL ACADEMY OF SCIENCES OF UKRAINE 511 (2001).

ILO, FREEDOM OF ASSOCIATION - COMPILATION OF DECISIONS OF THE COMMITTEE ON FREEDOM OF ASSOCIATION, Geneva: ILO 59 (6th edition, 2018).

HALIYA INSAFIYNA CHANYSHEVA, COLLECTIVE RELATIONS IN LABOUR ENVIRONMENT: THEORY AND LAW MATTER, Odesa: Yurydychna literatura (2001).

Viktoriya Ivanivna Ivancho, *Right of Aliens to Organize in Political Parties and Civil Associations in Ukraine, Poland and the Federal Republic of Germany: Benchmark Analysis*, 29(1) SCIENTIFIC BULLETIN OF UZHHOROD NATIONAL UNIVERSITY, Series: Law (2014).

Volodymyr Ivanovych Kozlov, COLLECTIVE POLITICAL RIGHTS AND FREEDOMS OF CITIZENS OF UKRAINE: CONSTITUTIONAL AND LEGAL ANALYSIS, Kharkiv (2009).

Yuriy Viktorovych Kyrychenko, *Freedom to organize in trade unionds: Compliance of Constitutional Practice of Ukraine with European Standards*, 10(1) SCIENTIFIC HERALD OF INTERNATIONAL HUMANITARIAN UNIVERSITY, Series: Legal science 71 (2014).

DENIS MALYI, CONSTITUTIONAL RIGHT TO ASSOCIATION IN THE RUSSIAN FEDERATION, St. Petersburg: Yuridicheski Tsentr Press (2003).

Oleksandr Oleksandrovych Pifko, *The Peculiarities of the Realization of the Constitutional Right to Form and Join Trade Unions in Ukraine and in Some EU Member Countries: a Comparative Study*, 2 COMPARATIVE AND ANALYTICAL LAW 80 (2018).

BRONISLAV STANISLAVOVYCH STYCHYNSKYI, IHOR VOLODYMYROVYCH ZUB, VOLODYMYR HAVRYLOVYCH ROTAN, SCIENTIFIC AND PRACTICAL COMMENTARY TO LABOUR LAWS OF UKRAINE, REVISED AND EXTENDED, Kyiv: A.C.K (2 ed. 2000).

DAVID TAJGMAN, KAREN CURTIS, FREEDOM OF ASSOCIATION: A USER`S GUIDE – STANDARDS, PRINCIPLES AND PROCEDURES OF THE INTERNATIONAL LABOUR ORGANIZATION, Geneva: ILO (2007).

Oksana Anatoliivna Triukhan, *Realization of the Right of Workers to Association to Trade Unions*, 1(2) SCIENTIFIC HERALD OF KHERSON STATE UNIVERSITY, Series: Legal sciences 96 (2016).

NATALIYA ANTONIVNA TSIGANCHUK, TRADE UNIONS AS SUBJECTS OF LABOUR LAW, Kharkiv (2004).

BORYS MYKOLAYOVYCH ZHARKOV, TRADE-UNION RIGHTS AND THEIR INTERNATIONAL LEGAL PROTECTION, Moscow: Nauka (1990).

Marieta Safta

# Prison Law and Human Rights: Interactions and Developments

*Key words:*
prison law | detention
condition | detainee rights |
European Court of Human
Rights | Court of Justice
of the European Union |
Constitutional Court of
Romania

Czech Yearbook of International Law®

*Abstract* | *Starting from the premise of a veritable 'prison law' in the context of systemic actions at the level of States targeting the conditions of detention and the rights of imprisoned persons, reference, within the present article, will be to the interactions and developments that determine the development of this area of law. With reference to the specific situation of Romania, emphasize, from this perspective, will be on the landmarks of the jurisprudence of the ECHR, of the CJEU, and of the Constitutional Court of Romania (CCR), concluding from the point of view of the influences produced upon the actions undertaken by the Romanian authorities in this field, including the process of lawmaking. Thus, the role of all these jurisdictional mechanisms is revealed at various levels – national, supranational, international, – in the shaping of legal systems, and a specific area of law, characterized here as prison law, in a continuous alignment with the highest standards of protection of fundamental rights.*

**Ph.D Marieta Safta** is an Associate Professor at ‹Titu Maiorescu› University of Bucharest, Faculty of Law, First Assistant-Magistrate of the Constitutional Court of Romania, former Secretary of State at the Ministry of Justice (2017-2018). E-mail: marietasafta@ yahoo.com

| | |

# I. Introduction

**10.01.** The 20th century and the beginning of the 21st century have brought to the forefront the exponential development of fundamental rights for imprisoned people, but more specifically, a focus on protection instruments as well as the guarantees established for enforcing them, and the issue of overcrowding and detention conditions, triggering systemic State actions as solutions. The concern arose in the context of European States, who are making sustained efforts to identify solutions regarding this issue and not just with the phenomenon of prison overcrowding. In Romania, one of the main topics on the agenda of both public authorities and civil society is also the detention conditions in prisons.

**10.02.** There have been several developments in this regard. First, there is the rich jurisprudence of the European Court of Human Rights (ECHR) in the application of Article 2 and 3 of the Convention for the Protection of Rights and Fundamental Freedoms (the Convention), which protect the right to life and prohibit inhuman or degrading punishments or treatments. Additionally, there have also been recent cases involving the same issue pending before the Court of Justice of the European Union (CJEU) that put in a new light the principle of legitimate trust between the Member States of the European Union.[1] Such developments entitle us to support the opinion expressed by other authors suggesting the growth of a veritable ‚*prison law*'.[2] Seen in a broad sense as being ‚the law governing all aspects of imprisonment',[3] the emergence of *prison law* is recent, associated to the period to which we made reference to at the beginning of the article.

**10.03.** This article will not proceed to a theorization, in itself, of *prison law* but will refer to the interactions and developments that determine its development. With reference to the specific situation of Romania, the emphasize, from this perspective, will be landmarks of the jurisprudence of the ECHR, of the CJEU, and of the CCR, concluding from the point of view of the influences produced upon the actions undertaken by the Romanian authorities in this field, including in the field of lawmaking. We believe it is necessary to emphasize these

---

[1] For developments see SÉBASTIEN PLATON, CONFIANCE MUTUELLE ET CRISE DE L´ÉTAT DE DROIT DANS LÚNION EUROPÉENNE, L'Observateur de Bruxelles (2019), et. 16-23, available at: https://www.dbfbruxelles.eu/wp-content/uploads/2019/02/SOMMAIREOBS115.pdf (accessed on 29 January 2020).

[2] See eg. Dirk van Zyl Smit, *Prison Law*, THE OXFORD HANDBOOK OF CRIMINAL LAW, Oxford University Press 988, 1008 (Markus D. Dubber, Tatjana Hörnle ed., 2014).

[3] *Ibid.*, at 988.

developments, precisely because, as has been shown, at least at the level of the European Union, the issue of prisoners' rights and detention conditions has emerged in recent years in the context of the assessment and reassessment of the principle of legitimate expectations. As this principle stands at the foundation of the European Union, the edification of a *prison law* that is structured and aligned with the highest standards of protection of fundamental rights in the field contributes to strengthening the foundations of European construction in its entirety.

## II.     ECHR Jurisprudence with Incidence Regarding *Prison Law*

### II.1.     General Considerations

**10.04.** The ECHR has developed extensive jurisprudence in the application of Articles 2 and 3 of the Convention.[4] Of course, this jurisprudence itself is of major importance in the evolution of *prison law*, taking into account the place and role of the ECHR in the system of the Convention for the Protection of Human Rights and Fundamental Freedoms.

**10.05.** In particular for Romania, the constitutional provisions establish the mandatory value of the interpretations that the ECHR establishes for the texts of the Convention, the latter being obligatory under Article 20 of the Constitution. These confer constitutional interpretative value to international treaties in the field of human rights to which Romania is a party and makes them a priority, including in relation to constitutional provisions, where they contain more favorable provisions. Therefore, as will be seen below, ECHR jurisprudence and, within its framework, the pilot judgments, have fundamentally influenced the evolution of regulations in the field of *prison law*.

### II.2.     The Rights of Detainees - Jurisprudential Developments

### II.2.1.     Detention Conditions

**10.06.** Underlying the general issues concerning detention conditions are specific issues, distinctly analyzed in ECHR jurisprudence. These include the overcrowding of cells, the lack of sanitary

---

[4]    Article 2 of the Convention for the Protection of Human Rights and Fundamental Freedoms governs the right to life, and Article 3 provides that ,no one can be subjected to torture or to inhuman or degrading treatments.

facilities and of natural and/or artificial light, minimal hygiene conditions and living conditions in general. Other issues often referred to include the isolation of detainees in cells, the fact that they do not benefit from a program of activities outside of their detention rooms, and the behavior of authorities, prison staff and other detention centers towards prisoners undergoing custodial sentences[5]. In numerous cases, the ECHR found violations of Article 3 of the Convention. At the same time it ruled on its interpretation in relation to the particular circumstances of the judgment, developing criteria and standards that have influenced and continue to influence the evolution of the legislative system at the level of member States of the Council of Europe.

10.07. Thus, as regards the first category of issues mentioned, the ECHR has found in multiple judgments that there have been violations of Article 3 of the Convention resulting from the plaintiffs detention conditions. Examples include the following:

- lack of ventilation, windows, and use of the toilet in the presence of other inmates;[6]
- passive smoking as a result of detention in the same cell with smokers;[7]
- the inability to sleep properly because the TV and the light in the cell having never been shut/turned off, the presence of cockroaches and ants in cells;[8]
- cold, inappropriate hygiene;[9]
- overcrowding and sanitary conditions, in particular the problem of access to running water and toilets.[10]

10.08. The systemic problems identified have in some cases determined the application of the *pilot judgments* procedure by the ECHR.[11] Thus, for example, through the 10 January 2012 judgment in *Ananyev and Others* v. *Russia,* the Court found structural problems, recurrent in what concerned detention conditions. These included the blatant lack of space in cells, the lack of bed

---

[5]  For a systematic presentation of case-law, see the factsheets of the European Court of Human Rights, available at: https://www.echr.coe.int/Pages/home.aspx?p=press/factsheets&c= (accessed on 30 January 2020).

[6]  For example, *Peers* v. *Greece* of 09 April 2001.

[7]  For example, *Elefteriadis* v. *Romania* of 25 January 2011, *Florea* v. *Romania* of 14 September 2010.

[8]  For example, *Kalashnikov* v. *Russia* of 15 July 2002.

[9]  For example, *Canali* v. *France* of 25 April 2013.

[10]  For example, *Vasilescu* v. *Belgia* of 18 March 2014, *Valentin Baştovoi* v. *the Republic of Moldova* of 28 November 2017.

[11]  Over the past few years the European Court of Human Rights has developed a new procedure known as the pilot-judgment procedure as a means of dealing with large groups of identical cases that derive from the same underlying problem. (...) The way in which the procedure operates is that when the Court receives a significant number of applications deriving from the same root cause, it may decide to select one or more of them for priority treatment. In dealing with the selected case or cases, it will seek to achieve a solution that extends beyond the particular case or cases so as to cover all similar cases raising the same issue. The resulting judgment will be a pilot judgment, available at: https://www.echr.coe.int/Documents/Pilot_judgment_procedure_ENG.pdf (accessed on 29 January 2020).

space, limited access to light and air, the lack of privacy in the use of hygiene and sanitation needs, and overcrowding with a personal space of 1, 25 m² or 2 m² per detainee. They decided that the defendant State in cooperation with the Committee of Ministers of the Council of Europe, within a period of 6 months, should adopt a rigorous timetable for the application of preventive and compensatory measures due to violation of Article 3 of the Convention. This encouraged the Russian authorities to look for an integrated solution to the problem of overcrowding in detention centers, a solution that should include changes in the legal framework, as well as in practices and behaviors. Likewise, on 08 January 2013, in the case of *Torreggiani and others* v. *Italy*, the court condemned the Italian State for violating Article 3 of the Convention. The structural nature of the problem had been confirmed by the existence of several hundred pending claims at the Court of Justice which required verification of the compliance of detention conditions in several Italian prisons with the provisions of Article 3 of the Convention. The Court held, *inter alia*, that the standard for the living space in the cell recommended by the European Committee for the Prevention of Torture (ECPT) is of 4 m² per person. The Court asked the Italian Government to institute, within one year of the final judgment, an effective internal remedy or a combination of such remedies capable of providing adequate and sufficient reparation, in accordance with the principles stated in the Convention, in the cases which the overcrowding of detention facilities is proven to be true. Similarly, in the judgment of 27 January 2015 in *Neshkov and Others* v. *Bulgaria*, it was stated that overcrowding and extremely poor material conditions in Bulgarian prisons constituted violations of Article 3 of the Convention. In view of the serious and persistent nature of the violations, and finding that there was a systemic problem within the Bulgarian penitentiary system, the Court set an 18-month period for the Government to implement measures that would, *inter alia*, solve the problem of overcrowding. The measures recommended to the Bulgarian State were the construction of new penitentiaries, the implementation of penalties for short periods of time and the replacement of imprisonment with other sanctions. They also recommended the introduction of specific legislative measures, such as the establishment of an independent body to monitor detention centers and carry out effective investigations into the complaints lodged by detainees, as well as to provide compensation and make binding and enforceable decisions. Similarly, in its judgment of 10

March 2015 in the case of *Varga and Others* v. *Hungary*, the ECHR found that there had been a violation of Article 3 of the Convention, noting, in particular, that the limited personal space available to all the six detainees in this case, was aggravated by the lack of privacy during toilet use, inadequate sleeping structures, inadequate ventilation and shower restrictions or time spent away from their cells, and that these constituted degrading treatment. The Court recommended a combination of remedies, both preventive and compensatory, and to ensure effective remedies for the violations of the Convention caused by the overcrowding of penitentiaries. The situation of Romania – in the case of which numerous judgments were pronounced, including a pilot-judgment, in the matter, will form the subject of a distinctive chapter. In any case, there is a common denominator for all the examples presented, namely obliging the convicted States to adopt legislative measures as well as criminal policies. Basically, compliance with ECHR judgments has influenced and continues to influence, among other things, criminal policy of the States - the types and duration of sentences, as well as the method through which they were enforced.

10.09. As regards the second category of above-mentioned problems, the ECHR found violations of Article 3 of the Convention. These included the following:

- failure by the authorities to fulfill their positive obligation to adequately ensure the physical and mental integrity, and well-being of the applicant;[12]
- a violation of Article 3 with reference to a prisoner's complaint that he was ill-treated by prison officers when he refused to comply with orders;[13]
- plaintiffs beaten with rubber batons during the time their cell was searched;[14]
- repeated transfer from one prison to another, long-term isolated detention and frequent searches.[15]

## II.2.2. Exercise of Fundamental Rights under Detention Conditions

10.10. The exercise of **the right of prisoners to vote**[16] has given rise to several judgments, again with direct influence on national regulations. In the case of *Hirst (No 2)* v. *the United Kingdom of*

---

[12] For example, *Premininy* v. *Russia* of 10 February 2011.
[13] For example, *Tali* v. *Estonia* of 13 February 2014.
[14] For example, *Milic and Nikezic* v. *Montenegro* of 28 April 2015.
[15] For example, *Khider* v. *France* of 09 July 2009.
[16] For a systematic presentation of case law, see the thematic sheet at: https://www.echr.coe.int/Documents/FS_Prisoners_vote_FRA.pdf (accessed on 29 January 2020).

*Great Britain* of 06 October 2005 – the Grand Chamber, it was held that in the case of a person sentenced to life imprisonment for murder, there had been a violation of Article 3 (the right to free elections) of Protocol no. 1 of the Convention, because of the automatic and discriminatory restriction of the applicant's right to vote because of his status as a convicted prisoner. Subsequently, in a number of cases, the ECHR found that there had been a violation of Article 3 of Protocol No. 1, due to the fact that the United Kingdom did not implement the Grand Chamber judgment in the case of Hirst (No 2) against the United Kingdom. In particular, given the significant number of repeated claims it received shortly before the general elections in May 2010 and the next six months, the Court decided to apply the pronouncement procedure of the pilot-judgment on this case. In accordance with Article 46 of the Convention, the United Kingdom was asked to introduce legislative proposals to amend the legislation concerned within six months, the decision in this case becoming definitive, with the mention of the adoption of an electoral law to ensure compliance with the provisions of the Court in the judgment given in the case of Hirst (No 2), and according to a determined period of time by the Committee of Ministers of the Council of Europe (see *Greens and M.T* v. *the United Kingdom of Great Britain* of 23 November 2010). [17]

**10.11.** **The right to health** (of prisoners) has been the subject of the ECHR's analysis and statutes in several cases. In one example, a prisoner diagnosed with lymphatic leukemia was put in chains during transportation to the hospital and claimed that during his chemotherapy sessions his legs were chained. The Court pointed out, in connection with the applicant's handcuffs, that their application was disproportionate in comparison to the security risk presented, finding that there had been a violation of Article 3 of the Convention.[18] Various situations where the state of health of the applicants was held to be incompatible with detention were brought to the attention of the ECHR in cases such as *Tekin Yildiz* v. *Turkey* of 10 November 2005 or *Serfis* v. *Greece*, of 02 November 2006. Also, the lack of adequate medical assistance was found in cases such as *Holomiov* v. *the Republic of Moldova* of 07 November 2006, *Tarariyeva* v. *Russia of* 14 December 2006, *Testa* v. *Croatia* of 12 July 2007, *Hummatov* v. *Azerbaijan of* 29 November 2007, *Kotsaftis* v. *Greece of* 12 June 2008, *Slyusarev* v. *Russia* of 20 April 2010, *Ashot Harutyunyan* v.

---

[17] The reasoning of the ECHR was further developed in such cases as *Scoppola (No 3). Italy* (22 May 2012) - The Grand Chamber of *Soyler* v. *Turkey* (17 September 2013), *Anchugov and Gladkov* v. *Russia* (04 July 2013), *Murat Vural* v. *Turkey* (21 October 2014), *Kulinski and Sabev* v. *Bulgaria* of 21 July 2006).
[18] *Mouisel* v. *France* of 14 November 2002.

*Armenia* of 15 June 2010, *Xiros* v. *Greece* of 09 September 2010, *Vladimir Vasilyev* v. *Russia of* 10 January 2012, *Iacov Stanciu* v. *Romania* of 24 July 2012, *Mozer* v. *the Republic of Moldova and Russia* of 23 February 2016 – Grand Chamber, *Dorneanu* v. *Romania* of 28 November 2017. The specific situation of HIV-infected detainees has been examined in such cases as *Kats and others* v. *Ukraine* of 18 December 2008, *Aleksanyan* v. *Russia* of 22 December 2008, *Khudobin* v. *Russia* of 26 October 2010, *Salakhov și Islyamova* v. *Ukraine* of 14 March 2013 or Martzaklis and others v. Greece of 09 July 2015. Insufficient diet has been the subject of the analysis, for example in the case of *Moisejevs* v. *Letoniei* of 15 June 2006. There is also situations where systemic problems such as structural inadequacy of medical care in prisons were found. Also consider the case of Georgia when, observing that there were almost forty notifications of lack of medical care in Georgian prisons, the ECHR found that there was a systemic problem in administering adequate medical care, with detainees being infected with viral hepatitis C, among other things. Consequently, it invited Georgia, under Article 46 of the Convention, to adopt legislative and administrative measures without delay to prevent the transmission of the hepatitis C virus in prisons and to introduce screening arrangements for this disease and ensure timely, and efficient treatment.[19] A case with Turkey was similarly judged, where the ECHR recommended under Article 46 of the Convention that the authorities take the necessary measures to protect the health of prisoners with incurable diseases, regardless of whether they were detained during the trial or after a final conviction.[20]

### II.2.3.  The Specific Situation of Detainees

10.12.  There are also situations where **minors are in detention**, namely cases in which the ECHR found violations of Articles 3 and 2 of the Convention. In one example, the Court found that the applicant has been subjected to inhuman and degrading treatments given their age, the duration of imprisonment for adults and the lack of adequate health care or to take measures to prevent repeated suicide attempts (*Guvec* v. *Turkey* of 20 January 2009). In another situation, the suicide of a minor occurred, and the authorities were found responsible for the deterioration of the prisoner's mental state by detaining him in

---

[19]  See e.g. *Poghosyan* v. *Georgia* of 24 February 2009.
[20]  See e.g. *Gulay Cetin* v. *Turkey* of 05 March 2013.

a prison for adults, without providing medical or special care, thus leading to his suicide (*Coselav* v. *Turkey*, 09 October 2012).

10.13. The **treatment of people with disabilities** poses additional situations. The ECHR found, for example, that having a disabled person under degrading conditions in a cold room created the risk of developing injuries because the bed was too hard or untouched. In the same case, the prisoner was unable to go to the toilet or clean, and these constituted degrading treatment contrary to Article 3 of the Convention (*Price* v. *the United Kingdom of Great Britain*, 10 July 2001). Such violations have also been found, for example, in the case of a deaf-mute person (*Z.H.* v. *Hungary*, 08 November 2011) or of a person immobilized to a wheelchair who had numerous health problems, including the need for a kidney transplant, very poor vision, diabetes and serious obesity (*Arutyunyan* v. *Russia*, 10 January 2012), the case of a paraplegic (*D.G.* v. *Poland*, 12 February 2013), and of a person suffering from lower limb paraplegia and urinary and fecal incontinence (*Helhal* v. *France* of 19 February 2015).

10.14. Likewise, **the detention of mentally ill persons** may raise issues under Article 3 of the Convention, where failure to provide appropriate medical treatment may constitute treatment contrary to that provision. For example, in the case of Albania, the Court has held that there have been violations of Article 3 of the Convention, noting, in particular, that the applicant's psychological nature/condition made him more vulnerable and that his detention had exacerbated feelings of distress, pain and fear. The fact that the Albanian government acknowledged that the applicant was treated as other detainees, regardless of his or her particular health status, also showed a failure to comply with the Council of Europe recommendations on the treatment of prisoners with mental illnesses. In addition, pursuant to Article 46 of the Convention, the Court urged Albania to urgently adopt the necessary measures to ensure appropriate conditions of detention and, in particular, to ensure adequate medical treatment for detainees requiring special care on account of their state of health (*Dybeku* v. *Albania* of 18 December 2007). Similarly, in the case of Poland, pursuant to Article 46, given the gravity and structural nature of the problem of overcrowding, inadequate living conditions and sanitary conditions in Polish detention, the Court considered that urgent legislative and administrative measures must be taken to ensure adequate conditions of detention, especially for detainees in need of special care because of their health. Given the specific circumstances of the case and the urgent need to put an end to the breach of Article 3 of the Convention, the Court also stated that Poland had to ensure as soon as possible the transfer of the applicant to a specialized institution able to provide him with the necessary psychiatric treatment and constant medical supervision (*Slawomir Musial* v. *Poland* of 20 January 2009).

**10.15.** In this context, a number of cases specifically refer to prisoners with suicidal tendencies. The ECHR noted in particular that prisoners with severe mental disorders and suicidal tendencies require special measures adapted to their condition, irrespective of the seriousness of the offense for which they were convicted (for example see *Riviere* v. *France* of 11 July 2006, *Renolde* v. *France* of 16 October 2008, *Guvec* v. *Turkey* of 20 January 2009, *Jasinka* v. *Poland* of 01 June 2010, the Association for the Defense of Human Rights in Romania – *the Helsinki Committee in the name of Ionel Garcea* v. *Romania* of 24 March 2015).

**10.16.** Obviously, these cases, in particular the pilot-judgments that the ECHR has issued, have laid down as many standards for the States as to the conditions of detention and the rights of detainees. The efforts to align with these standards have prompted profound transformations in States that have suffered convictions, including, or perhaps – especially – regarding the regulatory framework, contributing to the development *prison law*.

## III. The Role of the CJEU

**10.17.** Both developments at the level of the European Union and, in this framework, the CJEU jurisprudence influences the legal systems of the Member States.

**10.18.** The judgment of 05 April 2016 in the joint cases C-404/15 and C-659/15 PPU, concerns claims of preliminary decision made under Article 267 TFEU by Hanseatisches Oberlandesgericht in Bremen (Superior Regional Court of Bremen, Germany), in procedures for the execution of European arrest warrants issued against Pál Aranyosi (C-404/15) and Robert Căldăraru (C-659/15 PPU).[21] The CJEU stated on that occasion that,

> Article 1(3), Article 5 and Article 6(1) of Council Framework Decision 2002/584/JHA of 13 June 2002 on the European arrest warrant and the surrender procedures between Member States, as amended by Council Framework Decision 2009/299/JHA of 26 February 2009, must be interpreted as meaning

---

that, where there is objective, reliable, specific and properly updated evidence with respect to detention conditions in the issuing Member State that demonstrates that there are deficiencies, which may be systemic or generalized, or which may affect certain groups of people, or which may affect certain places of detention, the executing judicial authority must determine, specifically and precisely, whether there are substantial grounds to believe that the individual concerned by a European arrest warrant, issued for the purposes of conducting a criminal prosecution or executing a custodial sentence, will be exposed, because of the conditions for his detention in the issuing Member State, to a real risk of inhuman or degrading treatment, within the meaning of Article 4 of the Charter, in the event of his surrender to that Member State. To that end, the executing judicial authority must request that supplementary information be provided by the issuing judicial authority, which, after seeking, if necessary, the assistance of the central authority or one of the central authorities of the issuing Member State, under Article 7 of the Framework Decision, must send that information within the time limit specified in the request. The executing judicial authority must postpone its decision on the surrender of the individual concerned until it obtains the supplementary information that allows it to discount the existence of such a risk. If the existence of that risk cannot be discounted within a reasonable time, the executing judicial authority must decide whether the surrender procedure should be brought to an end.'[22]

**10.19.** By way of another reference for a preliminary ruling, addressed to the CJEU by a court in Germany,[23] in the case of *C-128/18, Dorobanțu*[24] the CJEU was recently requested to detail the

---

[22] See also the developments in the case of C-216/18 PPU, having as subject an application for a preliminary ruling formulated under Article 267 TFEU by the High Court (High Court, Ireland), by the judgment of 23 March 2018, received by the Court on 27 March 2018, in proceedings relating to the execution of European arrest warrants issued against LM, The judgment of the Court (Grand Chamber) of 25 July 2018 (see: http://curia.europa.eu/juris/document/document. jsf;jsessionid=34450CF5D91663AA3E76B98075CC6EFF?text=&docid=204384&pageIndex=0&doclang =RO&mode=lst&dir=&occ=first&part=1&cid=5172108#Footnote* (accessed on 02 February 2020)). This raises another problem, namely that of the rule of law, in terms of the independence of the courts.

[23] Henceforth known as, ,The court of referral', Hanseatisches Oberlandesgericht Hamburg.

[24] Available at: http://curia.europa.eu/juris/document/document.jsf?text=&docid=204484&pageIndex=0 &doclang=RO&mode=lst&dir=&occ=first&part=1&cid=426534 (accessed on 29 January 2020).

interpretation given to the Framework Decision EAW by the judgment of 05 April 2016 in the joint Cases, C-404/15, *Aranyosi* and C-659/15 PPU, *Căldăraru*. Essentially, in the context of executing an EAW issued by Romanian judicial authorities, on behalf of a Romanian citizen, for the purpose of conducting criminal proceedings, the referring court wished to know what were the minimal requirements regarding detention conditions, as well as the evaluation criteria of the respective conditions, from the perspective of observing the right of the person to not be subjected to inhuman or degrading punishments or treatments.[25]

10.20. The route of this case is also interesting. The referring court was in fact bound by the German Federal Constitutional Court to address the CJEU by its judgment in the case of 2 BvR 424/17.[26] The constitutional complaint was formulated by the plaintiff against the judgment of the German court, claiming that in Romania the conditions of detention imposed by the Romanian authorities violated the guarantee of human dignity - both in terms of preventive detention and imprisonment. By ruling

---

[25] C-128/18, Dorobanţu- the preliminary questions are the following:
1. In the context of the FDEAW,[1] what are the minimum standards for custodial conditions required under Article 4 of the Charter?
a. Specifically, is there, under EU law, an 'absolute' minimum limit for the size of custody cells, pursuant to which the use of cells under that limit will always constitute an infringement of Article 4 of the Charter?
i. When determining an individual's portion of a custody cell, should the fact that a given cell is being used for single or multiple occupancy be taken into account?
ii. When calculating the size of the custody cell, should areas covered by furniture (beds, wardrobes, etc.) be discounted?
iii. What infrastructural requirements, if any, are relevant for the purposes of compliance of custodial conditions with EU law? Does direct (or only indirect) open access from the custody cell to, for example, sanitary facilities or other rooms, or the provision of hot and cold water, heating, lighting, etc. have any significance?
b. To what extent do the various 'prison regimes', such as differing unlock times and varying degrees of freedom of movement within a penal institution, play a role in the assessment?
c. Can legal and organisational improvements in the issuing Member State (introduction of an ombudsman system, establishment of courts of enforcement of penalties, etc.) also be taken into account, as the present Chamber did in its decisions on the permissibility of the extradition?
2. What standards are to be used to assess whether custodial conditions comply with EU law? To what extent do those standards influence the interpretation of the term 'real risk' within the meaning of the judgment of the Court of Justice in Aranyosi and Căldăraru?
a. In that regard, are the judicial authorities of the executing Member State authorised to undertake a comprehensive assessment of the custodial conditions in the issuing Member State, or are they limited to an 'examination as to manifest errors'?
b. To the extent that, in the context of its reply to the first question referred for a preliminary ruling, the Court of Justice concludes that there are 'absolute' requirements under EU law for custodial conditions, would a failure to meet those minimum standards be, in a sense, 'unquestionable', so that, as a result, such a failure would always immediately constitute a 'real risk', thereby prohibiting extradition, or can the executing Member State nevertheless carry out its own assessment? In that regard, can factors such as the maintenance of mutual legal assistance between Member States, the functioning of European criminal justice or the principles of mutual trust and recognition be taken into account?
[26] Available at: https://www.bundesverfassungsgericht.de/SharedDocs/Entscheidungen/EN/2017/12/rs20171219_2bvr042417en.html (accessed on 29 January 2020).

on the obligation to refer the CJEU, in accordance with Article 267(3) TFEU, taking into account that there is no domestic remedy against the decisions given in extradition proceedings, the German Constitutional Court held that

> it needs to be clarified to what extent it is required that Article 4 CFR be interpreted in light of the ECtHR's case-law (cf. Article 52(3) CFR) and if – as was apparently presumed by the Higher Regional Court – the review of whether detention conditions are compatible with the fundamental rights of the European Union requires an overall assessment that gives consideration to all the aspects drawn on by the Higher Regional Court.

**10.21.** The Federal Constitutional Court has also held that

> The Higher Regional Court untenably exceeded its margin of assessment in relation to its duty of referral, and thereby violated the complainant's right to his lawful judge (Article 101(1) second sentence GG). The court did not provide objective reasons for why it concluded that the legal situation with respect to the guarantee afforded by Article 4 CFR relating to specific detention conditions were clear from the outset or clarified beyond reasonable doubts. The Higher Regional Court assessed independently the standards of review deriving from fundamental rights under the Basic Law, European Union law and the ECHR, without establishing a connection to the specific requirements deriving from Article 4 CFR. In this respect, it failed to substantiate whether and in how far the minimum requirements deriving from Article 4 CFR are either fully clarified in the case-law of the ECJ or are so manifestly clear that clarification by the ECJ would be unnecessary.

**10.22.** Although they acknowledged that the insurance provided by Romania in the case of the applicant does not correspond to the minimum personal area requirements established by the ECtHR with regard to guaranteeing the conditions of detention of human rights detainees, on the basis of Article 3 ECHR, the Court concluded that deficient conditions of detention do not constitute a relevant risk for inhuman and degrading treatment under European Union law. While taking into account ECHR jurisprudence, additional considerations were added through an ‚overall assessment' which was considered able to eliminate the risk of inhuman or degrading treatment in the case of the applicant. The Federal Constitutional Court nevertheless considered that the CJEU should be asked because its jurisprudence is not clear in this respect.

10.23. It is important to note, with regard to the reasoning of the Federal Constitutional Court, the interference with ECHR and the CJEU jurisprudence, namely how the ECtHR case law influences the double test - the assessment of the real risk of inhuman or degrading treatment, in accordance with Article 4 CFR.

## IV.  The Development of *Prison Law* in Romania Following Developments in ECHR Case Law and the CJEU

### IV.1.  Romania at the ECHR – Detention Conditions

10.24. The first conviction of Romania for violating Article 3 of the Convention for the Protection of Human Rights and Fundamental Freedoms was passed on 06 December 2007 in the case of *Bragadireanu v. Romania* by which the Court found that material detention conditions did not meet the European standard.

10.25. During the period 2007-2012, 93 judgments were passed to condemn the Romanian State for violations of Article 3 in terms of overcrowding and inappropriate material detention conditions in both penitentiaries and detention centers and preventive arrest. On 24 July 2012 the Court pronounced a semi-pilot judgment in the case of *Iacov Stanciu v. Romania*. The Court found that overcrowding in prisons, lack of hygiene and the inadequacy of care and medical treatment constituted for the applicant inhuman and degrading treatment, the problems and difficulties experienced exceeding the 'inevitable level of inherent suffering in detention and the severity threshold provided for in Article 3 of the Convention'. Finding the existence of a recurring problem, the Court emphasized the need to introduce effective national remedies enabling national authorities to substantively establish violations of the Convention's provisions, as well as to order the cessation of the infringement and to pay compensation. Recognizing that the matter is a recurring one, the Court has held that, beyond the general measures aimed at improving the prison system, it is necessary to ensure an effective internal remedy to enable effective compensation for the damage suffered as a result of inadequate detention conditions, both by ending the situation which leads to violation of Article 3 of the Convention, as well as by granting moral damages.

10.26. In subsequent years, both the number of cases filed and those in which the Court concluded that Article 3 of the Convention had been infringed in terms of overpopulation and inappropriate material detention conditions increased. In the pilot judgment of 25 April 2017 in the joined cases of *Rezmiveş and Others* v. *Romania* (no. 61467/12, 39516/13, 48231/13 and 68191/13) the Court also found, under Article 46 of the Convention, that the applicants' situation was part of a general problem caused by a structural dysfunction specific to the Romanian penitentiary system. The situation persisted, although it was signaled by the Court in 2012 (*Iacov Stanciu* v. *Romania* of 24 July 2012). In order to remedy the situation, the Court has ruled that Romania has the obligation to implement two types of general measures: (1) measures to reduce overcrowding and improve material conditions of detention; and (2) legal methods (a preventive mode of appeal and specific reparatory measures). The Court requested the Romanian State to provide, in cooperation with the Committee of Ministers of the Council of Europe, and within six months of the final date of the judgment, an exact timetable for the implementation of appropriate general measures capable of resolving the problem of overcrowding and inadequate detention conditions, in accordance with the principles of the Convention as set out in the pilot judgment. The Court also decided to postpone similar cases that have not yet been communicated to the Government of Romania until the necessary national measures have been taken.

10.27. As seen in section 3 of this article, these systemic problems have also triggered the referral of the CJEU in the case of *Dorobanţu*. At the time of application (2016), the Romanian authorities only offered the guarantee of a space of 2 m² in the semi-open regime of execution of punishments. Meanwhile, both detention conditions as such and the legal system in Romania have seen significant changes.

## IV.2. Measures taken by the Romanian State to Eliminate Overcrowding and Improve Detention Conditions, and the Protection of the Rights of Prisoners[27]

### IV.2.1. The Period up to the Delivery of the Pilot Judgment in the Joint Cases of Rezmiveş and others v. Romania

**10.28.** During the reference period, the Government of Romania adopted a series of Memoranda, namely in 31 August 2012, on 'The Effects of Romania Determining the Ban on Inhuman or Degrading Treatment in the Case of *Iacov Stanciu* v. *Romania*, the Decision of the European Court of Human Rights of July 24, 2012. Proposed solutions', in 19 January 2016 on the 'ECHR's intention to apply the pilot judgment in cases concerning detention conditions' and in 26 April 2016 on 'The approval of the timetable for measures to improve detention conditions and the probation system, elaborated on the basis of the Memorandum approved by the Government on 19 January 2016'. Practically, the problems of the penitentiary system have been identified and the directions of action have been established in terms of legislation, budget, and management.

**10.29.** As a general rule, for the reference period, the following main developments have taken place:[28]

- a new legislative framework (Criminal Code and Criminal Procedure Code) - including measures to strengthen the exceptional nature of deprivation of liberty as a preventive measure during the criminal proceedings;
- the inclusion of alternatives to the preventive arrest measure (house arrest);
- the efficiency of judicial control institutions;
- judicial control on bail;
- regulation of new institutions to encourage the evasion of the penitentiary system (recognition of guilt);
- the extension of the powers of the judge for the supervision of the deprivation of liberty, as well as the establishment in Romania of the National Mechanism for the prevention of torture in the places of detention, by extending the powers of the Ombudsman;

---

[27] Marieta Safta, Beatrice Drăghiciu, *Measure To Solve Prison Overcrowding And Improve Detention Conditions*, REVISTA ANALELE UNIVERSITĂȚII ,TITU MAIORESCU', LAW SERIES (2018), available at: http://analedrept.utm.ro/Numere/AnaleDrept2018.pdf.

[28] See the press release of the Ministry of Justice, available at: http://www.just.ro/hotararea-pilot-pronuntata-de-cedo-privind-conditiile-de-detentie/ (accessed on 29 January 2020).

- measures for identifying financial resources for repair and investment works;
- measures to modernize detention facilities and extend accommodation capacity in order to comply with international standards with respect to the minimum area of 4 m² per prisoner;
- measures for the social reintegration of detainees through the development of a new evaluation and planning system for the execution of punishment;
- increased participation of detainees in activities.

**10.30.** The measures adopted by the Romanian authorities led, on the one hand, to a decrease in the number of persons in custody of the prison system and under arrest, and, on the other hand, the increase of the places of detention and the improvement of the general conditions. As a result, the detention deficit has fallen from 18,000 in 2012 to 4,300 in 2017.

### IV.2.2. *The Period after the Delivery of the Pilot Judgment in the Joint Cases of Rezmiveş and others v. Romania*

**10.31.** With all these measures, the ECHR pronounced the aforementioned pilot judgment, which determined the adoption by the Government of Romania of the Memorandum of January 16, 2018 on the '*Approval of the Timetable for Measures 2018-2024 to resolve overcrowding and detention conditions in the execution of the ruling Rezmiveş and Others v. Romania issued by the ECHR on 25 April 2017.*'[29] The Government also decided to transmit the Calendar to the Committee of Ministers and, for information, to the European Court of Human Rights prior to 25 January 2018.

**10.32.** The timetable for proposed measures to reduce overcrowding and improve prison conditions sets out five main lines of action: (1) legislative changes aimed at reducing the prison population and improving prison conditions; (2) investments in physical infrastructure of penitentiaries aimed at expanding the number of places of detention and modernizing existing ones; (3) the effective functioning of the probation system to facilitate the application of community sanctions and measures to reduce the prison population; (4) implementing programs and strategies for inserting people from the penitentiary system and; (5) legislative

---

[29] Published on the Ministry of Justice website, available at: http://www.just.ro/wp-content/uploads/2018/01/calendar-masuri.pdf (accessed on 29 January 2020) as Secretary of State at the Ministry of Justice during the reference period, I participated in the drafting of the Measure Timetable and I was a member of the ministerial delegation to the ECHR.

measures to ensure an effective appeal for the harm suffered. The Memorandum also established a monitoring mechanism through a Working Group which included the Ministry of Justice, the Ministry Foreign Affairs, the Government Agent for the ECHR, the Ministry of Public Finance, the National Penitentiary Administration, and the National Penitentiary Directorate. The Secretariat of the Group is provided by the Ministry of Justice.

Numerous **administrative measures** were adopted such as:

- the construction of a penitentiary with the capacity to accommodate 1000 detainees;
- the adoption of the Memorandum entitled *'Decision on the Opportunity to Financing the Physical Infrastructure of the Romanian Penitentiary System through a project financed by reimbursable external funds'*, of 05 December 2017, proposing the concept of a national project on investments in prison infrastructure;
- the adoption of Government Ruling no. 791/2017 approving the transfer of real estate found in the public domain of the State, from the administration of the Ministry of National Defense (MAPN) in the administration of the Ministry of Justice for the NAP, for the purpose of being transformed into penitentiaries, with a capacity of accommodating 900 persons;
- the adoption of the Memorandum on the Principle Agreement on a loan of up to EUR 223 million from the Council of Europe Development Bank to support the project *'Investments in Prison Infrastructure'* of 07 March 2018, which provides for the financing of some of the measures set out in the Timetable for Measures approved by the Government of Romania on 17 January 2018.

**10.33.** At the same time, it is worth mentioning the development measures of the probation system,[30] as well as the social reintegration of convicted persons. Government Decision no. 389/2015 on the approval of the National Strategy for Social Reintegration of Persons deprived of their liberty, 2015-2019[31] contained a series of actions aimed at reducing the recidivism rate. These were implemented and the Inter-ministerial Commission was set up and functioning to coordinate and implement the provisions of the National Social Reintegration Strategy for

---

[30]    Law no. 252/2013 on the organization and functioning of the probation system, published in the Official Gazette of Romania, Part I, no.

[31]    Published in the Official Gazette of Romania, Part I, no. 532 bis/16 July 2015.

Persons deprived of their liberty, 2015-2019. According to Article 6(1) and (4) of G.O. no. 389/2015, the Commission is made up of a representative with a leading position in the Ministry of Justice, the Ministry of Internal Affairs, the Ministry of National Education, the Ministry of Labor and Social Justice, the Ministry of Health, the National Probation Directorate and the National Administration of Penitentiaries. The Presidency of the Commission is provided by the Ministry of Justice.

10.34. The administrative measures were supported by **legislative measures**. Thus, during the reference period the State adopted Law no. 169/2017 regarding the modification and completion of the Law no. 254/2013 on the execution of sentences and detention measures ordered by the judicial bodies during the criminal proceedings.[32] It mainly establishes a compensatory mechanism for granting a benefit, meaning 6 days considered to be executed for a period of 30 days in custody in inadequate detention facilities. It shall also apply accordingly to the calculation of the punishment actually executed as a preventive measure or punishment in imprisonment and detention centers in inappropriate conditions. Inappropriate punishment is considered to be accommodation in any of the following situations:

- accommodation in an area less than or equal to 4 m / inmate, calculated excluding the area of sanitary groups and food storage areas, by dividing the total area of detention rooms to the number of persons accommodated in the respective rooms, irrespective of how equipped the space in question is;
- lack of access to outdoor activities;
- lack of access to natural light or sufficient air or availability of ventilation;
- lack of adequate room temperature;
- the lack of the possibility to use the private toilet and to comply with the basic sanitary standards as well as the hygiene requirements or;
- the existence of infiltrations, dampness and mold in the walls of detention rooms.

10.35. If a person was admitted to the infirmary at the places of detention, or hospitals in the sanitary network of the National Penitentiary Administration, or the Ministry of Internal Affairs or the public health network or in transit, that time is not considered the execution of the punishment under improper conditions. Settlement provisions do not apply if the person

---

[32] Published in the Official Gazette of Romania, Part I, no. 571/18 July 2017.

Czech Yearbook of International Law®

has been compensated for improper conditions of detention by final judgments of national courts or the European Court of Human Rights for the period for which compensation has been granted and has been transferred or moved in a detention facility with inadequate conditions. The period for which days considered as executed to compensate for inappropriate accommodation are calculated starting from 24 July 2012. As a result of the enforcement of this law, with the total number of 187 accommodation spaces, 156 were established as inadequate by the Order of the Minister of Justice no. 2773/2017, or 83%.

**10.36.** Similarly, another law adopted was Law no. 61/2018 amending and supplementing the Government Ordinance no. 26/1994 on the right to food, in peacetime, of the personnel in the national defense sector, public order and national security,[33] which updates the provisions of the Government Ordinance and took into consideration aspects such as the equalization of the caloric norms of food of people detained or in preventive custody with that of convicted persons and the setting minimum calorie scales for food standards of people deprived of their liberty.

**10.37.** Several legal provisions were likewise adopted. Order of the Minister of Justice no. 2771/C/2017 on the approval of minimum standards on the accommodation of persons deprived of their liberty[34] establishes that places intended to accommodate persons deprived of their liberty should respect human dignity and meet minimum sanitary and hygienic standards, taking into account the area inhabited, air volume, lighting, heating and ventilation sources, related to climatic conditions and correlated with the provisions of Law No. 169/2017 regarding the definition of inadequate conditions of detention. Additionally, the Order of the Minister of Justice no. 2773/C/2017 for the approval of the centralized situation of buildings which are inadequate in terms of detention conditions[35] changes the number of days calculated for persons deprived of their liberty, as 6 days executed for a number of 30 days of custody in detention facilities was considered inadequate. A prisoner's situation will be updated annually or whenever changes which generate a reclassification of accommodation occur.

**10.38.** According to the timetable for measures is also expected to be adopted other legislative measures, namely the introduction of the electronic supervision measure as a measure to reduce the penitentiary population and to grant financial compensation to

---

[33] The Official Gazette of Romania, Part I, no. 227 of 14 March 2018.
[34] The Official Gazette of Romania no. 822 of 18 October 2017.
[35] The Official Gazette of Romania no. 822 of 18 October 2017.

persons who have pending actions before the European Court of Human Rights or who are called upon to bring an action before the Court to ensure an effective appeal for repairing the harm suffered.

## IV.3. The Current Legislative Framework in Romania Regarding the Execution of Punishments

10.39. The framework regulation in this area is Law no. 254/2013 regarding the execution of punishments and deprivation measures ordered by the judicial bodies during the criminal trial,[36] with subsequent modifications and completions. It is a new, modern law, in line with the above-mentioned international standards, as evidenced by the jurisprudence of the Romanian Constitutional Court.

10.40. Comprising a total of 191 articles, Law no.254/2013 develops over seven sections: (1) rules and general principles, (2) the institution of the judge supervising the deprivation of liberty, (3) the execution of the custodial sentences (including organization, security, execution regimes, conditions of detention, rights of convicted persons, the work done by persons sentenced to custodial sentences, educational activities, psychological assistance and social assistance, school education, university education and professional training of condemned persons, conditional release, rewards, and offenses and disciplinary sanctions), (4) the execution of preventive custodial measures, (5) provisions on the execution of educational custodial measures, (6) offenses and contraventions, and (7) final provisions.

10.41. We underline the express regulation of respect for human dignity, in Article 4, according to which 'sentences and detention measures are executed under conditions that ensure respect for human dignity', the prohibition of subjection to torture, inhuman or degrading treatment or other ill-treatments (Article 5) as well as discrimination of any kind in Article 6. According to Article 7 of the law the detainees exercise all their civil and political rights, with the exception of those who were forbidden, according to the law, by the final conviction decision, as well as those whose lack of exercise or restricted exercise results inherently from the deprivation of liberty or for reasons of maintaining the security of the detention.

10.42. In this regard, reference is made to domestic legislation, the application of which resulted in several convictions to the

---

[36] Published in the Official Gazette of Romania, Part I, no. 514 of 14 August 2013.

ECHR in cases involving the exercise of the right to vote of the detainees (see, in particular, *Calmanovici* v. *Romania*, no. 42250/02, pt. 152-154, 01 July 2008 *Pleş* v. *Romania* (dec.), no. 15275/10, pt. 14, 08 October 2013. In those cases, the High Court of Cassation and Justice by Decision no. LXXIV (74), admitting an appeal in the interest of the law, held that the provisions of Article 71 of the Criminal Code regarding the ancillary penalties is interpreted as meaning that the prohibition of the rights provided by Article 64 let. a sentences I-c of the Criminal Code shall not be made automatically by the effect of the law. Instead they shall be subject to the court's assessment, according to the criteria set out in Article 71(3) of the Criminal Code. The ECHR took note of a change in the interpretation of the legislation in question, brought by the judgment of the High Court of Cassation and Justice of 5 November 2007 (see, for example, *Nenciu* v. *Romania*, 17 January 2017).

10.43. Moreover, Law no.254/2013 grants a broader scope to the rights of convicted persons such as:
- freedom of conscience;
- opinions and freedom of religious beliefs;
- the right to information;
- the right to consultation of personal documents;
- ensuring the exercise of the right to legal assistance;
- the right to petition and the right to correspondence;
- the right to telephone conversations;
- the right to online communications;
- the right to receive visits and the right to be informed about special family situations;
- the right to conjugal visits;
- the right to receive, buy and hold assets;
- the right to diplomatic assistance;
- the right to marry;
- the right to vote;
- the right to rest and weekly rest;
- the right to work;
- the right to education; and
- the right to food, clothes, beds and minimum accommodation conditions.

10.44. With reference to these provisions, The Constitutional Court has admitted a single exception to unconstitutionality regarding the rules governing the right to conjugal visits. In essence, the Court found that, with regard to conjugal visits, Law no.254/2013 provides for a different legal regime for persons executing the preventive custody measure than for those who are convicted to final custodial sentences. The maximum duration of preventive arrest in the first instance is 5 years, representing a sufficiently long period for the lack of the right to conjugal visits of persons in preventive custody to substantially affect their family relationships. This impairment of family life is not justified by limitations specific to the detention regime, and the Constitutional Court of Romania has applied the constitutional norms of reference in line with ECHR jurisprudence. Thus, by the judgment of 09 July 2013, delivered in the case of *Varnas* v. *Lithuania,* the European Court found that while the deprivation of liberty of a person implies limitations of his private and family life, the right of the person concerned to maintain close contact with his family is essential and that restrictions on the number of visits, to the supervision of such visits and, if the nature of the deed justifies it, the subjection of a person in detention to a certain execution regime or certain types of visits constitute interference with the right to respect for private and family life, provided for in Article 8 of the Convention for the Protection of Human Rights and Fundamental Freedoms, without constituting infringements of this right (paragraph 108). The European Court of Human Rights has also noted that more than half of Council of Europe member States have provided in their domestic law the right of detainees to conjugal visits, with specific limitations and restrictions, while simultaneously stating that the provisions of the Convention should not be interpreted as obliging signatory States to regulate such visits. It has been shown that this is an aspect on which States Parties have a wide margin of discretion, having the freedom to determine on their own the measures to be taken to implement the provisions of the Convention in relation to the needs and resources of the community or individual (paragraph 109). By the same judgment, the European Court held that convicted and arrested persons are in different situations, according to Article 14 of the Convention (paragraph 111), but that the person concerned who has been deprived of the right to conjugal visits during the pre-trial detention period was, from this point of view, in a situation similar to that of persons serving a criminal custodial sentence who benefited from different treatment (paragraphs 112 and 114). Similarly, by the judgment of 06 June 2009, delivered in the case of *Moiseyev* v. *Russia,* paragraphs 258-259, the European Court of Human Rights found regarding the lack of contact with the visitors, that the person detained during the criminal proceedings who was physically deprived from contact with the visitors during his three-and-a-half year detention, in the absence of a demonstrated need for isolation, such as security reasons, has suffered undue interference with the right to private and family life. In this case submitted for resolution, the Court ruled that the long period of detention (which was 2 years on the date when the applicant requested, for the first time, the right to a conjugal visit) reduced his family life to an extent that cannot be justified by the limitations specific to the detention regime and that the authorities' refusal to grant the detainee the right to a marital visit was based on theoretical security considerations, but also in equal measure the lack of necessary facilities, arguments which cannot constitute the basis for the Court's ruling, (paragraph 121, *Moiseyev* v. *Russia*). Consequently, the European Court held that restricting the right to marital visits during detention without objective and reasonable justification by the authorities for the difference of treatment created constitutes discrimination contrary to the provisions of Article 14 on the prohibition of discrimination in conjunction with Article 8 on the right to respect for private and family life of the Convention (paragraphs 121 and 122).

**10.45.** For the same reasons, the CCR found that the difference in legal treatment regarding the right to conjugal visits, as provided for in Article 69 and Article 110(1)(b) of Law no. 254/2013, in the regulation of the regime of the execution of the preventive custody measures, respectively of the final sentence, has no objective and reasonable justification and is not based on security considerations of the activities carried out in the detention places. This difference, therefore, discriminates between persons in preventive custody in relation to those sentenced to criminal custodial sentences, being likely to contravene the provisions of Article 16 of the Basic Law, in relation to those of Article 26 of the Constitution.[37]

**10.46.** We emphasize here the influence and interference of the jurisprudence of the two Courts, and effects on the legal framework in Romania, taking into account the *erga omnes* obligation Constitutional Court decisions, as well as the obligation of the legislature to reconcile the rules found to be unconstitutional with the decision of the constitutional litigation court, enshrined in paragraph (1) of the same Article 147.

---

[37] Decision no.222 of 02 April 2015, Published in the Official Gazette of Romania, Part I, no.380 of 02 June 2015.

# V. Conclusions

**10.47.** From the perspective of *prison law*, the issues discussed, namely the problem of prison overcrowding, the improvement of detention conditions, and the rights of detainees, are all challenges that will inevitably lead to the development of this area of law. It has already been shown that in the cases that have been resolved, the ECHR has requested from the State legislative measures on several levels, and with reference to Romania, what substantive changes occurred even in the legal framework and in the criminal policy of the Romanian State.

**10.48.** All of these jurisdictional mechanisms at various levels – national, supranational, international – have shaped legal systems, and a specific area of law, characterized here as *prison law*, in continuous alignment with the highest standards of fundamental human rights protection. The evolution of this specific area of law, as well as of the public policies that influence the configuration of criminal law, is of major importance at all mentioned levels, especially at the level of the European Union, whose law is thus based on the fundamental premises that each Member State shares with all the other Member States, and recognizes that they share with it a set of common values on which the EU is founded, as stated in Article 2 TEU. That premise implies and justifies the existence of mutual trust between the Member States that those values will be recognized, and therefore that the law of the EU that implements them will be respected. (Judgment of 06 March 2018, *Achmea*, C-284/16, EU:C:2018:158, paragraph 34 and the case-law cited). As the CJEU has stated, both the principle of mutual trust between member States, as well as the principle of mutual recognition of the latter (see 10 August 2017, *Tupikas*, C-270/17 PPU, EU:C:2017:628, paragraph 49), have, in Union law, a fundamental importance, since they allow the creation and maintenance of an area without internal frontiers. More specifically – as the CJEU emphasizes - the principle of mutual trust requires, in particular with regard to the area of freedom, security and justice, for each of these States to consider, save in exceptional circumstances, that all other Member States respect Union law and, in particular, the fundamental rights recognized by it (10 November 2016, *Poltorak*, C-452/16 PPU, EU:C:2016:858, paragraph 26 and the case-law cited). Thus, when implementing Union law, Member States may, on the basis of that provision, presume to observe the fundamental rights of the other Member States, so that they are deprived not only of the possibility of claiming from another Member State a higher level of national protection of fundamental rights than that provided by Union law, but also, save for exceptional situations, of the possibility to assess another Member State has effectively observed, in a concrete case, the fundamental rights guaranteed by the Union [Opinion 2/13 (Accession of the EU to the ECHR) of 18 December 2014, EU:C:2014:2454, paragraphs 192].

**10.49.** The discussed cases, respectively *C-128/18, Dorobanțu,* as well as the other two cases from which the problem originated (the joint cases, *C-404/15, Aranyosi and C-659/15 PPU, Căldăraru)* have had a significant impact on the balance between the three important legal principles of the EU legal order as well as the national legal orders: (1) the principle of respect for human rights, (2) the principle of mutual trust and mutual recognition among EU Member States, and (3) the principle of the rule of law. Clarifications requested by the referring courts, in the case of *C-128/18, Dorobanțu,* have had a direct impact on Romania as a State issuing European arrest warrants but certainly affect all Member States, the interpretation of the EAW Framework Decision being relevant as regards judicial cooperation in criminal matters between EU Member States. In any case, the progress made by Romania in this respect, including in the field of criminal policy and incidental legislation, is in our opinion obvious and is also seconded by a policy in being open to solving the punctual problems in relations with the other Member States.[38]

| | |

---

[38] For example, in a press release on the bilateral meeting with the Danish Minister of Justice in the margins of the JHA Council (Justice session) in Luxembourg on 12 October 2017, it is expressly stated that

Based on these recent developments at national level, the issue of the transfer of Romanian citizens convicted from Denmark to Romania can find a rapid solution, respecting legal requirements and European standards on detention conditions. Consequently, in the immediate future, the transfer procedures will be initiated at the request of the Danish authorities, based on the applicable procedural legal framework. The Danish Minister appreciated the efforts of the Romanian authorities, especially the Minister of Justice, in solving this case and the issue of the conditions in the Romanian penitentiaries. At the expert level, contacts were established to initiate the necessary correspondence between the two ministries. Taking note that a similar issue is also high on the agenda of Romanian judicial cooperation in relations with other EU Member States, the Ministry of Justice will do the same in the other cases.' Available at: http://www.just.ro/transferul-cetatenilor-romani-detinuti-in-penitenciarele-din-alte-state/ (accessed on 29 January 2020).

## Summaries

**DEU** *[Gefängnisrecht und Menschenrechte: Interaktion und Entwicklung]*
*Dieser Beitrag basiert auf der Annahme eines „Gefängnisrechts" im Kontext systematischer Maßnahmen auf nationaler Ebene, die auf die Strafvollzugsbedingungen und die Rechte der Gefangenen ausgerichtet sind, und sich dann auf die Interaktion und Entwicklung fokussiert, die die weitere Richtung dieses Rechtsbereichs bestimmen. Angesichts der spezifischen Situation in Rumänien liegt der Schwerpunkt auf den Schlüsselentscheidungen der EMRK, des EuGH und des rumänischen Verfassungsgerichts, wobei die Schlussfolgerung hinsichtlich der Auswirkungen auf die in diesem Bereich von den rumänischen Behörden eingeleiteten Maßnahmen, einschließlich des Gesetzgebungsprozesses, erörtert wird. Der Beitrag hebt daher die Rolle all dieser Rechtsprechungsmechanismen auf verschiedenen Ebenen – der nationalen, transnationalen, internationalen – bei der Gestaltung der Rechtsordnungen und des spezifischen Rechtsbereichs, der in diesem Beitrag als Gefängnisrecht bezeichnet wird, in ständiger Übereinstimmung mit den höchsten Standards des Grundrechtsschutzes hervor.*

**CZE** *[Vězeňské právo a lidská práva: interakce a vývoj]*
*Tento článek vychází z předpokladu existence „vězeňského práva" v kontextu systémových opatření na úrovni států, která jsou zaměřena na podmínky výkonu trestu odnětí svobody a práva vězněných osob, a následně se zaměřuje na interakci a vývoj, které určují další směřování této oblasti práva. Vzhledem ke specifické situaci v Rumunsku se z tohoto pohledu klade důraz na klíčová rozhodnutí ESLP, SDEU a Ústavního soudu Rumunska (ÚSR), přičemž závěr je pojednán z hlediska vlivů na opatření přijímaná v této oblasti rumunskými orgány, včetně zákonodárného procesu. Článek tedy poukazuje na úlohu všech těchto jurisdikčních mechanismů na nejrůznějších úrovních – vnitrostátní, nadnárodní, mezinárodní – při utváření právních řádů a specifické právní oblasti, charakterizované v tomto příspěvku jako vězeňské právo, při neustálém zajišťování souladu s nejvyššími standardy ochrany základních práv.*

I I I

Czech Yearbook of International Law®

**POL** [*Prawo więzienne a prawa człowieka: interakcja i rozwój*]

*Niniejszy artykuł wychodzi z założenia, że istnieje „prawo więzienne" w kontekście rozwiązań systemowych na poziomie państwa, regulujących warunki odbywania kary pozbawienia wolności i prawa osadzonych, a następnie analizuje interakcję i rozwój ukierunkowujący ten obszar prawa. Ze względu na specyficzną sytuację w Rumunii szczególną uwagę zwraca się tutaj na kluczowe orzeczenia ETPC, TSUE i Trybunału Konstytucyjnego Rumunii, przy czym wnioski przedstawiono z perspektywy wpływu na środki wprowadzane w tej dziedzinie przez władze rumuńskie, w tym na proces ustawodawczy.*

**FRA** [*Le droit pénitentiaire et les droits de l'homme : leurs interactions et évolutions*]

*Le présent article part du concept de « droit pénitentiaire », ensemble de mesures systémiques prises au niveau de l'État et visant les conditions d'exécution de la peine privative de liberté et les droits des prisonniers. Il analyse les interactions et les évolutions qui façonnent ce domaine de droit. Compte tenu des spécificités de la Roumanie, il se focalise sur les grandes décisions de la CEDH, de la CJUE, ainsi que de la Cour constitutionnelle de Roumanie. En conclusion, il examine l'impact de ces décisions sur les mesures prises en la matière par les institutions roumaines, y compris la procédure législative.*

**RUS** [*Тюремное право и права человека: взаимодействие и развитие*]

*Данная статья исходит из предпосылки существования «тюремного права» в контексте системных мер на уровне государств, направленных на условия отбывания тюремного заключения и права заключенных. Затем в ней анализируется взаимодействие и развитие, которые определяют последующее направление этой области права. С учетом особой ситуации в Румынии в данной области, акцент делается на ключевые решения ЕСПЧ, СЕС и Конституционного суда Румынии. Причем в заключении статьи учитываются влияния на меры, принимаемые в этой области румынскими органами власти, а также законодательный процесс.*

**ESP** [*Derecho penitenciario y derechos humanos: interacción y evolución*]

*Este artículo parte del supuesto de la existencia del «derecho penitenciario» en contexto de las medidas sistémicas a nivel de los estados que contemplen las condiciones de la ejecución de las penas privativas de libertad  y de los derechos de la población carcelaria. A continuación, el texto analiza la interacción y la evolución que determinan el rumbo a seguir de esa rama del derecho. Dada la situación específica en que se encuentra Rumania, se pone énfasis en las resoluciones judiciales de TEDH, TJUE y el Tribunal Constitucional de Rumania. En las conclusiones se da cuenta de la influencia de estas resoluciones en las medidas adoptadas por las autoridades rumanas, incluido el proceso legislativo.*

| | |

*Notwithstanding its somewhat chaotic emergence as a recognizable field of legal study, prison law now has a core set of administrative principles and human rights values that allow it to address questions of how prisoners should be treated in prison. (...) However, there are major systematic challenges that prisons are likely to face that will require further development of prison law, which may go beyond the claims of individual prisoners for the recognition of their rights.*[39]

| | |

## Bibliography

SÉBASTIEN PLATON, CONFIANCE MUTUELLE ET CRISE DE L´ÉTAT DE DROIT DANS L´UNION EUROPÉENNE, L'Observateur de Bruxelles (2019).

Marieta Safta, Beatrice Drăghiciu, *Measure To Solve Prison Overcrowding And Improve Detention Conditions,* REVISTA ANALELE UNIVERSITĂŢII ,TITU MAIORESCU', LAW SERIES (2018).

Dirk van Zyl Smit, *Prison Law,* THE OXFORD HANDBOOK OF CRIMINAL LAW, Oxford University Press 988, 1008 (Markus D. Dubber, Tatjana Hörnle ed., 2014).

---

[39]    Dirk van Zyl Smit, *Prison Law,* THE OXFORD HANDBOOK OF CRIMINAL LAW, Oxford University Press 988, 1008 (Markus D. Dubber, Tatjana Hörnle ed., 2014).

Czech Yearbook of International Law®

Albertas Šekštelo

# Impact of Decisions of European Court of Human Rights on International Investment Arbitration

**Key words:**
*Achmea | arbitral tribunal | arbitration | BIT | court | fair trial | human rights | ICSID | investment arbitration | VCLT*

**Abstract |** *In this period of increasing globalisation, large corporations play a vital role not only in business, but also in the social sphere. Thus, their activity becomes very important for increasingly larger populations. By invoking the concept of social responsibility, the international dispute adjudicating bodies pay more and more attention to the protection of fundamental human rights.*

*International investment arbitration is no exception. Nowadays, the arbitral tribunals interfere time to time in the human right protection field. Human rights are also protected by many international treaties, such as the European Convention on Human Rights. Such treaties establish autonomous dispute resolution bodies like the European Court of Human Rights, and an overlap is inevitable between the jurisdictions of international investment arbitral tribunals and specific international courts. Consequently, such an overlap may affect the validity of the arbitral awards in question.*

*This article explores the possible impact of decisions of the European Court of Human Rights on international investment arbitration. The author argues that overlapping jurisdictions can exist between arbitral tribunals and, for instance, the European Court of Human Rights. Moreover, as fundamental human rights are ius cogens in terms of applicable public international law, arbitral tribunals must apply such rules. The duty of the arbitrators to comply with fundamental human rights embodied in international treaties*

**Albertas Šekštelo** is a senior associate in PLP Motieka & Audzevičius. He has considerable experience in both international investment and commercial arbitrations under ICSID, ICC, SCC, UNCITRAL, LCIA, VIAC, MKAS, BelCCI, VCCA rules, as well as in complex cross-border litigations with a focus on international insolvency, asset-tracing proceedings and human rights. Šekštelo has a master's degree in Law from the Faculty of Law, Vilnius University (2005) and a PGDip (with distinction) in International Arbitration from Queen Mary University of London (2011). In 2013, he became a Fellow of the Chartered Institute of Arbitrators (FCIArb). Šekštelo is a candidate for LLM in International Dispute Resolution at the Queen Mary University of London and the author of many publications in the field of arbitration. He is a lecturer in the Vilnius University where he teaches courses in civil law and business dispute resolution.
E-mail: albertas.sekstelo@motieka.com

Czech Yearbook of International Law®

*other than bilateral investment agreements not only brings jurisdictions of the arbitral tribunals and the specialised international courts closer together, but can also impact, as in the Achmea case, the validity of the arbitral award in question.*

*The role of the specialised international courts such as the European Court of Human Rights might be vital in reviewing the proceedings of the Courts of a Member State related to the challenge of the award in question. In compulsory arbitrations prescribed by law, the European Court of Human Rights could interfere even into the arbitral proceedings by reviewing its compliance with the requirements of the European Convention on Human Rights at the stage of review of the Member State's Highest court decision. Such a review can have a considerable impact on international investment arbitration, at least on the regional European level. However, the European Court of Human Rights should not exercise jurisdiction upon any dispute related to direct or indirect review of the ICSID awards.*

| | |

## I.    Introduction

**11.01.**    More and more arbitral tribunals in international investment arbitrations overlap with the domain of international human rights. In December 2016 the ICSID tribunal in *Urbaser* v. *Argentina*[1] made significant findings on the role of international human rights law in investment treaty arbitration. Following the decision in *Urbaser*, several tribunals have been called upon to consider the relevance of allegations concerning human rights and environmental issues.[2]

**11.02.**    However, protection of fundamental human rights also falls within the scope of other international conventions, such as the European Convention on Human Rights (the Convention). International instruments such as Bilateral Investment Treaties (BIT) and the Convention have similar ambits but different methods to resolve disputes. Thus, jurisdiction of dispute resolution bodies, such as arbitral tribunals and specialised courts, may overlap. If so, two different adjudicators may come

---

[1]    *Urbasser S.A. and Consorcio de Aguas Bilbao Bizkaia, Bilbao Biskaia Ur Partzuergoa* v. *the Argentine Republic*, ICSID Case No. ARB/07/26, Award of 08 December 2016.

[2]    See e.g., *Bear Creek Mining Corporation* v. *Republic of Peru*, ICSID Case No. ARB/14/21, Award of 30 November 2017; *Burlington Resources Inc.* v. *Republic of Ecuador*, ICSID Case No. ARB/08/5, Award of 07 December 2017; *David Aven et al.* v. *the Republic of Costa Rica*, UNCITRAL Arbitration Case No. UNCT/15/3, Final Award of 18 September 2018; *Cortec Mining Kenya Limited, Cortec (Pty) Limited and Stirling Capital Limited* v. *Republic of Kenya*, ICSID Case No. ARB/15/29, Award of 22 October 2018.

to opposite conclusions when dealing with the same issue of protection of human rights (**II.**).

**11.03.** This may lead to set aside proceedings. Moreover, set aside proceedings may lead to an application to the European Court of Human Rights the Court, or ECHR in the situations when the Convention is applicable. The judgement of the Court may trigger the annulment of the award in question, as happened in the *Achmea*[3] case (**III.**).

**11.04.** Thus, the scope of this article is to analyse how the Court could interfere in international investment arbitration and what impact such interventions would have on the arbitration (**IV.**).

## II.     Overlapping Jurisdictions

**11.05.** Different international instruments, e.g. BITs, and international multilateral agreements, such as the Convention, may cover the same scope of protections for human rights. However, such instruments provide for different forums and bodies that resolve disputes between the parties.

**11.06.** In this chapter we will analyse how the Convention might be relevant when dealing with the human rights protection in the international investment arbitration (**II.1.**). We also will look into the similar scope of protection vested in the BITs and the Convention (**II.2.**). Finally, we will analyse how the proceedings in international investment arbitration may be scrutinized later by the Court because of the 'Fair trial' requirement (**II.3.**).

### II.1.     Reliance on the Convention when Interpreting BITs

**11.07.** An issue of application of the Convention may occur when the arbitral tribunal deals with applicable law standards related to the merits[4] in a particular international investment arbitration. For both the State and the investor, the determination of the law applicable to the contract and the agreement on dispute resolution are often the most sensitive legal issues.[5]

---

[3]   ECJ Judgement of 06 March 2018, C-248/16, *Achmea* [2018] EU:C:2018:158; For more information regarding the impact of this Judgement on the International Commercial Arbitration see Albertas Šekštelo, *A Prophecy of the Crisis of International Commercial Arbitration in Europe?*, CYARB VOL. IX, CZECH (& CENTRAL EUROPEAN) YEARBOOK OF ARBITRATION, RECOGNITION AND ENFORCEMENT OF ARBITRAL AWARDS 271 (Alexander J. Bělohlávek, Naděžda Rozehnalová eds., 2019).
[4]   In terms of jurisdiction, it is the predominant position that the relevant BIT and international standards are sufficient to determine competence of the Arbitral Tribunal, see Christoph Schreuer, *Jurisdiction and Applicable Law in Investment Treaty Arbitration*, 1(1) REVUE DE RÉGLEMENT DES DIFFÉRENDS DE MCGILL (2014); *CMS Gas Transmission Company* v. *the Republic of Argentina*, ICSID Case No. ARB/01/8, Award of 17 July 2014, paragraphs 42, 88.
[5]   RUDOLF DOLZER, CHRISTOPH SCHREUER, PRINCIPLES OF INTERNATIONAL INVESTMENT LAW, Oxford University Press (2008), et. 73-74.

**11.08.** First of all, every contract must have a basis in a national legal order.[6] However, reference only to domestic law might be problematic, because the State-respondent can amend or repeal the relevant legal acts.[7] Thus, historically, international guarantees,[8] such as the system of Article 42 of the Convention on the Settlement of Investment Disputes between States and Nationals of other States (the ICSID Convention), envisage (in the absence of express choice of law) the concurrent application of the law of the host State and international law in lieu of diplomatic protection.[9]

**11.09.** Secondly, as the international legal order becomes applied, the arbitral tribunals may be faced with the application of other international conventions. This may lead to treaty interpretation issues. The *Urbaser* tribunal noted that treaties must be interpreted pursuant to Article 31(3)(c) of the Vienna Convention on the Law of Treaties (VCLT Convention). This provides that when interpreting treaties, account must be taken of 'any relevant rules of international law applicable in the relations between the parties':[10]

> [t]he Tribunal further retains that the [ICSID Convention] has to be interpreted in the light of the rules set out in the [VCLT Convention] and that Article [31(3)(c)] of that Treaty indicates that account is to be taken of 'any relevant rules of international law applicable in the relations between the parties'. The BIT cannot be interpreted and applied in a vacuum. The Tribunal must certainly be mindful of the BIT's special purpose as a Treaty promoting foreign investments, but it cannot do so without taking the relevant rules of international

---

[6] Judgment of the Permanent Court of International Justice of 12 July 1929 in Serbian Loans Case, PCIJ Ser.A. No. 20 1929, 41: '[a]ny contract which is not a contract between States in their capacity as subjects of international law is based on the municipal law of some country'.

[7] In relation to foreign investments, applicable law has been internationalized not because it is less unclear than national law, but because national law is found to be inadequate; see MARC BUNGENBERG ET AL., INTERNATIONAL INVESTMENT LAW, C.H.Beck-Hart-Nomos (2015), et. 1389-1390.

[8] See e.g., Statute of the International Court of Justice, Article 38.

[9] DOAK R. BISHOP, JAMES R. CRAWFORD, MICHAEL W. REISMAN, FOREIGN INVESTMENT DISPUTES. CASES, MATERIALS AND COMMENTARY, Kluwer Law International (2005), et. 632; see also e.g., *AGIP Spa* v. *The Government of the Popular Republic of the Congo*, ICSID Case No. ARB/77/1, Award of 30 November 1979, paragraph 43; *Bienvenuti and Bonfant Srl* v. *The Government of the People's Republic of the Congo*, ICSID Case No. ARB/77/2, Award of 15 August 1980, paragraph 4.2.; *Amco Asia* v. *Indonesia*, ICSID Case No. ARB/81/1, Decision on the Application for Annulment of 16 May 1986, paragraph 19; *Kloeckner Industrie-Anlagen GmbH* v. *Republic of Cameroon*, ICSID Case No. ARB/81/2, Decision on Annulment of 03 May 1985, paragraph 69; *Southern Pacific Properties (Middle Esat) Limited* v. *Arab Republic of Egypt*, ICSID Case No. ARB/84/3, Award of 20 May 1992, (Dissenting Opinion of Dr El Mahdi), section 3.

[10] *Urbasser S.A. and Consorcio de Aguas Bilbao Bizkaia, Bilbao Biskaia Ur Partzuergoa* v. *the Argentine Republic*, ICSID Case No. ARB/07/26, Award of 08 December 2016, paragraph 1200.

law into account. The BIT has to be construed in harmony with other rules of international law of which it forms part, including those relating to human rights.[11]

**11.10.** In investment cases involving parties to the Convention, some tribunals relied only on the ICSID Convention and its case law.[12] In other cases involving non-parties, that case law was used as authority on a number of points concerning individual rights.[13] In a similar way, investment tribunals have relied on the Inter-American Convention on Human Rights and on the practice of its court.[14] One tribunal undertook an extensive examination of the right to a fair trial in international human rights instruments, especially the International Covenant on Civil and Political Rights, for purposes of interpreting a treaty provision on fair and equitable treatment.[15] In one case, the tribunal took into account the Universal Declaration of Human Rights.[16] Thus, it is more than evident that the tribunals takes due account of provisions of the international human rights law.

**11.11.** Thirdly, another issue is whether, when interpreting the BIT, the provisions of international human rights are the peremptory norms of general international law (*ius cogens*). If so, such norms must certainly prevail over any contrary provision of the BIT, as per the express statement in Article 53 of the VCLT

---

[11] See also *Tulip Real Estate and Development Netherlands B.V.* v. *Republic of Turkey*, ICSID Case No. ARB/11/28, Decision of Annulment dated of 30 December 2015, paragraphs 86-92.

[12] *Ronald S. Lauder* v. *Czech Republic*, UNCITRAL, Award of 03 September 2001, paragraph 200; *ADC Affiliate Limited and ADC & ADMC Management Limited* v. *Republic of Hungary* Award, ICSID Case No. ARB/03/16, Decision of 02 October 2006, paragraph 497; *The Rompetrol Group N.V.* v. *Romania*, ICSID Case No. ARB/06/3, Decision on the Participation of a Counsel of 14 January 2010, paragraph 20. In *Frontier Petroleum* v. *the Czech Republic*, the Tribunal indicated that the Convention was applicable but had not been pleaded properly by the parties. *Frontier Petroleum Services Ltd.* v. *the Czech Republic*, UNCITRAL, Final Award of 12 November 2010, paragraph 338.

[13] *Mondev International Ltd.* v. *United States of America*, ICSID Case No. ARB(AF)/99/2, Award of 11 October 2002, paragraph 143; *Técnicas Medioambientales Tecmed, S.A.* v. *United Mexican States*, Award of 29 May 2003, paragraph 122; *Saipem S.p.A.* v. *People's Republic of Bangladesh*, ICSID Case No. ARB/05/7, Decision on Jurisdiction dated 21 March 2007, paragraphs 130, 132; *Azurix* v. *Argentina*, Award of 14 July 2006, paragraph 311; *International Thunderbird Gaming Corporation* v. *United Mexican States*, UNCITRAL, Award, Dissenting Opinion Wälde of 26 January 2006, paragraph 27; *Société Générale in respect of DR Energy Holdings Limited and Empresa Distribuidora de Electricidad del Este, S.A.* v. *Dominican Republic*, LCIA Case No. UN 7927, Award on Jurisdiction of 19 September 2008, paragraph 93; *Perenco Ecuador Limited* v. *Republic of Ecuador*, ICSID Case No. ARB/08/6, Decision on Provisional Measures of 08 May 2009, paragraph 70; *Total S.A.* v. *Argentine Republic*, ICSID Case No. ARB/04/1, Decision on Liability of 27 December 2010, paragraph 129; *El Paso* v. *Argentina*, Award of 31 October 2011, paragraph 598. In *Fireman's Fund* v. *Mexico*, the Tribunal questioned whether the case law under the ECHR is aviable source to interpreting Article 1110 of the North American Free Trade Agreement (NAFTA). *Fireman's Fund Insurance Company* v. *United Mexican States*, ICSID Case No. ARB/02/1, Award of 17 July 2006, footnote 161.

[14] *IBM World Trade Corp.* v. *Republic of Ecuador*, ICSID Case No. ARB/02/10, Decision on Jurisdiction of 22 December 2003, paragraph 72; *El Paso* v. *Argentina*, Award of 31 October 2011, paragraph 598.

[15] *Hesham Talaat M. Al-Warraq* v. *Republic of Indonesia*, UNCITRAL, Final Award of 15 December 2014, paragraphs 556-621.

[16] *Ioan Micula, Viorel Micula and others* v. *Romania*, ICSID Case No. ARB/05/20, Decision on Jurisdiction and Admissibility of 24 September 2008, paragraph 88.

Convention.[17] Article 53 is also called 'an empty box' as it defines the peremptory norm but gives no examples.[18] Commentators rightly believe that human rights fall within *ius cogens*.[19]

**11.12.** Thus, by virtue of interpreting the BIT other international provisions on human rights are mandatory as a form of *ius cogens*. Therefore, the arbitral tribunals must pay due attention to the violation of human rights or the Convention in international investment disputes.

## II.2.    Similar Scope of Protection

**11.13.** At the first sight, the ambits of BIT and the Convention are different. The purpose of the BIT is to give protection for investments, which is not necessarily the same as protection of human rights. On the contrary, interests of the corporation are not always in line with human rights.

**11.14.** However, globalisation is confronting new global challenges such as climate change. Some issues such as access to a clean water supply and sanitary conditions become more and more vital and can affect investments.

**11.15.** For instance, the dispute in *Urbaser*[20] arose out of a concession granted to the claimants for the provision of drinking water and sewerage services in the province of Buenos Aires.

**11.16.** In recent years, the Court, which bases its jurisprudence on the Convention, has handled an increasing number of cases in the context of the right to clean water and sanitation.

**11.17.** In the aftermath of the Second World War, environmental problems – amongst them access to clean water and sanitation - were not yet considered a significant threat to human rights and were thus not included in the Convention.[21] But this did not

---

[17]    *Urbasser S.A. and Consorcio de Aguas Bilbao Bizkaia, Bilbao Biskaia Ur Partzuergoa* v. *the Argentine Republic*, ICSID Case No. ARB/07/26, Award of 08 December 2016, paragraph 1203. Article 53 of the VCTL Convention explains that a peremptory norm of general international law is a norm accepted and recognized by the international community of States as a norm from which no derogation is permitted and which can be modified only by a subsequent norm of general international law having the same character.

[18]    Such norm was criticized by the International Law Commission stating that '[t]he formulation of the article is not free from difficulty, since there is no simple criterion by which to identify a general rule of international law as having the character of *ius cogens*'; see INTERNATIONAL LAW COMMISSION, DRAFT ARTICLES ON THE LAW OF TREATIES WITH COMMENTARIES, Yearbook of the International Law Commission vol. II (1966), et. 247-248.

[19]    *Ibid.*, at 248. See also RUEDIGER WOLFRUM (ED.), THE MAX PLANCK ENCYCLOPEDIA OF PUBLIC INTERNATIONAL LAW VOL. VI, Oxford: Oxford University Press (2012), et. 444. In the Barcelona Traction Case the ICJ gave examples of obligation *erga omnes* which by their nature must also form part of *ius cogens*: '[s]uch obligations derive, for example, in contemporary international law, ... from the principles and rules concerning the basic rights of the human person'; *Barcelona traction, Light and Power Co. Ltd (Belgium* v. *Spain) (Second Phase)*, Judgement, I.C.J. Rep 3, 1970, paragraph 34.

[20]    *Urbasser S.A. and Consorcio de Aguas Bilbao Bizkaia, Bilbao Biskaia Ur Partzuergoa* v. *the Argentine Republic*, ICSID Case No. ARB/07/26, Award of 08 December 2016.

[21]    KATHARINA FRANZISKA BRAIG, THE EUROPEAN COURT OF HUMAN RIGHTS AND THE RIGHT TO CLEAN WATER AND SANITATION, Water Policy, IWA Publishing 20 (2018), paragraph 284.

prevent the Court from establishing pan-European minimum standards relating to the rights to a clean environment.[22]

**11.18.** The Court has dealt with environmental issues as components of Article 2 (the right to life) and Article 8 (the right to respect of private and family life), as well as Article 10 (the right to freedom of expression and information) and Article 1 of Protocol I (the right to property) of the Convention. It has also addressed the procedural guarantees such as the right to fair trial and effective remedy (Articles 6(1) and 13 of the Convention).[23] Thus, environmental issues are related to such fundamental rights as the right to life, private and family life and others. In turn, such fundamental rights form part of *ius cogens* and, therefore, are mandatory for any dispute resolution body.

**11.19.** As fundamental human rights are part of *ius cogens*, there are situations where the scope of protection under the BIT and the Convention are similar. Two examples can illustrate this. The first is a case held by the arbitral tribunal under the BIT, and the other is a situation that might arise before the Court.[24]

**11.20.** In the *Urbasser* case,[25] a dispute arose over the privatisation of drinking water supply services in Argentina. Before the privatization, Argentina's Federal Government provided drinking water and sewage services through its company. But because of budgetary restraints, such services underwent great difficulties. Then, the Federal Government promoted the decentralization of these services to the provinces, and some of them in turn transferred services to the Municipalities.[26] As the legal, operational and economic situation of the drinking water and sewage sector in Argentina remained unhealthy,[27] Argentina promoted private-sector involvement though privatization on both the national level and in the Provinces. But such privatisations resulted in many investment disputes between the investors and Argentina.[28]

---

[22] *Ibid.*, at 285; see also *Kyrtatos v. Greece*, Judgement, No. 41666/98, 22 May 2003, paragraph 52; *Fadeyeva v. Russia*, No. 55723/00, 09 June 2005; *Ivan Atanasov v. Bulgaria*, No. 12853/03, 02 December 2010, paragraphs 66, 75–76; *Dubetska and others v. Ukraine*, No. 30499/03, 10 February 2011 (final on 10 October 2011).
[23] KATHARINA FRANZISKA BRAIG, THE EUROPEAN COURT OF HUMAN RIGHTS AND THE RIGHT TO CLEAN WATER AND SANITATION, Water Policy, IWA Publishing 20 (2018), paragraph 285.
[24] There are many other scopes of protection of the fundamental rights that might overlap under the BITs and the Convention, such as fair and equitable treatment, full protection, fair trial, and expropriation.
[25] *Urbasser S.A. and Consorcio de Aguas Bilbao Bizkaia, Bilbao Biskaia Ur Partzuergoa v. the Argentine Republic*, ICSID Case No. ARB/07/26, Award of 08 December 2016.
[26] *Ibid.*, at 39.
[27] *Ibid.*, at 40.
[28] *Ibid.*, at 41-51. The following disputes arose over privatization processes: *Suez, Sociedad General de Aguas de Barcelona, S.A. and Vivendi Universal S.A. v. Argentine Republic*, ICSID Case No. ARB/03/19, Award of 9 April 2015; *Compañía de Aguas del Aconquija S.A. and Vivendi Universal S.A. v. Argentine Republic*, ICSID Case No. ARB/97/3, Award of 20 August 2007, also known as 'Vivendi II', the Tribunal found that the Argentine Republic had violated principles of fair and equitable treatment and that the Argentine

Czech Yearbook of International Law®

**11.21.** Claimants got a concession contract for the Buenos Aires area. During Argentina's financial crisis, the State instituted emergency measures that caused financial loss to the claimants, and ultimately led to Argentina terminating the concession agreement. The claimants commenced ICSID proceedings against Argentina under the Spain-Argentina bilateral investment treaty. Argentina subsequently filed a counterclaim, alleging that the claimants' failure to make necessary investments violated obligations under international law, in particular the human right to clean water and sanitation.[29] In an award issued in December 2016, the tribunal accepted jurisdiction over Argentina's human rights counterclaim, rejecting the claimants' argument that any claim on the basis of alleged human rights violations was outside the tribunal's competence. Although it ultimately dismissed the counterclaim, the tribunal rejected the claimants' 'principled objection' that the asymmetric nature of the BIT meant that it does not impose any obligations on the investor. The tribunal considered that the BIT must be 'construed in harmony with other rules of international law... including those relating to human rights'.[30]

**11.22.** More importantly, the tribunal in *Urbasser* stated that[31]

> ... international law accepts corporate social responsibility as a standard of crucial importance for companies operating in the field of international commerce. This standard includes commitments to comply with human rights in the framework of those entities' operations conducted in countries other than the country of their seat or incorporation. In light of this more recent development, it can no longer be admitted that companies operating internationally are immune from becoming subjects of international law. [Quotations omitted]

**11.23.** A major aspect of water- and sanitation-related international case law concerns discrimination against members of a

---

Republic had taken unlawful expropriation measures and the Republic was ordered to pay USD 105 million; *Suez, Sociedad General de Aguas de Barcelona S.A., and InterAguas Servicios Integrales del Agua S.A. v. the Argentine Republic*, ICSID Case No. ARB/03/17, Decision on Liability of 30 July 2010; *Aguas Cordobesas S.A., Suez, and Sociedad General de Aguas de Barcelona S.A. v. Argentine Republic*, ICSID Case No. ARB/03/18, Order Taking Note of the Discontinuance of the Proceedings (not public) of 24 January 2007.

[29] *Urbasser S.A. and Consorcio de Aguas Bilbao Bizkaia, Bilbao Biskaia Ur Partzuergoa v. the Argentine Republic*, ICSID Case No. ARB/07/26, Award of 08 December 2016; HUMAN RIGHTS IN ISDS: WHERE ARE WE NOW, Global Arbitration Review (2019), available on: https://globalarbitrationreview.com/article/1194453/human-rights-in-isds-where-are-we-now (accessed on 07 August 2019).

[30] *Ibid.*

[31] *Urbasser S.A. and Consorcio de Aguas Bilbao Bizkaia, Bilbao Biskaia Ur Partzuergoa v. the Argentine Republic*, ICSID Case No. ARB/07/26, Award of 08 December 2016, paragraph 1195.

vulnerable population.[32] On a global level, governments have been held responsible for protecting vulnerable groups' access to water and sanitation.[33] Although in Europe, these issues are rarely addressed by the Court,[34] the Court might investigate more closely the minority rights at stake in future cases and might come to similar conclusions as the Human Rights Committee. The latter, for instance, held in communication No. 20173/2011 that Sofia's municipality would violate the applicants' rights if it enforced an eviction order without providing satisfactory replacement housing immediately.[35] One of the issues brought before the Committee was the cutting of the water supply. In an attempt to force the Roma community to leave, the Municipality of Sofia ordered its water company, Sofiyska Voda, to cut off the water supply to the community.[36]

11.24. Thus, clean water-supply is a part of fundamental human rights and thus is protected by the Convention provisions. These, in turn have an *ius cogens* effect upon the BIT.[37] Consequently, the tribunals must take into consideration these mandatory provisions of the Convention as far as such provisions are interlinked with investment protection.[38]

11.25. In a following section we will explore how arbitration proceedings and also the right to be heard fall within the 'fair trial' requirements of the Convention.

## II.3.  Arbitration Falls within 'Fair Trial' Requirements of the Convention

11.26. Article 6(1) of the Convention provides that:

> [i]n the determination of his civil rights and obligations ... everyone is entitled to a fair and public hearing within a reasonable time by an independent and impartial *tribunal* established by law. [Emphasis added].

---

[32] KATHARINA FRANZISKA BRAIG, THE EUROPEAN COURT OF HUMAN RIGHTS AND THE RIGHT TO CLEAN WATER AND SANITATION, Water Policy, IWA Publishing 20 (2018), paragraph 297.

[33] *Ibid.*, at 297.

[34] *Ibid.*, at 297.

[35] *Naidenova* v. *Bulgaria*, Human Right Committee Communication No. 20173/2011 dated 27 November 2012, CCPR/C/106/D/2073/2011.

[36] *Ibid.*, at 9.

[37] The Court protects access to clean water and holds States liable for water contamination, see e. g., *Zander* v. *Sweden*, No. 1482/88, 25 November 1993; *Tătar* v. *Romania*, No. 67021/01, 27 January 2009; *Băcilă* v. *Romania*, No. 19234/04, 30 March 2010; *Dubetska and others* v. *Ukraine*, No. 30499, 10 February 2011; *Dzemyuk* v. *Ukraine*, No. 42488/02, 04 September 2014.

[38] The Tribunals also might have to consider other applicable mandatory rules of environmental protection, e.g. those prescribed by the European Union. The impact of the European Union rules on the jurisdiction of the Tribunals is beyond the scope of this publication.

**11.27.** The Court held that,[39]

> ... [t]he word 'tribunal' in Article [6(1)] is not necessarily to be understood as signifying a court of law of the classic kind, integrated within the standard judicial machinery of the country ... thus, it may comprise a body set up to determine a limited number of specific issues, provided always that it offers the appropriate guarantees. The Court also notes that ... the proceedings before the Arbitration Tribunal were similar to those before a court and that due provision was made for appeals.

**11.28.** Therefore, the Court recognises the arbitral tribunals as having the status of a 'tribunal' within the meaning of Article 6(1) of the Convention.[40]

**11.29.** Article 6(1) of the Convention defines certain procedural rights ensuring a fair trial. The provision notably established:

    a) The right of access to court;

    b) The right to an independent and impartial tribunal;

    c) The right to present one's case, including the right to be heard, the principle of equal treatment and the right to obtain a reasoned decision;

    d) The right to obtain a decision within a reasonable time;

    e) The right to a public trial.[41]

**11.30.** Moreover, apart from these procedural rights, certain substantive rights guaranteed by the Convention may have an impact on a case submitted to arbitration. If, for instance, the protection of property established in Protocol No. 1 of the Convention can affect the resolution of a civil dispute before the court, then it might also have an impact on the resolution of the same dispute before the arbitral tribunal.[42]

**11.31.** If we look into purely procedural rights protected by the Convention, and in particular, by Article 6(1), there is the following link between Arbitration and the Convention. First, an agreement to arbitrate is permissible under the Convention, provided it was not reached under constraint.[43] Second, Article 6(1) is fully applicable to compulsory arbitration, in

---

[39] *Lithgow and others* v. *the United Kingdom*, No. 9006/80; 9262/81; 9263/81; 9265/81; 9266/81; 9313/81; 9405/81, 8 July 1986, paragraph 201.

[40] See also *Mutu and Pechstein* v. *Svitzerland*, No. 40575/10 and 67474/10, 02 October 2018 (final on 04 February 2019) paragraph 149.

[41] Sébastien Besson, *Arbitration and Human Rights*, ASA BULLETIN, Kluwer Law International (2006).

[42] *Ibid.*, at 397.

[43] 'La clause compromissoire litigieuse aurait pu, toutefois, se révéler contraire à la Convention si X. ne l'avait signée que sous la contrainte'; see Commission, *X* v. *Germany*, No. 1197/61, 05 March 1963, paragraph 68.

other words, arbitration imposed on the parties by law.[44] It might be argued that an arbitration stipulated in the BIT becomes compulsory arbitration to the State-respondent in international investment arbitration, because it is incumbent upon the investor to opt-in to the dispute resolution forum and the BIT itself is an international treaty. Thus, application of Article 6(1) of the Convention becomes even more vital in investment treaty arbitration. Third, Article 6(1) of the Convention applies directly to the arbitrators.[45] Fourth, Article 6(1) of the Convention is applicable to court proceedings related to arbitration. A court of a contracting State requested to appoint or to challenge an arbitrator, or to review an arbitral award is hence bound by the Convention.[46]

**11.32.** The issue of when the Convention is applicable to the court proceedings related to arbitration (in this case the set-aside procedure), will be subject of further examination in the next part of this article.

## III. Set-aside Proceedings and Application to ECHR

**11.33.** Although there are many scenarios within arbitration-related court proceedings,[47] the set-aside proceedings when the award

---

[44] 'A distinction must be drawn between voluntary arbitration and compulsory arbitration. Normally Article 6 poses no problem where arbitration is entered into voluntarily. ... If, on the other hand, arbitration is compulsory in the sense of being required by law, ... the parties have no option but to refer their dispute to an arbitration Board, and the Board must offer the guarantees set forth in Article 6(1)'; see Commission, *Bramelid and Malmstrom* v. *Sweden*, No. 8588/79; No. 8589/79, 12 December 1983, paragraph 30.

[45] See e.g. Sébastien Besson, *Arbitration and Human Rights*, ASA BULLETIN, Kluwer Law International 404 (2006); MANUEL ARROYO (ED), ARBITRATION IN SWITZERLAND: THE PRACTITIONER'S GUIDE, Kluwer law International 717 (2013); Jean-Hubert Moitry, *Right to Fair Trial and the European Convention on Human Rights: Some Remarks on the République de Guinée Case*, JOURNAL OF INTERNATIONAL ARBITRATION, Kluwer Law International (1989), et. 116-117.

[46] Sébastien Besson, *Arbitration and Human Rights*, ASA BULLETIN, Kluwer Law International (2006), paragraph 399 '... [T]he Commission considers that the State cannot be held responsible for the arbitrator's actions unless, and only insofar as, the national courts were required to intervene ...'; see Commission, *R* v. *Switzerland*, No. 10881/84, 04 March 1987, paragraphs 83-93, where the Paris Court of Appeal held: '[c] elui-ci [le juge étatique] ayant rempli sa mission légale d' assistance ou de coopération technique, se doit de laisser les arbitres épuiser leur pouvoir propre et exclusif de juger et assurer eux-mêmes, en conscience et sous leur responsabilité propre, les conditions d'un 'procès équitable', conforme aux principes généraux et fondamentaux et, en tant que de besoin, aux dispositions de l'article 6 de la Convention de Sauvegarde des Droits de l'Homme ...', quoted in Jean-Hubert Moitry, *Right to Fair Trial and the European Convention on Human Rights: Some Remarks on the République de Guinée Case*, JOURNAL OF INTERNATIONAL ARBITRATION, Kluwer Law International 4 (1989).

[47] Such proceedings include those concerning the validity of the arbitration agreement, anti-suit injunctions, proceedings related to the composition of the Arbitral Tribunal, court involvement during the arbitral proceedings such as assistance in taking of evidence, an application of interim measures, an extension of time limits, and preliminary determination of questions of law. There are also proceedings after the award has been rendered, including challenges, appeals and enforcement; for more details see JULIAN D. M. LEW, LOUKAS A. MISTELIS, STEFAN M. KROELL, COMPARATIVE INTERNATIONAL COMMERCIAL ARBITRATION, Kluwer Law International 355 (2003).

in question is being challenged before the courts of *lex arbitri* is of particular interest for the purpose of this article.

**11.34.** The purpose of challenging an award before a national court at the seat, or place, of arbitration is to have it modified in some way by the relevant court, or more usually to have that court declare that the award is to be disregarded (*i.e.* 'annulled' or 'set-aside') in whole or in part.[48]

**11.35.** Thus, many national arbitration statutes, including the UNCITRAL Model Law, permit the annulment of international awards if:

a) There was no valid arbitration agreement;

b) The award-debtor was denied an adequate opportunity to present their case;

c) The arbitration was not conducted in accordance with the parties' agreement or, failing such agreement, the law of the arbitral seat;

d) The award dealt with matters not submitted by the parties to arbitration;

e) The award dealt with a dispute that is not capable of settlement by arbitration; or

f) The award is contrary to public policy.[49]

**11.36.** Also, the annulment of the international investment award may also be subject to special annulment proceedings, for example those embodied in the ICSID Convention. Article 52(1) of the ICSID Convention prescribes separate grounds for the annulment of an ICSID Award:

a) That the arbitral tribunal was not properly constituted;

b) That the arbitral tribunal has manifestly exceeded its powers;

c) That there was corruption on the part of a member of the arbitral tribunal;

d) That there has been a serious departure from a fundamental rule of procedure; or

e) That the award has failed to state the reasons on which it is based.[50]

**11.37.** In almost all these situations, grounds to set aside the arbitral award correlate with the Fair Trial standards embodied in the Convention. Therefore, we will briefly examine the grounds to set aside that are mostly connected with Article 6(1)

---

[48] ALLAN REDFERN, MARTIN HUNTER ET AL., LAW AND PRACTICE OF INTERNATIONAL COMMERCIAL ARBITRATION, Thomson Sweet & Maxwell 404 (4th ed. 2004).

[49] GARY B. BORN, INTERNATIONAL COMMERCIAL ARBITRATION, International Arbitral Awards vol. III, Wolters Kluwer Law & Business 3165 (2nd ed. 2014).

[50] See also CHRISTOPH H. SCHREUER ET AL., THE ICSID CONVENTION. A COMMENTARY, Cambridge University Press 898 (2nd ed. 2011).

of the Convention (**III.1.**) and application to the Court proceedings (**III.2.**).

## III.1.  Grounds to Set-aside Connected with Article 6(1) of the Convention

**11.38.** It would be fair to say that the grounds to set aside exist to safeguard due process in arbitral proceedings. So does Article 6 of the Convention. Thus, unsurprisingly, there are many grounds to challenge an award related to the Fair Trial protection enshrined in the Convention, such as forced conclusion of the arbitration agreement (***III.1.1.***), lack of the arbitral tribunal's jurisdiction *ratione personae* and *ratione materiae* (***III.1.2.***), violations of the right to be heard (***III.1.3.***), lack of impartiality and independence of the arbitral tribunal (***III.1.4.***), and issues related to the *ordre public* (***III.1.5.***).

### III.1.1.  Arbitration Agreement

**11.39.** An arbitration agreement is a fundamental prerequisite for the arbitral proceedings. Even in international investment arbitration, the State parties to the BIT offer consent to arbitration to investors who are nationals of the other contracting party. The arbitration agreement is perfected through the acceptance of that offer by an eligible investor. Thus, technically, the agreement to arbitrate may be concluded not between two contracting States, but between such a State and the investor of another contracting State. In this regard, there is no fundamental difference between arbitration clauses contained in a BIT and in a commercial contract; for instance, when a State concludes a Private-Public Partnership contract.[51]

**11.40.** The State's consent to arbitration usually has three origins: an arbitration clause in an investor-State contract,[52] a provision in a national investment code or law[53] and the dispute-settlement provision of a bilateral or multilateral treaty.[54]

**11.41.** Thus, if the arbitral agreement is concluded without the party's free will, e.g. by bribing State officials,[55] this may affect the validity

---

[51]  Albertas Šekštelo, *A Prophecy of the Crisis of International Commercial Arbitration in Europe?*, CYARB VOL. IX, CZECH (& CENTRAL EUROPEAN) YEARBOOK OF ARBITRATION, RECOGNITION AND ENFORCEMENT OF ARBITRAL AWARDS 271 (Alexander J. Bělohlávek, Naděžda Rozehnalová eds., 2019), et. 289-290.

[52]  *Mobil* v. *New Zeland*, ICSID Case No. ARB/87/2, Award of 04 May 1989; *Vacuum Salt* v. *Ghana*, ICSID Case No. ARB/92/1, Award of 16 February 1994.

[53]  *SPP* v. *Egypt*, ICSID Case No. ARB/84/3, Decision on Jurisdiction II of 14 April 1988; *Tradex* v. *Albania*, ICSID Case No. ARB/94/2, 24 December 1996.

[54]  ANDREA MARCO STEINGRUBER, CONSENT IN INTERNATIONAL ARBITRATION, Oxford University Press 196 (2012).

[55]  See e.g. *Cortec Mining Kenya Limited, Cortec (Pty) Limited and Stirling Capital Limited* v. *Republic of*

of such agreement. Such an action would constitute a breach of the Fair Trial requirements of Article 6(1) of the Convention. Thus, if the arbitral tribunal disregards the clear evidence of lack of will by the parties to enter into the arbitration agreement, this may infringe, *inter alia*, on Article 6(1) of the Convention.

### III.1.2. Jurisdiction Ratione Personae and Ratione Materiae

**11.42.** There are several indicators of jurisdiction of the arbitral tribunals in investment treaty arbitration. Among them is jurisdiction *ratione personae* (whether the claimant is an investor) and jurisdiction *ratione materiae* (whether the investor has made investments).

**11.43.** The first indicator is the jurisdiction *ratione personae* of investment tribunals. Two issues are of considerable importance: nationality and the protection of shareholders.[56]

**11.44.** The investor must be a national of a State which is a party to a treaty with the State which interfered with the property rights of the investor. The investor's nationality is decisive for the jurisdiction of an arbitral tribunal, as well as for the applicability of the substantial protection standards.[57] However, the nationality of the claimant is irrelevant for the question of whether they are eligible to present their claim before the Court. The necessary link for protection is not the nationality of the person to be protected, but the fact that the inferring State is a party to the Convention.[58]

**11.45.** In international investment law it is not disputed that corporations are protected, if only they have the right nationality, and the same is true for shareholders,[59] including minority shareholders.[60] At the same time, the Courts have adopted a restrictive attitude towards shareholders who acted independently of the company in pursuit of claims arising from acts that adversely affected the company. Moreover, claims by

---

*Kenya*, ICSID Case No. ARB/15/29, Award of 22 October 2018.

[56] PIERRE-MARIE DUPUY, FRANCESCO FRANCIONI, ERNST-ULRICH PETERSMANN (EDS.), HUMAN RIGHTS IN INTERNATIONAL INVESTMENT LAW AND ARBITRATION, Oxford University Press 220 (2010).

[57] *Ibid.*, at 220.

[58] *Ibid.*, at 222.

[59] *Ibid.*, at 223.

[60] See e.g., *Asian Agricultural Products LTD (AAPL) v. Republic of Sri Lanka*, ICSID Case No. ARB/87/3, Final award of 27 June 1990; *Lanco International Inc. v. The Argentine Republic*, ICSID Case No. ARB/97/6, Preliminary Decision: Jurisdiction of the Arbitral Tribunal of 18 December 1998; *Compañía de Aguas del Aconquija S.A. and Vivendi Universal S.A. v. Argentine Republic*, ICSID Case No. ARB/97/3, Decision on Annulment of 03 July 2002; *CMS Gas Transmission Company v. the Republic of Argentina*, ICSID Case No. ARB/01/8, Decision of the Tribunal on Objections to Jurisdiction of 17 July 2003.

minority shareholders were declared inadmissible even though the value of their shares had been affected.[61]

**11.46.** Thus, there are divergences in the case law of the Court and the arbitral tribunals in terms of *ratione personae* that may lead to different approaches and scopes of protection under a BIT and the Convention.

**11.47.** The second decisive indicator for the jurisdiction of an investment tribunal is the existence of an investment (*ratione materiae*). Usually, BITs contain a very broad notion of investments. Besides, national law or multilateral agreements[62] can also stipulate additional characteristics of the investment.

**11.48.** On the contrary, Article 1 of the First Additional Protocol to the Convention speaks of 'possessions' and 'property'.[63]

**11.49.** Although there are certain differences between 'investments' and 'property', only rarely will claims of investors be protected by Article 1 of the First Protocol and not qualify as investments under the applicable BIT or other investment protection treaties.[64]

### III.1.3. The Right to be Heard

**11.50.** The Right to be heard is a fundamental principle, sometimes called the 'Magna Carta of arbitral procedure'.[65] This principle is also protected by Article 6(1) of the Convention. Thus, if the principle is not respected by the arbitral tribunal, it can be a ground to set aside the award in question solely on the breach of Fair Trial.

### III.1.4. Composition of the Arbitral Tribunal

**11.51.** As with the right to be heard, an independent and impartial arbitral tribunal is a key requirement of both international investment arbitration and human rights law. The requirement of such an independent and impartial tribunal is expressly

---

[61]  PIERRE-MARIE DUPUY, FRANCESCO FRANCIONI, ERNST-ULRICH PETERSMANN (EDS.), HUMAN RIGHTS IN INTERNATIONAL INVESTMENT LAW AND ARBITRATION, Oxford University Press 227 (2010); see also Commission, *Yarrow Plc ors* v. *United Kingdom*, No. 7598/76, 28 January 1983.

[62]  See e.g., Article 1 of the Energy Charter Treaty.

[63]  Every natural or legal person is entitled to the peaceful enjoyment of their possessions. No one shall be deprived of their possessions except in the public interest and subject to the conditions provided for by the law and by the general principles of international law.

[64]  PIERRE-MARIE DUPUY, FRANCESCO FRANCIONI, ERNST-ULRICH PETERSMANN (EDS.), HUMAN RIGHTS IN INTERNATIONAL INVESTMENT LAW AND ARBITRATION, Oxford University Press 234 (2010).

[65]  DR. PETER BINDER, INTERNATIONAL COMMERCIAL ARBITRATION AND CONCILIATION IN UNCITRAL MODEL LAW JURISDICTIONS, Sweet & Maxwell 227 (3rd ed. 2010).

embodied in Article 6(1) of the Convention. The Court commonly considers the two requirements together.[66]

**11.52.** The issue of independence and impartiality is prominent in the appointment of conciliators and arbitrators to particular commissions or tribunals.[67]

**11.53.** Consequently, if the requirements of independence and impartiality of the adjudicators are disrespected, a breach of such requirements can constitute a violation of a Fair Trial guaranteed by the Convention and could be a separate ground to set aside the award in question.

### III.1.5. Ordre Public

**11.54.** The Court has emphasised the Convention's role as a 'constitutional instrument of European public order' in the field of human rights.[68] As was mentioned earlier in this publication, the protective provisions of the Convention are *ius cogens* in terms of applicable international public law. Therefore, a breach of fundamental human rights would constitute a breach of *ordre public* as prescribed in Article V(2)(b) of the New York Convention and in Article 34(2)(b)(ii) of the UNCITRAL Model Law and could lead to the refusal to recognize or set aside of the challenged award.

### III.2. Application to the Court

**11.55.** In principle, application to the Court is possible only if the challenge of the award in question is pursued in the courts of the *lex arbitri*, or later, at the enforcement stage. This is because of the principle of exhaustion of local remedies embodied in Article 35(1) of the Convention.

**11.56.** However, the rule allows for certain limited exceptions, such as:
a) If the victim is denied access to the remedies;
b) If the victim has been prevented from exhausting them, or
c) With regard to remedies which are certain not to be effective or adequate.[69]

**11.57.** Thus, a party which is unsuccessful with the challenge of the award in question at the place of arbitration within the territory

---

[66] *Findlay v. the United Kingdom*, No. 22107/93, 25 February 1997, paragraph 73.
[67] CHRISTOPH H. SCHREUER ET AL., THE ICSID CONVENTION. A COMMENTARY, Cambridge University Press 48, 49 (2nd ed. 2011); see also *Compañía de Aguas del Aconquija S.A. and Vivendi Universal S.A. v. Argentine Republic*, ICSID Case No. ARB/97/3, 03 October 2001, paragraphs 14,18.
[68] *Bosphorus Hava Yollari Turizm ve Ticaret Anonim Şikreti v. Ireland*, No. 45036/98, 30 June 2005, paragraph 156.
[69] See e.g., *Vernillo v. France*, No. 11889/85, 20 February 1991, paragraph 27; *Dalia v. France*, No. 26102/95, 19 February 1998, paragraph 38; *Horvat v. Croatia*, No. 51585/99, 26 July 2001, paragraph 38.

the Member State may apply to the Court with, *inter alia*, a request to declare a breach of the Convention's provisions. Here, the party might argue either that the State in question had to annul the challenged award as it breaches the Convention, or that the State has breached the Convention by annulling the award in question. In turn, the State could resume the annulment proceedings and make necessary decisions in terms of the award in question. Consequently, a Court's decision could have an impact on other pending or prospective similar arbitrations.[70]

## IV.  How Could the Court Interfere with International Investment Arbitration?

**11.58.** If the seat of international investment arbitration under the BIT is in the Member State of the Convention, the unsuccessful party may apply to the Court once it exhausts all domestic remedies for the annulment of the award in question. The Court can rule that parties' procedural rights to a Fair Trial might be infringed (**IV.1.**). Moreover, the award in question may breach substantive human rights (**IV.2.**). Consequently, the Member State in question may resume the proceedings and, for example, annul the award (**IV.3.**). For example, the ICSID Convention establishes a de-located annulment proceeding, so a possible impact of the Court's judgement on an ICSID award will be considered separately (**IV.4.**).

### IV.1.  Issues of Due Process

**11.59.** Due process or Fair Trial are fundamental procedural safeguards provided by the Convention. Such safeguards must be respected not only by the domestic courts, but also by the arbitral tribunals. If the place of arbitration is in a Member State of the Convention, the party believing that due process was infringed by the tribunal may challenge such an award stating, *inter alia*, that such an award infringes Article 6(1) of the Convention. If such a challenge is not successful and national remedies are exhausted in this regard, the party can refer to the Court and plead that the Member State has breached the Convention.

**11.60.** It is not disputed that the contracting States must in any case enact a law which imposes on arbitration respect for

---

[70]  As in *Achmea* case with the Court of Justice of the European Union.

the procedural guarantees of Article 6(1).[71] The European Commission on Human Rights held that[72]

> ... the applicant company had voluntarily entered into an arbitration agreement and thereby renounced its right to have its civil rights determined in court proceedings for the conduct of which the State is responsible under the Convention.

> This does not mean, however, that the respondent State's responsibility is completely excluded ... as the arbitration award had to be recognized by the German courts and be given executory effect by them. The courts thereby exercised a certain control and guarantee as to the fairness and correctness of the arbitration proceedings which they considered to have been carried out in conformity with fundamental rights and in particular with the right of the applicant company to be heard.

11.61. Thus, the State's liability in terms of the Convention can arise in two scenarios. In first scenario, the State could quash the arbitral award in question and thus breach Article 6(1).[73] In the second scenario, the State's intervention could be required by arguing that the arbitral proceedings were conducted in breach of the Convention and the court of the Member State ignored that.[74] The last scenario is of particular interest in terms of this publication.

11.62. Besides the fundamental procedural rights that can be infringed, the arbitral proceedings can breach substantive rights.

## IV.2. Issue of the Protection of Fundamental Human Rights

11.63. The Convention protects not only procedural rights, but also substantive rights such as property. So might the BIT.

11.64. There is a basic rule in international investment arbitration. When awards fall within the New York Convention regime, such awards cannot be reviewed on their merits.

11.65. In this situation, a fundamental issue arises – if the arbitral tribunal breaches the substantive provisions of the Convention, e.g. those enshrined in the Article 1 Protocol No. 1 of the Convention and the State courts do not react to such a breach,

---

[71] Sébastien Besson, *Arbitration and Human Rights*, ASA BULLETIN, Kluwer Law International (2006).
[72] Commission, *Jacob Boss Sohne KG v. Germany*, No. 18479/91, 02 December 1991.
[73] See e.g., *Stran Greek Refineries and Stratis Andreadis v. Greece*, No. 13427/87, 09 December 1994.
[74] See e.g., *Suovaniemi and others v. Finland*, No. 31737/96, 23 February 1999.

can the Court intervene by punishing the Member State for non-compliance with the Convention?

**11.66.** The breach of the substantive rights of the Convention may be one of the issues on the merits. It may be noted that the Court has ruled that where incoherent reasoning by a court is then repeated on appeal, a breach of Article 6(1) of the Convention can result. However, the arbitral awards usually cannot be reviewed on the merits or *de novo* at the appellate instance.

**11.67.** Thus, if we could say that the arbitral tribunals must to apply the Convention, the court reviewing the award in question should be entitled to review whether the rights vested in the Convention have been breached by the arbitral tribunal. Otherwise, the Member State in question may breach the relevant procedural and substantive provisions of the Convention (e.g. Article 6(1) and Article 1 Protocol No. 1, respectively).

**11.68.** What then are implications of such a breach and intervention?

### IV.3.  Consequences of Intervention

**11.69.** The consequences of such intervention may be like those in the *Achmea* case.

**11.70.** If the State has ratified Protocol No. 16 of the Convention, then "the highest court before which the challenge of the disputed award is pending, may request the Court to give advisory opinions on questions of principle relating to the interpretation or application of the rights and freedoms defined in the Convention or the protocols thereto".

**11.71.** Such proceedings are very similar to that which occurred in the *Achmea* case. The Highest court suspended the case and refers for the opinion to the Court. The only significant difference is that, contrary to the proceedings before the Court of Justice of the European Union, the Court delivers only an advisory opinion which is thus not binding upon the national court. Then, upon receipt of an advisory Court's opinion, the Highest court should resume the case and render a decision.

**11.72.** In this scenario, if the Court advises upon the breach of the Convention, the domestic court could react accordingly. If the breach of the Convention is inherited in the arbitral award, to the court should quash the award in question thus protecting the State from subsequent liability for the breach of the Convention.

**11.73.** Another scenario is when a national supreme court renders a final decision related to the challenged award. Then the unsuccessful party applies to the Court because of the breach of the Convention. Subsequently, the Court renders that there is a breach of the Convention.

**11.74.** Then, assuming that the breach of Convention occurred because a breach of its provisions by the arbitral tribunal, the successful party can reopen the proceedings before the national court and request to annul the award in question.

**11.75.** As case-law of the Court is accessible world-wide and thus would be highly discussed in the arbitration community, such case-law would have a global effect on other arbitrations where the Member States of Convention are involved as the parties.

**11.76.** Consequently, an Achmea-like situation could occur because of the intervention of the Court into the arbitration-related proceedings.

**11.77.** However, a different situation could be in the regime where the review of the award in question is put on supra-national level, e.g. as prescribed in the ICSID Convention.

## IV.4. The ICSID Regime

**11.78.** As noted by Prof. Emmanuel Gaillard,[75]

> [N]ational legal orders are thus gradually abandoning the idea that the source of validity of arbitral awards necessarily lies in the legal order of the seat, conceived as a forum, or even in any national legal order, and moving towards the conception that recognizes the existence of an arbitral legal order.

**11.79.** Thus, certain international agreements provide for independent and de-localised review and enforcement of arbitral awards. One such example is ICSID Convention regime. The ICSID Convention provides for its own self-contained system of review of awards.[76]

**11.80.** Thus, contrary to the New York Convention regime, ICSID awards are outside of review by national courts. If the unsuccessful party wants to raise human rights issues, and in particular, the issue of breach of the Convention, can the party apply to the Court?

**11.81.** Article 26 of the ICSID Convention states that consent of the parties to arbitration under this Convention shall, unless

---

[75] EMMANUEL GAILLARD, LEGAL THEORY OF INTERNATIONAL ARBITRATION, Leiden 66 (2010). This is so-called autonomous (*sui generis*) or de-localization theory. It acknowledges jurisdictional and contractual elements in the arbitration regime, but shifts the focus from the control that the law of the seat of arbitration may exercise and the autonomy of parties, to the business and legal level where parties agree to and participate in the arbitration process; see JULIAN D. M. LEW, LOUKAS A. MISTELIS, STEFAN M. KROELL, COMPARATIVE INTERNATIONAL COMMERCIAL ARBITRATION, Kluwer Law International 82 (2003).

[76] CHRISTOPH H. SCHREUER ET AL., THE ICSID CONVENTION. A COMMENTARY, Cambridge University Press 1096, 1102 (2nd ed. 2011), see also Article 53 of the ICSID Convention, on enforcement see Article 54 of the ICSID Convention.

otherwise stated, be deemed consent to such arbitration to the exclusion of any other remedy. However, a Contracting State may require the exhaustion of local administrative or judicial remedies as a condition of its consent to arbitration under the ICSID Convention. This is an example of a flexible exclusive jurisdiction clause.[77]

**11.82.** Another arrangement, of perhaps greater significance to this publication, is found in Article 27(1) of the ICSID Convention that addresses diplomatic protection. It provides that:

> [n]o Contracting State shall give diplomatic protection or bring an international claim in respect of a dispute which one of its nationals and another Contracting State shall have failed to abide by and comply with the award rendered in such a dispute.

**11.83.** Article 26 creates a presumption that the parties intended to resort to ISCID arbitration to the exclusion of all other means of dispute settlement. This is expressed in the Report of the Executive Directors to the Convention:[78]

> It may be presumed that when a State and an investor agree to have recourse to arbitration, and do not reserve the right to have recourse to other remedies or require the prior exhaustion of other remedies, the intention of the parties is to have recourse to arbitration to the exclusion of any other remedy. This rule of interpretation is embodied in the first sentence of Article 26.

**11.84.** Article 27(1) must be seen in the context of the exclusive remedy rule of Article 26 of the ICSID Convention.[79] Article 27(1) provides a strong indication of the intent of the drafters to strengthen the exclusivity of the ICSID regime as the only forum for settling investment disputes, and thereby to prevent the rendering of conflicting judgements.[80] Thus, an international court or tribunal before which a claim is brought in violation of Article 27 will have to decline jurisdiction.[81]

**11.85.** Most multiple proceedings regulation provisions, including *electa una via* provisions, can be found in the human rights

---

[77] YUVAL SHANY, THE COMPETING JURISDICTIONS OF INTERNATIONAL COURTS AND TRIBUNALS, Oxford: Oxford University Press 192 (2004).
[78] CHRISTOPH H. SCHREUER ET AL., THE ICSID CONVENTION. A COMMENTARY, Cambridge University Press 348, 380 (2nd ed. 2011).
[79] *Ibid.*, at 416.
[80] YUVAL SHANY, THE COMPETING JURISDICTIONS OF INTERNATIONAL COURTS AND TRIBUNALS, Oxford: Oxford University Press 194 (2004).
[81] CHRISTOPH H. SCHREUER ET AL., THE ICSID CONVENTION. A COMMENTARY, Cambridge University Press 414, 416, 421-422 (2nd ed. 2011).

sphere.[82] The most significant factors have probably been the relatively large number of bodies operating in this area with palpable jurisdictional overlaps and the wish of the drafters of the instruments to reduce the risk of inconsistent decisions on human rights issues, which might adversely affect the authority and legitimacy of the courts and tribunals involved.[83]

**11.86.** The prototype *electa una via* provision, barring multiple submissions of the same claim, can be found in the Convention. Article 35(2) provides that:

> [t]he Court shall not deal with any application submitted under Article 34 [i.e. individual application] that
>
> ...
>
> [i]s substantially the same as the matter that has been examined by the Court or has *already been submitted to another procedure* of international investigation or settlement and contains no relevant new information. [Emphasis added].

**11.87.** On several occasions the Court and the Commission held, by virtue of Article 35(2) of the Convention which contains an *electa una via* clause that petitions previously presented before other dispute-settlement procedures were inadmissible.[84]

**11.88.** Therefore, it seems that the ICSID Convention excludes the jurisdiction of the Court. Following the rule *lex posterior derogat legi priori*, Article 30(3) of the VCLT Convention provides that when all the parties to an earlier treaty are parties also to a later treaty but the earlier treaty is not terminated or suspended, the earlier treaty applies only to the extent that its provisions are compatible with those of the later treaty. The Convention became effective on 3 September 1953. The ICSID Convention entered into force on 14 October 1966. Thus, in terms of Article 30(3) of the VCLT Convention, the ICSID Convention is *lex posteriori* and jurisdiction of the arbitral tribunals constituted under that convention should prevail over the Court's jurisdiction under the Convention.

---

[82] YUVAL SHANY, THE COMPETING JURISDICTIONS OF INTERNATIONAL COURTS AND TRIBUNALS, Oxford: Oxford University Press 213 (2004).

[83] *Ibid.*, at 213.

[84] *Dušan Vojnović and Dragica Vojnović v. Croatia* (Dec.), No. 4819/10, 26 June 2012, paragraph 31; *Leonicio Calcerrada Fornieles and Luis Gabeza Mato v. Spain* (Dec.), No. 17512/90, 06 July 1992.

**11.89.** Therefore, the review of or intervention to the ICSID awards is inadmissible under the Convention.

| | |

*Summaries*

FRA  [*L'impact des décisions de la Cour européenne des droits de l'homme sur l'arbitrage international d'investissement*]

En cette période de mondialisation, les grandes entreprises jouent un rôle essentiel non seulement au niveau du commerce, mais aussi au niveau social, et leurs activités revêtent une importance capitale pour une part grandissante de la population. Ainsi, les organes chargés de trancher les litiges internationaux, conscients de leur responsabilité sociale, portent une attention particulière à la protection des droits de l'homme fondamentaux. À cet égard, la procédure d'arbitrage international d'investissement n'est pas une exception. En effet, les chambres arbitrales statuent aujourd'hui, à titre occasionnel, sur des questions ayant trait à la protection des droits de l'homme. Les droits de l'homme sont protégés par plusieurs conventions internationales, dont la Convention européenne des droits de l'homme. Ces conventions prévoient la création d'organes spécialisés pour trancher les litiges, comme par exemple la Cour européenne des droits de l'homme. Dans le cas des litiges d'investissement, un certain chevauchement entre les compétences des instances arbitrales internationales et celles des juridictions internationales spécialisées est inévitable. Ce chevauchement peut compromettre la validité des sentences arbitrales en question. Le présent article examine les impacts potentiels des décisions de la Cour européenne des droits de l'homme sur l'arbitrage international d'investissement. Selon l'auteur, le chevauchement de compétences peut survenir, par exemple, entre les chambres arbitrales et la Cour européenne des droits de l'homme. Par ailleurs, les chambres arbitrales sont tenues d'appliquer les normes relatives aux droits de l'homme fondamentaux, car il s'agit de normes impératives (ius cogens) dans le sens du droit international public applicable. L'obligation des arbitres de statuer dans le respect des droits de l'homme fondamentaux, tels que définis par les conventions internationales, qui ne sont pas des accords bilatéraux de protection des investissements, a pour conséquence le fait que les compétences des chambres arbitrales et celles des juridictions internationales spécialisées se rapprochent ; de plus, elle peut *affecter la validité des sentences arbitrales, comme cela a été le cas dans l'affaire Achmea. Le rôle des juridictions internationales spécialisées, dont la Cour européenne des droits de l'homme, peut s'avérer crucial lors de l'examen des procédures menées devant les tribunaux des pays membres suite à un recours contre la sentence arbitrale en question. En ce qui concerne les procédures d'arbitrage obligatoires, prévues par des normes juridiques contraignantes, la Cour européenne des droits de l'homme peut aller jusqu'à intervenir dans ces procédures d'arbitrage, en examinant leur conformité avec les dispositions de la Convention européenne des droits de l'homme. Une telle intervention, qui peut se réaliser lors de l'examen d'une décision rendue par la cour suprême de l'État membre en question, peut avoir une répercussion importante sur l'arbitrage international d'investissement, tout au moins au niveau européen. La Cour européenne des droits de l'homme ne devrait cependant pas être compétente en matière de litiges ayant pour objet l'examen direct ou indirect des sentences arbitrales du CIRDI.*

CZE  *[Dopady rozhodnutí Evropského soudu pro lidská práva na mezinárodní investiční arbitráž]*
*V tomto období rostoucí globalizace hrají velké korporace klíčovou úlohu nikoli pouze v oblasti obchodní, ale rovněž v oblasti sociální. Jejich činnost se proto stává nanejvýš důležitou pro stále větší části populace. Orgány příslušné pro rozhodování mezinárodních sporů tak s odkazem na koncepci sociální odpovědnosti věnují stále větší pozornost ochraně základních lidských práv. Ani mezinárodní investiční arbitráž není výjimkou. Rozhodčí senáty se v dnešní době příležitostně dotýkají i oblasti ochrany lidských práv. Lidská práva chrání i řada mezinárodních úmluv, například Evropská úmluva o lidských právech. Na základě těchto úmluv vznikají zvláštní orgány pro řešení sporů, jako například Evropský soud pro lidská práva, přičemž určité překrývání se pravomocí mezinárodních rozhodčích orgánů pro řešení sporů z investic a zvláštních mezinárodních soudů je nevyhnutelné. Toto překrývání tak může negativně ovlivnit platnost dotčených rozhodčích nálezů. Tento článek zkoumá možné dopady rozhodnutí Evropského soudu pro lidská práva na mezinárodní investiční arbitráž. Autor uvádí, že k překrývání pravomocí může docházet například mezi rozhodčími senáty a Evropským soudem pro lidská práva. Navíc platí, že rozhodčí senáty jsou povinny normy týkající se základních lidských práv aplikovat, neboť se jedná o ius cogens ve smyslu použitelného mezinárodního práva veřejného. Povinnost rozhodců rozhodovat v souladu se základními*

*lidskými právy zakotvená v mezinárodních úmluvách, které nejsou dvoustrannými dohodami o ochraně investic, je nejen příčinou vzájemného sbližování pravomoci rozhodčích senátů a pravomoci zvláštních mezinárodních soudů, ale může mít dopad i na platnost dotčeného rozhodčího nálezu, jako například ve věci Achmea. Úloha specializovaných mezinárodních soudů, jako například Evropského soudu pro lidská práva, může být klíčová při přezkumu řízení u soudů členského státu vedených v souvislosti s žalobou podanou proti dotčenému rozhodčímu nálezu. V případech mandatorních rozhodčích řízení, která jsou závazně stanovena právními předpisy, může Evropský soud pro lidská práva zasahovat dokonce i do samotných rozhodčích řízení tím, že může přezkoumávat jejich soulad s požadavky Evropské úmluvy o lidských právech, a to ve fázi přezkumu rozhodnutí vydaného nejvyšším soudem daného členského státu. Takový přezkum může mít citelný dopad na mezinárodní investiční arbitráž, a to přinejmenším na regionální evropské úrovni. Evropský soud pro lidská práva by však neměl vykonávat pravomoc ve vztahu k žádnému sporu, který se týká přímého nebo nepřímého přezkumu rozhodčích nálezů ICSID.*

| | |

POL    [*Wpływ orzeczeń Europejskiego Trybunału Praw Człowieka na międzynarodowy arbitraż inwestycyjny*]
*Artykuł został poświęcony problematyce pokrywania się kompetencji trybunałów arbitrażowych orzekających w międzynarodowych sporach inwestycyjnych i kompetencji wyspecjalizowanych sądów międzynarodowych, powołanych w celu ochrony praw człowieka. Pokrywają się one często m.in. w konsekwencji globalizacji i rosnącej roli korporacji międzynarodowych, czego skutki są objęte przez obszar międzynarodowej ochrony praw człowieka. W rezultacie trybunały arbitrażowe mogą wydać opinię odmienną niż np. Europejski Trybunał Praw Człowieka, co może prowadzić do scenariuszy takich, jak w sprawie Achmea.*

DEU    [*Auswirkungen der Entscheidungen des Europäischen Gerichtshofs für Menschenrechte auf die internationale Investitionsschiedsgerichtsbarkeit*]
*In diesem Beitrag wird das Problem der Überschneidung der Befugnisse von Schiedsgerichten bei der Beilegung von internationalen Investitionsstreitigkeiten mit der Zuständigkeit*

*spezialisierter internationaler Gerichte zum Schutz der Menschenrechte erörtert. Eine solche Überschneidung ist manchmal auch das Ergebnis der Globalisierung und der zunehmenden Rolle internationaler Unternehmen, deren Auswirkungen in den Bereich des internationalen Menschenrechtsschutzes fallen. Dies kann zu unterschiedlichen Ansichten der Schiedsgerichte einerseits und beispielsweise des Europäischen Gerichtshofs für Menschenrechte andererseits führen, was zu ähnlichen Szenarien wie im Fall Achmea führen kann.*

**RUS** [*Влияния решений Европейского суда по правам человека на международный инвестиционный арбитраж*]

*В настоящей статье рассматривается проблематичный вопрос пересечения юрисдикций арбитражных трибуналов по разрешению международных инвестиционных споров с юрисдикцией специализированных международных судов по защите прав человека. Такое пересечение возможно из-за глобализации и возрастающей роли международных корпораций, действия которых попадают в сферу международной защиты прав человека. Последствием может быть различная позиция арбитражных трибуналов и, например, Европейского Суда по Правам Человека, что может привести к сценариям, похожим на ситуацию по делу Achmea.*

**ESP** [*Las consecuencias de la resolución del Tribunal Europeo de Derechos Humanos en el arbitraje internacional de inversiones*]

*Este texto da cuenta del conflicto de jurisdicciones de los tribunales de arbitraje con los tribunales internacionales especializados, establecidos con el objetivo de proteger los derechos humanos, a la hora de resolver los pleitos internacionales de inversión. Ese tipo de conflictos puede ser, en algunos casos, la consecuencia de la globalización, y el papel cada vez más destacado de las empresas multinacionales, cuyos efectos pertenecen a la esfera de la protección internacional de los derechos humanos. Estos factores pueden provocar divergentes perspectivas legales entre los tribunales de arbitraje y, por ejemplo, el Tribunal Europeo de Derechos Humanos, lo que puede dar lugar a situaciones como el caso Achmea.*

| | |

## Bibliography

MANUEL ARROYO (ED), ARBITRATION IN SWITZERLAND: THE PRACTITIONER'S GUIDE, Kluwer law International (2013).

ALBERT JAN VAN DEN BERG, THE NEW YORK ARBITRATION CONVENTION OF 1958, the Hague: Kluwer Law International (1981).

Sébastien Besson, *Arbitration and Human Rights*, ASA BULLETIN, Kluwer Law International (2006).

DR. PETER BINDER, INTERNATIONAL COMMERCIAL ARBITRATION AND CONCILIATION IN UNCITRAL MODEL LAW JURISDICTIONS, Sweet & Maxwell (3rd ed. 2010).

DOAK R. BISHOP, JAMES R. CRAWFORD, MICHAEL W. REISMAN, FOREIGN INVESTMENT DISPUTES. CASES, MATERIALS AND COMMENTARY, Kluwer Law International (2005).

GARY B. BORN, INTERNATIONAL COMMERCIAL ARBITRATION, International Arbitral Awards vol. III, Wolters Kluwer Law & Business (2nd ed. 2014).

KATHARINA FRANZISKA BRAIG, THE EUROPEAN COURT OF HUMAN RIGHTS AND THE RIGHT TO CLEAN WATER AND SANITATION, Water Policy, IWA Publishing 20 (2018).

MARC BUNGENBERG ET AL., INTERNATIONAL INVESTMENT LAW, C.H.Beck-Hart-Nomos (2015).

RUDOLF DOLZER, CHRISTOPH SCHREUER, PRINCIPLES OF INTERNATIONAL INVESTMENT LAW, Oxford University Press (2008).

PIERRE-MARIE DUPUY, FRANCESCO FRANCIONI, ERNST-ULRICH PETERSMANN (EDS.), HUMAN RIGHTS IN INTERNATIONAL INVESTMENT LAW AND ARBITRATION, Oxford University Press (2010).

EMMANUEL GAILLARD, LEGAL THEORY OF INTERNATIONAL ARBITRATION, Leiden 66 (2010).

INTERNATIONAL LAW COMMISSION, DRAFT ARTICLES ON THE LAW OF TREATIES WITH COMMENTARIES, Yearbook of the International Law Commission vol. II (1966).

JULIAN D. M. LEW, LOUKAS A. MISTELIS, STEFAN M. KROELL, COMPARATIVE INTERNATIONAL COMMERCIAL ARBITRATION, Kluwer Law International (2003).

Jean-Hubert Moitry, *Right to Fair Trial and the European Convention on Human Rights: Some Remarks on the République de Guinée Case*, JOURNAL OF INTERNATIONAL ARBITRATION, Kluwer Law International (1989).

ALLAN REDFERN, MARTIN HUNTER ET AL., LAW AND PRACTICE

OF INTERNATIONAL COMMERCIAL ARBITRATION, Thomson Sweet & Maxwell (4th ed. 2004).

HUMAN RIGHTS IN ISDS: WHERE ARE WE NOW, Global Arbitration Review (2019).

YUVAL SHANY, THE COMPETING JURISDICTIONS OF INTERNATIONAL COURTS AND TRIBUNALS, Oxford: Oxford University Press (2004).

Christoph Schreuer, *Jurisdiction and Applicable Law in Investment Treaty Arbitration*, 1(1) REVUE DE RÉGLEMENT DES DIFFÉRENDS DE MCGILL (2014).

CHRISTOPH H. SCHREUER ET AL., THE ICSID CONVENTION. A COMMENTARY, Cambridge University Press (2nd ed. 2011).

ANDREA MARCO STEINGRUBER, CONSENT IN INTERNATIONAL ARBITRATION, Oxford University Press (2012).

Albertas Šekštelo, *A Prophecy of the Crisis of International Commercial Arbitration in Europe?*, CYARB, CZECH (& CENTRAL EUROPEAN) YEARBOOK OF ARBITRATION, RECOGNITION AND ENFORCEMENT OF ARBITRAL AWARDS (Alexander J. Bělohlávek, Naděžda Rozehnalová eds., 2019).

Jaques Werner, *Limits of Commercial Investor-State Arbitration: The Need for Appellate Review, in* Human Rights in International Investment Law and Arbitration, Oxford: Oxford University Press 115, 117 (Pierre-Marie Dupuy, Francesco Francioni, and Ernst-Urlich Petersmann eds., 2010).

RUEDIGER WOLFRUM (ED.), THE MAX PLANCK ENCYCLOPEDIA OF PUBLIC INTERNATIONAL LAW VOL. VI, Oxford: Oxford University Press (2012).

Natalia N. Viktorova

# Protection of Foreign Investments and Human Rights

**Key words:**
*international investment
disputes | bilateral investment
treaties | human rights |
environmental protection
| settlement of investment
disputes | foreign investments
| foreign ownership |
nationalization | promotion
and protection of foreign
investments | the European
Court of Human Rights*

Czech Yearbook of International Law®

**Abstract |** *This article addresses the challenges of protecting human rights in foreign investment. The activities of transnational corporations can often harm the ecology of the host State. Based on the analysis of arbitration practice and international treaties, the article investigates whether the host State is entitled to restrict the activities of foreign investors to protect the health of its citizens. The analysis of decisions from the practice of the European Court of Human Rights shows that investors can apply for the protection of their rights in case of nationalization of their property. Special attention is paid to the analyses of the provisions of bilateral investment treaties of a new generation that contain the obligations of investors concerning the protection of the environment of a host State. This article analyses several famous international investment disputes regarding human rights.*

**Natalia N. Viktorova** has a PhD in Law and is a senior lecturer at the Chair of Private International Law at Kutafin Moscow State Law University.
E-mail: vozgik@mail.mipt.ru

| | |

# I. Introduction

**12.01.** One of the basic principles of international law is the principle of respect for human rights and freedoms.[1] This principle is based on many international documents that reinforce international standards of human rights and freedoms. These include the Universal Declaration of Human Rights (1948), the International Covenant on Economic, Social and Cultural Rights, and the International Covenant on Civil and Political Rights. Many States have incorporated these standards into their constitutions and other legal acts. Thus, the Constitution of Russia (Article 2) regards a person's rights and freedoms as the having the highest value.

**12.02.** Human rights are inalienable. The modern world cannot be imagined without human rights, which are based on the principles of freedom, equality, justice and are universal.[2] Human rights can be classified into three groups: personal, political, socio-economic.[3] For example, the Declaration provides for the right to life, liberty, and personal integrity (Article 3), the right to own one's property both individually and in association with others (Article 17) and other rights. The personal (civil) rights and freedoms of a person include, the right to life and dignity of the person and the right to liberty and security of a person. This block of rights embraces the fundamental aspects of individual freedom, expressing the humanistic principles of any democratically organized society.[4] Personal rights are designed to ensure the freedom of the individual as a member of civil society, and their legal protection from any unlawful external interference.[5]

**12.03.** The right to life forms the fundamental principle of all other rights and freedoms taking shape in this sphere. It represents the absolute value of world civilization, because all other rights lose their meaning and value in the event of human death. All other rights somehow unite around this pivotal right. For example, rights such as the right to social security, to health protection, to a favorable environment, as well as the right to freedom from cruel treatment and punishment, act as additional tools to ensure its effective implementation.[6]

---

[1]  МЕЖДУНАРОДНОЕ ПУБЛИЧНОЕ ПРАВО (International Public Law), Moscow 227 (K.A. Bekyashev ed., 2007).
[2]  ELENA ANDREEVNA LUKASHEVA, ПРАВА ЧЕЛОВЕКА (HUMAN RIGHTS), Moscow (1st ed. 1999).
[3]  EKATERINA I. KOZLOVA, OLEG E. KUTAFIN, КОНСТИТУЦИОННОЕ ПРАВО РОССИИ (CONSTITUTIONAL LAW OF RUSSIA), Moscow 258 (2003).
[4]  *Supra* note 2 at 143.
[5]  *Supra* note 2 at 142.
[6]  *Supra* note 2 at 143.

**12.04.** This article examines the relationship between human rights and investment, showing what human rights violations transnational corporations can entail in the territory of the States that receive investments. The question of whether international investment treaties provide for the responsibility of investors for violating human rights is explored. The article analyzes the practice of the European Court of Human Rights in protecting the property rights of investors.

## II.    Human Rights in Investment Arbitration

**12.05.** Transnational corporations are actively involved in the investment process. However, at the same time, there is regular evidence of investigations carried out by human rights groups that report various violations by such corporations in the host country. These include, crimes against humanity, and environmental disasters.[7] Human rights issues are often connected with the problem of environmental protection, since the human right to life includes the right to a clean environment. If a foreign investor pollutes the environment, they violate the right to life of the local population. In developing countries, where environmental standards are lax, multinational corporations have been responsible for causing pollution.[8] Let us consider several cases where the activities of foreign investors have led to gross violations of the rights of people in the territory of host States.

### II.1.    The Bhopal Gas Disaster

**12.06.** **On 3 December 1984, a p**oisonous gas leaked from Union Carbide's pesticides factory in Bhopal, an Indian subsidiary of the American company Union Carbide Corporation (UCC). In three days around 8,000 people died, more than 150,000 people were left severely disabled, and 22,000 people have since died of their injuries. The safety systems at the plant were not functional. Union Carbide and the Government of India reached a settlement in 1989 under which each survivor would be awarded USD 500 for injuries – an inadequate compensation. Many people lost their ability to work because of health problems. 'Recent reports confirm that the contamination is getting worse. The rate of birth defects in the contaminated areas is ten times higher

---

7    E.A. ARISTOVA, ОТВЕТСТВЕННОСТЬ ТРАНСГРАНИЧНЫХ КОРПОРАТИВНЫХ ГРУПП: ТЕОРИЯ И ПРАКТИКА (RESPONSIBILITY OF TRANSNATIONAL CORPORATE GROUPS), Moscow 77 (2014).
8    MUTHUCUMARASWAMY SORNARAJAH, THE INTERNATIONAL LAW ON FOREIGN INVESTMENT, Cambridge 260 (2nd 2007).

than in the rest of India. Cancers and other diseases are rife.'[9] As Amnesty International reported, the gas leak 'killed between 7,000 and 10,000 men, women and children just in the first three days. Many have suffered severe health impacts, including gynaecological and reproductive health disorders.'[10]

**12.07.** According to Amnesty International: 'The Bhopal case illustrates how companies evade their human rights responsibilities and underlines the need to establish a universal human rights framework that can be applied to companies directly.'[11] The investor violated the right to life, that includes the right to health and the right to protection from environmental pollution. As the Indian Supreme Court determined 'Companies are responsible for environmental damage and for compensating anyone harmed by their activities.'[12]

## II.2. *Chevron v. Ecuador*

**12.08.** *Chevron* v. *Ecuador* is an infamous case. In 1964, Ecuador granted oil exploration and production rights in Ecuador's Oriente region to TexPet, an American company and the Ecuadorian Gulf Oil Company under a Concession Agreement. They formed a Consortium. Oriente lies in the Amazon Basin. In 1967, this Consortium discovered oil in Oriente and drilled its first well; and in 1972, nine oil fields were developed and an oil pipeline constructed. In 1993, a group of Ecuadorian citizens of the Oriente region filed a class action lawsuit in US federal court against Texaco. The complaint alleged that between 1964 and 1992 Texaco's oil operations polluted the rainforests and rivers in Ecuador. This resulted in environmental damage and damage to the health of those who live in the region.[13] This story of the environmental pollution of the Ecuadorian Amazon by Chevron-Texaco is known as the "Amazonian Chernobyl". Chevron used a system of investment protection, and filed a lawsuit arguing that the Ecuadorian government should pay the company a multimillion-dollar compensation. It was stated that 'the Chevron case in Ecuador highlights the need for a legally binding international instrument to put an end to the impunity

---

[9] International Campaign for Justice in Bhopal, available at: https://www.bhopal.net/what-happened/contamination/timeline-us-court-cases/ (accessed on 06 December 2019).
[10] https://www.amnesty.org/en/latest/news/2012/12/years-later-women-bhopal-still-waiting-justice/ (accessed on 06 December 2019).
[11] International Campaign for Justice in Bhopal, available at: https://www.bhopal.net/what-happened/contamination/timeline-us-court-cases/ (accessed on 23 January 2020).
[12] International Campaign for Justice in Bhopal, available at: https://www.bhopal.net/what-happened/contamination/timeline-us-court-cases/ (accessed on 23 January 2020).
[13] Available at: https://www.business-humanrights.org/en/texacochevron-lawsuits-re-ecuador (accessed on 06 December 2019).

with which companies operate, and to offer adequate guarantees to the communities that are resisting and protecting the land'.[14]

**12.09.** In the mid-1970s, the international community attempted to create a document restricting the activities of transnational corporations, and a code of conduct regulating the activities of such corporations. In 1974, the UN Center and the UN Commission on Transnational Corporations (TNCs) were created. These bodies were to develop a code of conduct for TNCs. Work on the document was completed in 1990. The Code proclaimed that corporations should respect the human rights, values, and traditions of the countries in which they operate. However, the code contained only declarative language; it did not oblige the governments of the host countries to adhere to strict rules regarding the confiscation of property of companies. Code negotiations are at a standstill, as the Code was never accepted.[15] Subsequently, within the framework of the Organisation for Economic Co-operation and Development (OECD), a declaration on international investment and transnational enterprises was developed and signed by the member countries of this organization, which included the OECD Guidelines.

**12.10.** The problem of correlation of the protection of human rights and foreign investment is that international investment agreements 'thus confer substantive and procedural rights only on investors'. The authors also say that 'the international investment regime is a one-way road where only investors are allowed to drive'.[16] The scholars propose a reform that 'rests upon two alternative pillars: The first is to reform investment-treaty arbitration by including both obligations for investors and enforceable rights for investment-affected individuals and groups. The second is to replace investor-state arbitration with public alternative complaint mechanisms'.[17] Another problem is that investor-state arbitral tribunals 'rarely examine human rights based against investors'.[18]

**12.11.** Muthucumaraswamy Sornarajah considers that human rights are seldom in bilateral investment treaties. 'There are few treaties

---

[14] Aldo Orellana López, *Chevron* v. *Ecuador*, international arbitration and corporate impunity, 27 March 2019. Available at: https://www.opendemocracy.net/en/democraciaabierta/chevron-vs-ecuador-international-arbitration-and-corporate-impunity/ (accessed on 06 December 2019).

[15] See *Supra* note 7, at 93.

[16] Alessandra Arcuri, Francesco Montanaro, Federica Violi, Proposal for a human rights-compatible international investment agreement: arbitration for all, available at: https://www.ohchr.org/Documents/Issues/Business/Forum2018Submission2.pdf (accessed on 06 December 2019).

[17] *Ibid.*

[18] International Investment Law and Human Rights: *Urbaser* v. *Argentina*, available at: https://www.iisd.org/event/international-investment-law-and-human-rights-urbaser-v-argentina (accessed on 06 December 2019).

Czech Yearbook of International Law®

which address this issue. The saving of issues of health, morals and public welfare, a formula that is used in international trade law, has found its way into some investment treaties. But, the scope of the use of the phrase in investment treaties has yet to be determined.'[19]

**12.12.** The Bilateral Investment Treaty (BIT) between Morocco and Nigeria is called by some scholars 'one of the most innovative and balanced bilateral investment treaties ever concluded'. It 'is a valuable response from two developing countries to the criticism raised in the last few years against investment treaties, most prominently unbalanced content, restrictions on regulatory powers and inadequacies of investment arbitration'.[20]

**12.13.** The treaty contains obligations upon investors in the field of environment protection and protection of human rights.[21]

**12.14.** According to BIT Morocco-Nigeria

> Investors or the investment shall comply with environmental assessment screening and assessment processes applicable to their proposed investments prior to their establishment, as required by the laws of the host state for such an investment or the laws of the home state for such an investment, whichever is more rigorous in relation to the investment in question. 2) Investors or the investment shall conduct a social impact assessment of the potential investment...Investments shall, in keeping with good practice requirements relating to the size and nature of the investment, maintain an environmental management system. (Article 14).[22]

**12.15.** Article 18(2) envisages that investments 'shall uphold human rights in the host state' while Article 18(3) states that 'Investors and investments shall act in accordance with core labour standards as required by the ILO[23] Declaration on Fundamental Principles and Rights of Work, 1998'.[24]

**12.16.** Several countries presented a proposal to the UN Human Rights Council to create a binding international instrument on human

---

[19] *Supra* note 8, at 261.
[20] Tarcisio Gazzini, *The 2016 Morocco-Nigeria BIT: An Important Contribution to the Reform of Investment Treaties*, 8(3) INVESTMENT TREATY NEWS (2017), available at: www.iisd.org/itn (accessed on 06 December 2019).
[21] Available at: https://investmentpolicy.unctad.org/international-investment-agreements (accessed on 06 December 2019).
[22] RECIPROCAL INVESTMENT PROMOTION AND PROTECTION AGREEMENT BETWEEN THE GOVERNMENT OF THE KINGDOM OF MOROCCO AND THE GOVERNMENT OF THE FEDERAL REPUBLIC OF NIGERIA signed on 03 December 2016 not in force.
[23] International Labour Organization.
[24] Available at: https://investmentpolicy.unctad.org/international-investment-agreements (accessed on 23 January 2020).

rights violations by multinationals. This 'instrument could advance international human rights protection and extend responsibility from states to private companies...'[25]

**12.17.** The problem of the balance of interests of a foreign investor and a host State is difficult and important. Can the measures taken by the State to protect the health of its citizens be considered a violation of investment agreements? The answer to this question can be examined in an arbitration award in the case of *Philip Morris* v. *Uruguay.*

## II.3.   *Philip Morris* v. *Uruguay*[26]

**12.18.** The dispute was submitted to the International Centre for Settlement of Investment Disputes (ICSID or the Centre) based on Article 10 of the Switzerland-Uruguay BIT[27] by Philip Morris Products S.A. (Switzerland) and Abal Hermanos S.A. The claimants alleged that 'through the tobacco-control measures Uruguay violated the BIT in its treatment of the trademarks associated with cigarettes brands in which the Claimants had invested'. These measures included the 'Government's adoption of a single presentation requirement precluding tobacco manufacturers from marketing more than one variant of cigarette per brand family and the increase in the size of graphic health warnings appearing on cigarette packages'.[28] The Claimants allege that the measures 'caused a deprivation of their intellectual property rights' and 'substantially impacted the value of their investments'.[29] According to Uruguay, the measures 'were adopted in compliance with Uruguay's international obligations, including the BIT, for the single purpose of protecting public health', and that 'both regulations were applied in a nondiscriminatory manner to all tobacco companies, and they amounted to a reasonable, good faith exercise of Uruguay's sovereign prerogatives'.[30]

---

[25]   26/9 Elaboration of an international legally binding instrument on transnational corporations and other business enterprises with respect to human rights, available at: https://digitallibrary.un.org/record/775715/files/A_HRC_RES_26_9-EN.pdf (accessed on 06 December 2019).

[26]   *Philip Morris Brand Sárl, Philip Morris Products s.a., Abal Hermanos s.a.* v. *Oriental republic of Uruguay,* ICSID Case No. ARB/10/7, Award of 08 July 2016. Available at: https://www.italaw.com/sites/default/files/case-documents/italaw7417.pdf (accessed on 06 December 2019).

[27]   Agreement between the Swiss Confederation and the Oriental Republic of Uruguay on the Reciprocal Promotion and Protection of Investments (including Ad Article 10 of the Protocol thereto) dated 07 October 1988.

[28]   *Philip Morris Brand Sárl, Philip Morris Products s.a., Abal Hermanos s.a.* v. *Oriental republic of Uruguay,* ICSID Case No. ARB/10/7, Award of 08 July 2016. Available at: https://www.italaw.com/sites/default/files/case-documents/italaw7417.pdf (accessed on 06 December 2019).

[29]   *Ibid.,* at 2-3.

[30]   *Ibid.,* at 3.

**12.19.** Protecting public health has long since been recognized as an essential manifestation of the State's police power, as also indicated by Article 2(1) of the BIT which permits contracting States to refuse to admit investments 'for reasons of public security and order, public health and morality'.[31] As the tribunal stated, the measures had been 'adopted in fulfilment of Uruguay's national and international legal obligations for the protection of public health'. According to the Uruguayan Constitution: 'The State shall legislate in all matters appertaining to public health and hygiene, to secure the physical, moral and well-being of all the inhabitants of the country'.[32] So, it is the duty of the State 'to protect public health' and to guarantee the human rights to health, and 'the State has the authority to prevent, limit or condition the commercialization of a product or service, and this will consequently prevent, limit or condition the use of the trademark that identifies it'.[33] The tribunal stated that the measures 'were taken by Uruguay with a view to protect public health in fulfilment of its national and international obligations'. The measures were 'a valid exercise by Uruguay of its police powers for the protection of public health. As such, they cannot constitute an expropriation of the Claimants' investment'.[34]

## III. The European Court of Human Rights and Investments

**12.20.** The work of the European Court of Human Rights is of particularly important for the protection of human rights. The European Convention for the Protection of Human Rights and Fundamental Freedoms of 04 November 1950 '[created] not only the world's most effective system of international standards for the protection of human rights, but also one of the most advanced forms of international judicial procedure in the world'.[35]

**12.21.** Protocol No. 1 of 20 March 1952 in Article 1 provides for the protection of property:

> Every natural or legal person is entitled to the peaceful enjoyment of his possessions. No one shall be deprived of his possessions except in the public interest and subject to the conditions provided for

---

[31] Available at: https://www.italaw.com/sites/default/files/case-documents/italaw7417.pdf (accessed on 23 January 2020), et 82.
[32] *Ibid.*, at 86.
[33] *Supra* note 30.
[34] *Ibid.*, at 88.
[35] I.V. MINGAZOVA, ПРАВО СОБСТВЕННОСТИ В МЕЖДУНАРОДНОМ ПРАВЕ (OWNERSHIP RIGHT IN INTERNATIONAL LAW), Moscow 157 (2007).

by law and by the general principles of international law. The preceding provisions shall not, however, in any way impair the right of a State to enforce such laws as it deems necessary to control the use of property in accordance with the general interest or to secure the payment of taxes or other contributions or penalties.

**12.22.** Based on the analysis of this article, experts identify three types of norms involved in the mechanism for the protection of human rights. This is a general rule enshrining the principle of respect for property rights (follows from the first sentence of the Protocol); the second provides for the possibility of deprivation of property only under certain conditions; the third recognizes the state the right to regulate the use of property in the general (public) interests.[36]

**12.23.** Under the ECHR, property means 'various types of property, as well as non-property rights, for example, economic interests associated with the use of various rights, the right to social insurance, etc.'[37] Consequently, investments, as they are understood in BITs and other investment agreements, fall under the concept of 'property' in the context of the interpretation of the ECHR.

**12.24.** In *Trektörer Aktienbolag* v. *Sweden*, Swedish authorities have withdrew a license to sell alcohol from a legal entity that owned a restaurant. The court recognized that the economic interests affected as a result of the withdrawal of a license fell within the concept of 'property' as provided for in Article 1 of the Protocol.[38]

**12.25.** Not every State intervention in the exercise of a person's property rights is a violation of the Convention. This is allowed in accordance with the 'public interest', as specified in Article 1 of Protocol No. 1. In the *Sporrong and Lönnroth* v. *Case Sweden* dated 23 September 1982, the ECHR established the principle that was later used in the application of Article 1: 'For the purposes of this provision [of Protocol No. 1], the Court must establish whether a fair balance has been maintained between the requirements of public interest and the protection requirements of key individuals.'[39]

---

[36] *Ibid.*, at 166.
[37] *Ibid.*, at 182-183.
[38] MIKHAIL LOBOV, ЗАЩИТА ИМУЩЕСТВЕННЫХ ПРАВ В РАМКАХ ЕВРОПЕЙСКОЙ КОНВЕНЦИИ О ЗАЩИТЕ ПРАВ ЧЕЛОВЕКА И ОСНОВНЫХ СВОБОД (PROTECTION OF PROPERTY RIGHTS UNDER THE EUROPEAN CONVENTION ON HUMAN RIGHTS) in The Role of Constitutional Courts in Securing of Property Rights: Digest of Lectures, Moscow 121 (2011).
[39] *Supra* note 36, at 122.

**12.26.** Consequently,

> any lawful interference of the state with the right of unhindered use of property must meet the following mandatory criteria (criteria): a) legality; b) the implementation of actions in the public interest; c) maintaining a fair balance between the interests of society and the need to protect individual interests (the balance of private and public interest).[40]

**12.27.** The court also developed the principle of compensation for the alienation of property (e.g. nationalization, expropriation). In the decision in *the Lithgow Case*, the Court indicated that 'the nationalization of property without compensation is carried out only in exceptional circumstances. According to the Court, a measure depriving a person of his property should ensure a fair balance between the needs of the community as a whole and the requirements for the protection of individual fundamental rights'. The court further emphasized that 'the nationalization of property without reasonable compensation, in the normal state of affairs, will constitute a disproportionate intervention that cannot be considered as complying with Article 1 of Protocol 1 of the ECHR'.[41]

**12.28.** According to experts, the European Convention is a 'unique legal mechanism providing a collective guarantee of a single minimum standard in the protection of fundamental human rights and freedoms,'[42] including property rights, and therefore investments.

## IV.    Conclusion

**12.29.** The activity of foreign investors may lead to the violation of human rights. Mainly it comes in the form of a violation of the environment, which can adversely affect the health and well-being of the local population. At the same time, the protection of its population is the responsibility of each State, and the State has the right to take measures restricting the activities of foreign investors.

**12.30.** Recently, human rights issues have been raised in the resolution of investment disputes. The problem is that, as a rule, in investment agreements there are no provisions obliging foreign investors to take measures to protect the environment in the territory of the host State.

---

[40]   *Supra* note 33, at 190.
[41]   *Supra* note 36, at 125.
[42]   *Ibid.*

**12.31.** Foreign investors should respect human rights. It is vital to elaborate an international legal binding instrument on business enterprises with respect to human rights.

**12.32.** As M. Sornarajah says, 'There is little room the believe that the situation will be any different when the phrase is considered in relation to investment treaties. The general trend to interpret these treaties as giving primacy to investment protection will probably be continued. But, the seeds of discontent will multiply as a result.'[43]

| | |

*Summaries*

FRA    [*La protection des investissements étrangers et les droits de l'homme*]
*Le présent article se propose de réfléchir sur la protection des droits de l'homme au regard des investissements étrangers. Les activités d'entreprises supranationales sont susceptibles de mettre en péril l'environnement de l'État hôte. Partant de l'analyse de la pratique arbitrale et des conventions internationales, nous nous interrogeons si l'État hôte est en droit de restreindre les activités des investisseurs étrangers afin de protéger la santé de ses citoyens. L'analyse des décisions rendues par la Cour européenne des droits de l'homme montre que les investisseurs peuvent réclamer la protection de leurs droits en cas d'expropriation de leurs biens. Nous nous focalisons en particulier sur l'analyse des accords bilatéraux de nouvelle génération relatifs aux investissements, qui prévoient des engagements des investisseurs en matière de protection de l'environnement de l'État hôte. Par ailleurs, nous examinons plusieurs grands litiges internationaux d'investissement ayant trait à la question des droits de l'homme.*

CZE    [*Ochrana zahraničních investic a lidská práva*]
*Tento článek se zabývá otázkami ochrany lidských práv v souvislosti se zahraničními investicemi. Aktivity nadnárodních korporací mohou často ohrozit životní prostředí hostitelského státu. Na základě rozboru arbitrážní praxe a mezinárodních úmluv tato stať pátrá po tom, zda je hostitelský stát oprávněn omezit aktivity zahraničních investorů za účelem ochrany zdraví svých občanů. Rozbor rozhodnutí z praxe Evropského soudu pro lidská práva ukazuje, že investoři se mohou domáhat ochrany svých práv v případě vyvlastnění jejich majetku. Zvláštní*

---

[43]    *Supra* note 8, at 261.

*pozornost článek věnuje analýze ustanovení dvoustranných investičních smluv nové generace, které obsahují závazky investorů ohledně ochrany životního prostředí hostitelského státu. Tento článek rozebírá několik známých mezinárodních investičních sporů týkajících se problematiky lidských práv.*

| | |

POL    [*Ochrona inwestycji zagranicznych a prawa człowieka*]
*Niniejszy artykuł omawia problem ochrony praw człowieka w związku z realizacją inwestycji zagranicznych. Zwraca uwagę na potencjalną szkodliwość działań korporacji ponadnarodowych dla środowiska naturalnego państwa przyjmującego. Artykuł na podstawie analizy praktyki arbitrażowej i międzynarodowych umów bada, czy państwo przyjmujące może ograniczyć działalność inwestorów zagranicznych w imię ochrony zdrowia swoich obywateli. Ponadto artykuł analizuje orzeczenia Europejskiego Trybunału Praw Człowieka. Z powyższych badań wynika, że inwestorzy mogą dochodzić ochrony swoich praw przed sądem w razie przejęcia ich własności przez państwo.*

DEU    [*Schutz ausländischer Investitionen und Menschenrechte*]
*Dieser Beitrag beschäftigt sich mit dem Problem des Schutzes der Menschenrechte bei Auslandsinvestitionen. Es wird darauf hingewiesen, dass die Aktivitäten multinationaler Unternehmen häufig der Umwelt des Gaststaates schaden können. Basierend auf einer Analyse der Schiedsgerichtsbarkeit und internationaler Verträge wird in diesem Beitrag erörtert, ob der Gaststaat das Recht hat, die Tätigkeit ausländischer Investoren zum Schutz der Gesundheit seiner Bürger einzuschränken. Der Beitrag befasst sich auch mit den Entscheidungen des Europäischen Gerichtshofs für Menschenrechte, und deren Analyse zeigt, dass Anleger zum Schutz ihrer Rechte, wenn ihr Eigentum nationalisiert wird, vor Gericht gehen können.*

RUS    [*Защита иностранных инвестиций и права человека*]
*В настоящей статье рассмотрены проблемы защиты прав человека при осуществлении иностранных инвестиций. Показано, что, зачастую, деятельность, транснациональных корпораций может причинять вред экологии государства, принимающего инвестиции. На основе анализа арбитражной практики и международных договоров исследовано, вправе ли государство, принимающее инвестиции, ограничивать деятельность иностранных*

Czech Yearbook of International Law®

*инвесторов для защиты здоровья своих граждан. Сделан анализ решений из практики Европейского суда по правам человека, который показывает, что инвесторы могут обращаться за защитой своих прав в случае национализации их собственности.*

ESP    [*Protección de las inversiones y los derechos humanos*]
*El artículo trata el tema de la protección de los derechos humanos en el contexto de la inversión extranjera. El texto resalta el hecho de que las actividades económicas llevadas a cabo por las empresas multinacionales pueden a menudo causar daños medioambientales en los países receptores de la inversión. Partiendo del análisis de la actuación de los tribunales de arbitraje y de los convenios internacionales, se hace la reflexión sobre si el país afectado tiene derecho a restringir las empresas multinacionales con el objetivo de proteger el medio ambiente y la salud de los ciudadanos. El artículo también analiza las resoluciones del Tribunal Europeo de Derechos Humanos concluyendo que los inversores pueden acudir al tribunal para reclamar la protección de sus derechos en caso de que sus bienes hayan sido nacionalizados.*

| | |

## Bibliography

EKATERINA A. ARISTOVA, ОТВЕТСТВЕННОСТЬ ТРАНСГРАНИЧНЫХ КОРПОРАТИВНЫХ ГРУПП: ТЕОРИЯ И ПРАКТИКА (RESPONSIBILITY OF TRANSNATIONAL CORPORATE GROUPS), Moscow: Infotropik 77 (2014).

EKATERINA I. KOZLOVA, OLEG E. KUTAFIN. КОНСТИТУЦИОННОЕ ПРАВО РОССИИ (CONSTITUTIONAL LAW OF RUSSIA), Moscow 258 (2003).

MIKHAIL LOBOV, ЗАЩИТА ИМУЩЕСТВЕННЫХ ПРАВ В РАМКАХ ЕВРОПЕЙСКОЙ КОНВЕНЦИИ О ЗАЩИТЕ ПРАВ ЧЕЛОВЕКА И ОСНОВНЫХ СВОБОД (PROTECTION OF PROPERTY RIGHTS UNDER THE EUROPEAN CONVENTION ON HUMAN RIGHTS) in The Role of Constitutional Courts in Securing of Property Rights: Digest of Lectures, Moscow 121 (2011).

ELENA ANDREEVNA LUKASHEVA, ПРАВА ЧЕЛОВЕКА (HUMAN RIGHTS), Moscow (ed. 1999).

IRINA V. MINGAZOVA, ПРАВО СОБСТВЕННОСТИ В МЕЖДУНАРОДНОМ ПРАВЕ (OWNERSHIP RIGHT IN INTERNATIONAL LAW), Moscow 157 (2007).

МЕЖДУНАРОДНОЕ ПУБЛИЧНОЕ ПРАВО (International Public Law), Moscow 227 (K.A. Bekyashev ed., 2007).

MUTHUCUMARASWAMY SORNARAJAH, THE INTERNATIONAL LAW ON FOREIGN INVESTMENT, Cambridge 260 (2nd edition 2007).

# Book Reviews

Czech Yearbook of International Law®

Petr Dobiáš

## Insurance in Cross-Border Entrepreneur Relationships
*POJIŠTĚNÍ PODNIKATELŮ VE VZTAZÍCH S MEZINÁRDNÍM*
*PRVKEM, Prague: Leges (2019), 324 pages, ISBN 978-80-7502-348-3*

In the field of private international law some sub-fields and topics have been analyzed and studied many times. The professional and scientific community has provided studies and critiques in many specialized monographs and articles, published in specialized journals or excellent books, and has provided analysis and discussion topics regarding aspects of private international law, international business and international arbitration. However, there are not a significant number of books or correspondent literature in the Czech international private law area at present, especially in the field of insurance relationships of the entrepreneurs with an international or cross-border aspect. The book by Petr Dobiáš under review here is an interesting and important work, not only for its addressing of this lack, but also for its artistry and elaboration.

For the purpose of this review it is not important to analyze the reasons why the presented topic has been overlooked and only partially analyzed. Rather, it is a professional pleasure to reflect on the structure, subject matter and importance of the presented monograph. This book is presenting a much-needed analysis of selected legal aspects and also discussing a very important subject for international business actors. These aspects include issues of the procedural law arising not only from cross-border contracts, but also from cross-border relationships touched by problems of insurance and reinsurance.

The monograph is not only aimed at practitioners and private international lawyers, but also to scholars and students of private international law and it is also a helpful source of information for the insurance lawyers. All of the above-mentioned groups have had to deal with the question of the applicable law of insurance contracts and reinsurance contracts covering critical circumstances situated outside of national borders. Additionally, the question of the choice of law provisions and most important aspects of the legal sources applicable to contractual obligations are covered by this work.

The book is divided into eight chapters or parts. Each part considers the special topics that are important for analysis of the special insurance questions related to aspects of private international law. The first part considers the aspects of European Union conflict of law rules in insurance contracts. This part describes the Rome Convention of 1980 and also selected conflict of law codifications in the close relationship to the insurance contracts in selected European countries. Also mentioned are countries outside the European Union and differences in the national legislative steps because of the special position of those countries. The first chapter also handles the law applicable to insurance contracts following the regulation Rome I. It is clear that in connection with the Rome I regulation many member States of the EU are not capable of identifying problems regarding the scope of Rome I regulation application today. The monograph successfully describes the application of the Rome I regulation including insurance contracts. The question of excluding some special types of insurance contracts and other important aspects are also mentioned. Chapter 2 of the monograph handles the aspects of selected judicatory, realized by the Court of Justice of the European Union, with the connection to the contracts of insurance for motor vehicles. After an interesting and extensive presentation of the decisions of the Court of Justice of the European Union, the author presents the rules for selecting the applicable law under the Hague convention 1971 and also the regulations of Rome II, as well as the rules for the selection of the applicable law for traffic accidents.

Chapter 3 is not only important but also interesting, handling the content and purpose of the regulation Brussel Ia. In a step-by-step analysis, it explores the jurisdictional problems and possible solutions of Brussel Ia. Jurisdictional problems are combined with the analyses of prorogation and other important or significant foundations of the Brussel Ia regulation. In a similar fashion to Chapter 2, Chapter 3 introduces selected decisions of the Court of Justice of the European Union and the most important judicatory practice in this field. A special chapter of this monograph is devoted to the Principles of European Insurance Contract Law (PEICL) from the year 2016. These have been drafted so as to complete the international market for insurance products. The intention was for the PEICL to apply when parties have agreed that their contract shall be governed by them. In this Chapter are important analytical sections describing the primary terminology and basic definitions, not to mention the final conclusions to the contemporary, past, and future importance of the Principles of European Insurance Contract Law. Chapter 6 is devoted to the problems of international arbitration and insurance contracts. The author of the monograph has already written many publications handling insurance aspects and also the problems of international arbitration by resolving disputes arising from international insurance contracts. These publications are used for an interesting synthesis in this book.

The chapter on international arbitration in insurance contracts is important for providing a practical point of view on the subject, as well as for situations where a dispute is arising and has to be handled by an arbitration institution or arbitrator. Chapter 7 is devoted to the INCOTERMS 2010 (2020) of the International Chamber of Commerce - ICC and to the Institute cargo clauses 2009, as well as to the selected terms of insurance contracts used by the international transportation of goods. Finally, chapter 8 describes insurance in relation to cybernetic security, focusing on terminology and classification, insurance and the risks in the Internet, as well as other important practical and theoretical aspects. It also discusses the differences between the risks on the Internet, online insurance contracts and online contracting. It is important to note that these problematical aspects concern not only subjects in business to business - B2B relationships but also the broad legal sphere of business-to-consumer - B2C legal regulation. Last but not least, the problematical aspects of the applicable law in mass risk and large risk insurance are also richly described.

This book provides a useful and clear introduction and guide for the applicable legal regimes and also relevant rules implemented by the laws of private international law, concerning the most important aspects of insurance with cross border elements. These are important not only for B2B relations, but also for the insurers and in some cases re-insurers as well. This book will be practically relevant not only for entrepreneurs but also for scholars and policymakers, not to mention legal practitioners who are involved in cross-border relations that have insurance components. This monograph not only touches on important parts of private international law, but it also is one of a small number of books dedicated to this subject. It is also an interesting reference to a complex area of legal questions. It identifies the applicable legal regimes and relevant rules of private international law in the international relations concerning insurance questions and dispute resolution in this field.

[*JUDr. Mag. iur. Michal Malacka, PhD., MBA*]
*Department of International and Private Law Faculty of Law,*
*Palacky University Olomouc*
*E-mail: Michal.Malacka@upol.cz*

Czech Yearbook of International Law®

Ian Iosifovich Funk | Inna Vladimirovna Pererva
**Human Rights and Principles of Humanity in the Consideration of Disputes at the International Arbitration Court at BelCCI........303**

# News & Reports

# Human rights and principles of humanity in the consideration of disputes at the International Arbitration Court at BelCCI

The principle of humanity and protection of human rights is inherent to all modern legal institutions in almost all European countries, including the Republic of Belarus.

The activities of international arbitration courts, including the International Arbitration Court at the BelCCI, are also based on the same humanistic principles. This is despite the fact that the vast majority of disputes in the International Court of Arbitration at BelCCI are disputes between legal entities, and only about 10% of disputes involve individuals, mostly with the status of individual entrepreneurs (merchants). However, legal entities as a legal construct exist, first of all, in order to simplify "communication" in the property turnover between people, and if so, then the activity of the International Court of Arbitration at the BelCCI is ultimately an activity for the sake of people and for the satisfaction of the property interests of people, and not of some abstract legal category.

At the same time, the activities of the International Arbitration Court at the Belarusian Chamber of Commerce and Industry respect the property rights of a person, allowing them to realize human capabilities in the production and distribution of wealth, aimed at ensuring their property independence, decent living standards and social security. In particular, we are talking about proprietary rights, including the right to own, use and dispose of our own property alone as well as jointly with other persons, the right to entrepreneurial activity, the right to choose a profession, occupation and work in accordance with vocation, abilities, education, training, as well as healthy and safe working conditions, and guaranteed remuneration for work in accordance with its quantity, quality and social value, but not lower than the level, ensuring present work for someone else and his family a free and decent life, the right to housing, right to inheritance, the right to social security, the right to the protection of health and medical care.

Further the International Court of Arbitration at the Belarusian Chamber of Commerce and Industry also deals directly with disputes related to the protection of the interests of specific people, for example, in the framework of their right to the protection of health and medical care.

It should be noted that due to globalization, a person can enjoy medical services not only in his own country but also in other countries in order to exercise his right to health protection.

The Republic of Belarus is a country in which a high and at the same time inexpensive level of medicine enables it to attract patients from almost the entire post-Soviet space and even from the countries in Eastern Europe.

Thus, in the line of medical tourism or treatment, the Republic of Belarus was visited:

in 2010 — by more than 100,000 foreign citizens;
in 2011 — 115,500 foreign citizens;
in 2012 — 130,000 foreign citizens;
in 2013 — about 160,000 foreign citizens;
in 2014 — more than 160,000 foreign citizens;
in 2015 — about 160,000 foreign citizens;
in 2016 — more than 150,000 foreign citizens;
in 2017 — over 190,000 foreign citizens.

With the availability of such an extensive medical practice, disputes between patients and hospitals are inevitable.

Moreover, these disputes may arise both due to the fact that the patient is dissatisfied with the quality of medical services rendered to him, and due to the fact that the patient does not pay for the services rendered to him properly.

Given the international, as well as extra-economic, from the point of view of Belarusian law, the nature of these disputes, the International Court of Arbitration at the BelCCI is quite often chosen as the body to deal with disputes between medical institutions in the Republic of Belarus and patients.

This approach can be explained by Article 4 of the Law of the Republic of Belarus "On the International Arbitration Court", according to which, by agreement of the parties, civil law disputes between any subjects arising from the implementation of foreign trade and other types of international economic relations can be transferred to the international arbitration court, if the location or residence of at least one of them is located abroad (outside of the Republic of Belarus), as well as other disputes of an economic nature, if an agreement provides for the resolution of the dispute by an international arbitration court and if it arbitrable under the legislation of the Republic of Belarus.

The existence of foreign economic relations in the contract between the medical institution and the patient is from a Belarusian legal point of view based on the provisions of Presidential Decree of 27 March 2008 No. 178 "On the procedure for conducting and controlling foreign trade operations", as well as the Law of the Republic of Belarus of 25 November 2004 No. 347-3 "On the state regulation of foreign trade".

Thus, in accordance with clause 1.1 of the Decree of the President of the Republic of Belarus of 27 March 2008 No. 178 "On the Procedure for Conducting and Controlling Foreign Trade" foreign trade agreement - is an agreement between a resident and a non-resident, which provides for a paid transfer of goods, protected information, exclusive rights to the results of intellectual activity, performance of work, provision of services.

At the same time, non-residents may be individuals, including individuals - foreign citizens and stateless persons, with the exception of foreign citizens and stateless persons who have a residence permit in the Republic of Belarus.

Article 1 of the Law of the Republic of Belarus "On the State Regulation of Foreign Trade" contains the definition of foreign activity as an activity for carrying out foreign trade in goods, and (or) services, and (or) objects of intellectual property. Foreign trade in services, as indicated in Article 25 of this Law, is carried out in the following ways:

- from the territory of the Republic of Belarus to the territory of a foreign state;
- from the territory of a foreign state to the territory of the Republic of Belarus;
- on the territory of the Republic of Belarus to a foreign customer of services;
- in the territory of a foreign state to the Belarusian service customer;
- Belarusian service provider who does not have a commercial presence in the territory of a foreign state, by providing services to them or an authorized person acting on his behalf in the territory of a foreign state;
- a foreign service provider who does not have a commercial

presence in the territory of the Republic of Belarus by providing services to them or an authorized person acting on his behalf in the territory of the Republic of Belarus;

- Belarusian service provider by commercial presence in the territory of a foreign state;
- foreign service provider through commercial presence in the Republic of Belarus.

At the same time, clause 1.16 of Article 1 of the named legislation also refers to the number of non-residents, including individuals who have permanent residence outside the Republic of Belarus.

Thus, the services of the Belarusian entity to a non-resident, including on the territory of the Republic of Belarus, are the export of services, and, therefore, the activity described in this article is a foreign trade (foreign economic) activity, the disputes within which can be considered by the International Arbitration Court BelCCI.

Let us give an example from the practice of the International Court of Arbitration at the BelCCI.

The dispute arose between the health institution "A" (Republic of Belarus), which entered as a plaintiff, and a citizen of Georgia, who is the defendant, of the agreement concluded by the parties on 27 October 2011, the subject of which was to provide the defendant with liver transplant medical services (hereinafter — the Contract).

Clause 5.3 of the Agreement provides that "if the parties do not reach an agreement through mutual negotiations, the disagreements are subject to arbitration in accordance with the legislation of the Republic of Belarus".

According to clause 5.4 of the Agreement "location of the arbitration court — International Arbitration Court at the Belarusian Chamber of Commerce and Industry in Minsk".

The plaintiff "M" claimed that the operation on liver transplantation was successfully performed on 27 October 2011. However, the defendant has fulfilled the obligation under the Agreement only partially.

According to the claimant's calculation, the principal debt of the respondent under the contract was $ 28 670,00.

As a legal rationale for its claim for the recovery of the principal under the contract in the above amount, the plaintiff specified Articles 290, 295 and 733 of the Civil Code of the Republic of Belarus.

Since Clause 7.1 of the Contract stipulates the responsibility of the defendant in the form of a penalty in the amount of 0.1% of the debt amount for each day of delay in payment, the claimant claimed a penalty from the defendant as of 30 August 2013 in the amount of $ 18 819,48.

The plaintiff asked to assign the costs of the arbitration fee to the defendant in connection with the filing of a claim with the International Arbitration Court at BelCCI.

Before applying for judicial protection, the parties exchanged letters.

Thus, the defendant, in his letter of 28 February 2012, indicated that he had paid $23,000.00 for a liver transplantation, and remains to pay $ 28,670.00.

The defendant stated that he was hoping for help from the Parliament and the Ministry of Health of Georgia, but he was refused help. To fulfill his obligations to pay the remaining debt, he will sell a house in Tbilisi. This takes time.

In the letter, the respondent asked for some time and pledged to pay the debt.

In the claim from 27 March 2012, the plaintiff invited the respondent to pay the debt under the contract before 30 April 2012, in the amount of 28 670,00 US dollars, provided for by clause 7.1 of the Agreement, a penalty in the amount of 2 609,00 US dollars and interest for using other people's funds in the amount of 3013,00 US dollars.

Since the parties did not succeed in resolving the dispute in the pre-trial (arbitration) procedure, the claimant submitted a claim to the International Court of Arbitration at the BelCCI.

Since in paragraph 5.3 of the Agreement the parties chose the legislation of the Republic of Belarus as the applicable law, when resolving a dispute between the parties, the Court was guided by the civil law of the Republic of Belarus.

In the proceeding, the Court established the following.

The contract stipulated that the service provided by the plaintiff to the defendant was a liver transplantation and its cost was 51,670.00 US dollars.

Clause 2.1 of the Agreement provides for the following obligations of the claimant:

- to perform (carry out) the work (services) specified in clause 1 of the Agreement;
- to draw up the results of the work performed (services) in accordance with the procedure established by the legislation of the Republic of Belarus.

The defendant, in accordance with clause 2.2 of the Agreement, assumed the obligation to pay all the expenses of the claimant to fulfill obligations under the Agreement in the manner and within the time provided for in Chapter 3 of the Agreement.

Clause 3.2 of the Agreement states that the respondent makes payment under the Agreement within 10 banking days from the date the service is provided by the claimant on the basis of the invoice issued by him.

According to clause 1.1 of the Decree of the President of the Republic of Belarus of 27 March 2008 N178 "On the Procedure for Conducting and Controlling Foreign Operations", the date of performance of work (provision of services) is the date of signing by the parties of the Certificate of Delivery and Acceptance of Rendered Services.

The Court concluded that the fact of the provision of medical services by the plaintiff. on liver transplantation in the amount of 51 670,00 US dollars is confirmed by the act of acceptance of the work signed by the parties on 11 November 2011, and also recorded in the medical card of the patient B.

The defendant fulfilled the obligation to pay for the services rendered to him in accordance with clause 3.2 of the Agreement by transferring funds to the claimant's account on 02 December 2011 in the amount of US $ 10,000.00 according to the payment order, and on 14 December 2011 - money in US $ 10,000.00 according to the payment order and on December 27, 2011 - in the amount of 3000.00 US dollars according to the payment order, and all in the amount of 23,000.00 US dollars.

Thus, the sum of the principal debt of the defendant under the contract amounted to 28,670.00 US dollars.

The defendant confirmed the existence of the debt under the contract in the above amount in a letter dated 28 February 2012.

Clause 1 of Article 733 of the Civil Code of the Republic of Belarus provides that under an onerous services agreement, one party (contractor) undertakes, on the instructions of the other party (customer), to provide services (perform certain actions or carry out certain activities), and the customer undertakes to pay for these services.

Clause 1 of Article 735 of the Civil Code of the Republic of Belarus contains the provision that the customer is obliged to pay for the services rendered to him within the time limits and in the manner specified in the legislation or under the contract for provision of services.

On the basis of the foregoing, the Court considered that the plaintiff's claim to recover the principal debt under the Agreement in the amount of 28,670.00 US dollars was justified and subject to satisfaction.

In resolving the claim for the recovery of a penalty from the defendant, the Court was guided by Article 311 of the Civil Code of the Republic of Belarus.

According to clause 1 of Article 311 of the Civil Code of the Republic of Belarus, the amount of money determined by the legislation or the contract, which the debtor is obligated to pay to the creditor, unless otherwise provided by legislation, is recognized as a penalty (fine, interest), unless otherwise provided for by the performance of the obligation execution. Upon request for payment of the penalty, the lender is not obliged to prove the loss caused to him.

Clause 7.1 of the Agreement establishes the responsibility of the defendant, including for late payment provided for by the agreement. In the event of a delay in payment in accordance with clause 2.2 of the Agreement, the defendant shall pay a penalty in the amount of 0.1% of the debt amount for each day of delay in payment.

As previously indicated, in accordance with clause 3.2 of the contract, the defendant was obliged to make payment within 10 banking days from the date of service, which took place on 11 November 2011 according to the work acceptance certificate, that is no later than 25 November 2011.

According to the opinion of the Court, the plaintiff's claim for the recovery of a penalty in the amount of USD 18,819.48 from the defendant is reasonable and subject to satisfaction.

Based on the above and in accordance with Article 311, clause 1 of Article 733, clause 1 of Article 735 of the Civil Code of the Republic of Belarus, the Court decided to satisfy the claim.

To recover in favor of health care institution "A" (Republic of Belarus) from B (Georgia) the principal debt in the amount of 28 670,00 US dollars, a penalty in the amount of 18 819,48 US dollars and expenses related to the payment of the arbitration fee in the amount of 2 822,17 Euro, and a total of 47 489,48 US dollars and 2,822.17 euros.

[*Jan Iosifovich Funk, LL.D.*]
is a Professor, Chairman of the International Arbitration Court at the BelCCI.
E-mail: funk25@mail.ru

[*Inna Vladimirovna Pererva, Ph.D.*]
is the Head of Information and Consultation Centre of the International Arbitration Court at the BelCCI
E-mail: iac@cci.by

Alexander J. Bělohlávek

# I.    Selected Bibliography for 2019[1]

**Opening Remarks:**

This overview lists only works published in 2019. The individual chapters into which this overview is divided always cover both substantive and procedural issues.

Titles in translations are indicative.

## I.1.    (Public) international law, including constitutional issues and other public-law areas with transnational dimensions and including the legal issues of international business relations, international relationships.

### I.1.1. [CZE] – [CZECH REPUBLIC] – Titles published within the Czech Republic

<u>Monographs and Collections</u>

TOMÁŠ MACH, VADEMECUM OF INTERNATIONAL LAW, Prague: Wolters Kluwer ČR (2019), ISBN: 978-80-7598-358-9.

**Bulletin advokacie [*Bulletin of the Czech Bar*], Prague: Česká advokátní komora [*Czech Bar Association*], 2019, ISSN: 1210-6348**[2]

Daniel Hrčka, *Soumrak (nejen) investiční arbitráže? – Rozhodnutí SD EU C-284/16 a jeho důsledky* [title in translation – *Twilight of investment (and other) arbitration? – Decision of the CJ EU in C-284/16 and the Consequences Thereof*], 2019, No. 7-8, p. 42-46.

**Mezinárodní vztahy [International Relations], Prague: Institute of International Relations Prague, 2019, Vol. LIIV**[3]

Michael Baun, Dan Marek, *Making Europe Defend Again: The Relaunch of European Defense Cooperation from a Neoclassical Realist Perspective,* No. 4, p. 27-46.

---

[1]    Collected by: Alexander J. BĚLOHLÁVEK, Prague (Czech Republic). Translations of titles to English are for easy reference only. In certain cases (exceptionally), the translation is not a *literal* translation, but an adapted translation of the title intended to best express the actual contents of the publication in English.

[2]    Papers published in Czech with abstracts in a foreign language. Abstracts in English and in German.

[3]    Majority of papers published in Czech, summary in English.

Vít Beneš, *Foreign Policy Analysis: Coneptualizing Temporality and Otherness in the Role Theory*, No. 3, p. 5-21.

Jakub Charvát, **Degressive Representation in the European Parliament:** *the Union Law vs. Reality,* No. 3, p. 22-40.

Jan Karlas, **National Reporting in the Framework of Human Rights** *Treties: Analysis of the Core Universal Treaties,* No. 3, p. 5-27.

Kamil Klosek, *Indirect Interventions in Civil Wars: The Use of States as Proxies in Military Interventions,* No. 4, p. 5-26.

Sarah Komasová, *Threat and Security Production at Václav Havel Airport Prague,* No. 3, p. 50-69.

Michal Kouřil, *Democracyand Social Conflict in Burma,* No. 3, p. 41-56.

Josef Mlejnek, *The Intertwining of Religion and Nationalism in the Struggle for an Autocephalous Status for Ukrainian Orthodoxy,* No. 3, p. 28-48.

Blanka Nyklová, Kateřina Cidlinská, Nina Fárová, *International Relations in the Czech Republic: Where Have All the Women Gone?,* No. 3, p. 5-23.

Nikita Odintsov, *Nabucco Swept Away by South Stream: Was the Securitization of the Russian Pipeline Successful?,* No. 3, p. 49-69.

Míla O´Sullivan, *The Women, Peace and Security Agenda: The Unfinished Story of Feminist Revolution versus Compromise in Global Politics,* No. 4, p. 47-65.

Michal Parizek, Ekaterina Ananyeva, *Central and Eastern Europe and the Decline of Russia in the United Nationas Administrative Bodies: 1996-2015,* No. 3, p. 24-49.

**The Lawyer Quarterly, Prague: Ústav státu a práva Akademie věd České republiky [Institute of State and Law of the Academy of Sciences of the Czech Republic], 2019, Vol. IX, ISSN: 0231-6625**[4]

---

[4]  A subsidiary title to the monthly periodical Právník [in translation – *The Lawyer*] which will be published by the Institute of State and Law of the Academy of Science of the Czech Republic in Czech. Papers published in *The Lawyer Quarterly* are in English, exceptionally in other languages (German, for instance); abstracts are in English. For papers published in the periodical *"Pravnik"* [in translation – *The Lawyer*], issued monthly, see the separate excerpt from papers listed under the heading of the respective periodical.

Refia Kaya, *European Court of Human Rights on Addressing Environmental Discrimination Against Collectivities*, No 4, p. 283-298.

**Obchodní právo [*Commercial Law*], Prague: Prospektrum, 2019, Vol. 28, ISSN: 1210-8278[5]**

Tomáš Mach, *Ochrana investic v době Post-Achmea: lze očekávat ransatlantickou rozštěpenost ochrany investic?* [title in translation – *Investment protection in the Post-Achmea times: Can one expect atransatlantic split of investment protection?*] No. 10, p. 18-33.

**Právní rozhledy [*Law Review*], Prague: C. H. Beck, 2019, Vol. 27, ISSN: 1210-6410[6]**

Markéta Bednářová, *Právo na soudní přezkum rozhodnutí o neudělení dlouhodobého víza za účelem studia dle směrnice 2004/114/ES* [title in translation – *Right to Judicial Review of a Decision Denying a Long-Term Student Visa under Directive 2004/114/EC*], No. 11, p. 403-407.

Sandra Brožová, *Mezinárodní smlouvy za první republiky a dnes: koordinace sociálního pojištění a zamezení dvojího zdanění* [title in translation – *International Agreements in the First Republic and Today: Coordination of Social Insurance and Avoidance of Double Taxation*], No. 4, p. 128-133.

**Právník [Title in translation - *The Lawyer*], Prague: Ústav státu a práva Akademie věd České republiky [Institute of State and Law of the Academy of Sciences of the Czech Republic], 2019, Vol. 158, ISSN: 0231-6625[7]**

Jan Bárta, *Istanbulská úmluva o prevenci a porítání násilí vůči ženám – dočká se naší ratifikace?* [title in translation – *The Istanbul Convention on Combating Violence Against Women – is it Going to be Ratified by the Czech Republic?*], No. 8, p. 803-818.

Jan Petr Kosinka, *Nebezpečí totalitarismu universalistických koncepcí* [title in translation – *Totalitarian Threat of Universal Ontological Conceptions*], No. 3, p. 283-306.

Jiří Malenovský, *Problémy svrchovanosti a nezávislosti miniaturního státu na příkladu Monackého knížectví* [title in translation – *Problems*

---

[5]   Papers published in Czech. Abstracts in English.
[6]   Papers published in Czech.
[7]   Papers published in Czech with abstracts in a foreign language. The abstract is most often in English (exceptionally in German or French).

*of Sovereignty and Independence of a Micro-State on the Example of the Principality of Monaco*], No 02, p. 141-162.

Zdeněk Nový, *Mezinárodní investiční arbitráž a vláda práva v hostitelských státech* [title in translation – *International Investment Arbitration and the Rule of Law in Host States*], No 10, p. 909-933

Šárka Ošťádalová, Martin Faix, *Aspekty uprchlické a azylové problematiky v kontextu správy území mezinárodními organizacemi: Kosovo pod správou UNMIK* [title in translation – *Selected Asylum and Refugee Aspects in the Context of Territorial Administration by International Organizations: Kosovo under the UNMIK Administration*], No 06, p. 555-574.

Jan Petrov, *Vnitrostátní soudy a způsoby argumentace judikaturou ESLP* [title in translation – *Domestic Courts and Methods of Argumentation with the ECtHR´s Case Law*], No 02, p. 163-181.

Eva Procházková, *Je univerzalita přísně střežených hodnot lidství v Evropě ohrožena?* [title in translation – *Is the Universality of High Values of Humanity Endangered in Europe?*], No 02, p. 217-220.

Michal Radvan, *Internacionalizace výuky práva na Právnické fakultě Masarykovy univerzity* [title in translation – *Internationalization of Legal Education at the Faculty of Law, Masaryk University*], No 01, p. 119-128.

Ondřej Svoboda, *Systém investičního soudu: Překotný rozchod Evropské unie s investiční arbitráží* [title in translation – *Investment Court System? European Union´s Abrupt Divorce with Investment Arbitration*], No 04, p. 390-405.

Jindřiška Syllová, *K metodám zkoumání judicializace politiky ve střední Evropě* [title in translation – *Methods of Examining Judicialization of Politics in Central Europe*], No. 5, p. 445-455.

**The Lawyer Quarterly, Prague: Ústav státu a práva Akademie věd České republiky [Institute of State and Law of the Academy of Sciences of the Czech Republic], 2018, Vol. VIII, ISSN: 0231-6625**[8]

---

[8] As subsidiary title to the monthly periodical Právník [in translation – *The Lawyer*], which will be published by the Institute of State and Law of the Academy of Science of the Czech Republic in Czech. Papers published in *The Lawyer Quarterly* are in English, exceptionally in other languages (German for instance); abstracts are in English. Papers published in the monthly issued periodical "*Pravnik*" [in translation – *The Lawyer*] see separate extract of papers under the particular periodical.

Martin Madej, *The Charter of Fundamental Rights of the EU in the Czech Judicial Decisions: Falling Short of Expectations?*, No 3, p. 213-228.

Walled Fuad Mahameed, Jamal Barafi, *The Legal Impact of the Lack of a Theoretical Definition of Terrorism Rowards Rights Enshrined in the Charter of the United Nations*, No 1, p. 97-108.

**Other titles published in the Czech Republic:**

Alexander J. Bělohlávek, *Autonomní výklad mezinárodních smluv* [title in translation – *Autonomous Interpretation of International Agreements*]. In: TEREZA KYSELOVSKÁ, DAVID SEHNÁLEK, NADĚŽDA ROZEHNALOVÁ (eds.). *IN VARIETATE CONCORDIA*: SOUBOR VĚDECKÝCH STATÍ K POCTĚ PROF. VLADIMÍRA TÝČE [title in translation – *IN VARIETATE CONCORDIA*: COLLECTION OF SCIENTIFIC PAPERS TO COMMEMORATE PROF. VLADIMÍR TÝČ]. Brno [Czech Republic]: Masaryk University, Collected Papers of the Masaryk University, Scientia Edition: Theoretical Series, (2019), No. 651, p. 31-61.

Ján Klučka, *K niektorým špecifikám súčasného medzinárodného súdnictva* [title in translation – *Selected Specifics of the Contemporary International Judiciary*]. In: TEREZA KYSELOVSKÁ, DAVID SEHNÁLEK, NADĚŽDA ROZEHNALOVÁ (eds.). *IN VARIETATE CONCORDIA*: SOUBOR VĚDECKÝCH STATÍ K POCTĚ PROF. VLADIMÍRA TÝČE [title in translation – *IN VARIETATE CONCORDIA*: COLLECTION OF SCIENTIFIC PAPERS TO COMMEMORATE PROF. VLADIMÍR TÝČ]. Brno [Czech Republic]: Masaryk University, Collected Papers of the Masaryk University, Scientia Edition: Theoretical Series, (2019), No. 651, p. 105-120.

Zdeněk Nový, *Úvahy nad smyslem maximy in claris non fit interpretation v soudobém právu mezinárodních smluv* [title in translation – *Essays Concerning the Meaning of the In Claris Non Fit Interpretation Maxim in the Contemporary Law of International Agreements*]. In: TEREZA KYSELOVSKÁ, DAVID SEHNÁLEK, NADĚŽDA ROZEHNALOVÁ (eds.). *IN VARIETATE CONCORDIA*: SOUBOR VĚDECKÝCH STATÍ K POCTĚ PROF. VLADIMÍRA TÝČE [title in translation – *IN VARIETATE CONCORDIA*: COLLECTION OF SCIENTIFIC PAPERS TO COMMEMORATE PROF. VLADIMÍR TÝČ]. Brno [Czech Republic]: Masaryk University, Collected Papers of the Masaryk University, Scientia Edition: Theoretical Series, (2019), No. 651, p. 121-130.

Jan Ondřej, *Vztah mezinárodního a vnitrostátního práva – na základě učení prof. Vladimíra Týče* [title in translation – ***Relationship Between International and National Law – Based on the Teachings of Prof. Vladimír Týč***]. In: TEREZA KYSELOVSKÁ, DAVID SEHNÁLEK, NADĚŽDA ROZEHNALOVÁ (eds.). *IN VARIETATE CONCORDIA*: SOUBOR VĚDECKÝCH STATÍ K POCTĚ PROF. VLADIMÍRA TÝČE [title in translation – *IN VARIETATE CONCORDIA*: COLLECTION OF SCIENTIFIC PAPERS TO COMMEMORATE PROF. VLADIMÍR TÝČ]. Brno [Czech Republic]: Masaryk University, Collected Papers of the Masaryk University, Scientia Edition: Theoretical Series, (2019), No. 651, p. 121-130.

Miroslav Slašťan, ***Uplatňovanie medzinárodných zmlúv Spojeného kráľovstva a členských štátov Euroópskej únie po BREXITE*** [title in translation – ***Application of International Agreements of the United Kingdom and the European Union Member States after BREXIT***]. In: TEREZA KYSELOVSKÁ, DAVID SEHNÁLEK, NADĚŽDA ROZEHNALOVÁ (eds.). *IN VARIETATE CONCORDIA*: SOUBOR VĚDECKÝCH STATÍ K POCTĚ PROF. VLADIMÍRA TÝČE [title in translation – *IN VARIETATE CONCORDIA*: COLLECTION OF SCIENTIFIC PAPERS TO COMMEMORATE PROF. VLADIMÍR TÝČ]. Brno [Czech Republic]: Masaryk University, Collected Papers of the Masaryk University, Scientia Edition: Theoretical Series, (2019), No. 651, p. 121-130.

Ondřej Svaček, ***Kosovo jako laboratoř užití síly v mezinárodním právu*** [title in translation – ***Kosovo as the Laboratory of the Use of Force in International Law***]. In: TEREZA KYSELOVSKÁ, DAVID SEHNÁLEK, NADĚŽDA ROZEHNALOVÁ (eds.). *IN VARIETATE CONCORDIA*: SOUBOR VĚDECKÝCH STATÍ K POCTĚ PROF. VLADIMÍRA TÝČE [title in translation – *IN VARIETATE CONCORDIA*: COLLECTION OF SCIENTIFIC PAPERS TO COMMEMORATE PROF. VLADIMÍR TÝČ]. Brno [Czech Republic]: Masaryk University, Collected Papers of the Masaryk University, Scientia Edition: Theoretical Series, (2019), No. 651, p. 367-384.

Michal Tomášek, ***Dvacet let od zavedení eura a prvního setkání s prof. Týčem*** [title in translation – ***Twenty Years after the Introduction of Euro and the First Meeting with Prof. Týč***]. In: TEREZA KYSELOVSKÁ, DAVID SEHNÁLEK, NADĚŽDA ROZEHNALOVÁ (eds.). *IN VARIETATE CONCORDIA*: SOUBOR VĚDECKÝCH STATÍ K POCTĚ PROF. VLADIMÍRA TÝČE [title in translation – *IN VARIETATE CONCORDIA*: COLLECTION OF SCIENTIFIC PAPERS TO COMMEMORATE PROF. VLADIMÍR TÝČ]. Brno [Czech Republic]: Masaryk University, Collected Papers of the Masaryk University, Scientia Edition: Theoretical Series,

(2019), No. 651, p. 397-412.

Kateřina Uhlířová, *Zásada zákazu použití síly a „počítačový útok" proti kritickým infrastrukturám státu: vaccum iuris či výkladová výzva?* [title in translation – *Principle of Non-Use of Force and "Computer Attack" Against the Critical Infrastructure of the State: Vacuum Iuris or Interpretation Challenge?*]. In: TEREZA KYSELOVSKÁ, DAVID SEHNÁLEK, NADĚŽDA ROZEHNALOVÁ (eds.). *IN VARIETATE CONCORDIA*: SOUBOR VĚDECKÝCH STATÍ K POCTĚ PROF. VLADIMÍRA TÝČE [title in translation – *IN VARIETATE CONCORDIA*: COLLECTION OF SCIENTIFIC PAPERS TO COMMEMORATE PROF. VLADIMÍR TÝČ]. Brno [Czech Republic]: Masaryk University, Collected Papers of the Masaryk University, Scientia Edition: Theoretical Series, (2019), No. 651, p. 413-464.

Peter Vršanský, *Jedna gratulácia a dve úvahy k aktuálnym problémom medzinárodného práva* [title in translation – *Congratulations and Two Essays on the Current Issues of International Law*]. In: TEREZA KYSELOVSKÁ, DAVID SEHNÁLEK, NADĚŽDA ROZEHNALOVÁ (eds.). *IN VARIETATE CONCORDIA*: SOUBOR VĚDECKÝCH STATÍ K POCTĚ PROF. VLADIMÍRA TÝČE [title in translation – *IN VARIETATE CONCORDIA*: COLLECTION OF SCIENTIFIC PAPERS TO COMMEMORATE PROF. VLADIMÍR TÝČ]. Brno [Czech Republic]: Masaryk University, Collected Papers of the Masaryk University, Scientia Edition: Theoretical Series, (2019), No. 651, p. 479-514.

Jiří Zemánek, *Uplatnění Listiny základních práv EU při přezkumu zákona o pobytu cizinců Ústavním soudem* [title in translation – *Application of the EU Charter of Fundamental Rights in a Constitutional Court Review of the Act on the Residence of Foreign Nationals*]. In: TEREZA KYSELOVSKÁ, DAVID SEHNÁLEK, NADĚŽDA ROZEHNALOVÁ (eds.). *IN VARIETATE CONCORDIA*: SOUBOR VĚDECKÝCH STATÍ K POCTĚ PROF. VLADIMÍRA TÝČE [title in translation – *IN VARIETATE CONCORDIA*: COLLECTION OF SCIENTIFIC PAPERS TO COMMEMORATE PROF. VLADIMÍR TÝČ]. Brno [Czech Republic]: Masaryk University, Collected Papers of the Masaryk University, Scientia Edition: Theoretical Series, (2019), No. 651, p. 515-520.

## I.1.2. [CZE] – [CZECH REPUBLIC] – Selected titles of Czech authors published outside the Czech Republic:

See also selected papers published in: JOZEF SUCHOŽA, JÁN HUSÁR, REGINA HUČKOVÁ (eds.), PRÁVO OBCHOD EKONOMIKA IX, Košice:

Právnická fakulta Univerzity Pavla Jozefa Šafárika v Košiciach [Title in translation - LAW- *TRADE - ECONOMICS - IX. COLLECTION OF SCIENTIFIC WRITINGS*] – cited in part I.1.3 below.

## I.1.3. [SVK] – [SLOVAK REPUBLIC] – Selected titles published in the Slovak Republic:

### Monographs

JOZEF SUCHOŽA, JÁN HUSÁR, REGINA HUČKOVÁ (eds.), PRÁVO OBCHOD EKONOMIKA IX, Košice: Právnická fakulta Univerzity Pavla Jozefa Šafárika v Košiciach [Title in translation - LAW- *TRADE - ECONOMICS - IX. COLLECTION OF SCIENTIFIC WRITINGS*], Košice [Košice], Slovenská republika [Slovak Republic]: Univerzita Pavla Jozefa Šafárika [Pavol Jozef Šafárik University], (2019) , ISBN: 978-80-8152-775-3 (print) / ISBN: 978-80-8152-776-0 (ePublication) / ISSN 2453-921 X.

### Selected papers published in the book

Alexander J. Bělohlávek, *Vyloučení rozhodce v řízení před stálým rozhodčím soudem a v řízení ad hoc* [title in translation – *Arbitrator Challenge in Proceedings before a Permanent Arbitral Institution and in Ad Hoc Arbitration*], p. 249-260.

Jaroslav Čolák, *Rozhodcovské konanie ako prejav vôle účastníkov – (posledná?) vôla ruší skoršiu alebo – niekoľko procesnoprávnych úvah o možnosti zrušenia rozhodcovského rozsudku a súvisiacich hmotnoprávnych následkov* [title in translation – *Arbitration as Expression of Will of the Parties – (Final?) Will Cancels Subsequent aka – Procedural Essays on the Possibility of Annulment of an Arbitral Award and Associated Consequences under Substantive Law*], p. 261-285.

Pavel Horák, *Limity možnosti stran zvolit si rozhodce* [title in translation – *Limitations of the Parties' Freedom to Choose Arbitrator*], p. 298-308.

Pavol Kubíček, *Stále rozhodcovské súdy verzus rozhodcovské konanie ad hoc v právnej úprave Slovenskej republiky* [title in translation – *Permanent Arbitral Institutions versus Ad Hoc Arbitration in Slovak law*], p. 309-316.

Tereza Profeldová, *Výše a způsob určení nákladů řízení a odměny rozhodce v řízení před stálým rozhodčím soudem a v řízení ad hoc* [title in translation – *Amount and Calculation of the Costs of Arbitration and*

*Arbitrator's Fee in Proceedings before a Permanent Arbitral Institution and in Ad Hoc Arbitration*], p. 317-328.

Naděžda Rozehnalová, *Autonomie vůle stran vs. intervence soudů* [title in translation – *Party Autonomy versus Court Intervention*], p. 340-352.

David Řezníček, *Opatření proti nečinnosti rozhodce v režimu řízení před stálým rozhodčím soudem ve srovnání s řízením ad hoc* [title in translation – *Remedies against Arbitrator Inaction in Proceedings before a Permanent Arbitral Institution Compared to Ad Hoc Arbitration*], p. 329-339.

Ľudmila Albert, Adam Giertl, Ján Klučka, *Repetitórium medzinárodného práva verejného* [title in translation – *Public International Law Handbook*], Bratislava: Iuris Libri (2018), ISBN: 978-80-89635-38-2.[9]

Peter Lysina, *Medzinárodná zmluva ako nástroj vonkajšej činnosti Európskej únie* [title in translation – *International Treaty as an Instrument of External Activities of the European Union*], Bratislava: Wolters Kluwer (2018), ISBN: 978-80-8168-890-4.[10]

Peter Vršanský, Jozef Valuch, Daniel Bednár, *Dokumenty k štúdiu medzinárodného práva veřejného. 1. část* [title in translation – *Documents for Public International Law Studies. Part 1*], Bratislava: Wolters Kluwer (2018), ISBN: 978-80-8168-874-4.[11]

**Bulletin slovenskej advokacie** [*Bulletin of the Slovak Bar*]**, Bratislava: Slovenská advokátska komora** [*Slovak Bar Association*]**, 2019, Vol. 25, ISSN: 1335-1079**[12]

Kristína Absolonová, *Viedenský dohovor o diplomatických stykoch a jeho súvislosť s návratovým konaním v zmysle § 123 a nasl. CMP* [title in translation – *Vienna Convention on Diplomatic Relations in the Context of Child Return Procedure under Section 123 et seq. of the Civil Non-Litigation Procedure Code*], No. 3, p. 6-10.

# I.2. (Private) international law, European private international law and legal relations in foreign trade relations, including international arbitration and other private-law areas with transnational dimensions

---

[9]   Published in Slovak.
[10]  Published in Slovak.
[11]  Published in Slovak.
[12]  Papers published in Slovak with abstracts in a foreign language. Abstracts in English and in German.

## I.2.1. [CZE] – [CZECH REPUBLIC] – Titles published within the Czech Republic

### Monographs, Collections and Conference Proceedings

Martin Janků, *WTO a právo mezinárodního obchodu* [title in translation – *WTO and Law of International Trade*], Prague: C. H. Beck (2019)

Jan Ondřej et al., *Zahájení podnikání (právní, ekonomické, účetní, daňové aspekty)* [title in translation – Starting Business (legal, economic, accounting, tax aspects)], Praha: Wolters Kluwer ČR (2019), ISBN 978-80-7598-337-4.

Magdalena Pfeiffer, Monika Pauknerová, Květoslav Růžička et al., *Mezinárodní obchodní práva* [title in translation – *International Commercial Law*], Plzeň [Pilsne / Czech Republic]: Aleš Čeněk (2019), ISBN 978-80-7380-764-1.[13]

Květoslav Růžička, Bohumil Poláček, P. Dostalík, *Geneze kodifikací mezinárodního práva soukromého. Soukromoprávní úpravy mezinárodních poměrů* [title in translation – *Genesis of the Private International Law Codifications. Private-Law Regulations of International Affairs*], Prague: Leges (2019), ISBN 978-80-7502-330-8.[14]

### Obchodněprávní revue [Commercial Law Review], Prague: C.H.Beck, 2019, Vol. 11, ISSN: 1211-0558[15]

Alexander J. Bělohlávek, *Koordinační řízení jako nový typ řízení podle nařízení 2015/848 o insolvenčním řízení: Koordinace nezávislých insolvenčních řízení proti dlužníkům ve skupině* [title in translation – *Coordination Proceedings as a New Type of Proceedings under Regulation 2015/848 on Insolvency Proceedings: Coordination of Independent Insolvency Proceedings against Debtors in a Group*], No. 10, p. 241-251.

Moritz Brinkmann, *Vývoj insolvenčního práva v EU* [title in translation – *Development of Insolvency Law in the EU*], No. 10, p. 241-251.

---

13    Book published in Czech.
14    Book published in Czech.
15    Papers published in Czech. Summary in German.

Právní rozhledy [Law Review], Prague: C. H. Beck, 2019, Vol. 29, ISSN: 1210-6410, Reg.No Ministry of Cultural Affairs Czech Republic] E 18487[16]

Alexander J. Bělohlávek, *Mezinárodní příslušnost pro vedení řízení souvisejících s insolvenčním řízením v režimu evropského insolvenčního nařízení* [title in translation – *International Jurisdiction to Conduct Proceedings Related to Insolvency Proceedings under the European Insolvency Regulation*], No. 19, p. 662-671.

Zdeňka Králíčková, Lucie Zatloukalová, *Dokud nás smrt nerozdělí: úvahy nad právem na rozvod* [title in translation – *Till Death Do Us Part: Essays on the Right to Divorce*], No. 17, p. 573-580.

Romana Rogalewiczová, *Určení místa bydliště jako významná záležitost dítěte* [title in translation – *Determination of the Place of Residence as an Important Issue Concerning a Child*], No. 19, p. 649-654.

Právník [Title in translation - *The Lawyer*], Prague: Ústav státu a práva Akademie věd České republiky [Institute of State and Law of the Academy of Sciences of the Czech Republic], 2018, Vol. 157, ISSN: 0231-6625[17]

Lenka Bezoušková, Monika Pauknerová, *Systém investičního soudu: Překotný rozchod Evropské unie s investiční arbitráží* [title in translation – *Mahr ("Dowry") in the Right of Muslim Countries and International Private Law*], No 04, p. 349-369.

Magdalena Pfeiffer, *Předběžná otázka v kolizi právních řádů* [title in translation – *Incidental Question in Conflicts of Laws*], No. 1, p. 65-79.

Monika Pauknerová, *Prostor pro uvážení v českém mezinárodním právu soukromém: ohlédnutí se za mezinárdním právem soukromým k výroční Antnína Hobzy* [title in translation – *Judicial Discretion in the Czech Private International Law: Looking Back at Czech Private International Law in Honour of Antonín Hobza*], No. 1, p. 12-28.

Soukromé právo [Title in translation – Private Law], Prague: Wolers Kluwer ČR, a.s., 2019, ISSN: 2533-4239[18]

Alexander J. Bělohlávek, *Institut provozovny při aplikaci evropského*

---

[16] Papers published in Czech.
[17] Papers published in Czech with abstracts in a foreign language. The abstract is most often in English (exceptionally in German or French).
[18] Papers published in Czech.

*insolvenčního nařízení jako autonomní právní konstrukce* [title in translation – *Concept of Establishment in the Application of the European Insolvency Regulation as an Autonomous Legal Construct*], No. 11, p. 5-16.

Jan Brodec, *Vybrané aspekty právních účinků insolvenčního řízení na probíhající rozhodčí řízení v oblasti právních poměrů s mezinárodním prvkem* [title in translation – *Selected Aspects of the Legal Effects Which Insolvency Proceedings Have on Pending Arbitration in Legal Relationships with an International Dimension*], Issue No. 7-8.

## Other publications

Alexander J. Bělohlávek, *Autonomní výklad mezinárodních smluv* [title in translation – *Autonomous Interpretation of International Agreements*], In: TEREZA KYSELOVSKÁ, DAVID SEHNÁLEK, NADĚŽDA ROZEHNALOVÁ (eds.). *IN VARIETATE CONCORDIA*: SOUBOR VĚDECKÝCH STATÍ K POCTĚ PROF. VLADIMÍRA TÝČE [title in translation – *IN VARIETATE CONCORDIA*: COLLECTION OF SCIENTIFIC PAPERS TO COMMEMORATE PROF. VLADIMÍR TÝČ], Brno [Czech Republic]: Masaryk University, Collected Papers of the Masaryk University, Scientia Edition: Theoretical Series, (2019), Collected Papers of the Masaryk University, Scientia Edition: Theoretical Series, No. 651, p. 31-61.

Alexander J. Bělohlávek, *Jiné výdělečné činnosti státních zaměstnanců: výkon činnosti rozhodce zaměstnancem státní správy a ve srovnání s dalšími činnostmi (znalecká činnost, tlumočnická činnost aj.)* [title in translation – *Other Gainful Activities of Civil Servants: a State administration Employee Acting as Arbitrator, also in Comparison with other Activities (Expert Witness, Sworn Interpreter etc.)*], XXVII Časopis pro právní vědu a praxis 3, Brno [Czech Republic]: Masarykova univerzita [Masaryk University] (2019), p. 311-331.[19]

Petr Bříza, *Moderace smluvní pokuty po zápočtu a její kolizně-právní reflexe* [title in translation – *Moderation of a Contractual Penalty after Set-Off and Its Conflict-of-Laws Reflections*]. In: REKODIFIKACE OBCHODNÍHO PRÁVA – 5 LET POTÉ, SVAZEK II., POCTA PROF. IRENĚ PELIKÁNOVÉ [title in translation – RECODIFICATION OF BUSINESS LAW – 5 YEARS AFTER, VOLUME II, IN HONOUR OF PROF. IRENA PELIKÁNOVÁ]. Wolters Kluwer ČR (2019), p. 429-438.

Klára Drličková, *Arbitrabilita sporů vyžadujících aplikaci unijních*

---

[19] Papers published in Czech, Annotation in Czech and English.

*pravidel hospodářské soutěže* [title in translation – *Arbitrability of Disputes Requiring the Application of EU Competition Rules*]. In: TEREZA KYSELOVSKÁ, DAVID SEHNÁLEK, NADĚŽDA ROZEHNALOVÁ (eds.). *IN VARIETATE CONCORDIA*: SOUBOR VĚDECKÝCH STATÍ K POCTĚ PROF. VLADIMÍRA TÝČE [title in translation – *IN VARIETATE CONCORDIA*: COLLECTION OF SCIENTIFIC PAPERS TO COMMEMORATE PROF. VLADIMÍR TÝČ]. Brno [Czech Republic]: Masaryk University, Collected Papers of the Masaryk University, Scientia Edition: Theoretical Series, (2019), No. 651, p. 63-82.

Michaela Garajová, *Rozhodovanie podľa zásad spravodlivosti v prípadoch dotknutých korupciou v medzinárodnej obchodnej arbitráži* [title in translation – *Decision-making according to Ex Aequo Et Bono in Cases Tainted by Corruption in the International Commercial Arbitration*], XXVII Časopis pro právní vědu a praxis 2, Brno [Czech Republic]: Masarykova univerzita [Masaryk University] (2019), p. 227-242.[20]

Radim Charvát, *Primát unijních zeměpisných označení a jeho vliv na mezinárodní zápisy označení původu podle Lisabonské dohody* [title in translation – *Primacy of EU Geographical Indications and Its Influence on International Registration of Appellations of Origin under the Lisbon Agreement*]. In: TEREZA KYSELOVSKÁ, DAVID SEHNÁLEK, NADĚŽDA ROZEHNALOVÁ (eds.). *IN VARIETATE CONCORDIA*: SOUBOR VĚDECKÝCH STATÍ K POCTĚ PROF. VLADIMÍRA TÝČE [title in translation – *IN VARIETATE CONCORDIA*: COLLECTION OF SCIENTIFIC PAPERS TO COMMEMORATE PROF. VLADIMÍR TÝČ]. Brno [Czech Republic]: Masaryk University, Collected Papers of the Masaryk University, Scientia Edition: Theoretical Series, (2019), No. 651, p. 84-104.

Monika Pauknerová, *Dvojí exequatur a mezinárodní právo soukromé* [title in translation – *Double Exequatur and Private International Law*]. In: TEREZA KYSELOVSKÁ, DAVID SEHNÁLEK, NADĚŽDA ROZEHNALOVÁ (eds.). *IN VARIETATE CONCORDIA*: SOUBOR VĚDECKÝCH STATÍ K POCTĚ PROF. VLADIMÍRA TÝČE [title in translation – *IN VARIETATE CONCORDIA*: COLLECTION OF SCIENTIFIC PAPERS TO COMMEMORATE PROF. VLADIMÍR TÝČ]. Brno [Czech Republic]: Masaryk University, Collected Papers of the Masaryk University, Scientia Edition: Theoretical Series, (2019), No. 651, p. 249-264.

Monika Pauknerová, *Obchodní společnosti v evropském mezinárodním právu soukromém – nové trendy* [title in translation – *Business*

---

[20] Papers published in Czech, Annotation in Czech and English.

*Companies in European Private International Law – New Trends*]. In: REKODIFIKACE OBCHODNÍHO PRÁVA – 5 LET POTÉ, SVAZEK II., POCTA PROF. IRENĚ PELIKÁNOVÉ [title in translation – RECODIFICATION OF BUSINESS LAW – 5 YEARS AFTER, VOLUME II, IN HONOUR OF PROF. IRENA PELIKÁNOVÁ]. Wolters Kluwer ČR (2019), p. 101-111.

Magdalena Pfeiffer, *Kolizní nástrahy smluveného majetkového režimu manželů* [title in translation – *Conflict-of-Laws Pitfalls of the Contractual Matrimonial Property Regime*], Ad Notam, (2019), Issue No. 1, p. 20-26.

Magdalena Pfeiffer, *Mezinárodní příslušnost soudů dle čl. 24 bod 2 nařízení Brusel I a ve světle rozhodnutí SDEU ve věci Dědouch* [title in translation – *International Court Jurisdiction pursuant to Article 24(2) of the Brussels I Regulation and in Light of the CJ EU Ruling in Dědouch.*] In: REKODIFIKACE OBCHODNÍHO PRÁVA – 5 LET POTÉ, SVAZEK II., POCTA PROF. IRENĚ PELIKÁNOVÉ [title in translation – RECODIFICATION OF BUSINESS LAW – 5 YEARS AFTER, VOLUME II, IN HONOUR OF PROF. IRENA PELIKÁNOVÁ]. Wolters Kluwer ČR (2019), p. 395-403.

Naděžda Rozehnalová, *Evropské mezinárodní právo soukromé – hledání formální a neformální harmonie* [title in translation – *European Private International Law – Searching for Formal and Informal Harmony*]. In: TEREZA KYSELOVSKÁ, DAVID SEHNÁLEK, NADĚŽDA ROZEHNALOVÁ (eds.). IN VARIETATE CONCORDIA: SOUBOR VĚDECKÝCH STATÍ K POCTĚ PROF. VLADIMÍRA TÝČE [title in translation – IN VARIETATE CONCORDIA: COLLECTION OF SCIENTIFIC PAPERS TO COMMEMORATE PROF. VLADIMÍR TÝČ]. Brno [Czech Republic]: Masaryk University, Collected Papers of the Masaryk University, Scientia Edition: Theoretical Series, (2019), No. 651, p. 31-61.

Květoslav Růžička, *Urychlené řízení v obchodních sporech* [title in translation – *Fast-Track Proceedings in Business Disputes*]. In: TEREZA KYSELOVSKÁ, DAVID SEHNÁLEK, NADĚŽDA ROZEHNALOVÁ (eds.). IN VARIETATE CONCORDIA: SOUBOR VĚDECKÝCH STATÍ K POCTĚ PROF. VLADIMÍRA TÝČE [title in translation – IN VARIETATE CONCORDIA: COLLECTION OF SCIENTIFIC PAPERS TO COMMEMORATE PROF. VLADIMÍR TÝČ]. Brno [Czech Republic]: Masaryk University, Collected Papers of the Masaryk University, Scientia Edition: Theoretical Series, (2019), No. 651, p. 285-294.

Jiří Valdhans, *Mezinárodně-soukromoprávní tvář profesora Týče, neboli od lex loci delicti commissi k lex loci damni infecti* [title in translation – *International Private-Law Face of Professor Týč aka from Lex Loci Delicti Commissi to Lex Loci Damni Infecti*]. In: TEREZA KYSELOVSKÁ, DAVID SEHNÁLEK, NADĚŽDA ROZEHNALOVÁ (eds.). *IN VARIETATE CONCORDIA*: SOUBOR VĚDECKÝCH STATÍ K POCTĚ PROF. VLADIMÍRA TÝČE [title in translation – *IN VARIETATE CONCORDIA*: COLLECTION OF SCIENTIFIC PAPERS TO COMMEMORATE PROF. VLADIMÍR TÝČ]. Brno [Czech Republic]: Masaryk University, Collected Papers of the Masaryk University, Scientia Edition: Theoretical Series, (2019), No. 651, p. 465-479.

Marta Zavadilová, *Spotřebitel v jurisdikčních normách nařízení Brusel I a aneb kde žalovat migrujícího spotřebitele* [title in translation – *Consumer in the Jurisdiction Rules of the Brussels Ia Regulation aka Where to Sue a Migrant Consumer*]. In: REKODIFIKACE OBCHODNÍHO PRÁVA – 5 LET POTÉ. SVAZEK II. [title in translation – RECODIFICATION OF BUSINESS LAW – 5 YEARS AFTER. VOLUME II]. Wolters Kluwer ČR (2019).

## I.2.2. [CZE] – [CZECH REPUBLIC] – Selected titles of Czech authors published outside the Czech Republic

Alexander J. Bělohlávek, **Беспристрастность и независимость арбитра и его обязанность уведомлять о наличии связей со сторонами в свете международных стандартов** [transcript – *Bespristrannost i nezavisimost arbitra i jevo objazannost uvjedomlat o nalichiji svjazej so storonami v svjete mezhdunarodnych standartov*] [title in translation – *Impartiality and Independence of Arbitrator and His Duty of Disclosure pursuant to International Standards*] In: N. G. MARKALOVA ET A.I. MURANOV (EDS.) ARBITRATION AND REGULATION OF INTERNATIONAL TRADE: RUSSIAN, FOREIGN AND CROSS-BORDER APPROACHES. Moscow: Statut (2019), p. 71-96.[21]

Petr Bříza, Marta Zavadilová, *Czeska kodyfikacja prawa prywatnego międzynarodowego z 2012 roku* [title in translation – *Czech Codification of Private International Law as of 2012*], 2 Kwartalnik Prawa Prywatnego (2019), p. 467-496.

MONIKA PAUKNEROVÁ, MAGDALENA PFEIFFER, PRIVATE INTERNATIONAL LAW IN THE CZECH, Kluwer Law International (2nd ed. 2019), ISBN 978-94-035-1332-4.

---

[21]  УДК 341 [UDK 341] - ББК 67.412.2 – BBK 67.412.2 / A79. Total no of pages: 736.

Monika Pauknerová, *Treatment of Foreign Law – Past and Future*, In: AGUSTIN PARISE, EVGENY V. POPOV, GLOBALISATION AND PRIVATE INTERNATIONAL LAW (2017), Annual Symposium of the Association of Legal Science (IALS), Moscow (2019), p. 37-59, ISBN 978-5-94103-425-3.

Magdalena Pfeiffer, *Perspective of EU States – Czech Republic*, In ANATOL DUTTAX, WOLFGANG WURMNEST (EDS.), EUROPEAN PRIVATE INTERNATIONAL LAW AND MEMBER STATE TREATIES WITH THIRD STATES: THE CASE OF THE EUROPEAN SUCCESSION REGULATION, Cambridge: Intersentia (2019), p. 85-119, ISBN 978-1-78068-664-6.

### I.3. EU Law (general, not classified under Chapter I.1 or I.2 above)

### I.3.1. [CZE] – [CZECH REPUBLIC] – Titles published within the Czech Republic

**Bulletin advokacie [*Bulletin of the Czech Bar*], Prague: Česká advokátní komora [*Czech Bar Association*], 2016, ISSN: 1210-6348**[22]

Daniel Hrčka, *Soumrak (nejen) investiční arbitráže? – Rozhodnutí SD EU C-284/16 a jeho důsledky* [title in translation – *Twilight of investment (and other) arbitration? – Decision of the CJ EU in and the Consequences Thereof*], Bulletin advokacie (2019), Nos. 7-8, p. 42-46.

**The Lawyer Quarterly, Prague: Ústav státu a práva Akademie věd České republiky [Institute of State and Law of the Academy of Sciences of the Czech Republic], 2019, Vol. IX, ISSN: 0231-6625**[23]

Iva Čípová, *Patient´s rights in cross-border health care in the European Union*, No. 1, p.25-46.

Ian Edmond, Tereza Kunertová, *European Union Regulation of Insurance Industry in the Aftermath of the Financial Crisis*, No 1, p. 140-149.

Daniel Houska, *Dusk Over The European Contract Law?*, No 4, p. 359-

---

[22] Papers published in Czech with abstracts in a foreign language. Abstracts in English and in German.

[23] A subsidiary title to the monthly periodical Právník [in translation – *The Lawyer*] which will be published by the Institute of State and Law of the Academy of Science of the Czech Republic in Czech. Papers published in *The Lawyer Quarterly* are primarily in English, exceptionally in other languages (such as German); abstracts are in English. For papers published in the periodical "*Pravnik*" [in translation – *The Lawyer*], issued monthly, see the separate excerpt from papers listed under the heading of the respective periodical.

368.

Refia Kaya, *European Court of Human Rights on Addressing Environmental Discrimination Against Collectivities,* No 4, p. 283-298.

Martin Madej, *The Charter of Fundamental Rights of the EU in the Czech Judicial Decisions: Falling Short of Expectations?*, No 3, p. 213-228.

**Mezinárodní vztahy [International Relations], Prague: Institute of International Relations Prague, 2019, Vol. LIIV**[24]

Jakub Charvát, *Degressive Representation in the European Parliament: the Union Law vs. Reality*, No. 3, p. 22-40.

**Obchodněprávní revue [Commercial Law Review], Prague: C. H. Beck, 2019 Vol. 11 ISSN: 1803-6554**[25]

Alexander J. Bělohlávek, *Koordinační řízení jako nový typ řízení podle nařízení 2015/848 o insolvenčním řízení: Koordinace nezávislých insolvenčních řízení proti dlužníkům ve skupině* [title in translation – *Coordination Proceedings as a New Type of Proceedings under Regulation 2015/848 on Insolvency Proceedings: Coordination of Independent Insolvency Proceedings against Debtors in a Group*], No. 10, p. 241-251.

Moritz Brinkmann, *Vývoj insolvenčního práva v EU* [title in translation – *Development of Insolvency Law in the EU*], No 10, p. 241-251.
**Obchodní právo [Commercial Law], Prague: Prospektrum, 2019, Vol. 27, ISSN: 1210-8278**[26]

Sandra Brožová, *Interpretace společenské smlouvy a stanov obchodních korporací po rekodifikaci* [title in translation – *Interpretation of a Corporation's Memorandum of Association and Articles of Association after Recodification*], No 6, p. 2-14.

Petr Fabian, *Kolektivní vymáhání náhrady škody způsobené porušením soutěžního práva Evropské unie v České republice a Portugalsku* [title in translation – *Collective Enforcement of Compensation for Damage Caused by Breach of EU Competition Law in the Czech Republic and in Portugal*], No. 4, p. 20-31.

---

[24]    Majority of papers published in Czech, summary in English.
[25]    Papers published in Czech. Abstracts in English, exceptionally in German.
[26]    Papers published in Czech. Abstracts in English.

Kateřina Holečková, *Určování mezinárodní příslušnosti v případech deliktní odpovědnosti podle nařízení Brusel I bis* [title in translation – *International Jurisdiction in Cases Involving Liability for Torts under the Brussels Ia Regulation*], No. 6, p. 15-14.

Iva Fellerová Palkovská, *Pravomoc Evropské Unie k europeizaci soukromého práva se zaměřením na právo nekalé soutěže* [title in translation – *Power of the European Union to Europeanise Private Law with Special Focus on Unfair Competition Law*], No. 5, p. 11-22.

**Právník [Title in translation - *The Lawyer*], Prague: Ústav státu a práva Akademie věd České republiky [Institute of State and Law of the Academy of Sciences of the Czech Republic], 2019, Vol. 158, ISSN: 0231-6625**[27]

Andej Beleš, *Zásada subsidiarity a zásada proporcionality pri prijímaní nariadenia o Európskej prokuratre* [title in translation – *The Subsidiarity Principle and the Proportionality Principle by Adopting the Regulation on the European Public Prosecutor's Office*], No. 5, p. 456-471.

Eva Procházková, *Je univerzalita přísně střežených hodnot lidství v Evropě ohrožena?* [title in translation – *Is the Universality of High Values of Humanity Endangered in Europe?*], No 02, p. 217-220.

Ondřej Svoboda, *Systém investičního soudu: Překotný rozchod Evropské unie s investiční arbitráží* [title in translation – *Investment Court System? European Union´s Abrupt Divorce with Investment Arbitration*], No 04, p. 390-405.

**Právní rozhledy [Title in translation – *Law Review*], Prague: C. H. Beck, 2019, Vol. 27, ISSN: 1210-6410**[28]

Jan Balarin, Anežka Janoušková, *K fenoménu hromadné žaloby* [title in translation – *Regarding the Phenomenon of Class Action*], Nos. 13-14, p. 489-496.

Alexander J. Bělohlávek, *Mezinárodní příslušnost pro vedení řízení souvisejících s insolvenčním řízením v režimu evropského insolvenčního nařízení* [title in translation – *International Jurisdiction to Conduct Proceedings Related to Insolvency Proceedings under the European*

[27] Papers published in Czech with abstracts in a foreign language. The abstract is most often in English (exceptionally in German or French).
[28] Papers published in Czech.

*Insolvency Regulation*], No. 19, p. 662-671.

Markéta Bednářová, *Právo na soudní přezkum rozhodnutí o neudělení dlouhodobého víza za účelem studia dle směrnice 2004/114/ES* [title in translation – *Right to Judicial Review of a Decision Denying a Long-Term Student Visa under Directive 2004/114/EC*], No. 11, p. 403-407.

Jiří Fuchs, *Diskriminace z důvodu věku v judikatuře Soudního dvora EU* [title in translation – *Age Discrimination in the Case-Law of the Court of Justice of the EU*], No. 11, p. 397-400.

Martina Kopcová, *Moderní funkce ochranných známek a jejich vliv na posouzení konfliktu ochranné známky s obchodní firmou v judikatuře SDEU* [title in translation – *Modern Functions of Trade Marks and Their Influence on the Examination of a Conflict between a Trade Mark and a Company Name in CJ EU Case-Law*], No. 8, p. 282-287.

Jiří Malenovský, *Protichůdné zájmy v řízení o předběžné otázce a jejich důsledky* [title in translation – *Contrary Interests in Preliminary Ruling Proceedings and Their Consequences*], No. 6, p. 191-197.

Romana Rogalewiczová, *Určení místa bydliště jako významná záležitost dítěte* [title in translation – *Determination of the Place of Residence as an Important Issue Concerning a Child*], No. 19, p. 649-654.

<u>**Soukromé právo [Title in translation – *Private Law*], Prague: Wolers Kluwer ČR, a.s., 2019, ISSN: 2533-4239**</u>[29]

Alexander J. Bělohlávek, *Institut provozovny při aplikaci evropského insolvenčního nařízení jako autonomní právní konstrukce* [title in translation – *Concept of Establishment in the Application of the European Insolvency Regulation as an Autonomous Legal Construct*], No. 11, p. 5-16.

Jan Brodec, *Vybrané aspekty právních účinků insolvenčního řízení na probíhající rozhodčí řízení v oblasti právních poměrů s mezinárodním prvkem* [title in translation – *Selected Aspects of the Legal Effects Which Insolvency Proceedings Have on Pending Arbitration in Legal Relationships with an International Dimension*], Issue No. 7-8.

**Other publications**

Radim Charvát, *Primát unijních zeměpisných označení a jeho vliv na*

---

[29]   Papers published in Czech.

*mezinárodní zápisy označení původu podle Lisabonské dohody* [title in translation – *Primacy of EU Geographical Indications and Its Influence on International Registration of Appellations of Origin under the Lisbon Agreement*]. In: TEREZA KYSELOVSKÁ, DAVID SEHNÁLEK, NADĚŽDA ROZEHNALOVÁ (eds.). *IN VARIETATE CONCORDIA*: SOUBOR VĚDECKÝCH STATÍ K POCTĚ PROF. VLADIMÍRA TÝČE [title in translation – *IN VARIETATE CONCORDIA*: COLLECTION OF SCIENTIFIC PAPERS TO COMMEMORATE PROF. VLADIMÍR TÝČ]. Brno [Czech Republic]: Masaryk University, Collected Papers of the Masaryk University, Scientia Edition: Theoretical Series, (2019), No. 651, p. 83-104.

Richard Král, *Rozsudek SDEU Metock v kontextu Brexitu* [title in translation – *CJ EU Judgment in Metock in the Context of Brexit*]. In: TEREZA KYSELOVSKÁ, DAVID SEHNÁLEK, NADĚŽDA ROZEHNALOVÁ (eds.). *IN VARIETATE CONCORDIA*: SOUBOR VĚDECKÝCH STATÍ K POCTĚ PROF. VLADIMÍRA TÝČE [title in translation – *IN VARIETATE CONCORDIA*: COLLECTION OF SCIENTIFIC PAPERS TO COMMEMORATE PROF. VLADIMÍR TÝČ]. Brno [Czech Republic]: Masaryk University, Collected Papers of the Masaryk University, Scientia Edition: Theoretical Series, (2019), No. 651, p. 121-130.

Jiří Malenovský, *Jedno kolo ve věcném zápasu o autonomii unijního práva z křesel unijních soudců* [title in translation – *One Round of the Material Fight for Autonomy of EU Law from the EU Judges' Chairs*]. In: TEREZA KYSELOVSKÁ, DAVID SEHNÁLEK, NADĚŽDA ROZEHNALOVÁ (eds.). *IN VARIETATE CONCORDIA*: SOUBOR VĚDECKÝCH STATÍ K POCTĚ PROF. VLADIMÍRA TÝČE [title in translation – *IN VARIETATE CONCORDIA*: COLLECTION OF SCIENTIFIC PAPERS TO COMMEMORATE PROF. VLADIMÍR TÝČ]. Brno [Czech Republic]: Masaryk University, Collected Papers of the Masaryk University, Scientia Edition: Theoretical Series, (2019), No. 651, p. 183-196.

Ján Mazák, *Súdny dvor EÚ zrušil vnútroštátny právny akt: Rodí sa nová doktrína alebo výnimka potvrdzuje pravidlo?* [title in translation – *Court of Justice of the EU Annulled a National Legal Act: A New Doctrine is Born or Exception Proves the Rule?*]. In: TEREZA KYSELOVSKÁ, DAVID SEHNÁLEK, NADĚŽDA ROZEHNALOVÁ (eds.). *IN VARIETATE CONCORDIA*: SOUBOR VĚDECKÝCH STATÍ K POCTĚ PROF. VLADIMÍRA TÝČE [title in translation – *IN VARIETATE CONCORDIA*: COLLECTION OF SCIENTIFIC PAPERS TO COMMEMORATE PROF. VLADIMÍR TÝČ]. Brno [Czech Republic]: Masaryk University, Collected Papers of the Masaryk University, Scientia Edition: Theoretical Series, (2019), No. 651, p. 197-210.

Magdalena Pfeiffer, *Mezinárodní příslušnost soudů dle čl. 24 bod 2 nařízení Brusel I a ve světle rozhodnutí SDEU ve věci Dědouch* [title in translation – *International Court Jurisdiction pursuant to Article 24(2) of the Brussels I Regulation and in Light of the CJ EU Ruling in Dědouch*]. In: REKODIFIKACE OBCHODNÍHO PRÁVA – 5 LET POTÉ. SVAZEK II. [title in translation – RECODIFICATION OF BUSINESS LAW – 5 YEARS AFTER.VOLUME II], Wolters Kluwer ČR (2019), p. 395-403.

Naděžda Rozehnalová, *Evropské mezinárodní právo soukromé – hledání formální a neformální harmonie* [title in translation – *European Private International Law – Searching for Formal and Informal Harmony*]. In: TEREZA KYSELOVSKÁ, DAVID SEHNÁLEK, NADĚŽDA ROZEHNALOVÁ (eds.). *IN VARIETATE CONCORDIA*: SOUBOR VĚDECKÝCH STATÍ K POCTĚ PROF. VLADIMÍRA TÝČE [title in translation – *IN VARIETATE CONCORDIA*: COLLECTION OF SCIENTIFIC PAPERS TO COMMEMORATE PROF. VLADIMÍR TÝČ]. Brno [Czech Republic]: Masaryk University, Collected Papers of the Masaryk University, Scientia Edition: Theoretical Series, (2019), No. 651, p. 285-294.

Miroslav Slašťan, *Uplatňovanie medzinárodných zmlúv Spojeného kráľovstva a členských štátov Euroópskej únie po BREXITE* [title in translation – *Application of International Agreements of the United Kingdom and the European Union Member States after BREXIT*]. In: TEREZA KYSELOVSKÁ, DAVID SEHNÁLEK, NADĚŽDA ROZEHNALOVÁ (eds.). *IN VARIETATE CONCORDIA*: SOUBOR VĚDECKÝCH STATÍ K POCTĚ PROF. VLADIMÍRA TÝČE [title in translation – *IN VARIETATE CONCORDIA*: COLLECTION OF SCIENTIFIC PAPERS TO COMMEMORATE PROF. VLADIMÍR TÝČ]. Brno [Czech Republic]: Masaryk University, Collected Papers of the Masaryk University, Scientia Edition: Theoretical Series, (2019), No. 651, p. 325-346.

Václav Stehlík, *Ohlédnutí se (nejen) za řízením o předběžné otázce v prvních 15 letech členství České republiky v Evropské unii* [title in translation – *Preliminary Ruling (And Other) Proceedings during the First 15 Years of the Czech Republic's Accession to the EU in Retrospect*]. In: TEREZA KYSELOVSKÁ, DAVID SEHNÁLEK, NADĚŽDA ROZEHNALOVÁ (eds.). *IN VARIETATE CONCORDIA*: SOUBOR VĚDECKÝCH STATÍ K POCTĚ PROF. VLADIMÍRA TÝČE [title in translation – *IN VARIETATE CONCORDIA*: COLLECTION OF SCIENTIFIC PAPERS TO COMMEMORATE PROF. VLADIMÍR TÝČ]. Brno [Czech Republic]: Masaryk University, Collected Papers of the

Masaryk University, Scientia Edition: Theoretical Series, (2019), No. 651, p. 347-366.

Naděžda Šišková, *Několik glos k ochraně zásad právního státu na úrovni EU* [title in translation – *Notes on the Protection of the Rule of Law Principles at the EU Level*]. In: TEREZA KYSELOVSKÁ, DAVID SEHNÁLEK, NADĚŽDA ROZEHNALOVÁ (eds.). *IN VARIETATE CONCORDIA*: SOUBOR VĚDECKÝCH STATÍ K POCTĚ PROF. VLADIMÍRA TÝČE [title in translation – *IN VARIETATE CONCORDIA*: COLLECTION OF SCIENTIFIC PAPERS TO COMMEMORATE PROF. VLADIMÍR TÝČ]. Brno [Czech Republic]: Masaryk University, Collected Papers of the Masaryk University, Scientia Edition: Theoretical Series, (2019), No. 651, p. 385-396.

Marta Zavadilová, *Spotřebitel v jurisdikčních normách nařízení Brusel Ia aneb kde žalovat migrujícího spotřebitele* [title in translation – *Consumer in the Jurisdiction Rules of the Brussels Ia Regulation aka Where to Sue a Migrant Consumer*]. In: REKODIFIKACE OBCHODNÍHO PRÁVA – 5 LET POTÉ. SVAZEK II. [title in translation – RECODIFICATION OF BUSINESS LAW – 5 YEARS AFTER.VOLUME II], Wolters Kluwer ČR (2019).

Jiří Zemánek, *Uplatnění Listiny základních práv EU při přezkumu zákona o pobytu cizinců Ústavním soudem* [title in translation – *Application of the EU Charter of Fundamental Rights in a Constitutional Court Review of the Act on the Residence of Foreign Nationals*]. In: TEREZA KYSELOVSKÁ, DAVID SEHNÁLEK, NADĚŽDA ROZEHNALOVÁ (eds.). *IN VARIETATE CONCORDIA*: SOUBOR VĚDECKÝCH STATÍ K POCTĚ PROF. VLADIMÍRA TÝČE [title in translation – *IN VARIETATE CONCORDIA*: COLLECTION OF SCIENTIFIC PAPERS TO COMMEMORATE PROF. VLADIMÍR TÝČ]. Brno [Czech Republic]: Masaryk University, Collected Papers of the Masaryk University, Scientia Edition: Theoretical Series, (2019), No. 651, p. 515-520.

# II.  CURRENT EVENTS

## II.1.  Selected scientific conferences, seminars, academic lectures and other professional events in the Czech Republic and in the Slovak Republic[1]

**[CZE] Kroměříž, 04 – 06 October 2019**
Joint International Symposium of the Czech Society of International Law and of the Slovak Society of International Law on **Amicable Dispute Settlement in International Law.**
Speakers Doc. JUDr. Vladimír Balaš, JUDr. Daniel Bednár, JUDr. Dagmar Beňaková, JUDr. Milan Beránek, JUDr. Sandra Brožová, JUDr. Monika Feigerlová, Mgr. Martina Filippiová, Doc. JUDr. Katarína Chovancová, Doc. JUDr. Jan Ondřej, Dr. Klára Poláčková Van der Ploeg, JUDr. Zdeněk Nový, JUDr. Milena Nosková, JUDr. Emil Ruffer, JUDr. Petra Ruffer Lustigová, JUDr. Michaela Sýkorová, JUDr. Metod Špaček, prof. JUDr. Pavel Šturma, JUDr. JUDr. Petr Válek, Jaroslav Větrovský.

**[CZE] Prague, 11 November 2019**
Conference on **Ten Years of the Charter of Fundamental Rights of the European Union.** Organized by the Department of EU Law of the Faculty of Law, Charles University in Prague.

---

[1]    Contributions mentioned herein represent a selection from papers related to issues with an international element. CYIL editors hereby apologize to the lecturers for omitting some of them and their topics due to the limited space provided for this section. Editors referred especially to published and other accessible information. Readers are specifically warned that the information about papers presented at the individual conferences and other academic and scientific events is only a selection and definitely does not provide a full report on the entire proceedings and the academic scope of each particular event.

# III.   Important Web sites

http://www.czechyearbook.org; http://www.lexlata.pro

<u>Czech Yearbook of International Law®</u> and <u>Czech (& Central European) Yearbook of Arbitration®</u>

The website is currently available in sixteen languages: English, Bulgarian, Czech, Chinese, Japanese, Korean, Hungarian, German, Polish, Romanian, Russian, Portuguese, Slovenian, Spanish, Ukrainian, Vietnamese. This website allows access to the annotations of all core articles and to information about the authors of these articles as well as to the entire remaining contents (except core articles) of both yearbooks (CYIL and CYArb®).

## III.1.   [CZE] – [CZECH REPUBLIC]

- http://www.cnb.cz. Česká národní banka [Czech National Bank as the Central bank of the Czech Republic].[1]
- http://www.compet.cz. Office for the protection of competition.[2]
- http://www.concourt.cz. The Constitutional Court of the Czech Republic.[3]
- http://www.csesp.cz. Czech Society for European and Comparative Law.[4]
- http://www.csmp-csil.org. The Czech Society Of International Law.[5]
- http://www.czech.cz. Portal „Hello Czech Republic". Basic information about the Czech Republic and news interesting for foreigners. Rather a promotional portal.[6]
- http://www.czso.cz. Czech Statistical Office.[7]
- http://dtjvcnsp.org. Česko-německý spolek právníků. [Czech-German Lawyers Association]. Deutsch-Tschechische Juristenvereinigung e.V.[8]
- http:// ekf.vsb.cz. Faculty of Economics, VŠB Technical University of Ostrava.[9]

---

[1]   Website available in English and Czech.
[2]   Website available in English and Czech. Basic laws and regulations on the protection of competition in the Czech Republic are also available at the website, both in Czech and in English (unofficial translation).
[3]   Website available in English and Czech. Part of the (significant) case law also available in English.
[4]   Website available in English and Czech.
[5]   Website available in Czech. In English only a brief summary of the webpages.
[6]   Website available in English, Czech, French, German, Russian and Spanish.
[7]   Website available in English and Czech.
[8]   Website available in German.
[9]   Website available in English and Czech. Some information (regarding post-graduate studies) also available in German. Department of Law see http://en.ekf.vsb.cz/information-about/departments/structure/departments/dept-119 (in English).

- http://www.hrad.cz.[10] Website of the Office of the President of the Czech Republic.
- http://www.icc-cr.cz. ICC National Committee Czech Republic.
- http://www.iir.cz. Institute Of International Relations Prague.[11]
- http://www.ilaw.cas.cz. Ústav státu a práva Akademie věd ČR, v.v.i. [Institute of State and Law of the Academy of Sciences of the Czech Republic][12]
- http://www.jednotaceskychpravniku.cz. Jednota českých právníků [Czech Lawyers Union]
- http://justice.cz. Czech justice portal including both courts and the Ministry of Justice, prosecution departments, Judicial Academy, Institute of Criminology and Social Prevention, as well as the Probation and Mediation Service and the Prison Service.[13]
- http://www.law.muni.cz. Faculty of Law, Masaryk University, Brno.[14]
- http://www.mzv.cz. Ministry of Foreign Affairs of the Czech Republic.[15]
- http://www.nsoud.cz. The Supreme Court of the Czech Republic.[16]
- http://www.nssoud.cz. The Supreme Administrative Court of the Czech Republic.[17]
- http://www.ochrance.cz. Public Defender of Rights (Ombudsman).[18]
- http://www.ok.cz/iksp/en/aboutus.html. Institute of Criminology and Social Prevention.[19]
- http://portal.gov.cz. Portal of the Public Administration.[20] This website allows access to the websites of most supreme public administration authorities (including ministries).
- http://www.prf.cuni.cz. Faculty of Law, Charles University in Prague.[21]
- http://www.psp.cz. Parliament of the Czech Republic. Chamber of Deputies.[22]
- http://www.senat.cz. Parliament of the Czech Republic. Senate.[23]
- http://www.society.cz/wordpress/#awp. Common Law Society.[24]

---

[10] Website available in English and Czech. This website also allows access to the personal webpage of the President of the Czech Republic.
[11] Website available in English and Czech. This Institute was founded by the Ministry of Foreign Affairs of the Czech Republic.
[12] Website available in English and Czech.
[13] Website available in Czech. The individual websites of the institutions covered by this portal also contain pages or summary information in English.
[14] Website available in English and Czech.
[15] Website available in Czech. Important information from this portal also available in English.
[16] Website available in Czech. Some basic information also in English and French.
[17] Website available in English and Czech.
[18] Website available in English and Czech.
[19] Website available in English and Czech.
[20] Website available in English and Czech.
[21] Website available in Czech. Basic information available in English.
[22] Website available in English and Czech.
[23] Website available in English and Czech.
[24] Website available in Czech.

- http://www.soud.cz. Arbitration Court attached to the Economic Chamber of the Czech Republic and Agricultural Chamber of the Czech Republic.[25]
- http://www.umpod.cz. Office for International Legal Protection of Children.[26]
- http://www.upol.cz/fakulty/pf/. Faculty of Law. Palacký University, Olomouc.
- http://www.vse.cz. The University of Economics, Prague.[27]
- http://www.zcu.cz/fpr/. Faculty of Law, Western Bohemia University in Pilsen.[28]

## III.2.    [SVK] – [SLOVAK REPUBLIC]

- http://www.concourt.sk. Constitutional Court of the Slovak Republic.[29]
- http://www.flaw.uniba.sk. Faculty of Law, Comenius University in Bratislava (SVK).[30]
- http://iuridica.truni.sk. Faculty of Law. Trnava University in Trnava (SVK).[31]
- http://www.justice.gov.sk. Ministry of Justice of the Slovak Republic.[32]
- http://www.nbs.sk. Národná banka Slovenska [National Bank of Slovakia as the Central bank of Slovak Republic].[33]
- http://www.nrsr.sk. National Council of the Slovak Republic [Slovak Parliament].[34]
- http://www.prf.umb.sk. Faculty of Law. Matej Bel University, Banská Bystrica (SVK).
- http://www.prezident.sk. President of the Slovak Republic and Office of the President (SVK).[35]
- http://www.uninova.sk/pf_bvsp/src_angl/index.php. Faculty of Law, Pan European University (SVK).[36]
- http://www.upjs.sk/pravnicka-fakulta. Faculty of Law, Pavol Jozef

---

[25]   Website available in English, Czech, German and Russian.
[26]   The Office is the Central authority responsible for protection of children in civil matters having cross-border implications. Website available in English and Czech.
[27]   Website available in English and Czech.
[28]   Website available in Czech.
[29]   Website available in English and Slovak.
[30]   Website available in English and Slovak.
[31]   Website available in English and Slovak.
[32]   Website available in English and Slovak. This website also allows access to the following portals: Courts, Slovak Agent before the European Court for Human Rights, Slovak Agent before the Court of Justice of the European Union, The Judicial Academy.
[33]   Website available in English and Slovak.
[34]   Website available in English, French, German and Slovak.
[35]   Website available in English and Slovak.
[36]   Website available in English, German and Slovak.

Šafárik University in Košice (SVK).[37]

- http://www.usap.sav.sk. Institute of State and Law, Slovak Academy of Science.[38]

---

[37] Website available in English and Slovak.
[38] Website available in Slovak.

# Index

Czech Yearbook of International Law®

# CALL FOR PAPERS FOR VOLUMES 2021/2022

Did you find the articles in the eleventh volume of CYIL interesting?
Would you like to react to a current article
or contribute to future volumes?

We are seeking authors for both
the Czech Yearbook on International Law® and the
Czech (& Central European) Yearbook of Arbitration®.

The general topics for the 2021/2022 volumes are following:

### CYIL 2021
*Immunities and Privileges*

### CYArb® 2021
*(Best) Practices in Arbitration*

### CYIL 2022
*International Justice
and International
Enforcement*

### CYArb® 2022
*Jurisdiction of Arbitral
Tribunals*

More general and contact information available at:

**www.czechyearbook.org**
**www.lexlata.pro**

## CYIL – Czech Yearbook of International Law®, 2021
## Immunities and Privileges

The issues relating to immunities and privileges will be discussed from the public and private law point of view, addressing the immunity of a state, as well as personal and special immunities, their content, and manifestations. The needs of the globalized environment namely suggest that immunities often manifest in situations that international law was previously not concerned with at all, or only marginally. Attention will for example therefore be given to immunities from the perspective of how the Vienna Convention on Diplomatic Relations is applied in practice, immunities in the case of civil and criminal Court proceedings, but also immunities in special situations. Although privileges do not prime facie pose that significant of a question in international law, they cannot be ignored as they are a significant attribute of state representation, diplomatic employees, but also other representatives of the state in international relations.

## CYArb® – Czech (& Central European) Yearbook of Arbitration®, 2021
## (Best) Practices in Arbitration

Although we are talking about international standards of arbitration, the course of every arbitration is highly influenced by the place (seat) of arbitration. The so called denationalization of arbitration seems to be a debunked idea. Or is this not the case? In any event, despite a high degree of standardization of procedures in arbitration, the influence of national and regional standards cannot be ignored. The standardization of procedures is evident throughout the entire duration of arbitral proceeding. It is evident in commencement of proceedings, in the preparation for hearings, in the hearing themselves, in the burden of proof, as well as in the termination of proceedings. Every state and every region, same as every permanent arbitral institution, has its own "time-tested" procedures through which it influences the culture of arbitration.

## CYIL – Czech Yearbook of International Law®, 2022
## International Justice and International Enforcement

The broad topic of the 2022 edition deals with the enforcement of rights in a transnational environment, according to the views of courts established by international treaties, as well as from the views of forums established under international organizations, their specifics and proceedings before these bodies. The purpose of this work is to examine forums established *ad hoc*, as well as institutionalized justice, both general and specific. At the same time, another goal is to address the specifics of the enforcement of judgements of such forums and guarantees for the enforcement of claims adjudicated by these courts in cross-border and transnational contexts.

## CYArb® – Czech (& Central European) Yearbook of Arbitration®, 2022
## Jurisdiction of Arbitral Tribunals

The issue of the jurisdiction of arbitral tribunals has so far overlapped to some extent with almost all topics that have been the main ideas of all editions of this yearbook over the past decade. The main aim of the 2022 edition is to focus mainly on the nature of the jurisdiction of arbitral tribunals, its specifics in a transnational environment, as well as on questions of the effects of jurisdiction in terms of *lis pendens*, etc. It will also cover the power to order interim reliefs and to render decisions in expedited procedures and in disputes of a *sui generis* nature.